842-14

McGraw-Hill Series in Education

HAROLD BENJAMIN, *Consulting Editor*

Adult Education

McGraw-Hill Series in Education

HAROLD BENJAMIN, *Consulting Editor*

ADULT EDUCATION

Homer Kempfer

EXECUTIVE DIRECTOR, NATIONAL HOME STUDY COUNCIL
FORMERLY SPECIALIST FOR GENERAL ADULT
AND POST-HIGH-SCHOOL EDUCATION
U.S. OFFICE OF EDUCATION

McGRAW-HILL BOOK COMPANY, INC.

New York   Toronto   London

1955

ADULT EDUCATION

Library of Congress Catalog Card Number 54–12679

Preface

This book has been written primarily as a practical guide for directors of adult education in a broad range of agencies and community organizations. It draws upon research findings and pulls together experience from practitioners in a variety of situations. It suggests solutions to many recurring problems of program administrators.

In addition, this book emphasizes the changing nature of adult education. The central focus of adult education is no longer on narrow remedial functions, even though millions of adults in this country are illiterate and tens of millions more are below the educational levels desirable in a democracy. Likewise, the acquisition of salable skills no longer provides the exciting growing edge of the adult-education movement. Instead, the greatest growth in recent years has been in public affairs, in human relations, and in liberal studies.

The impact of an accelerating science and technology on patterns of living is so great that old means of adjusting to change no longer suffice. Millions of adults are finding in the concept of lifelong learning a strategy both for adjusting to changes and for creating new patterns of living. At the adult level, education is becoming less a way of passing on the cultural heritage and more a method for solving the problems of the present and future. In addition, both voluntary groups and governmental units are recognizing that changes are integrated most easily through educational processes. As a consequence, adult education is the most rapidly growing segment of American education. Adults are literally demanding that educational opportunities continue throughout life.

In our democracy an expanding adult education is rightly the business and responsibility of the total citizenry working together in many ways and in many organizations. A primary source of strength in the adult-education movement lies in the scores and hundreds of national organizations and in the hundreds of thousands of local groups engaged in providing adult education.

Moreover, there are signs of added strength as new cooperative relationships evolve to reduce confusion, duplication, and lack of coordination and to increase the effectiveness of methods and approaches. While the ultimate shapes of these new patterns are not clear and are not blueprinted in detail, this book discusses principles and practices which should help administrators better relate their programs to the total community pattern of need for adult education.

vii

If this volume seems to stress the role of directors of adult education in public schools, this emphasis has a twin origin: First, the author has had most experience in the public-school field. Second, he believes that the public schools, as society's specialized organ for education, are in a strategic position to provide much of the leadership and program service required by the emerging adult-education movement.

This book has grown primarily out of two types of experience: (1) work with local community leaders in starting and expanding programs of adult education, and (2) research and analysis of data from adult-education programs throughout the United States.

Six years of work with the local directors of adult education, superintendents, advisory committees, adult-education councils, and community leaders in New York State provided the groundwork. The stimulation of coworkers in the Bureau of Adult Education, New York State Education Department, has been of inestimable value.

The privilege of spending 5 years in the U.S. Office of Education, with its breadth and richness of contact with educators both in this country and abroad, cannot be overestimated. Much of the material reported herein has been drawn from studies made during that period. The author has always felt especially grateful to the many unheralded local directors of adult education and adult-school principals who contributed so generously in supplying data for studies made under Office of Education auspices.

The author wishes that he could thank personally the many hundreds of people whose ideas and thinking have gone into this volume. In addition to the many practitioners who have contributed, appreciation is due for the stimulation provided by graduate students in classes at the University of Buffalo; Teachers College, Columbia University; the New York University summer session, Chautauqua Institution; and Johns Hopkins University.

With deep gratitude, I acknowledge the many painstaking hours spent on the manuscript by my first tutor in adult education, Carolina A. Whipple, retired chief, New York State Bureau of Adult Education. Thanks go, too, to Esther Anson, late of the Continuing Education Center, Michigan State College, for the many constructive suggestions made while the manuscript was in process. John Holden of the same staff contributed suggestions from the point of view of a local director.

Special thanks are due Dr. William G. Carr, executive secretary, National Education Association, who, when secretary of the Educational Policies Commission, gave permission to use material prepared for another purpose.

For aid in editorial preparation of the manuscript, I am indebted especially to Grace S. Wright of the U.S. Office of Education, to Helen Allion, and to Alice Y. Scates.

HOMER KEMPFER

Contents

Contents

PART ONE

The Task of Adult Education

CHAPTER 1 *The Expanding Role of Adult Education in Modern Society*

Lifelong learning is the most significant educational idea of this generation—indeed, of the twentieth century. No educational movement in the United States since the beginning of free public schools has offered more promise for the future than does adult education. As an influence on the further development of our culture, it may prove equal to public education itself. Its possibilities are almost beyond comprehension.

GROWTH OF A CONCEPT

Man has always learned throughout life. Organized education for adults has existed since early colonial times, but for the most part it has consisted of courses preparing for occupations or compensating for deficiencies in earlier training. Following the War between the States, as appreciable numbers of adults came to realize the value and the necessity of systematic learning beyond the school years, lyceums, Chautauquas, reading circles, and literary societies sprang up. Only within the past generation, however, have the various trends combined into a distinct movement.

Adult education emerges from a long cultural tradition of expanding educational opportunity. The idea of free education for all children germinated early in the colonies and came into fruition under the promotional efforts of such leaders as Horace Mann (1796–1859) and Henry Barnard (1811–1900). Starting over a century ago, the spread of public schools had already begun to assure a basic education for practically all children. Since then educational opportunities have been extended upward until today high-school graduation is widely accepted as the birthright of every American youth, and a good majority now finish the twelfth grade. Throughout the world the American public-school system is looked upon as unique. Certainly the idea of providing free education for all the children of all the people has contributed greatly to our national strength and world stature.

The scope of democratic education continues to expand. Increasing numbers can now attend junior colleges and 4-year institutions, and the fast-developing community colleges openly embrace the idea of lifelong

3

learning for all. The question is being asked: "If unlimited education is good for youth, why should it not be good for adults as well?"

This concept does not require that all people be enrolled in formal classes every year. Neither does it suggest the study of organized knowledge for the sake of knowledge or even for diplomas and certificates. Instead, it means that people of all ages will voluntarily seek solutions to their problems of living through educational processes.

RECENT GROWTH IN ADULT EDUCATION

After World War II adult education became the most rapidly growing segment of American education. It grew faster than elementary schools, where enrollments reflected the postwar birth rate; faster than institutions of higher education responding to GI benefits; faster than community colleges and kindergartens. Even so, it has nowhere approached its saturation point. The potential participants in adult education include over two-thirds of the total population—or, according to the 1950 census, over 100 million adults.

Growth in Interest

Numerous surveys report a high and growing interest in adult education. In 1944 the American Institute of Public Opinion announced that 34 per cent of a national representative sample of the adult population had expressed a desire to enroll in adult-education courses. Thirty-one months later, in July, 1947, 41 per cent of a similar sample indicated the same desire. On March 18, 1950, after another sampling, the institute reported: "One phenomenon of life in the United States these days is the tremendous and growing interest in adult education courses. More than 45 million people are taking, have taken, or would take such courses. . . . This is approximately half of the total number of adults in the country."

Milestones in Adult Education

1661	Earliest reference to evening schools, New Amsterdam (New York)
1826	First lyceum started, Millbury, Massachusetts
1833	First tax-supported library, Peterborough, New Hampshire
1859	Cooper Union forums opened in New York City
1873	Society to Encourage Studies at Home founded
1874	Chautauqua institution founded
1876	University extension movement started
1883	The Correspondence University founded at Ithaca, New York
1911	State Board of Vocational and Adult Education established in Wisconsin
1914	Smith-Lever Act established Extension Service in the U.S. Department of Agriculture
1914	Moonlight schools established in North Carolina
1917	Smith-Hughes Act established vocational education in public schools for adults and youth above age fourteen

1918 First full-time state supervisors of adult education appointed, New York and South Carolina

1918 First vocational rehabilitation law enacted in Massachusetts

1924 Department of Adult Education established by the National Education Association

1926 American Association for Adult Education organized

1926 National Home Study Council organized

1932 Des Moines, Iowa, selected for 5-year forum experiment

1933 Federal emergency program of education started for youth and adults

1935 American Youth Commission organized by American Council on Education

1936 Federal forum project inaugurated by U.S. Office of Education

1940 Vocational and military training established for youth and adults through national defense plan

1942 The Armed Forces Institute (predecessor to USAFI) established

1946 UNESCO founded

1947 National Training Laboratory in Group Development organized by National Education Association

1951 Adult Education Association of the United States of America organized

1951 Fund for Adult Education established

These findings have been substantiated by numerous state and local surveys. A poll of adults in New Jersey by the Princeton Research Service in October, 1948, showed marked interest in further education. In answer to the question: "Would you like to attend and take special courses for adults in some school or college?" 44 per cent said yes. In the state of Washington 42 per cent of a representative sample of adults said they would take part in evening classes if they were available,[1] and in an unpublished sampling study directed by the author in 1947, approximately 36 per cent of the adults in Erie County, New York, expressed a desire to participate in adult-education groups. Other local surveys and spot checks report similar attitudes. Evidence is clear that adults interested in further education outnumber all the children and youth now enrolled in schools of all kinds.

Growth in Participation

Interest in adult education is not only verbal. Repeated demonstrations indicating its sincerity and strength belie the oft-heard remark that adults do not want to be educated. Seeming apathy reflects the ineptness of program planners. *Where the types of educational opportunity desired by adults are freely provided at convenient locations on suitable schedules and under competent leadership, adults participate in large numbers.* There is ample support for this statement.

Following World War II state education departments reported a strong

[1] Washington Public Opinion Laboratory, *Adult Education*, Bulletin 3, University of Washington, Seattle, Wash., 1948.

upsurge in adult enrollment in public schools. California, which doubled its adult enrollment in 7 years, had a 50 per cent increase in 1 year alone: The enrollment was 674,000 in 1946–1947, but approximately 1 million the following year. Enrollment in Wisconsin nearly doubled from 1944 to 1947, and in Connecticut the number participating in adult education rose steadily from 12,320 in 1944 to 35,889 six years later. Maryland, where the state pays the salaries of all teachers of adults, multiplied its budget 250 per cent in the postwar years to take care of enlarged enrollments. In Massachusetts there was a threefold increase in adult civic education, and New Jersey reported that both the number of adult schools and the enrollment had tripled in 3 years. In New York "in 1946–47 twice as many people spent four times as many hours studying twice as many subjects in three times as many communities of the state as was the case in 1944–45." [2] The numbers continue to mount.

Reports from local schools were often more astounding. Doubled and tripled enrollments within 1 year were a common story, and a five- or tenfold expansion was not unheard of where boards of education suddenly increased funds, facilities, and leadership. New York State officials announced that if the enrollment increase continued at the rate set, the public schools would be serving more adults than children and youth within a decade. A number of communities in scattered parts of the country already enroll more adults in public-school educational activities than they have youth in grades 1 to 12. Whereas conventional evening schools historically attracted from ½ to 1 per cent of the adult population, the expanded interests of adults and new opportunities have now increased the participation to 5 to 10 per cent of the total population in many communities.

Because of inadequate provisions for gathering enrollment and other recurring data on public-school adult education, a complete nationwide report is unavailable. A number of state education departments collect no information on adult education except in the federally aided vocational fields. In addition, the two sets of data which the U.S. Office of Education has compiled for some years are incomplete. Varied definitions, or none, often weaken such data as can be obtained. However, the most comprehensive study of public-school adult education ever made reported an increase in enrollment of 51 per cent from 1947 to 1951.[3] In the cities covered, the adult enrollment equaled 24 per cent of the total day-school enrollment. Only 15 per cent of the cities indicated a smaller number of participants in 1952 than in 1951. Table 1 shows enrollment trends and the proportion of the population served by various curriculum

[2] *Bulletin to the Schools,* New York State Education Department, Albany, N.Y., October, 1947, p. 49.

[3] Division of Adult Education Service of the NEA, *A Study of Urban Public School Adult Education Programs of the United States,* National Education Association, Washington, 1952, p. 7.

areas. The total enrollment in 1951 in public-school adult-education activities was estimated to be approximately 4,750,000.[4]

Although for decades a number of junior colleges have provided educational opportunities for adults, and lifelong learning is a recognized function of the expanding community college, statistics on adult enrollment have only recently been reported separately in the *Annual Directory* issued by the American Association of Junior Colleges. In 1940 only 55 public junior and community colleges served more adults than regular full-time students, but by 1951 the number had increased to 100. In that year approximately 50 per cent of their total enrollment was adult. The previously mentioned NEA study reported that enrollment had doubled in 5 years and predicted that 1 million adults would be attending community colleges by 1960.[5] It is widely believed that as public junior colleges develop into community colleges, the great majority of their students will be adults.

Member institutions of the Association of University Evening Colleges, in reporting continued growth in adult education, indicated that informal, noncredit, general university extension activities have expanded more rapidly than credit courses. The report of the President's Commission on Higher Education recognized this trend and suggested various types of educational services which college-grade institutions could well provide for adults. Both the demands of adults and the shrinkage of regular enrollment caused by the declining number of veterans have stimulated colleges and universities to expand their adult-education opportunities.

The cooperative Extension Service of the U.S. Department of Agriculture reaches increasing millions of farm families through the county-agent system. Educational programs of private agencies, such as the YMCA, YWCA, settlement houses, social agencies, clubs, private schools, and churches, all reflect the growing interest in lifelong learning.

Reasons for Growth

In the past, interest in adult education has often been sporadic. After periods of high immigration, evening schools filled with the foreign-born. During the 1930s the growth of enrollment in emergency adult programs was aided by involuntary leisure time. The current increase, however, has been in the face of high employment, and only a small fraction of the total enrollment is foreign-born. Early in World War II heavy participation in vocational-education courses was encouraged by Federal subsidies and the urgent need for workers, and after the war college enrollments mounted for a few years under the influence of veteran benefits. But the expiration of these benefits, while markedly noticed in higher education, has had little effect on the total adult-education enrollment.

[4] *Ibid.*, pp. 3–4.
[5] *Ibid.*, p. 158.

Except in agriculture and, in a few states, in elementary and secondary programs for adults, adult education has received relatively little benefit from veteran funds. In fact, most of the fields showing rapid growth in Table 1 do not qualify for Federal aid of any kind.

Table 1. Public School Adult-education Enrollment Trends and Enrollment by Curriculum Areas

Curriculum area	Per cent of increase in enrollment from 1946–1947 to 1950–1951	Per cent of adult-education enrollment in each area, 1950–1951
Safety and driver education....................	535.1	2.1
Civic and public-affairs groups *..............	428.1	22.4
Remedial and special education................	228.3	0.3
Health and physical education.................	190.8	8.3
Agriculture...................................	165.9	1.4
Practical arts and crafts......................	92.4	6.2
Americanization and elementary education......	79.0	9.9
Recreational skills...........................	76.8	4.4
Homemaking education.......................	69.8	13.4
Fine arts....................................	69.1	4.7
Personal improvement.......................	67.0	1.1
Parent and family-life education..............	50.8	6.6
Commercial and distributive education.........	27.7	17.4
Vocational and technical education other than agriculture...............................	16.1	14.8
General academic education...................	4.1	13.5

* This category is not directly comparable to the other fourteen areas.

SOURCE: Division of Adult Education Service of the NEA, *A Study of Urban Public School Adult Education Programs of the United States*, National Education Association, Washington, 1952, pp. 18–19.

This rapid growth in adult education has resulted more from public demand than from external promotion. Adult programs have grown because of pressures from the people, not because big money was available. Primarily the demand reflects response to basic stimuli in our culture which arise directly from the impact of science and technology on our human institutions and which are likely to grow stronger with the passing years. As a result of this impact great numbers of adults want to learn, and there is little reason to believe that the present accelerating interest will soon decline.

This hunger for learning among adults arises primarily from four causes:

1. *Rise in Educational Level.* As the general educational level rises decade after decade, more adults recognize the value of further education. Many who dropped out of school return to finish an elementary, high-school, or college education. Often this return to school is caused in part by the commercial advantages of having a diploma, although other considerations are frequently intermixed. As long as employers and society in general place a premium on academic credentials, many adults who lack diplomas will seek them.

Aside from these specific pressures, evidence is clear that the more education adults have, the more they want; for those with education recognize its intrinsic value. Directors of adult education usually find most of their enrollment above average in educational level. The unlettered, since they understand least the advantages, requirements, possibilities, and rewards of education, are least interested in further learning. As more people become familiar with educational processes, more will desire to continue their education throughout life. A nation with a rising educational level can expect a growing interest in lifelong learning.

2. *Demands of the Changing Culture.* Adults are becoming more aware of the accelerating tempo of modern life and of the value of education in helping them adjust to cultural change. Two world wars within a generation, an economic depression, European unrest, the struggle of people in underdeveloped areas, the Korean conflict, and other postwar events all underscore the facts of change. The world is moving, and people do not want to be left behind. Increasingly, adults are realizing that through continued learning they can keep up with the changing times, that they can gain a more desirable status and play more important roles.

As would be expected in an expanding democracy, more people are beginning to recognize that they have some control over events. They have a growing faith that by taking thought, by studying, by learning, they can make the world a better place in which to live. They have some hope that wars can be prevented and that a peaceful world can be built. They are willing to spend time and energy preparing to make the decisions which affect them, fitting themselves for new roles in the evolving world, acquiring an understanding of the changes going on, and helping to shape those changes. With new problems to solve, they find that they can no longer depend upon reservoirs of knowledge built up in youth. They must learn anew; they must, in fact, create new solutions to both old and new problems. In short, they must continue to learn throughout life.

3. *The Influence of War.* During World War II more adults engaged in systematic and intensive learning than at any previous time in history. When millions of men and women in both military and civilian life had to learn as never before, they found that they, as adults, could learn,

adjust, and adapt. They gained a new appreciation of the benefits and possibilities of adult education and discovered new worlds which, with additional training, they could better understand and master. Millions more engaged in learning incident to the occupational shifts accompanying reconversion to a peacetime economy, and the industrial and economic mobilization following the Korean outbreak called for still further learning.

4. *The Need for Human Association.* Urbanization, industrialization, increased mobility of the population, reduction of family size, fragmentization of family life, and related social and economic circumstances increase loneliness among adults. In a world subject to such rapid changes, educational programs are helping many people to maintain contact with the culture of their times and to avoid social and psychological isolation. Increasingly, adults are finding personal satisfaction and mental health through participation in educational groups, which provide both reputable circumstances and laudable reasons for companionship.

THE NECESSITY FOR LEARNING THROUGHOUT LIFE

Lifelong learning has become necessary because our constantly changing world presents a continuous stream of problems which must be solved if our culture is to endure. According to Toynbee, a civilization survives only so long as it makes adequate response to the challenges of its time.[6] In slowly changing cultures much of the learning that one needs to adapt to his cultural and physical environment can take place in the years of childhood and youth, and any further learning that is necessary can be acquired incidentally during a normal lifetime. Beyond this, the amount and nature of learning required depend largely upon the rapidity of change in the outer world. When major changes occur in the physical or cultural environment, man must adjust to them. Literally, he must learn or perish.

In a Rapidly Changing Culture

Systematic learning throughout life becomes necessary when the rate of change requires faster adaptations than can be made incidentally in a normal lifetime. Of all changes, physical ones are the most obvious. We live in a perpetual industrial revolution, for science and technology continue to make rapid and far-reaching alterations in our environment. We have learned to expect startling advances in transportation and communication, in health and life span, in laborsaving machines and gadgets, and in the application of new forms of energy. Without too much resistance, we accept the fact that we must learn to adjust to the changes in the physical world.

[6] A. J. Toynbee, *A Study of History,* Oxford University Press, New York, 1947.

In simpler frontier times, when families had to be largely self-sufficient, independence and self-reliance were high virtues. However, urbanization and the growing specialization of an expanding technology have multiplied the points of dependence among people. In one sense, we can no longer supply our physical needs as easily as our forebears did. Ability to cooperate with others is increasingly necessary for the satisfaction of most human needs.

The problems brought on by this interdependence and complexity are growing every year. Technology seems to feed upon itself, and the physical world races ahead. For several decades science and technology have been growing on a geometrically accelerating curve until they are now generations and, in some respects, centuries in advance of social mechanisms for their control. For example, Hornell Hart [7] has shown that modern weapons have expanded the "killing area" more than a million-fold since 1900 so that it now covers the entire surface of the earth. Since the human institutions that govern such destructive force have progressed only a small fraction of this amount, the gap between physical power and effective social controls is now dangerously wide. The survival of civilization probably depends upon closing this gap.

In many respects the real world and the world as it exists in the minds of men are far apart. Many traditional ideas, attitudes, and familiar expectations have become archaic in the light of new knowledge and are no longer appropriate to life today. It is true that many behavior patterns have stood the test of time, but it is also true that many others prevent wholesome and effective living in the modern world.

Technological changes, then, require adjustments in our social, economic, and political worlds. Human institutions, however, do not make such adjustments easily. Even under the impact of two world wars within one generation, the minds and habits of men change slowly. Embedded in constitutions, customs, folkways, law, theology, and tradition are a host of practices and beliefs which have little or no functional value. Often they stand in the way of man's aspirations, for he follows tradition long after the original reason for it has disappeared. New ways of thinking about human relationships and of carrying those thoughts into constructive action are necessary if man is to maintain an adequate social order and human dignity. He may feel secure in the familiar old, but often he could satisfy his ideals and aspirations better by developing or accepting something new.

For many people the result of this widening gap between the technological world and human institutions is conflict, defeat, demoralization, mental instability, and personality breakdown. Others, looking ahead, see the possibilities and challenge of growth if all the new knowledge

[7] Hornell Hart, "Social Science and the Atomic Crisis," *The Journal of Social Issues,* Supplement Series, 2:4–29, April, 1949.

can be adequately integrated and put to use. Interdependence, requiring the ability to work with others, demands a higher type of social maturity than does independence and, in our highly interrelated culture, probably yields more satisfactions to all concerned. The impact of technology on human institutions requires that we redefine and refine the principles underlying our relationships with our fellow men.

The lag in social control lies very largely within the field of social sciences—man's relations to man in economic, social, political, and personal aspects. Man can solve the problems of his physical environment more easily than he can his problems in human relations. He has learned more about moving mountains than about removing prejudices. Although he knows how to combine and pyramid research in the several physical sciences under an Einstein equation and thus release atomic energy, he has made no synthesis of similar import in the social sciences.

Adult education and research in human relations are both necessary to close the gap between the many technical advances and their social control. Developments in human relations are necessary to give us new insights, and adult education is necessary to help the new understanding spread among all people.

In our culture, of course, we believe that the greatest use of technology, as well as its best control, can come under a democratic philosophy and system. Since we believe that democracy offers the greatest opportunity for both individual and group growth and development, we have chosen to pursue happiness under the democratic ideal.

Democracy is challenged, however, by other ideologies. Communism and fascism are merely convenient labels for philosophies that are opposed to our own, that represent different attitudes and viewpoints, different ways in which people relate themselves to one another. Will people be regarded as human personalities of infinite worth, dignity, and respect or as pawns in a gigantic chess game? Will individual and group freedom be retained and extended, or will it be lost through ignorance and apathy? Will we be free men in the highest sense or slaves? Will we help ourselves and our fellow men to greater self-realization and higher development, or will we seek to control and exploit them as they seek to control and exploit us?

Seen in this way, the competing ideologies are responsible, not only for a two-world conflict, but for a greater conflict that is constantly going on within our own culture, country, communities, and face-to-face groups. Indeed, it goes on within a great many individual hearts as people strive to reconcile their cultural heritage with the consistencies and inconsistencies of an ever-changing physical and social order.

According to many leaders in our democracy, that ideology or set of human principles, however defined, will win out which best serves both the basic needs and ultimate aspirations of men. The continued existence of the free world depends upon making democracy work supremely better than any other ideology in satisfying the developmental needs of mankind.

Democracy can survive only if it maintains sufficient strength through vigorous growth. Many civilizations have grown old and perished because they failed to maintain within themselves adequate processes of regeneration. The free world must continue to rebuild and reconstruct its culture, striving always for higher levels of maturity. Specifically, our economic system must produce more products and distribute them more equitably; political democracy must be extended so that more people will be involved in making the decisions which affect them; our entire social order must contribute more to the development of people, to living the good life in every way.

Hundreds of millions of people all over the world are stirring restlessly in search of a better life. Competing ideologies are bidding for the minds of men. These facts give added reason for making the democracy of the free world serve better the aspirations of all people.

This situation requires a higher degree of social and political maturity than we have yet achieved. Such maturity cannot be achieved by reviewing old answers. Improvement is a learning process, and there is no time to lose. Questions of war and peace, of economic development, of equitable treatment of minority groups, of extension of political democracy, of labor-management relations, of helping the underdeveloped areas of the world raise their standard of living—all these and dozens of other problems face us every day. Many of them will be settled by adults now living—often by people now in policy-making positions. We must learn to meet these and similar challenges, or we cannot survive.

In the Development of Democracy

Our forefathers saw clearly that political democracy depends upon an educated citizenry. As our relationships grow more complex, this observation acquires more validity. In so far as government in a representative democracy rests broadly on public opinion, satisfactory solutions to public problems depend upon an intelligent citizenry. Adults must inform themselves and seek enlightenment as new issues arise, for the alternative is stagnation and decay. In a world of rapid change, problems multiply too fast to be postponed indefinitely. Since their solution cannot wait the growing up of a new generation of children equipped to handle them, the present generation of adults must find the answers. Education among a democratic people, therefore, cannot be confined to youth; it must go on throughout life. If the free world is to endure, the total citizenry must continuously engage in creative learning and put that learning into constructive action.

In the Development of the Individual

In a democracy individual development—a process that can and should go on throughout life—is the supreme end of education. If education is to achieve its goal of assisting each individual to fulfill his maximum potentialities, it must be available throughout all the years of life.

The young are not mature enough to acquire all the behavior patterns they need as adults, even if those patterns could be predicted safely. A junior-high-school girl cannot understand the problems she will face as a young mother or as a middle-aged housewife. A lad cannot feel the responsibility that comes to a man with a family. Even a middle-aged person is not able to understand some of the attitudes and changes that come with advanced years. The task of education at any age is to help people make adjustments which they must make to maintain psychological and social integration and personal effectiveness. It must help people ever to mature.

THE CHALLENGE AHEAD

As interest in lifelong learning grows, adult education has the opportunity of building upon generations of accumulated educational research and experience. It can start further development at a high level without having to trace the blind alleys of the past. It can short-circuit some of the errors made earlier in other branches of education. The last half century has given clearer insight into the psychology of learning, better educational approaches and methods, and improved techniques for helping people change. While much progress still remains to be made, adult education is fortunate in being able to capitalize upon significant developments in other branches of education and related fields.

The basic need for learning throughout life is not new. Only the amount and the extent of the learning needed are new. Man has always had to adjust to the forces of internal and external change. In recent decades, however, and especially since World War II, the pressures for continuous learning have greatly increased. Competing ideologies and the rapid changes brought by science and technology make lifelong learning more imperative than ever before. As life becomes more complex, more educational assistance is necessary to help make the necessary adjustments.

The full potentialities of lifelong learning, however, may affect not only man's adjustment to the forces around him, but also his ability to gain control over his environment. Through research and learning processes, dramatic and creative progress has been made in the physical sciences. Results fully as creative are still to be achieved in the social-science and human-relations areas.

Such achievement calls for a major reorientation of adult education—

the creation of important new elements, the establishment of new directions. In the past most adult education was designed to improve individual competence. Today a large share of man's problems have become group problems, requiring collective study and action for their solution. Adult education in the future must provide opportunity for adults to gain the understanding, insights, and skills necessary to diagnose and solve both their individual and their social problems. This kind of education will require a much greater emphasis on discussion methods and other group processes. Much of it will center on the whole field of human relations.

In addition to helping with adjustment to a changing environment, learning can provide a positive way of creating that environment. As man becomes more adept in using educational processes, he can learn to apply them to his problems before they reach an acute stage. Instead of becoming aware of difficulties only after they have developed, man can begin to anticipate them and work them out as they arise. Specifically, by wise use of the educational process throughout life, man can (1) assure his own maximum personal development, (2) learn how to control the products and processes of science and technology maximally for his own benefit, and (3) perfect his ability to live democratically in all areas of human relationships. Through educational processes America has a chance of building a democracy so strong that it will eventually become the predominant way of life throughout the world. By use of the proper kind of education, man can literally create the kind of world in which he wants to live. By purposeful and lifelong learning, man can assure his continuous growth, development, and happiness.

By consciously integrating learning with living, a nation will be using most intelligently the major tool for the perpetual re-creation of its culture. If man learns to use educational processes will enough, he can not only adapt to change, but create the change he wants. Through learning he can have a hand in controlling the changes that come. He can avoid periodic Dark Ages. In fact, by using education as a substitute for violent revolution, he can ensure a perpetual Renaissance. If through lifelong application of the educational processes, our free society can learn to solve our group problems as they arise, it will be meeting the challenge of our time. Failure to learn to meet the challenge of increased interdependency may cause the decay of Western civilization.

SELECTED REFERENCES

Adams, James Truslow: *Frontiers of American Culture: A Study of Adult Education in a Democracy*, Charles Scribner's Sons, New York, 1944.

Blakely, Robert J.: "Adult Education Needs a Philosophy and a Goal," *Adult Education*, 3:2–10, November, 1952.

Bodet, J. T.: "Adult Education and the Future of Our Civilization," *School and Society*, 70:210–212, Oct. 1, 1949.

Bryson, Lyman: *Adult Education,* American Book Company, New York, 1936.
——: *Reason and Discontent: The Task of Liberal Adult Education,* Fund for Adult Education, Pasadena, Calif., 1954.
Essert, Paul L.: "Adult Education in the United States," *The Annals of The American Academy of Political and Social Science,* 265:122–129, September, 1949.
Fund for Adult Education: *The Challenge of Lifetime Learning,* Pasadena, Calif., 1953.
Kelley, Earl: *Education and the Nature of Man,* Harper & Brothers, New York, 1952.
Lindeman, E. C.: *The Meaning of Adult Education,* The New Republic, Inc., New York, 1926.
Livingstone, Sir Richard: *The Future in Education,* Cambridge University Press, New York, 1941.
Mayo, Elton: *The Social Problems of an Industrial Civilization,* Harvard University, Graduate School of Business Administration, Boston, 1945.
Studebaker, John W.: *Adult Education: A Bulwark of the Free Society,* American School, Chicago, 1952.
See also General References: [8] Beals and Brody, Chap. 1; Division of Adult Education Service, chaps. 1, 2; Essert, chaps. 1, 3; Knowles, chap. 1; Sheats, Jayne, and Spence, chaps. 1, 2, 20, 21.

[8] The General References are listed in full at the end of this book.

CHAPTER 2 *The Kind of Adult Education Needed*

Education is essentially a process involving the acquisition of (1) new facts and (2) new attitudes and methods, and permitting a new and more confident approach to the problems of everyday living. It is questionable whether learning that emphasizes facts at the expense of methods and attitudes can truly be called "education." In acquiring facts, we must, for the most part, accept the experience of others; but when we learn new methods and attitudes, we are equipped to solve problems independently and to arrive at our own conclusions. New methods become tools which enable us to gain a deeper understanding of relationships and better control of our environment. Facts include what we have learned to date about the operation of our universe; new attitudes and methods become the means whereby new relationships can be discovered, just as Columbus through his methods of observation and empirical test disproved an earlier "fact" and demonstrated the spherical shape of the earth.

If we look upon education in this way, it becomes a continuing process infusing our whole lives—not as a possession but as a set of guiding principles which we can use to solve our problems of living. The process may go on within us consciously or unconsciously. Although to some extent we learn from any experience, we do not always consciously analyze it so that we can use it profitably in the future.

To illustrate: Salesman A calls on Mr. C, a crusty gentleman who certainly knows how to run his business better than any pipsqueak of a salesman who comes into the office. He so informs salesman A. Salesman A is crushed. If he meets many more customers like that, he decides, he will go back to teaching school.

When salesman B calls on Mr. C, he has the same experience but draws entirely different conclusions. He mentally reviews the entire episode, recalling step by step what occurred, and then decides how he should have altered his behavior to have a better chance of making his sale. Next time he will test his theories and see if the results are what he has predicted.

Both men have learned from the experience. Salesman A has learned to be afraid of his reception and to doubt himself. Salesman B has learned that a certain approach is ineffective and has laid plans for a new one. Salesman A learned unconsciously; salesman B consciously turned his rebuff into a learning experience. Since, however, it is unpleasant to be turned down on a sale and learning is much pleasanter when it can come from someone else's trial and error, salesman B decides further that he will suggest that the salesmen have weekly meetings to talk over their experiences and learn from one another. If he had been warned about Mr. C in advance, he might not have lost that sale.

The reactions of these two men to the same situation were not accidental. Salesman B had, in the past, *learned* his analytical, objective approach—either unconsciously through imitation of other good salesmen, or consciously through the training of his sales manager. Salesman A had not had this learning experience. Regardless of the amount of data stored away in salesman A's head, he was not an educated man in this particular area. Salesman B, though he may have had less general knowledge and perhaps even less knowledge of sales techniques, had learned how to acquire the techniques he needed.

It is primarily through adequate use of educational processes that we, both as individuals and as groups, can hope to realize our ultimate values and aspirations. We must *learn* to live. We cannot hope to cope with the problems of living and to maintain a normal place for ourselves in the world without learning. Continuous learning is as essential to us today as it was to our cave-dwelling ancestors. The cave man who did not learn found the consequences charging to meet him; in today's fast-changing, competitive world, continuous learning is essential, not only to improving our position, but to holding what position we have. The man who realizes the advantages of such learning and consciously seeks to improve his knowledge, methods, and attitudes gives himself an advantage over his fellow who blunders along increasing his skills only by the haphazard method of unconscious, undirected learning. The full meaning of life comes not from the milestones passed but rather from the process of living and learning.

Like all education, adult education needs a solid footing in a sound theory of learning. The process of learning has received more intensive study than has any other aspect of psychology and a great deal is known about the conditions necessary to bring about within ourselves a change in behavior, a change in attitudes and methods. As yet, however, there is no crystal-clear theory which satisfactorily explains the total learning process in all circumstances. Although learning can be as simple as the mechanically conditioned response, at times it is as complex as problem solving and invention, which require an insight that has never been explained. Stimulus and response, generalization and differentiation, memorization and selective forgetting, rote learning and insight—all are fragments of a complicated process of which no Einstein has yet explained all the interrelationships. Nevertheless, we can recognize them when they occur in the behavior of individuals and groups of people, as they react to external conditions and produce changes in themselves and in the conditions about them.

For it is very evident that people do learn, that they do acquire new ways of behaving and modify old ones. While growth and physical maturation are, up to a point, natural functions of increasing age, they do not in themselves account for or ensure behavior change. Growth usually makes change possible, while learning completes the adjustment.

Paul Essert, speaking as an adult educator, states this concept of learning: [1] "A learning experience is a series of activities and appraisals from which one gains meanings that can be used in facing new problems and planning new experiences. Action tends to accompany conviction and *doing* and *knowing* are interactive components of all learning pertaining to beliefs, attitudes, skills, and understandings."

THE EDUCATIVE PROCESS

Americans have been leaders in objective research. The experimental method, which demands that every theory be rigidly tested before acceptance, is a forte with us, and it applies just as well to our study of human relations as to our study of physical relationships. If a hypothesis has been tested and found valid, we accept it tentatively until such time as further study may lead us to discard or modify it. The typical American rejection of authoritarianism has stood us in good stead here; refusing to give blind acceptance to any idea or theory, we insist on the right to restudy it and make up our own minds. This process of reflective thinking, theorizing, studying, testing, and reaching tentative conclusions lies at the heart of much of the education needed for living in a changing world. Although systematic study of the cultural heritage, memorization of organized knowledge, acquisition of knowledge for the sake of knowledge, and similar mental activities also have useful roles to play in education, in problem solving they must be kept in perspective.

The emphasis upon reflective thinking and scientific inquiry in education does not rule out "nonintellectual" activities that are also important for human growth, development, and adjustment. Research in psychology and biology is leading us more and more to believe that thinking involves the total person interacting with his whole environment—environment in this case meaning the immediate and past external surroundings and experiences of the person, together with his internal responses to them.

Expressing emotion and sharing emotional experiences; associating with others in work, play, love, and worship; and participating in other activities all contribute to our education. While these elements may be

[1] Paul Essert, *Creative Leadership of Adult Education,* copyright, 1951, by Prentice-Hall, Inc., New York, 1951, p. 14. Reprinted by permission of the publisher.

even less well understood than mental activities, they point up the need for an integrated theory of learning.

One early analysis of the reasoning process set forth a sequence of five interrelated steps which were thought to be characteristic of individual thinking.[2] Since then, other psychologists and philosophers have reformulated the process in other ways, extending it beyond the making of individual decisions to methods of determining social policy and reconstructing basic patterns of human conduct.[3] While no precise formula can yet be proposed for general application, enough common elements seem present in democratic planning and in solving problems to make study of the process profitable. Analysis helps one to see its different parts in their relation to one another and to understand the role of education at each stage. Dovetailed with the brief descriptions of the several stages in the thinking and planning process outlined below is an attempt to suggest some of the tasks of education.

Stage 1. *Defining the Problem*

Thinking and planning begin and new behavior is called for when a person, a group, or a culture becomes frustrated, confused, or uncertain. When a situation arises for which inborn or previously learned responses are inadequate, the individual or group sometimes has sufficient internal resources to work out a solution but at other times requires outside help. Unless problems are resolved in some way, either with or without outside help, the personality of the individual or group may weaken or disintegrate, growth may be stymied, and life may be less happy. The need to solve a pressing problem can provide motivation and direction to a whole process of thinking and learning.

Out of frustration or the blocking of action usually comes an effort to gain a clearer understanding of the nature of the problem. This understanding may take either or both of two forms: (1) The problem may be identified as an obstacle to achieving previously accepted ideals and purposes, or (2) the validity of those ideals and purposes may be questioned.

In the first case, if no reexamination of the purposes is needed, as much insight as possible should be gained into the exact nature of the difficulty. Some problems are easy to identify and isolate; others almost defy definition. Often the problem is not clearly understood until the moment of solution. Only then can one see completely the nature of the difficulty.

In the second case, either an individual must redetermine his objective or the group must set up processes for redefining its goals. The demo-

---

[2] John Dewey, *How We Think*, D. C. Heath and Company, Boston, 1933.

[3] R. Bruce Raup et al., *The Improvement of Practical Intelligence*, Harper & Brothers, New York, 1950.

cratic philosophy theoretically provides for the latter, but in practice the procedures are often inadequate to produce a set of purposes representative of the total population which should be drawn into the process. Lewis Mumford speaks of this inadequacy: [4]

It is naïve to think that geographers, sociologists, or engineers can by themselves formulate the social needs and purposes that underlie a good regional plan: the work of the philosopher, the educator, the artist, the common man is no less essential; and unless they are actively brought into the process of planning, as both critics and creators, the values that will be imported into the plan, when it is finally made, will be merely those that have been carried over from past situations and past needs, without critical revision: old dominants, not fresh emergents.

Education has two major tasks in connection with problem definition. First, if the individual or group is aware of the problem, the educator can assist in thinning out irrelevant factors, in exploring and isolating the various elements of the problem, and in stating it. This includes defining the functional values which the solution must have whether it is to yield a narrowly conceived satisfaction or serve a broad social purpose. The educator can help achieve objectivity where detachment is important. All this mental exploration, of course, must be within the learner's perceptual field, although the educator—through suggestions, questions, and other devices—may help enlarge that field.

Second, education should help those who have unrecognized problems to become aware of their need.[5] In our culture this is recognized as a moral responsibility if the solution of the problem would help the learners advance toward socially desirable goals. Developing this awareness is sometimes extremely difficult because of the wide gap which often exists between the troubles experienced and their remote and complex origins. Illiterates and well-educated alike find it easier to understand immediate, visible, concrete, and simple reasons for their problems. The growth in number and interdependence of causes calls for ever-greater assistance in the discovery, clarification, and definition of problems.

Stage 2. *Finding the Facts*

Once a problem has been identified and at least partially defined, pertinent data should be collected. This is the systematic survey or data-

---

[4] Lewis Mumford, *The Culture of Cities*, Harcourt, Brace and Company, Inc., New York, 1938, p. 377.

[5] Many problems are unrecognized. For example, people accustomed to nutritional deficiencies, poor methods of rearing children, or little civic participation may be conscious of no particular difficulty. Reflected against improved levels of living, however, these conditions may seem serious problems. This viewpoint suggests the possibility that all people have problems of which they are unaware—problems which education might help them solve. Consequently, where new discoveries are being made every year, all adults potentially need to learn throughout life.

gathering stage of research. Only relevant facts need be assembled—those that have a cause or effect relationship to the problem as defined or to any of the hypothetical solutions. Pertinent data may come from such sources as visual exploration, memory, or recorded experience. They may be drawn from past experience with similar problems or from systematic observations of the problem at hand.

The task of education, at this stage, is to help set up procedures for finding out what data should be gathered, for locating them, and for assembling them. Although the educator should be astute in indicating possible sources otherwise likely to be overlooked, he must recognize that desired data may often be unobtainable.

Stage 3. *Analysis and Projection*

Analysis of data usually begins as soon as any become available. They are tested for pertinency as they are located. The heart of analysis, however, is seeing facts in relationship, weighing their relative importance, judging their reliability, and evaluating their worth. Analysis includes selecting relevant facts and placing them in various combinations that may yield possible hypotheses. During analysis, individual and social needs and purposes should be clearly in mind so that facts can be judged in relation to the values held important.

The task of education is to help the analyzer put the available facts in order, to consider all the pertinent data, to see the whole picture, to achieve balanced judgment, to maintain objectivity, to be aware of the influence of his emotions, to suspend judgment until sufficient facts are in, and if decision has to be made on the basis of insufficient data, to be aware of the general magnitude and quality of the missing information. Education must help the learner develop his own insights as a basis for reaching his own conclusions.

Stage 4. *Decision*

Decisions and plans stem directly from analysis. On the basis of known facts, relationships among them, clearly formulated purposes, and estimated needs, a selection must be made among alternatives. This imaginative projection, whether simple or complex, will represent the best possible theoretical solution to the problem defined earlier.

Alternative plans may be set up and tested mentally. Sometimes they can also be tested, in whole or in part, as pilot projects, trial balloons, or experiments, or by any of numerous other methods which may suit the circumstances. Since two or more hypotheses may prove equally sound, decision may be multiple, although usually only one plan can be adopted.

The task of education at this stage is to help in the process of arriving at a decision. The educator can assist groups with methods of arriving at a sound judgment, getting a consensus, and finding opinion through sampling surveys, a total census, or some other means. Although the educator helps with the process of formulating the decision or social policy, he does not unduly influence its content.

Stage 5. Action

A decision or plan has little value until it results in action. This stage, if it is at all creative, calls for "the intelligent absorption of the plan by the community and its transition into action." Mumford [6] continues by saying:

> In this stage, the plan undergoes a re-adaptation as it encounters the traditions, the conventions, the resistances, and sometimes the unexpected opportunities of actual life. No plan can automatically foresee all contingencies: moreover, it loses some of its efficacy as plan if it sacrifices, at the beginning, the clarity of the ideal by timidly anticipating all qualifications and reductions that ideals are subject to in the course of their translation. Nor can a plan, as such, provide for its own fulfillment: to emerge as a reorganizing agent, it must help conjure up and re-educate the very groups and personalities that will bring it to fruition. Weak plans, which hesitate to leave solid ground at all, are often far less effective than over-bold ones that awaken the popular imagination. . . .

Often much education is required during the action stage. If action calls for doing things differently, new behavior patterns, skills, and habits must be developed. A common error is the attempt to induce changes in behavior when the people concerned have not been involved in earlier parts of the process. The extent to which adults are permitted to share in defining their problems, finding the facts, analyzing the data, and formulating their plans is the degree to which they are free men. Those who have participated in these earlier stages are most likely to effect changes in their behavior easily, for they will be strongly motivated to do so.

Where the process has not involved all those affected by a decision, those who made it usually try to "sell" it to the remainder of the group. This situation gives rise to propagandists and public-relations experts. If they are to be avoided, educators must design ways for all concerned to participate from the first in the procedures preliminary to the action stage.

Stage 6. Evaluation

This final stage in the educative process is often slighted, even though it usually offers great potentialities for learning. If a decision or policy works, it is often evaluated so quickly that little further study is made

[6] *Op. cit.,* pp. 379–380.

of the process by which the satisfactory solution was achieved. A perfect solution, of course, gives little stimulus to further thinking, but the merit of solutions to many complex problems is a matter of degree. Always an essential part of the educative process, evaluation is particularly valuable when a solution is imperfect.

Evaluation consists of reviewing the results of action, assessing the elements of success and failure, attempting to identify points of weakness and error in the process, and mentally setting up improvements. If action is to be repeated or continued, improvements and adjustments may be incorporated. If it is a single event, modifications may be suggested for use in solving similar problems in the future. As a result of this stage, changes may be made anywhere along the process line.

The educational task in evaluation is to suggest and help utilize whatever methods and tools of appraisal may be applicable to a given situation. These may include historical records, production records, tests, interviews, comparisons, observations, questionnaires, informal conversations, or any of dozens of other resources.

The six phases of the problem-solving process usually are so interrelated that they are difficult to separate one from the other. Seldom do the various stages of the process follow the exact sequence in which they have been presented here. Each stage may be integrated with one or more other stages. In simple problems, two or more stages may be telescoped; in complex situations certain stages may be subdivided further. In complicated problems and in those that concern groups, many phases go on simultaneously; often there is much shuttling back and forth among them.

APPLICATION TO A COMMUNITY PROBLEM

Fifteen farm-club members in a marginal agricultural neighborhood felt discouraged. Yields were getting worse; prices received were low, and prices paid, high; youth left for the cities; no doctor was available. The club members asked the village superintendent of schools to meet with them to discuss their plight.

The superintendent, knowing the community well, could have announced reasons for its difficulties: poor land, no planned system of agriculture, no attempt at soil conservation, no exciting recreational activities. Such explanations, however, no matter how valid, would not have helped. Positively, he could have said: "Rotate your crops; stop erosion; use fertilizer; grow more grass and livestock." Such advice would have been only a little better. Instead, understanding the nature of education, he did not skip steps in the process. He remembered that giving the answers does not solve the problem and recognized that his solutions might not be the best. After discussing many aspects of their interrelated problems with the superintendent for an evening, the club members *identified their* top-priority *problem:* How can we materially improve the agriculture of this neighborhood?

As the discussion closed, the superintendent asked how other farmers and the villagers felt about the problem and whether they should be brought into the discussion. Opinion was divided, but a majority consented to another meeting to see what the outsiders thought.

At this second meeting the group agreed that the whole community needed to work out methods of gaining more cash income from the farms. The village banker and storekeepers thought such a project would help their business too. The last hour was spent in sketching out plans for getting answers to the many questions that were raised.

After further defining their problem, the enlarged group proceeded to *gather facts,* under the guidance of a committee on which the superintendent, the county agricultural agent, and the agriculture teacher from the county seat, served as consultants. The steering committee organized teams to collect data, and all members of the original club, as well as many from outside, soon had some responsibility. The number joining in fact finding grew weekly. With the help of the three educators, soils were analyzed and classified, studies were made of crops which would grow in that climate, market possibilities were investigated, and a survey of community livestock and machine resources was finished. Even a survey of agricultural skills was undertaken to identify those who could perform special jobs. These and other fact-finding tasks required hours of educational consultation and training.

Meetings to present and *analyze* the findings were started long before all the data were available. Each new session seemed to raise more problems requiring further information. Although it soon became apparent that certain lines of inquiry could not lead to profitable action, the growing of strawberries and certain bush fruits and the raising of grazing animals began to offer hope, although more thorough studies of markets had to be made. Fact finding was continued by sending teams to other regions having these types of agriculture, and consultants were brought from the state college of agriculture. Innumerable committee meetings analyzed detailed data and organized them for consideration by larger meetings. Fact gathering and analysis proceeded simultaneously.

As the agricultural problems received wider discussion, some committees felt that enough time had been spent in discussion and demanded a *decision.* Since some studies were not as far along as others, the superintendent suggested a general meeting to get a "test run" on three major projects that would determine whether any of them had enough community support to succeed. At the meeting the available facts pertinent to each project were outlined. Then, instead of voting on each project, every farm family present filled in a commitment sheet indicating how far it was ready to go on each enterprise. The results showed enough interest in one project to warrant starting it, and a follow-up among absent families led to beginning a second. Study on other projects was continued for later consideration.

As the new projects moved into *action*, many people were faced with the need to learn. Production and marketing problems, operation of different machines, use of new sources of power, farm bookkeeping, seasonal credit, and cooperative management of certain phases of agricultural projects all required new knowledge. Most of the necessary instruction was given informally. The county agent, the agriculture teacher, and three specialists from the state college did most of the demonstration and teaching, although at most sessions local farmers had special contributions to make. The home-demonstration agent was called in to show the women how to preserve unmarketable produce. This gave her entree to a community which she had previously considered difficult.

In *evaluating* their activities 2 years later, the superintendent and a committee compared data from early surveys with information from improved farm accounts. In addition to some property improvements, there had been a satisfying increase in income and in the number of livestock. Stores reported more business. Since, however, some mistakes were evident in group management as well as in individual projects and some ideas had not worked well, committees were appointed to study the reasons for failure and to devise improvements. Success in working together built morale, and the study of other projects continued. A half-dozen young men who had planned to leave for industrial centers had not gone. A neighborhood baseball team was organized and scheduled games with nearby villages. Church, school, and social activities increased as family acquaintance spread within the community. The six-teacher village school started a PTA. A committee started studying ways of inducing a physician to settle in the village. Recognizing that these changes for the better had come largely through their own efforts, most families were enthusiastic about the future program of the farm club.

WIDER APPLICATION OF THE PROCESS

The educative process is applicable to a wide range of human problems. While it is most often used by individuals, it can also be applied to the problems of small groups, large groups, nations, cultures, and civilizations. Science and technology, in making possible a closely interrelated world, have greatly multiplied the number of group problems. Increasingly, whether in the neighborhood or the international fields, human relations and group relationships have become important.

Formal educational institutions, while building competent, independent, and self-reliant individuals, often fail to do a comparable job with groups. Until recently, most people have been given little systematic preparation for living as group members, on the assumption that growing up in groups and learning by trial and error are training enough. In an increasingly interdependent world, however, methods of education are needed which stress group cooperation in defining problems, finding and analyzing facts, making decisions, taking action, and evaluating results.

This lack of educational opportunity in methods of working together is widespread. Two recent studies show that fewer than 5 per cent of the public schools providing adult education give any direct training in group leadership or even in parliamentary procedure.[7] Fewer still offer consultation services to leaders of community organizations. While about one-tenth utilize civic-education discussion groups and a few more hold group conferences, workshops, and short institutes, only one in twelve schools having adult programs participates in any kind of community council. The records of university extension divisions and the cooperative Extension Service of the Department of Agriculture are somewhat better in this regard.

Some private organizations and agencies train in group work and develop skills in human relations, but the numbers served are usually small. Although group-work agencies provide significant help in human-relations training, much of their work is designed for individuals.

Efficient group processes and democracy in human relations do not develop automatically. Without trained leadership and membership a laissez-faire situation often develops where democracy should be operating. This opens the way to anarchy. Democracy is not a biologically natural way of life; it has to be learned, worked at, and maintained.

While the American people are no doubt gradually learning more of the ways of democracy, growing up in a democratic atmosphere is not enough to assure higher forms of group behavior. Vocational educators and specialists in health, homemaking, guidance, literacy, and many other fields no longer depend upon atmosphere. Even if proper group behavior could be acquired through some osmosis process, there are enough undemocratic strains in our culture to play havoc. America is made up of people with many diverse cultural and religious backgrounds, only in some of which is democracy a major concern.

The result of insufficient training in group process shows up in unhappy families, labor-management trouble, crime, delinquency, and a host of other problems. In times past, serious economic difficulties have beset us because we have inadequately solved the group problem of distribution. Housing shortages have existed despite an ample supply of labor and materials. Although large school enrollments are anticipated years in advance, neighborhood and community collaboration has often

---

[7] Homer Kempfer, *Adult Education Activities of the Public Schools: Report of a Survey, 1947–48,* U.S. Office of Education Pamphlet 107, 1949; and Homer Kempfer and Grace S. Wright, *100 Evening Schools,* U.S. Office of Education Bulletin 1949, no. 4.

been so inept that buildings have not been ready in time. The need for suitable recreational facilities, consumer protection, improvement in community health, useful activities in old age, better traffic safety, intercultural understanding, and more adequate financial provision for retirement are illustrative of many group problems which often exist for years before significant headway is made toward their solution.

Adult education needs to build both awareness of and competence in group processes. Many community and national organizations have been established to assist in the solution of one or more group problems. However, some of them are more interested in propagating a specific solution than in formulating answers which will benefit the total public. The role of adult education in developing the ability to work for the common good is twofold:

First, adult education should help people become *aware* that an increasing number of their problems can be solved through cooperative group processes. For instance, many workers, especially labor-union members, have learned that individual employment security is tied up with that of the group—that there is a connection between the employment security of one man and the security of everyone in the plant, the industry, and the total economy. Many individualists, of course, have not yet learned this. Likewise, health—though still an individual matter in some respects—also demands responsible group action at the neighborhood, community, national, and international levels. World peace, too, is a group problem. After learning in school that their country's history has been one of relative isolation, Americans are becoming aware that peace and security are world-wide matters. They are finding out that loss of democracy in a Latin American country is a loss here, that the outbreak of fighting in Korea endangers peace everywhere, that supplying munitions to a country may be more costly than supplying technical assistance for industrial development. We have to become aware that our brothers are all around the globe and that the nature of our world requires us to become our brothers' helper. The isolated pioneer could very well concentrate on his own corner of the world and forget the rest; we cannot.

Second, adult education needs to help people develop competence in working together to *solve* their problems of group living. This involves cooperatively defining the problem, doing the necessary research, making a careful analysis, arriving at a true group decision, carrying out the necessary action, and evaluating both the outcomes and the process.

Democratic planning calls for methodological discipline not only on the part of those who draw up and administer plans but on the part of the community as a whole. It also calls for certain auxiliary educational agencies to lay the groundwork of general methods of thinking and working together—the ideals, understandings, and procedures necessary to intelligent participation on the part of all members of the community.[8]

This procedure does not mean that every person should expect to participate fully in the solution of all problems which affect him. Obviously, many problems are too complex to be understood easily without a special background. Total involvement in all revelant problems ranging from those of the neighborhood to those of the world is more than is humanly possible, and representative democracy makes such complete involvement unnecessary. Usually, however, the component issues and subproblems can be expressed in successive layers of simplicity so that ultimately even persons of less than average education and intelligence can help make crude but fundamentally sound choices.

The rewards of democracy, however, do depend upon the degree to which citizens become involved in understanding and solving their group problems. Representative government requires the development of skill and discrimination in selecting officials. When an individual is delegated the authority to perform certain functions for the group, a balance between mutual trust and eternal vigilance must be built up to help him carry out his responsibility.

Competent use of the educative process yields the best possible solution, and those who participate in this process are expressing their faith that a systematic approach is better than a haphazard one, that reflective thought and scientific inquiry are more reliable than making snap judgments, merely asking a friend, copying old answers, or accepting unquestioned authority. Likewise, democracy implies faith that participation by all in the educative process will result in solutions best for everyone. The success with which group problems are solved depends largely upon the degree to which the process can be applied and the extent to which all members of the group are involved in the process.

METHODS AND APPROACHES

The *process* of thinking provides the fundamental structure for method in adult education. Its elements enter deeply into learning. In so far as reflective thought and scientific inquiry provide the best means of solving problems, the process of thinking is all important in designing educational procedures.

Method is a specific activity used to accomplish any stage in the process. For example, the discussion method helped clarify the farm club's problems. Reading, conducting community surveys, consulting with experts, analyzing soils and markets, and making an inventory of agricultural skills were among the fact-finding methods. Discussion, followed by the use of commitment sheets, constituted part of the method em-

[8] Raup et al., *op. cit.*, pp. 46–47.

ployed in arriving at decisions. Comparison of income, improvements, and inventories with those of a previous year was a method of evaluation.

While the elements of a process are more or less constant, methods are variable. They should be selected or designed anew each time to fit the situation. The value of methods, like that of tools, depends upon their proper application. They serve best when used for the purposes for which they were designed.

Effective Approaches and Methods Needed [9]

Methods and approaches are often weak points in adult education. Under the subject-matter, cultural-heritage concept of education, certain methods, such as the lecture, the recitation, and the catechism, the copying of dictated answers and the memorization of facts for subsequent reproduction, have become relatively standardized. These techniques have their virtues but also their limitations. They are not always effective in changing human behavior.

Many methods currently used in adult education have been copied from the schoolroom without much adaptation. They may never have been thoroughly tested for effectiveness, or if tested, may continue to be used where they have little value. Schools restrict themselves to a limited repertory of methods because repetition is easier than invention.

Lifelong learning will grow when more creative approaches are developed than are currently used in the typical organized program. The evening school, for instance, makes extensive use of conventional teacher-class patterns of instruction, although some of them have only limited usefulness in adult education. Much learning in adult life goes on in noninstitutional and informal settings. Yet the classroom technique is so firmly fixed that it often prevents the development or adaptation of more effective approaches.

Two recent surveys, however, indicated that schools are expanding their use of other approaches. Forums, civic discussion groups, film showings, excursions, directed visits and observations, exhibits, supervised correspondence study, individual tutorial services, training-within-industry, group conferences, workshops, short institutes, community-center activities, adult-guidance services, lecture series, and concert series have been reported by 10 to 45 per cent of all adult-school programs.[10] Film-forum discussions, radio broadcasts for adults, young-adult programs, radio listeners' groups, directed individual reading, educational camps, little theaters, school-sponsored clubs, block-leader organizations, special

[9] An *approach*, as used in this book, is any organized way of providing educational activities or learning experiences. Thus, educational experiences may be organized as television shows, consultations, neighborhood-leader activities, club programs, directed reading, community surveys, exhibits, or classroom activities. Each approach may use any of a number of methods.

[10] Kempfer, *op. cit.*, pp. 8–9.

activities for people past retirement age, and other approaches were also used by a significant number of schools. Lecture procedures are declining, while workshops, counseling activities, informal discussion groups, forums, panels, and home study are growing, according to a recent NEA study.[11]

Schools with strong programs of lifelong learning are adapting or devising other educational approaches and methods. In a growing number of communities, adult schools are breaking beyond institutional walls and providing services in many locations. Large-group activities, techniques for meeting individual needs, discussion methods, socialized activities, informal procedures, and numerous other changes are converting many evening schools into general community programs of adult education. A great deal of imaginative energy still needs to be spent, however, in inventing better methods and in adapting methods from other fields.

Much learning comes through the interaction of personalities and the operation of the dynamic forces within groups. Psychiatry has discovered, for instance, that certain kinds of learning are possible only in interpersonal situations. Consequently, a large proportion of the new methods and approaches could well be rooted in the findings of the scientific study of relationships within groups—a field sometimes called *group dynamics*.

More research is badly needed in this field. If enough were known about the operation of groups, methods could almost be designed on order for accomplishing designated purposes. Method building might then be roughly similar to process development in industry. A competent research chemist familiar with plastics, for instance, can set up procedures for creating a new product having desired specifications. Until more research has been done, however, most new educational methods will be created haphazardly.

Characteristics of Education Desired by Adults

Adults demand education with intrinsic merit, education that serves their recognized needs. When an activity helps them solve their problems and make the behavior changes they want and need to make, they will participate in great numbers. Only when adults are forced by social or economic pressure to acquire a diploma will they pursue classroom activities that are unrelated to their real concerns.

Since they are in a position to demand suitable learning experiences, adults usually insist on the following conditions:

1. Adults, responsible for their own development, must be allowed to set their own purposes. Experts in special fields may advise, but they should seldom determine the scope and sequence of content apart from

[11] Division of Adult Education Service of the NEA, *A Study of Urban Public School Adult Education Programs of the United States,* National Education Association, Washington, 1952, pp. 53–62.

the desires of adults. Adults want to take out of each learning situation only that knowledge and those skills and attitudes which fit their recognized needs. The aims of the instructor, the course planner, or someone else may or may not be acceptable.

2. Adults want educational experience that will help them master life, not merely subject matter. They are not interested in storing away quantities of information that they are not likely to use. They want their learning to help solve their actual problems and gain the goals they have set for themselves. They will not stay long with a text-bound teacher who attempts to make situations and problems fit subject matter. Adults generally want to draw upon organized knowledge as a resource that gives more meaning to their experience; they do not want to learn organized knowledge as an avenue to experience.

3. Adults want their learning to be useful in the immediate or foreseeable future. They are in the midst of life's pressing problems which demand solutions. Deferred values have little appeal to them. They reject as wasteful the idea of learning without regard to accepted purposes, although such purposes may include broadened visions and appreciations.

4. Adults want to be actively involved in the learning process. They demand a rich, personal learning experience and the freedom to control the amount and kind of assistance they get. Giving the answers is not the best way of helping people learn; it is a substitute method used by those who do not know a better one.

5. Adults demand methods which most efficiently develop useful knowledge, skills, habits, and attitudes. Methods accompanying the subject approach are frequently laden with things done *to* people. Adult education is something which people do for themselves, sometimes with outside assistance.

6. Adults want the kind of education which helps them develop their ability to control and enjoy their changing environment.

7. Adults demand competent leaders who have a thorough knowledge of a special field and the ability to relate that field to the purposes of the learner. One who is weak in either respect will not long hold their attendance and interest.

Solutions to problems which adults face may or may not exist in the accumulated experience of the race. Many old problems have never been satisfactorily solved. In these cases searching the systematized knowledge and the unsuccessful attempts at solutions may yield limited satisfactions, but the approach can best be made through emphasis on process. While the past should be investigated for whatever contributions it can make, in itself it can do little to help people move into the future or develop new controls over their environment. For this reason courses and curricula based on the subject-matter tradition often fail to contribute very much to solving the problems of adults. Mere inculcation of greater quantities of organized knowledge is not sufficient. A lifetime of this type of education would not be enough.

This is not to say that traditional learning is worthless for adults. It is inadequate only in so far as educators are unable to use it in its proper framework. In noncompulsory situations in which the participants are the ultimate judges of worth, few adults will subject themselves to heavy doses of organized knowledge presented without regard to their problems or to their aspirations.

Education for adults must be dynamic and forward-looking. In a world as changing as ours, education can no longer have fixed goals in the old sense. It can have no stopping points. It cannot be thought of as an accomplishment—as something to be gained while young and used as needed for the remainder of life. A high-school diploma, a bachelor's degree, or a doctorate are not adequate end products, and the old emphasis on credits, certificates, diplomas, degrees, and graduations is largely worthless in adult education. To mature people, such extrinsic rewards are false goals. When accepted as evidence of education, they become terminal points that needlessly limit growth. The real boundaries of education are coterminous with life. At best, diplomas and degrees should serve only as milestones on the road of lifelong learning.

Adult education cannot be "more of the same." The typical school curriculum is focused heavily upon the past. While adult educators must recognize that the roots of the future are in the past, they must also recognize that what is past is prologue. Many beliefs and viewpoints which may have been reasonably satisfactory during the nineteenth and early twentieth centuries are not adequate for the present generation. If lifelong learning is to play any significant role in the perpetuation of our culture, it must draw upon the past but focus primarily on the present and future.

INFLUENCE OF LIFELONG LEARNING ON THE EDUCATIONAL SYSTEM

As the concept of lifelong learning grows, it seems destined to have a salutary effect on our total educational system. The kind of education desired by adults will undoubtedly have a considerable impact on the approaches, methods, techniques, and subject matter used in other levels of education. In addition, the integration of adult learning with life may hasten the evolution and extension of the community-school idea throughout all levels of education. It may likewise help establish a core of general educational activities which would help maintain the integration of our culture and our personalities.

Underlying most schooling is the implicit assumption that all the knowledge, skills, habits, and attitudes needed by people for use now, during the immediate future, and throughout the remainder of life should be acquired before they leave school, for they are not likely to have any further opportunity for organized learning. In practice, schools are still concerned greatly with preparation for life. For the most part, the dictum "Education is life" is only an academic phrase. It has gained too little real meaning in American public schools.

If the preparation-for-life assumption and its corollaries were replaced by more appropriate ones, fundamental and long-needed changes could come about in the educational system. Let us project three other assumptions and examine their probable influence. Let us assume:

1. That education can, does, and should go on throughout life. This idea is in keeping with the psychology, philosophy, and conditions of the twentieth century.

2. That suitable educational opportunities and assistance are available throughout life. A general affirmation of belief in lifelong learning is the first step toward making this possible.

3. That the purpose of education is the development of competence to deal with life's problems. Adjustment to changes that occur in the environment and in the individual and participation in the control of these changes are included in this purpose.

If these became its underlying assumptions, four major changes would be possible in our educational system:

1. *Better Distribution of the Learning Load.* If adult education were generally available, tradition and available leisure time would no longer fix the period of schooling. Freed from the necessity of carrying the entire educational burden, elementary and secondary schools and, to an extent, colleges and universities could devote their energies to the important growth needs appropriate to the age groups served. The learning needs of adulthood could be postponed with full assurance that they would be cared for as they arose.

The artificial pressures of a crowded curriculum could vanish. There would be no need to compress all the education required in a lifetime into the years of childhood and youth. Competition of subjects and courses for time and space in the secondary curriculum would be eased.

If the adult years contained their proper amount of educational activity, learning could take place at any time in life—whenever it became necessary and meaningful. Immediacy of need often gives a motivation which makes learning easier. The long-recognized principle of learning immediately before use could be put into general practice. Educational experience could be appropriately timed.

2. *Greater Harmony between Education and Human Development.* If organized learning opportunities were available throughout life, education could be planned in keeping with the facts of human development. Research in mental development has shown that the ability to learn

climbs steadily from infancy until it reaches its peak during the early twenties, and then declines very slowly to senescence. Under the present system most organized education is crowded into the years of relative inefficiency. In fact, youth are graduated from high school before they reach their prime learning ability. The prevailing practice largely ignores the growth that takes place during adulthood or else assumes that adults need no educational help in solving their problems of living. With a re-organized time sequence, much of the needed education would take place during the years of maximum learning ability.

The belief that the learning one requires to participate in his culture can or should take place during the early years of life is only partly valid. The fundamental tool skills, constructive methods of work, the habit of acquiring new interests, and similar education can and should be acquired reasonably early. However, it is entirely probable that the years from childhood to adolescence should be freed from much of the academic learning sometimes found there and devoted to broadening experience. Academic learning is possible during the early years, but the shortage of life experience often precludes understanding the real significance of what is learned.

Lifelong learning would help ensure that all age groups would have appropriate purposes in their learning. The preparation-for-life assumption invites the danger of imposed adult purposes, which may not seem vital to children and youth. To the extent that this is true, education tends to be artificial, misunderstood, resisted, and ineffective. When children and youth learn under these circumstances, all sorts of inducements are required to make the experiences palatable. Much of the artificial incentive system of conventional schooling is an attempt to make this type of learning more attractive. The imposition of adult purposes on youth violates the principle that learning is most efficient when the learner is guided by his own goals.

3. *A More Dynamic Curriculum.* If opportunities for learning were available at all ages, knowledge organized by subject-matter specialists would no longer be the center of attention, but rather a resource to be drawn upon as needed. The center of gravity for most learning could shift back from the more or less remote future to present and immediate needs. Much learning for the future, with its accompanying waste, could be abandoned altogether; the learning load could be materially reduced by sloughing off irrelevant matter. The present secondary-school curriculum, in anticipation of the knowledge and skills needed in adult life, is congested with subjects and courses. Most youth will never use parts of it, at least as currently organized and taught. Conversely, experience important to the proper development of young people is often crowded out. If needed educational opportunities were available at every age, the sequence of learning could be suited very largely to the develop-

mental tasks of life.[12] As more of the curriculum became determined by the needs and interests of the individual, learning could become more efficient.

Lifelong learning would encourage a curriculum centered on the developmental problems of children, youth, and adults. Heavy emphasis on preparation for the future in youth education leaves little time for applying the educational process to problems of young people. In a sense, the present system encourages preparation for a static world. Not knowing what the future will be like, present curriculum makers can only guess at what will be useful to know in the future. Most of this has to be based on the past and present. The situation encourages education to provide ready-made behavior patterns rather than to build competence in solving problems. Too much emphasis is on content—too little on process.

This system is all right as far as it goes. If perfectly carried out, it might be all right in so far as the future is like the past. It does little, however, either to develop behavior suitable to new situations or help individuals grow in competence to solve their problems. It is not very useful in facing the changing aspects of our culture.

Much curriculum theory of the past two decades has recognized the deficiencies of our conventional system. While a number of attempts have been made to escape the evils inherent in the preparation-for-life philosophy, few suggestions have been made for removing them through any fundamental reorganization. The child-centered school, the community school, the experience curriculum, the core curriculum, the fused curriculum, and similar approaches attempt to organize learning experiences differently, but most of them do not get away from the assumption that all education for life has to be acquired in youth. Although various corrective devices and revision schemes may keep the content of learning reasonably up to date, the idea of preparation for life, in spite of the future implied in its name, is limited largely to an education suitable to the past. For this reason a dynamic adult education will be concerned primarily with process and will develop its content as necessary.

4. *A New Curriculum Pattern.* It is doubtful that anyone has ever plotted out in any detail the desirable scope and sequence of education under the unrestricted concept of lifelong learning. In certain specific fields enough experience has accumulated to yield norms. The amount of training required to develop a carpenter, an aviator, or a stenographer is known and can be plotted, but less is known about how much education should go into making a competent mother or father. The amount of education necessary in preparing for retirement and the declining

---

[12] For a more detailed discussion of these tasks, see Robert J. Havighurst, *Human Development and Education*, Longmans, Green & Co., Inc., New York, 1953.

years and the sequence of that educational experience undoubtedly vary widely with individuals, but norms have never been established.

The time of the onset of many of life's problems can be located by median age and range. Each individual can recognize the presence of some of his own problems, but for the identification of certain others he may need educational help. The number of people facing identifiable problems or developmental stages in a given year can be at least roughly determined.

Any educational plan designed to meet the needs of people at the various developmental stages would have to maintain great flexibility. It would have to be adjustable to the demands of the times—the amount of learning required by changing economic, political, and social conditions. It would have to be adjustable to the changing needs of individuals through different life stages. The curriculum of elementary and secondary schools might change materially.

Inherent in lifelong learning should be provision for helping people accept, and even welcome, cultural change. Security should no longer reside in achieving a bachelor's degree and depending upon the education represented therein to carry the holder through life. Instead, security would exist in knowing that suitable educational opportunity is available at all times to assist with any necessary or desirable changes.

THE COMMUNITY APPROACH TO LIFELONG LEARNING

In a democracy a community approach to adult education is necessary. A very high proportion of learning takes place in the family, in the neighborhood, and in other face-to-face groups. Interaction of personalities within such groups shapes the individual and influences his character and activities throughout life. The neighborhood, the community, and their component groups are of the highest importance in individual growth and development.

The community is likewise very important in our American democracy. The assumptions upon which the American way of life is based require a maximum amount of participation by people in the solution of their problems. Group and neighborhood activities in tens of thousands of communities provide the base of our social and political structure. If a man can count anywhere, it ought to be in his own group, neighborhood, or community, and local groups offer most people their greatest opportunity to participate in the decisions which affect them.

Because the basis of culture rests heavily on face-to-face relationships in communities and neighborhoods, it follows that any organized provision for cultural renewal should be rooted in and oriented to the community. Elementary and secondary education are based on this principle; the same principle applies to education throughout life.

Adult education intended to affect the lives of people in any comprehensive way in a democracy must be rooted in the community. Community adult education possesses greater vitality, affords greater opportunity for participation in problem solving, and enjoys greater freedom from outside manipulation than do Federal and state programs. The latter have repeatedly run into difficulties when they have not had intimate regard for the local community situation. Adult education developed within the community, by and for local people, is more likely to bring about useful change in a community than anything imported from without. This principle of community orientation assumes that people know their own needs or can find them with outside assistance more easily than outsiders can identify them.

THE ROLE OF THE PUBLIC SCHOOL

If adult education is a community responsibility, how should it be provided? What organizations should be concerned with leadership? Under the democratic tradition he who first sees the need can bestir himself. Competent leadership is welcome from anywhere and may arise in any agency, and sensitivity to the need for adult education is growing among a variety of community leaders. The type of adult-education leadership required by the times, however, is too important to everyone to be left to chance. While a number of organizations and agencies see parts of the need and attempt to meet it with their limited resources, integrated and broad-scale community-wide programs of adult education are pitifully few. Continued neglect and confusion could be avoided if some agency would assume responsibility for leadership.

In several ways the most logical agency to assume this responsibility is the public school. Schools are geographically accessible to nearly everyone. Well-recognized lines of organization and administration exist as do channels for the distribution of funds and the collection of information. Numerically, the public-school staff represents the largest collection of educational competence in the country. The staff, facilities, and financial resources of the schools potentially give adult education a firm base.

In addition to being in a position of leadership, schools are finding a rising public demand that they provide more educational opportunities for adults. This demand cannot be safely ignored. For generations, schools have been active in adult education, and their responsibility in this regard is recognized by the laws of most states. Increasingly, the adult public has been expecting more direct educational service and has repeatedly demonstrated a willingness to pay for it through taxes.

Superintendents in districts having satisfactory adult-education programs almost invariably report that good support for the schools is a by-product of these programs. Without adult education, parents usually become acquainted with the schools only through their children or in other indirect ways. Adults without children in school—usually more than one-half the families at any given time—have even less direct information. If many adults of both groups are actively involved in significant learning activities, they will know the worth of the schools at first-hand. If the school enlarges its concept of adult education, its services to adults, its value to the community, and its prestige as an educational agency will grow. In light of the attacks on public schools in recent years, this objective is much to be desired.

Adult Education for All

Adult education, especially that under public auspices, is concerned with extending democracy far into all human relationships. To achieve this purpose, it must be democratically organized and operated. It must identify itself with and serve the tens of millions of industrial workers, farmers, miners, doctors, fishermen, teachers, clerical workers, lawyers, craftsmen—all occupational groups. It must be organized to serve men and women everywhere—in isolated rural areas, in mountain and plain hamlets, in villages, in industrial centers, in residential suburbs, and in the slums and gold coasts of great cities. It must serve people of all races, ethnic groups, educational levels, and religious faiths.

As its major task, adult education must help all people think through, plan for, and satisfy their personal and developmental needs, assisting them to gain the material necessities of food, shelter, clothing, and health, as well as the more intangible benefits, such as security, adventure, comradeship, recognition, and self-government. It must try to make all people see that they can achieve these values primarily through cooperative group endeavor rather than through competition and conflict.

In helping to extend and reconstruct democracy, adult education cannot pretend to have the substantive answers ready to teach to all. It does not and cannot have them. At best, it can offer only the answers of the past, and new and better answers can be had only by those who work them out in the process of living and learning. Since answers to problems are made, not found, the major responsibility of adult educators is to know how to go about making the answers and to become skilled in helping others make them.

SELECTED REFERENCES

Childs, J. L.: *Education and Morals: An Experimentalist Philosophy of Education,* Appleton-Century-Crofts, Inc., New York, 1950.

Coady, M. M.: *Masters of Their Own Destiny,* Harper & Brothers, New York, 1939.

Dickerman, Watson: *Outposts of the Public School,* American Association for Adult Education, Inc., New York, 1938.

Drucker, Peter F.: *New Society: The Anatomy of the Industrial Order,* Harper & Brothers, New York, 1949.

Hallenbeck, Wilbur C.: "Building Working Philosophies in Adult Education," *Adult Education,* 3:148–153, May, 1953.

Lewin, Kurt: *Resolving Social Conflict,* Harper & Brothers, New York, 1948.

McCharen, W. K.: *Improving the Quality of Living: A Study of Community Schools in the South,* George Peabody College for Teachers, Division of Surveys and Field Services, Nashville, Tenn., 1947.

Pell, O. A. H.: "Social Philosophy at the Grass Roots: The Work of the A.E.A.'s Committee on Social Philosophy," *Adult Education,* 2:123–132, April, 1952.

Spence, Ralph B.: "Education's Stake in Adult Education," *Teachers College Record,* 54:275–284, February, 1953.

United Nations Educational, Scientific, and Cultural Organization: *Adult Education: Current Trends and Practices,* Problems in Education, no. 2, Paris, 1949.

See also General References: [13] Division of Adult Education Service, chap. 6; Sheats, Jayne, and Spence, chap. 3.

[13] The General References are listed in full at the end of this book.

CHAPTER 3 *The Developmental Tasks of Adults*

Hard work, abundant natural resources, the faith and vision of free men, and an extensive system of public education have combined to give America a high economic standard of living. This combination has yielded a reasonably good, happy, and abundant life for many people. The American dream has been high, and it has inspired a corresponding level of achievement.[1] Any fair comparison of reality with the vision, however, would show the dream some distance ahead.

The American dream remains incompletely fulfilled largely because our social skills have not developed as rapidly as the demands of our technological culture. We have never fully marshaled the forces of education to help everyone acquire the understanding and skill necessary to adjust to our technological civilization. Educational systems have been developed for young people; but with certain exceptions, extensive education for adults has not been generally provided. To assist in making the American dream a reality is at once the central task and the primary challenge of adult education.

In fulfilling this dream, to what ends shall the education of adults be directed? The answer to this eternal question derives largely from social philosophy.

THE OBJECTIVES OF ADULT EDUCATION

The aims of education have been stated and restated from time immemorial. Among the better purposes are the "Golden Rules of Education" proposed by Professors Briggs and Justman, which can be paraphrased for adult education: [2] "The first duty of adult education is to help adults learn to do better the desirable things they will do anyway. Another duty of adult education is to help adults discover higher activities and to desire to achieve them."

The all-inclusive purpose of education in a democracy, of course, is to assist in the continuous growth and development of every individual—

[1] James Truslow Adams, *The Epic of America*, Little, Brown & Company, Boston, 1932, pp. 404–405.
[2] Thomas H. Briggs and Joseph Justman, *Improving Instruction through Supervision*, The Macmillan Company, New York, 1952.

the fulfillment of his maximum potentiality in directions thought desirable by society. The problems and situations which adults face in this process of growth and development can be grouped into the four major areas set forth by the Educational Policies Commission.[3] The objectives of self-realization, human relationships, economic efficiency, and civic responsibility are good for the education of persons of all ages in a democratic culture.

The larger objectives of education are most useful if they are thought of, not as fixed goals finally attainable, but as directions in which to move. While the doctrine of the infinite improvability of man may have limitations, especially when applied to narrow skills, it has general acceptance in our culture. Certainly such goals as further self-realization, improvement in human relations, increased economic efficiency, and greater competence in citizenship are within the reach of most people. Larger objectives may represent a receding horizon, but smaller objectives often represent step-by-step progress along the road.

Self-realization

Self-realization is the primary and immediate concern of every individual. It stems from the most basic drive—survival or self-preservation—and aims at development of the highest intellectual and aesthetic interests.

The objectives of self-realization include the whole range of communication skills—speech, reading, writing, listening, observing, and numerical calculation. Adults of all educational levels and degrees of competence who have the spirit of lifelong learning will continue to strive for improvement in these abilities.

Knowledge and habits of personal and community health constitute another cluster of self-realization objectives. The continuing advance of medicine provides one reason for lifelong learning in this area. In so far as diet and other health habits should change with age and with the discovery of new information, they represent an area of continuing need.

A great deal of self-realization is achieved during leisure time. Whether increased leisure is a benefit or a curse depends largely upon whether or not people learn to use it in constructive and creative ways. Much of the feeling of integration with one's culture is acquired during leisure time. Much of the richness of life comes through the development of a wide range of interests and activities throughout the years. Adults need to find congenial social groups, establish satisfactory relations with groups of their own and different ages, and acquire a repertory of suitable leisure-time and recreational skills.

Intellectual interests of the inquiring mind, aesthetic interests that arise

[3] Educational Policies Commission of the NEA, *The Purposes of Education in American Democracy*, National Education Association, Washington, 1938.

in the craving for beauty, and the conscious or unconscious search for a philosophy of life are parts of the continuing drive toward self-realization. Every person's desire to develop his own individuality and independence—his desire to understand the meaning of life—requires lifelong learning.

Human Relationships

Happiness depends largely upon human relationships. One who cultivates the art of personal friendship, maintains a rich and varied social life, enjoys warm family relationships, practices democracy, and has humanity-wide sympathies possesses the chief ingredients of happiness. These relationships extend throughout adult life and necessitate continuous learning partly because the passing years bring new experiences.

Few tasks are more important than selecting and learning to live with a marriage partner, starting a family, rearing children, and helping them to become responsible and mature adults. Managing a home and establishing and maintaining satisfactory living arrangements, however, are problems which change during life. As families expand and later decline in size, adjustments must be made, and learning is required.

In the past, organized education has not been greatly concerned with some of these problems. Until recently little educational assistance has been available in this field. Increases in personality breakdowns, however, indicate that many people do not learn to adjust as their culture and biologically maturing selves demand. Yet, every community has an easily estimated number of people passing through each of these life stages every year. They represent population groups highly receptive to learning and very likely to benefit from imaginative adult-education programs.

Family structures, too, are changing. Urbanization, fluctuations in size of families, the changing status of women, and other factors leave many adults for long periods without close family ties. Normal human companionship is important for mental health. Learning activities provide an opportunity to form and maintain personal friendships and often to develop specific skills and understandings in personal relationships.

Beyond the intimate face-to-face relationships are ever-widening circles of association—neighborhood and community groups, racial and cultural groups, religious groups, nations, and clusters of nations operating on differing philosophies. Since the increasing complexity of modern life multiplies the importance of relationships among groups, an important objective of adult education in recent decades has been to increase reciprocal understanding and appreciation among people with different cultural and ethnic backgrounds. There is a great and continuing need to develop a broad knowledge of conditions and aspirations in foreign nations and colonial outposts. The brotherhood of man can come as people learn, through education—to a considerable extent through adult education.

Economic Efficiency

The economic problems of adults are primarily concerned with production and consumption. Sometimes selection of, often preparation for, usually entrance upon, and almost surely progress in an occupation come during the adult years. With the rapid changes in the world of work, many adults find it necessary to learn new occupations or take major refresher courses once or more during their working lives.

Responsible Citizenship

Citizenship is a lifelong responsibility. The obligations one assumes at age twenty-one do not decline with age, and learning is required by the changing succession of civic problems and the evolving nature of our social, economic, and political world.

In this field, probably more than in any other, group and individual needs can be served at the same time. As groups face issues and solve problems of citizenship, individuals will be growing in their tasks of taking civic responsibility and meeting social and civic obligations. Specific learning demanded includes refreshing oneself about the structure and operation of government and becoming acquainted with the major current problems. In addition, good citizenship requires the development of skills in detecting and evaluating propaganda; selecting candidates; participating in the affairs of a political party and/or political-action group, taking part in group discussion and leadership, which involves knowledge of parliamentary procedure and public speaking; participating in a variety of community and autonomous groups, and working in a number of other group situations.

THE CONCEPT OF DEVELOPMENTAL TASKS

Educational objectives take on meaning when they are converted into experiences which help people change. The experiences constitute the curriculum. The general objectives of adult education, as expressed earlier, provide guidelines for curriculum development. However, broadly stated objectives, such as assisting the continuous growth and development of every individual, offer little concrete direction to curriculum builders.

A leader can most intelligently help adults engage in educational experiences when he understands their needs for growth and development. Basically, such needs in our culture arise from biological maturation, from social demands on adults as they grow older, and from the interaction of these two forces. Educators must discover and clearly define these problems and needs before they can design a program of assistance.

Meeting individual needs has long been a concern of educators. This aim has often been coupled with the theory that the individual develops best if he is left as free as possible. When this idea was carried to the extreme, cues were sometimes taken from the whims of children and youth.

Demands of the social order, too, have entered into curriculum building. Current theory holds that education should assist children to develop in harmony with the restraints imposed by society. In recent years these two aspects have come together in the concept of the *developmental task*.

"A developmental task is a task which arises at or about a certain period in the life of the individual, successful achievement of which leads to his happiness and to success with later tasks, while failure leads to unhappiness in the individual, disapproval of the society, and difficulty with later tasks." [4]

Developmental tasks arise both from the physical and psychological growth of individuals and from the expectations of society. Such tasks result from the interaction of the maturing person with the cultural environment—the interaction of organic and environmental forces. Physical and psychological maturation and cultural pressure together, in varying ratio, give rise to each task. Early in an individual's life, his personal values and aspirations begin to modify the definition of the task and its accomplishment. If each task is successfully accomplished at it arises, the individual can maintain adjustment and can be happy. If he cannot do this, he is likely to become maladjusted and unhappy. While the concept first arose from the science of human development as related to early childhood, it is applicable to all stages of life.

Educators find the concept useful in two ways. First, it helps in defining more concretely the purposes of education. Thus, adult education may be thought of as an effort to assist people, both as individuals and in groups, to achieve the developmental tasks they face during their mature years.

Second, the concept helps in timing educational activities. If life is looked upon as a series of developmental tasks, each to be faced in due time, education can bring its efforts to bear at the most appropriate moment. When the developmental stage has been reached, when society demands, and when the person is wholly ready, then is the most teachable moment. A study of developmental tasks will show when educational efforts can bring most fruitful results.

Certain developmental tasks, such as selecting an occupation, may become necessary at a given period in life, be accomplished, and not be faced again. Other tasks, such as those connected with citizenship, arise

[4] Robert J. Havighurst, *Human Development and Education*, Longmans, Green & Co., Inc., New York, 1953, p. 2.

slowly, reach a plateau, and thereafter remain constant throughout life. Still others, while enduring for a long period, may change in nature during successive stages of living. Relationship to a spouse, for instance, changes as people grow from young adulthood, through middle age, to old age.

TASKS OF PERSONAL DEVELOPMENT AND FAMILY LIVING

A large cluster of developmental tasks centers around human relations in the family and in other intimate groups. These tasks have special bearing on well-being in so far as satisfactory relationships to other human beings are a source of happiness.

By the time adulthood is reached, many tasks in human relations have already been achieved, and many others are in process. Some tasks of younger years, however, may have been achieved poorly, if at all, thereby laying the groundwork for later failure unless remedied by further education. Even in a population which has accomplished its earlier tasks well, a fair proportion of persons will not successfully accomplish all the tasks of adulthood unless further educational services are adequate. Increases in personality breakdowns and other personal difficulties in later years indicate that many people do not learn to adjust automatically to the demands of their culture and their biologically maturing selves. Without help a fair proportion of them do not learn to solve their problems. With educational help many more, who may adjust well

Table 2. Size and Age of Groups Engaging in Developmental Tasks Related to Family Living

Task	Approximate no. of persons per 1,000 total population *	Median age of persons first engaging in task	Approximate ages between which 50% of group engage
Selecting a mate (first marriage)........	21	22	19–25
Learning to live with spouse (first marriage).............................	21	23	20–26
Having first child....................	16	24	20–27
Entering first child in school...........	16	29	26–33
Helping first child enter teen ages......	15	38	33–44
Adjusting to aging parents.............	15	38	30–45
Adjusting to death of parents..........	14	42	55–77
Adjusting to one's spouse in middle age.	19	45	40–50
Adjusting to death of spouse..........	9	67	60–78

* Figures based on number of persons per 1,000 reaching the median age each year.

SOURCE: National summaries of vital statistics for 1949 and preliminary reports of characteristics of the population in the 1950 census.

enough to get by, could make far better adjustments and learn to live more fully. The following are the developmental tasks most likely to be faced by a high proportion of people through their adult years:

Selecting a Mate

Nine-tenths of all people surviving past middle age are married sometime in life, and nearly everyone at one time or another faces the task of mate selection or rejection. Few tasks hold greater potential happiness or sorrow. Arising out of both biological and social pressures, this most

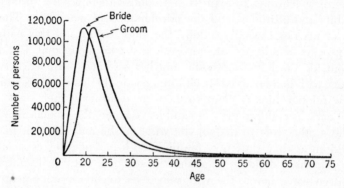

Fig. 1. Ages of brides and grooms at first marriage in a total of 15 states. (Source: *Statistics on Marriages: Specified States, 1949,* U.S. Public Health Service, National Office of Vital Statistics, Special Reports, National Summaries, vol. 36, no. 6, July 17, 1951, pp. 84–88.)

interesting and absorbing task often occupies the greater part of a decade. While most marriage partners are selected in the late teens and early twenties, many people marry for the first time at later ages. A number repeat the process after divorce or death of a spouse. While subsequent marriages may not present the same need for learning as the first, new elements are usually present on which educational assistance is useful.

Few tasks call for calmer thinking and greater care—or greater learning. It is ironical that our educational institutions give so much assistance in selecting a vocation and so little in selecting a life partner. To a large extent mate selection is still based on romantic tradition, folklore, and storybook concepts, coupled in some social classes with a complicated, almost ritualistic, courtship process. In spite of the romantic tradition, the human sciences have much light to throw on the mate-selection process. The findings of research in the biological and social sciences can contribute to the solution of problems of courtship, love, and mate choice without destroying the romantic glow. Surely education can contribute much more than it does to this highly important aspect of adult living.

If a mate is not selected, that choice, too, requires learning and adjustment—learning how to live alone and acquire satisfactory substitutes for what in most cultures is accepted as the normal state of life.

Learning to Live Together in Marriage

Both partners in a new marriage must learn new roles. Often they must draw further away from parents and the friends of younger years and transfer certain affections to each other. Each usually acquires a new set of relatives with whom personal relationships must be established. Failure in these family relations may jeopardize the marriage. Mutual adjustment requires learning to express and control feelings, the formation of new habits and attitudes, and the development of new skills. The early months of marriage usually require the most learning of this nature.

The process of adjustment, however, is a continuing one. If the wife works outside the home, both she and her husband must learn to combine work with homemaking. If children come, the man and woman must add new relationships without straining or destroying their own. In the middle years, as children grow up and leave home, the woman may revert from the mother role to that of the wife, or she may attempt to follow her children as they start new families. Both parents, but especially the mother, may have difficulty in assuming their new status as grandparents. As children leave home, the wife may seek outside employment which may require further man-wife adjustment. Both must adjust to the physiological changes of middle age, the climacterics of each, and the general diminution of youthful vigor as age increases.

One or the other, more often the woman, has to adjust to the death of the spouse. This may require acceptance of new living quarters and adjustment to other relatives, sometimes under crowded conditions. The woman may have to learn more about business and financial affairs. The man may have to develop the ability to care for his own clothes, to keep house, and to cook. In either case the remaining partner must learn to be alone and to do without or to find satisfactory substitutes for certain types of affection and companionship formerly enjoyed.

Through counseling, instruction, and discussion activities, an adult-education program can help couples learn to live together and get ready to face succeeding tasks. It can also prepare them to live alone when such a time comes.

Starting a Family and Rearing Children

The first pregnancy sets off a whole chain of learning tasks. Development of new attitudes toward life and acceptance of the unborn are probably more important than training in physical health. Both the father and mother must learn much both before and after the birth of the first child.

Whether the new baby is reared by folklore supplied by relatives and friends or by more scientific knowledge depends partly upon the parents and partly upon the organization of the community for parent education and child welfare. Certainly the sciences of human development can provide much information on infant care, the development of pre- and in-school children, and adolescent growth.

Parents must learn how to meet the changing physical, social, and emotional needs of their growing children. This learning includes knowledge and skills in child management, adaption of daily schedules to the needs of children, expression of affection without spoiling, and encouragement of an ever-maturing parent-child relationship. Later this relationship will

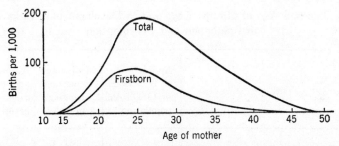

FIG. 2. Total birth rates and birth rates of firstborn, compared with age of mother: in the United States, 1949 (based on live births per 1,000 estimated female population in each specified group). (Source: *Births by Age of Mother, Race, and Birth Order*, U.S. Public Health Service, National Office of Vital Statistics, Special Reports, National Summaries, vol. 36, no. 9, Oct. 15, 1951, p. 145.)

involve learning how to help adolescents become independent and emotionally mature. The contrast between social and physical environments of present-day youth and conditions a generation ago point up the need for parent education. Methods that worked in 1925 may be ill adapted for today. Because the potential for improving human relations and happiness is so great, parent education and child development have become important parts of adult education.

Adjustment to Relatives and Aging Parents

The smaller families of recent decades tend to decrease the number of relatives to whom adjustment must be made, but increased longevity and the growing number of older people multiply the problems. Housing problems, economic and financial problems, the leisure time of retirement, two- and three-generation conflicts, and the slow deterioration of health from chronic diseases demand new adjustments and the learning of new ways of living. Lifelong learning can help adults adjust to their contemporaries as relationships evolve. Much of the involution of old age need not occur. Interests in the wider environment can continue, especially if the habit of acquiring new interests is engendered early and nurtured by learning throughout life.

The tasks connected with personal development and family living involve learning all along the line. Adult educators, together with social workers and others in human-relations occupations, have a responsibility for helping provide the conditions under which the necessary learning can take place.

DEVELOPMENTAL TASKS OF PRODUCTION AND CONSUMPTION

For most men and many women an occupation is a primary focal point. In our culture, wisely or not, an individual is often measured by his occupational success; vocational competence and the ability to achieve a good

Table 3. Size and Age of Groups Engaging in Developmental Tasks Related to Production and Consumption

Task	Approximate no. of persons per 1,000 total population *	Median age of persons engaging in task	Approximate ages between which 50% of group engage
Selecting first occupation..............	11	16	15–18
Preparing for first occupation..........	11	17	15–19
Entering the labor force, males........	7	17	16–19
Establishing first home...............	15	23	20–26
Learning how to manage first home.....	15	23	20–26
Participating as members of the labor force †.........................	413	38	27–48
Maintaining satisfactory living standards †...........................	642	40	27–54
First adjusting to reduced family size, middle-aged women...............	9	48	43–52
Retiring from labor force, males........	4	65	60–71

* Figures are based on number of persons per 1,000 reaching the median age each year, except for sixth and seventh category.

† Figures are cumulative, including all persons who have passed a certain age.

SOURCE: Census and U.S. Bureau of Labor Statistics data for 1950.

material life, therefore, are high in value. These abilities call for occupational training and consumer education. The tasks involved can be grouped under three headings.

Progressing in an Occupation

For middle-class people occupational life is usually only partly started, if at all, at the beginning of adulthood. Youth in the lower socioeconomic classes usually enter the labor force relatively early, while those in the upper classes enter it late. By the age of eighteen, a person may have definitely selected an occupation, have selected one only tentatively, or not have selected one at all. Educational and vocational guidance services, where available, are appreciated by many young people.

Occupational preparation may require only a little time or several years of study and work. Specific preparation often starts only after general day school is over, or—if begun earlier—may be continued in the out-of-school years. With the trend toward higher minimum wages, a longer span of formal schooling, later occupational entrance ages, reduction of child labor, higher educational requirements for work, and increased complexity of industrial processes, the period of occupational

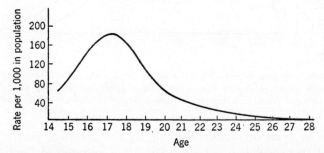

FIG. 3. Annual rates of labor force accession, total males, 1940, after age 14. (Source: *Tables of Working Life—Length of Working Life for Men*, U.S. Bureau of Labor Statistics Bulletin 1001, August, 1950, p. 7.)

training is being extended. Much of this education is now carried on past the normal age of high-school graduation, and often preparatory and upgrading periods are spread intermittently through the young-adult years.

Occupational progress may be made at any time during adulthood, but most preparation for it is likely to be concentrated in the first third of the working life. This explains the preponderance of young adults in vocational-education courses. The dying out of old occupations, the growth of new ones, and other changes brought on by developing technology, however, require an increasing number of older adults to seek occupational training throughout life. More adults than ever before are having to change occupations at age forty, fifty, or sixty. Many others repeatedly have to take in-service training courses to keep up with the progress in their occupations. All these changes call for additional guidance and educational programs.

Married women, too, as their children grow up, often go to work. Many of them who became employed during World War II are still working. In an expanding economy of high-level employment, their numbers are not likely to decline materially. Some who had a salable skill before marriage are able to refit themselves for employment by taking brush-up refresher courses. Others, including those who did no paid work before marriage, desire pre-employment training.

In an individual's later years, occupational activity declines. The widespread practice of abrupt retirement often creates hardships and unnecessary strain, especially for men. Transfer to part-time employment, to a self-managed business, or to an occupation permitting more gradual retirement are the solutions for some. Whenever possible, retirement

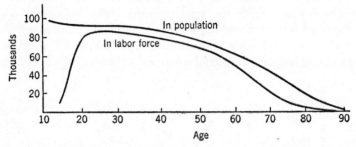

FIG. 4. Stationary population and labor force, total males, 1940 (number living, of 100,000 born alive). (Source: Reproduced from *Tables of Working Life—Length of Working Life for Men*, U.S. Bureau of Labor Statistics Bulletin 1001, August, 1950, p. 5.)

ought to be *to* an occupation suitable for the declining years. The substitute of increased leisure-time activity has recognized limitations for those who have lived active occupational lives.

These periods of change offer opportunities for education to assist with adjustment. Ewan Clague, U.S. Commissioner of Labor Statistics, has said, "Those over 45 give the educational institutions of the country their

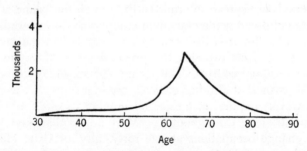

FIG. 5. Annual labor force separation due to retirement, total males, 1940 (number, of 100,000 born alive). (Source: Reproduced from *Tables of Working Life—Length of Working Life for Men*, U.S. Bureau of Labor Statistics Bulletin 1001, August, 1950, p. 9.)

greatest challenge. Vocational adjustment, guidance, and retraining are especially needed for those over 50."

Establishing and Managing a Home

While the number of independent households varies with economic conditions and available housing, 90 to 95 per cent of all married couples live in their own homes. Many single men and women also have their own households, either owned or rented. Setting up housekeeping for the first time calls for considerable learning. Purchase of furniture, equipment, and possibly the property itself requires decisions for which previous schooling can give only limited help. When growth or decline in family size, illness, or the absence of members from home for work or war necessitates reorganizing living arrangements, household routines, and home life, education can help people make these adjustments. The typical family changes residence about every 5 years, and each move may bring new problems requiring further learning.

Achieving a Satisfactory Living Standard

Every adult faces the task of adapting his level of living to his financial resources. Desire for more children, too, is often balanced against resources. The pressures of advertising, the psychology of keeping up with the Joneses, and cycles of inflation and deflation further complicate the task. Usually the standard of living is a compromise between income and expenditures. Within varying limits, income can sometimes be raised through greater occupational competence, larger investments, harder work, or longer hours.

Complementary to occupational training is consumer education. Either individually or in families, adults need to establish and maintain an economic standard of living. They need to learn to use available income wisely for food, clothing, shelter, health services, leisure activities, continued personal development, and economic security. For most individuals, family-budget management is an artificial task during the day-school years. It becomes real during early adulthood, and adjustments are necessary throughout life. Growing families sometimes bring increased expenses before maximum income is reached. Income often remains high during middle age until it is sharply reduced at retirement, when another major income adjustment must be made.

THE TASKS OF CITIZENSHIP

In a world of rapid change no amount or kind of citizenship education during youth can suffice for the half century of adulthood. The continual flow of problems over the civic horizon requires the constant study of an informed and concerned citizenry. Keeping well informed amid the strong pressures of conflicting propaganda is no simple task. Mass-media programs and political-party activities are not enough. Citizens need all the sound help which educational agencies can provide. A state using education for its own perpetuation will maintain educational programs to build enlightened citizens at all ages. At the same time it will encourage strong voluntary activities designed to spread civic information among its citizens.

Civic enlightenment, however, must be accompanied by action. People should register and vote in both primary and general elections. Many other democratic countries consistently demonstrate higher voting rates

Table 4. Size and Age of Groups Engaging in Developmental Tasks Related to Citizenship

Task	Approximate no. of persons per 1,000 total population *	Median age of persons engaging in task	Approximate ages between which 50% of group engage
Reaching voting age..................	15	21	
Invested with full citizenship †........	662	42	31–56
Acquiring citizenship responsibility through naturalization, etc...........	0.4	43	29–60
Aliens without full rights of citizenship..	20	52	

* Figures are based on number of persons per 1,000 reaching the median age each year, except for second category.

† Figures are cumulative, including all persons who have passed the legal voting age.

SOURCE: Census data and *Annual Report of the Immigration and Naturalization Service for 1950.*

than we produce in our most heated election contests. While voting is only a small part of citizenship responsibility, it is a specific index of the civic health of a community. The voting rate of young adults, those below the age of thirty or thirty-five, is usually much lower than that of older citizens. In one community, for example, very few young adults vote until 15 years after they become eligible.[5] Evidently the kind of citizenship education generally provided by the schools does not ensure that young adults will promptly assume full and active civic responsibility. The habits of citizenship built in the elementary and secondary schools are not strong enough to overcome the obstacles—preoccupation with court-ship, establishing homes, and getting started in occupational life. The appropriate time for most people to receive citizenship education focused on registration and voting should be when they reach voting age, which is twenty-one in all states except Georgia, where it is eighteen. Young adults with most of their lives ahead of them should be most concerned about formulating the social policies under which they will live. Yet, un-der pressures of other tasks, young adults all too often leave their govern-ment in the hands of their parents and grandparents.

Among every 1,000 inhabitants, approximately 15 each year reach the

[5] *Springfield, Massachusetts, Looks at Adult Education,* Adult Education Council, Springfield, Mass., 1951, p. 17.

voting age. A sizable number of them never vote—sometimes because of educational deficiencies. The training of young adults to discharge their citizenship responsibilities as new voters should be as seriously undertaken as is the military training of young men.

Citizenship responsibility, however, includes more than voting: Participation in governmental and community organizations is also essential. Studies show that one is likely to have more organizational affiliations as he grows older and improves his socioeconomic position. Many unskilled workers belong to no organized group, except possibly a labor union or a church. Young adults up to age thirty participate relatively little in organized groups and hold few leadership positions. The middle-aged are the most active in organized groups and civic affairs and often take the lead in community organizations. Many middle-aged people, however, never vote or take any other significant part in the formulation of public policy. Governmental positions, especially those dealing with policy making, are often held by older people. The general inactivity of young people in these specific citizenship activities makes it doubly imperative that effective adult-aducation programs be available to help the older groups keep abreast of the changing times.

THE TASKS OF LEISURE TIME

The amount of leisure time which people have varies somewhat with economic conditions. In periods of high employment, many have difficulty in getting enough leisure for adequate recreation. In years of unemployment, the enforced leisure of millions results in great economic waste, uncreative living, and personal unhappiness. In both cases, education has a responsibility for helping people to learn to use their available leisure to greatest advantage—in ways which contribute maximally to human development.

Unmarried young adults use much of their leisure in courtship. After marriage, children and the heavy schedule of serious work leave little time for leisure activities. This situation itself is a problem, as busy young married folk need to learn how to gain and use time for suitable recreation.

Family demands at middle age lessen and, unless the husband is too heavily involved in occupational life, more leisure is available. This time is suitable for expanding interests, although curiosity and the habit of developing new activities should be nurtured earlier. As the middle-aged develop new interests through the learning process, they should be afforded ample opportunity to participate in activities which are suitable for the years ahead. Preretirement guidance and the development of substitute occupations, new interests, and suitable leisure activities are among the responsibilities of education as older people move from full-time work to full leisure.

Use of time by middle-aged women is a growing problem as labor-saving machines, ready-made clothes, and ready-prepared foods simplify homemaking. Between the ages of forty and sixty, millions of married women enter the labor force. Those who remain unemployed spend their time in lightened housework, community activities, recreation, and a certain amount of idleness. The problem has caused James Wood, President of the Woman's Foundation, to propose the development of special colleges for middle- aged women.[6] The adult-education departments of community colleges and public-school systems can well develop programs for this population group. The potential energy for constructive civic and community work, for paid employment, and for creative forms of recreation is tremendous. Adequate educational programs slanted to this group undoubtedly could release energies which would materially strengthen both our economy and our democracy.

Table 5. Size and Age of Groups Engaging in Developmental Tasks Related to Leisure Time

Task	Approximate no. of persons per 1,000 total population *	Median age of persons first engaging in task	Approximate ages between which 50% of group engage
Establishing friendships and leisure activities in new neighborhood †........	126		
Establishing friendships and leisure activities in new communities †........	39		
Establishing friendships and leisure activities after marriage..............	25	23	20–26
Establishing friendships with younger people as contemporaries become fewer	7	65	55–75
Adjusting to increased leisure upon retirement, males....................	4	65	60–71

* Figures are based on number of persons per 1,000 reaching the median age each year, except for first and second categories.

† Figures for first category are based on census report of the number of persons per 1,000 who move to new locations within the same county; for second category, on the number who move outside the county.

SOURCE: National summaries of vital statistics and census data for 1950.

In the later years special problems arise as the tempo of living slows. Older people often reduce their activities in community organizations. They may find themselves in an isolated age group. While those who live past the normal life expectancy have more leisure time, they find that friends of their own age are thinning out. Consequently, they must make

6 *Woman's Home Companion*, May, 1948.

friends faster among their contemporaries, cultivate the acquaintance of younger adults, or make some other adjustment. Education can help older people make the necessary changes in their pattern of living.

Throughout life one has the ever-changing task of making and keeping friends. For those few who live in the same neighborhood all their lives this may require less learning than for the many who change residence periodically. In the teens and young-adult years many friends are of the same relative age. Mothers of young children may form groups on the basis of their common interests, and young couples often associate for recreational purposes.

During the middle years, especially in occupationally related activities, the age grouping becomes less important. Associations are maintained with all ages. Formally organized groups supplement the informal associations and provide the milieu in which individuals can find congenial friends.

Developmental tasks in regard to leisure time include establishing and maintaining congenial social relations and learning a repertory of recreational activities suitable for successive stages of life.

THE SIZE OF THE TASKS

Every director of adult education needs to know the size of the various population groups to be served. Statistics that give merely the total population of the community or the total adult population are not enough. Programs can be better tailored when the number of persons facing the various developmental tasks, their ages, and similar characteristics are known. Because conditions differ widely among communities, directors should, if possible, study the data reflecting local conditions. Most of the essential information on larger communities and political subdivisions can be found in census reports and similar sources. For local conditions in small communities, however, county and state figures are usually more helpful than national summaries. Tables 2 to 5 and Figures 1 to 5, drawn from national data, indicate what to expect in typical communities. By multiplying the approximate number of adults in every 1,000 persons who face a given task each year by the total population of his community or service area, the local director can estimate the number of adults concerned with each specific task.

Fluctuations in birth rates in recent decades have made marked irregularities in the population curve. Likewise, marriage rates have been severely affected by war and economic conditions. As a consequence, certain numbers in the tables are abnormally large or small. The indexes will not remain constant. As these irregularities move through their cycles, the relative size of the different age groups will change materially. This fluctuation is additional reason for every director of adult education to calculate the rates for his own community.

A major element has been omitted from Tables 2 to 5. In most cases the amount of educational time required to complete the task or the amount needed per year is not known. Decades of experience have standardized the amount of time required by persons of known competence to achieve specified goals in elementary, secondary, and higher education, but such norms have not yet been worked out in most areas of adult education. Wide individual differences, a multiplicity of methods, extreme variations in approach, differences in objectives, and many other factors make standardization difficult. Indeed, a great many adult educators think time standards in the conventional sense are to be avoided. As adult education becomes more universal, however, accumulated experience will indicate the time required for specific tasks. Many tasks, of course, are affected by the age of learners, changing times, economic circumstances, and other conditions, but the time required for adults to accomplish the following educational tasks has become relatively standardized:

Task	*Clock-hours*
Start as an illiterate and earn an eighth-grade equivalency certificate.......	800
Learn symbol shorthand with competence to take dictation of 120 words per minute..........	480
Pass Red Cross basic first-aid course..........	20
Participate in a Great Books Discussion group, first year..........	36
Complete a course in driving training..........	20

In theory, the amount of education required to assist all adults with all tasks they face during any one year should add up to the total education job for any given community. The field is so new, so few accurate data are available, and the effectiveness of methods is so variable that the total amount of adult education a community ought to provide cannot be carefully estimated. Certainly during the coming period of great adult-education expansion, a more practical measure is the amount in which adults will participate when the most ingenious approaches and effective methods are used.

SELECTED REFERENCES

Havighurst, Robert J.: *Human Development and Education,* Longmans, Green & Co., Inc., New York, 1953.

Horn, Francis: "International Understanding: The Lament of a Discouraged Adult Educator," *Adult Education Journal,* 9:109–118, July, 1950.

Kempfer, Homer: "How Much Adult Education Do 444 School Programs Provide?" *School and Society,* 75:26, Jan. 12, 1952.

Springfield, Massachusetts, Adult Education Council: *Springfield, Massachusetts, Looks at Adult Education,* 1951.

Wool, Harold: "Trends in Pattern of Working Life, 1900 to 1975," *Monthly Labor Review,* 71:438–442, October, 1950.

See also General References: [7] Beals and Brody, chap. 2; Essert, chap. 2; Knowles, chap. 2.

[7] The General References are listed in full at the end of this book.

PART TWO

Program Development

CHAPTER 4 *Identifying Educational Needs
and Interests of Adults*

"Adults in this town don't want to be educated. We publicized ten
courses last month and only a dozen people registered—no more than
three in any course." The superintendent who made this complaint
showed a list of offerings: American history, current events, arithmetic,
algebra, geometry, shorthand, Americanization, public speaking, French,
and chemistry.

Another superintendent looked over promotional materials of neighboring adult schools and listed thirty-two courses he thought would draw
sufficient registrations to start a local adult program. After the projected
curriculum had received some publicity, sixteen courses materialized, and
a new program got under way.

These two approaches to program building are dubious answers to the
question eternally facing directors of adult education: "What to offer?"
In elementary and secondary schools and in colleges, courses and curricula are often repeated year after year with only slight modification.
Entrance requirements of higher schools, state courses of study, widely
used textbooks, standardizing regulations, and accrediting systems encourage uniformity. Under these circumstances the director of instruction
can know with fair assurance what his total curriculum will look like a
year ahead.

There is no such uniform and exact guide for setting up adult programs. The adult curriculum, less firmly established in experience, cannot
be so standardized. Adults are not so likely as children to accept predetermined courses and curricula. In certain areas, such as vocational
education, outlines of content may be fairly well established, but even
then adults will choose only those courses that meet their special needs.
Although high-school and college courses for adults are often modifications of similar courses for youth, in some areas, the curriculum is much
more fluid, varying considerably among communities and even differing
from year to year within the same community.

The voluntary nature of adult education forces every program director
to be his own curriculum expert. Because adults do not have to go to
school, programs must be based on needs and interests which they them-

61

selves feel or can be led to recognize. They will accept organized instruction, even arduous curricula, provided they can thereby fulfill an ambition or satisfy a felt need. The adult educator's first task is to identify those needs.

The educational needs of adults cannot be identified once for all time. While some learning needs are basic and remain relatively stable for given age groups, others change greatly according to economic conditions, world tensions, the domestic situation, and the vicissitudes of our evolving civilization. These factors make program building a continuous job. In a very real sense, it is never finished.

Sound program building, then, requires the continuous identification and definition of adults' educational needs and interests. This work is the everlasting responsibility of the director of adult education. If he does it well, he will be on the road to developing a sound and thriving program. If he does it poorly, he is doomed to failure or, at best, to mediocrity. Inexperienced directors, especially, are in danger of making mistakes in identifying educational needs and interests. Needs that may seem obvious to a professional educator or to a social worker may not seem real to the adults in the neighborhood. On the other hand, if the program is limited to needs recognized by adults, it is likely to remain underdeveloped or to grow slowly. The director who tries everything under the sun without adequately determining need, however, will undoubtedly waste considerable time and money. To avoid these two extremes, the director must understand not only the needs felt by adults but those which they may not recognize. This skill comes best with experience, although the study of methods used by successful directors can give important clues.

In a recent study, administrators in 100 public junior colleges with adult-education programs stated that their most difficult problem was the lack of criteria to determine need for courses.[1] Directors in these institutions wanted to know most of all, "On what bases should the need for courses in adult education be determined?" The same problem was ranked second by private junior colleges. Without doubt the need is equally acute among directors of other adult programs. This chapter will discuss some tested ways by which directors can find out both what adults want and what they need to learn.

Involving Adults in the Identification of Need

Skill in bringing adults into the process of identifying their educational needs and interests is an earmark of outstanding directors of adult education. The extent to which a director has adults share in program planning may be expressed on a "scale of involvement." At one end of

---

[1] S. V. Martorana, "Problems in Adult Education in the Junior College," *Junior College Journal*, 18:115–123, November, 1947.

the scale the director sets up activities *for* adults. In extreme cases, he may set up courses quite arbitrarily based upon his own ideas of what is good for adults. He may go further by asking the board of control, faculty, or adults what courses should be given, or he may utilize one or a combination of techniques to identify and define adult needs. Educational activities planned according to these needs may be academic or problem-centered, depending upon the interpretation and orientation of the administrator. In so far as adults recognize that the activities serve their needs, they may participate. The success of such programs usually depends heavily upon effective publicity; under such circumstances, adult education is "sold."

At the other end of the scale, the director and the adults plan together. Adults are not merely studied and asked what their educational needs are. Instead they are *brought into the process* of identifying educational needs and setting up appropriate programs. They may make surveys, analyze their problems, ask others about their learning needs, and identify deficiencies which can be remedied by education.

The most advanced kind of program planning, of course, is that which makes identification of need an integral part of the educative process. Ideally, identifying need corresponds to the first step in the educative process, defining the problem. Program planning to meet the need embraces the remainder of the steps: gathering data, analysis, decision, action, and evaluation. Defining real problems and working out their solutions represent learning at its best. Under this system, the director of adult education is concerned, not with identifying needs in isolation, but with arranging conditions so that all adults will have maximum opportunity to identify and define their real problems and to work out their best solutions.

Even though under given conditions some ways of identifying educational needs are better than others, most directors must be familiar with a variety of methods. They will often have to use a combination of methods and may even fashion new ones to fit local circumstances. Likewise, they will have to operate at various points along the scale of involvement.

ADMINISTRATIVE PROCEDURES [2]

Receiving Requests

The easiest way for directors to find out what adults want to learn is to be alert to their individual requests for courses. More directors base their programs on individual requests than on any other indication of need. The Emily Griffith Opportunity School at Denver built its early

---

[2] Findings reported in this chapter are based largely on Homer Kempfer, *Identifying Educational Needs of Adults*, U.S. Office of Education Circular 330, 1951.

reputation largely upon its willingness to serve every request, even when only one person asked for a given course.

Ordinarily a course is opened only when enough adults have registered for it. Careful directors keep cumulative lists of all inquiries and encourage the inquirers to interest enough others to warrant starting the courses. The policy of offering any course requested by twelve or more, provided that a qualified teacher can be found, is effective primarily with organized groups. Persons not already in touch with others of similar interests are not likely to have the techniques for bringing together a dozen like-minded individuals. Often, if the director thinks a requested course might be of sufficient interest, he will publicize it as a possibility and open or drop it according to demonstrated interest. For activities which may appeal to selected groups, he may circularize specific lists of people most likely to be interested; he may check with a "consumer panel" as in market research; he may seek the opinion of an advisory committee or inquire among his present enrollment.

Directors who depend only upon individual requests are following the most conservative policy possible. Likewise, to consult individual laymen is a relatively poor way of identifying educational needs (see Table 6). If such a practice were followed in medicine, a physician might ask a patient to diagnose his own illness. To be sure, the patient can help, but he needs professional assistance. Programs based largely on individual requests are usually weak, especially if not widely publicized. A single request may represent only one person's interest and may not indicate a widespread need. Without strong encouragement, only a few adults are likely to make their interests known directly to the school.

Requests from business, industrial, labor, and community groups provide an excellent way of identifying adults' educational needs (see Table 6). Programs built upon such requests are ordinarily much larger than those catering merely to the expressed or implicit needs of individuals. Group requests by telephone, mail, or personal call are often based on considerable exploration and definition of adult interests. Usually they offer a ready-made group with definite motivation to participate in an educational activity designed to meet the request. This procedure saves the energy otherwise needed to form a group of people with allied interests. The requesting organization is often willing to help define needs further, advise on content, find leaders, and assume other cosponsoring responsibilities.

The practice of encouraging groups to voice their needs is especially useful in expanding going programs, but it may also be useful in starting new programs if leaders are sufficiently imaginative and facilities are adequate for meeting the requests. However, this practice is not highly effective in extending services to those who do not belong to organizations.

Identification of need in cooperation with organized groups is so profit-

Table 6. Relative Merits of Thirteen Methods of Identifying Educational Needs and Interests of Adults

Method	Composite superiority ratio *	No. of schools using method		
		Usually	Occasionally	Seldom or never
1. We systematically cultivate a group of "coordinators" in industry, business, and other community organizations and agencies who watch for every opportunity for education to perform a service..........	1.51	90	111	329
2. We receive requests from business, industrial, labor, and community groups.....	1.49	210	228	92
3. We study deficiencies of adults (e.g., poor nutrition, low educational level, lack of civic participation, poor methods of child rearing)............................	1.42	75	174	281
4. We maintain an extensive personal acquaintance with a wide range of community leaders and groups................	1.41	208	186	136
5. We examine data from the census and similar sources.......................	1.39	30	135	365
6. We make systematic surveys of the industrial, business, civic, and cultural life of the community...................	1.38	91	148	291
7. We examine published surveys of other communities and similar literature......	1.38	82	260	188
8. We examine catalogues, schedules, publicity materials, and programs of comparable institutions....................	1.32	127	249	154
9. We act on a "hunch."..............	1.28	28	104	399
10. We try to be sensitive to civic, personal, and social problems of people—problems which can be alleviated by education....	1.25	189	186	157
11. We check with other known interests of people (e.g., library reading interests, newspaper- and magazine-readership surveys)............................	1.20	58	150	322
12. We utilize check lists and other "interest finders."..........................	1.18	82	90	358
13. We receive individual requests..........	1.15	235	240	55

* The ratio indicates the superiority of schools which *usually* used the practice over those which *seldom or never* used it. Thus, the 90 schools usually using method 1 rated 51 per cent higher on a composite of the 6 indexes than did the 329 schools not using this practice. Six indexes entering into this "composite superiority ratio" were size of program, number of population segments served, flexibility of schedule, number of approaches used, number of coordinating practices, and number of cooperative practices.

SOURCE: Homer Kempfer, *Identifying Educational Needs of Adults*, U.S. Office of Education Circular 330, 1951, pp. 40–51.

able that directors of many successful programs have worked out a variety of relationships with these groups. In the evaluative study reported in Table 6, the best programs by every criterion were those in which directors systematically cultivated a group of coordinators in industry, business, and other community organizations, and those agencies that are alert to every opportunity for education to perform a service.

These coordinators are personnel managers, plant superintendents, training directors, program chairmen of large community groups, secretaries of councils, clergymen, prominent members of the chamber of commerce, labor-union officials, and other key people in business, industry, government, and community life who are in a position to be aware of educational needs. Directors of adult education can help these people become more sensitive to the educational possibilities in their daily work. The Phoenix Technical School in Arizona does this, in part, by periodically bringing groups of such coordinators into the school to show new equipment, to review training films, to demonstrate techniques, and to discuss their training problems. Group visits to their establishments and observation of their educational problems and activities stimulate the flow of ideas. In time, with several meetings per year, these coordinators become liaison agents, building strong relationships between the school and the community.

Looking at their problem from the educational point of view, coordinators multiply and extend the skills of the director. They are able to see what learning tasks are necessary, and they know where to turn for help. As their own competence in identifying educational needs increases, much of the work of defining the need is done before the problem reaches the director.

A few large adult programs, especially those sponsored by colleges and universities, employ field coordinators who keep in touch with the educational needs of community organizations and often work with advisory committees. Their relationship with these groups is largely informal, and it is sometimes based upon personal friendship. The use of field coordinators, while good, is only moderately effective in reaching unorganized portions of the population. It works best where both the policies and the direction of a program are relatively stable. Frequent turnover in leadership is obviously inimical to the development of strong liaison relationships with field coordinators.

Adults become aware of educational needs and interests in response to external or internal stimuli or to a combination of both. The director of adult education can provide some stimulation by publicizing the current program. Also, he can build among adults, and especially among their leaders, an awareness of the possibilities that new courses and additional educational services hold for enriching their lives and meeting their practical needs.

While systematic publicity of offerings is helpful, the best way to build awareness of the potential benefits inherent in new educational activities is to inform individuals and groups directly and personally. Many successful directors use this method even though it takes considerable time. Some supplement their own efforts by inviting leaders and groups to visit the school and see at first hand the varied programs in action.

Another common practice is to notify selected organization leaders and groups by mail of the desire to set up new activities. A number of directors do this annually or periodically in a covering letter sent with general publicity materials. Individual letters to newly appointed leaders can be well timed throughout the year.

About 85 per cent of all public-school directors use general publicity materials to announce the possibility of new courses. As statements of policy, such announcements are useful, but they do little to stimulate requests for new instructional groups. Competent directors build up the number and quality of requests from individuals and groups primarily through face-to-face interviews combined with direct-mail promotion.

Making Direct Inquiry

The obvious way of finding out what adults want and need to learn is to ask them. There are several ways of doing this. Results, however, are sometimes disappointing.

Newly appointed directors often depend more upon check lists and questionnaires to discover interests than do experienced program builders. Duplicated inquiry blanks seem simple and easy to use. They are most often distributed in classes or at the meetings of community groups, given out by libraries, or sent home with school children.

Inherent weaknesses, poor administration, and faulty interpretation make check lists tricky. They often start with program possibilities rather than with the needs of adults. This practice makes promotion of adult education much like selling stock available in the warehouse. It tends to disregard buyer demand. Highly conventional and rigid offerings are most easily thought of for listing, although courses that serve specific functional needs can also be included. Any long list of offerings, however, reduces the reliability of the questionnaire as an accurate reflection of interests, partly because bare titles with inadequate descriptive material give little information upon which to make an intelligent selection. Prospective students often take check lists lightly and soon forget the answers. This method of inciting interest frequently appeals to ephemeral desires. Changes in circumstances make questionnaires filled by registrants in the spring an unreliable guide to fall programming. Furthermore, check lists usually reach only a minor segment of the potential clientele so that returns are seldom representative.

These and other weaknesses have brought interest check lists into such disrepute that a majority of directors seldom, if ever, depend upon them. Nonetheless, when carefully planned, properly administered, and cautiously interpreted, such inquiries can help identify needs and interests. Check lists gain reliability if they ask for definite commitments in the presence of teachers or counselors. Inquiries limited to a few or even to one activity may yield a dependable response, but, like most forms of casual direct inquiry, they usually fail to uncover deeper educational needs. Even if these are really felt, only the bold will give more than polite responses to a questionnaire, particularly if respondents are asked to sign their names. Heavy dependence can rarely be placed upon them, even though they constitute one useful tool in the kit of professional program builders.

Direct inquiry can be systematized through surveys. For decades business firms have utilized market-research techniques to acquaint themselves with their potential customers. Such techniques constitute an important tool in the local director's kit when he thinks of the total population as his potential clientele. As a program planner and promoter, he will need reliable data on adult interests and needs. With these data he can design educational activities in much the same way as a product is designed to fit buyer demand.

Surveys using a questionnaire mailed to a representative cross section often result in a biased low return, provide too few data for sound analysis, and generally yield few clues helpful for course and program construction. Door-to-door surveys, while time-consuming, usually give better results. The steps in making such surveys are outlined in Chapter 6. With careful cross-section controls, an adequate number of return calls, and trained interviewers coached to probe wisely, surveys can give relatively reliable and systematic data. If the director and the interviewers hold a follow-up group discussion of results and experiences, they may gain further insight. Guided by a team of interviewers, conversations with small informal neighborhood groups meeting in homes may also indicate additional interests and needs.

The results of national and state sampling surveys of interest in adult education were cited in Chapter 1. On the local level, the cost of having an outside survey firm identify educational needs of adults is usually prohibitive except in the largest cities. In any case, the educational advantages of community participation in planning and conducting a survey are so great that the use of commercial surveys is usually ill advised. Outside consultants may be engaged, however, to help with the technical problems of developing a questionnaire, selecting the cross section, training interviewers, and analyzing of results.

Survey questions seeking directly to discover educational need and interest are most commonly used. They are often supplemented by other questions designed to determine leisure-time activities, vocational problems, difficulties in human relations and family living, inner motivations and ambitions, hidden desires, prejudices, and irritations. Significant insights into need and interest can usually be teased out of the data. The skill of the survey designer, the interviewers, and the analyzers determines in large part the effectiveness of such diagonal approaches. At best, in the hands of competent psychological research teams, such surveys become depth interviews applied to a representative cross section. At worst, they assemble a mass of data from which all sorts of erroneous conclusions can be drawn.

In addition to surveys of the adult population, systematic surveys of the industrial, business, civic, and cultural life of the community often lead to significant insights. Partial or comprehensive studies may be made of occupational trends, cultural resources, recreational activities, and community leadership structures. In a few communities the chamber of commerce or a similar agency keeps a perpetual inventory of payroll jobs. If the director of adult education can share in planning community surveys made by such agencies, he may be able to see that they are of maximum use in identifying the educational needs and interests of adults. Large programs, especially, can use this method to advantage.

Examinations of published surveys of other communities and similar literature are almost as revealing of educational need as are original surveys. Obviously directors find those surveys most useful that have been conducted in communities similar to their own. The value of this tool is limited by the difficulty of finding wholly comparable communities. The shortage of competently made and thoroughgoing surveys in small and middle-sized communities is a serious handicap which is another reason why directors should conduct their own studies.

Most directors occasionally test public interest in an educational activity by publicizing it. If there is enough response, the activity materializes; otherwise it fails. This is "trial-balloon" promotion, and it is warranted when the director has reason to believe that the activity will prove of sufficient interest. Sixty per cent of the courses given trial-balloon publicity by 350 adult schools actually materialized.[3]

Trial balloons may be based on little more than irresponsible guesswork, or they may be supported by good evidence. Often they are based on hunch. While apparently only a quarter of the public-school directors in the previously mentioned study claim to use the hunch even occasionally, its use, especially by experienced directors, is likely to prove profitable. Only a few directors are able to identify the components of a hunch. However, it seems to be an insight which comes to alert directors through clues from conversations, newspapers, radio programs, and travel, from mingling with the public and from observing hobbies. A few directors consciously develop hunches and take pride in those which

[3] Kempfer, *op. cit.*, pp. 47–48.

prove right. Through hunches experienced imaginations can move beyond tested facts. Where little time and money are at stake, hunches may pay dividends without too much costly experiment and pilot study. The few directors who frequently used this method had programs 75 per cent larger than those who did not use it. However, a hunch is of little value to the beginner who lacks enough experience to provide a subconscious guide to workable decisions.

In identifying the educational needs of adults, experienced directors know that there is no substitute for wide personal acquaintance with community leaders. Sensitivity to need cannot be developed in an ivory tower. Successful directors participate widely in groups as members, leaders, speakers, and advisers.

Directors of thriving programs devote considerable time to making and maintaining close acquaintance with leaders in their communities, and they encourage their staff to do likewise. Some members of large staffs spend almost full time in field work. Directors with wide personal associations have significantly larger programs and use more approaches than those lacking this advantage. Nearly 40 per cent of all directors usually depend upon personal acquaintance to yield valuable insights into adult needs and interests.

Studying Systematic Information

A surprising amount of systematic data has been compiled on medium- and large-sized communities. Even small communities and rural areas have been analyzed in numerous ways. This information, much of which is useful in identifying educational needs and interests, provides a solid base for program building.

Census reports are a mine of information for directors. The reports portray statistically the social and economic conditions in various major and many minor political subdivisions of the nation. National data are widely publicized, but local figures often show surprising variation from the national. These differences make it imperative to study the appropriate state, county, city, and census-tract data in detail. While the census points out directly few specific educational needs, imaginative directors see many implications which would be difficult to discover elsewhere. At best, census data provide stimulation to reflective thought. They help directors to look at these aspects of the adult community:

1. *Educational Level.* Nearly every community has illiterates, college graduates, and representatives of every other educational level. Their educational needs differ widely, and a program designed for the average person is not likely to appeal to either extreme. Those with the least formal education, even though they have the greatest need for learning, are often the most difficult to involve in any educational program. By studying each successive educational level, a director can design activities

that will serve needs at all levels. Such exploration will reveal not only the need for elementary education but also the levels at which other educational services should be directed.

2. *Age Structure.* While interest in education apparently declines with age, real educational need may not, although the respective needs of the young, middle-aged, and the old differ greatly. Activities tailored to the needs of specific age groups will serve the maximum number of people. Census data show how big the job is and keep one from forgetting important groups which may not show up at an evening school.

3. *Family Circumstances.* Educational needs change somewhat with marriage and the coming of a family. Data on the size and composition of families sharpen perception of need. The quality and characteristics of housing, the degree of crowding, family income, and many other data have implications for adult education.

4. *Occupational Breakdown.* A study of the various occupational groups may lead to an understanding of the educational needs of the gainfully employed and the unemployed. Ideas for the education and training of unskilled, skilled, and professional workers; proprietors; domestics; and others come to mind when one realizes the numbers involved. A director who frees his imagination soon realizes that there are many needs for occupational training beyond the Federally reimbursed vocational-education field.

5. *Cultural Background.* The typical American community is made up of a heterogeneous assortment of cultural groups. Roughly 7 per cent are foreign-born white. Some are still aliens, while others—technically citizens—are relatively unassimilated into our culture. Many more are children of foreign-born parents. Frequently communities will consist of several major foreign groups, each with its own language, social customs, political backgrounds, educational traditions, family pattern, and other cultural characteristics. Indians, Orientals, Puerto Ricans, Mexicans, and other distinct ethnic groups have unique educational needs which can often be served by specially designed activities.

6. *Socioeconomic Background.* The "upper 400," the "old-line aristocracy," and similar groups may not be clearly identified in census data, but they are there. So are the people across the tracks. The material standard of living is reflected in housing data, average rentals, employment status, economic statistics, and educational level. Study of people of low economic status may reveal educational needs which would never be discovered by waiting for requests. Paupers, inmates of county homes and prisons, and patients in hospitals are other groups with special needs. A rifle-shot approach in designing educational activities is more likely to serve these specific groups than is a blunderbuss attack.

7. *Geographic Location.* Neighborhoods within a community often offer striking differences in population characteristics and educational

needs.[4] An analysis of census-tract data often shows need for specialized and widely differing types of education.

These are only some of the ways to look at data about a community. In any analysis it is important (1) to break down the adult population in several ways so that the most useful grouping can be identified, (2) to analyze the educational needs and interests of each group, and (3) to develop educational activities in terms of those needs and interests. No one method of grouping is best for all purposes. For example, grouping by age may be most important for a new-voter preparation program, whereas family circumstances are more important data in most family-life education.

A great many directors overlook the importance of studying statistical information. Fewer than one-third of those studied depend even occasionally upon the census for insight into adult needs, although this method of need identification is better than most others. Programs are distinctly larger where census data are studied. Study of census reports will help prevent the myopia which may develop in a person whose acquaintance is largely with organized groups. Even better than a sampling survey, the census shows population characteristics in their true proportion and helps counterbalance biased observations. Census data both suggest specific needs and help show the human framework within which an educational program must operate. By making an analysis of these data, a director is less likely to leave out major groups; he can see specific educational challenges in sharper focus; and he can plan to serve a greater part of the total population.

Reports of many other governmental agencies at all levels contain information which illuminates educational needs and interests. Health and vital statistics are an example. Indexes of disease and chronic conditions may reveal educational needs which personal inquiry would not disclose. Birth statistics point up certain dimensions of the parent-education task, while marriage and divorce rates do the same for other aspects of family-life education. Frequently, information not publicly reported is available at agency headquarters.

Chambers of commerce, councils of social agencies, adult-education councils, labor unions, local foundations, and other private organizations often make recurring or special studies. Magazines, newspapers, and libraries are likely to have reliable information on the reading habits and interests of adults; the chamber of commerce, on economic conditions; social agencies, on the welfare load and the specifics of family and community disorganization; the housing office and real-estate people, on the migration pattern. Indeed, it is difficult to find a private agency which cannot throw some light on the educational needs and interests of adults.

[4] Perdue B. Graves, *An Investigation of Adult Education Needs and Interests in Topeka,* doctoral dissertation, University of Kansas, Lawrence, Kans., 1949.

Deficiencies often indicate educational needs and provide one point of departure in program building. Adults may be largely unaware of inadequacies which show up in surveys and statistics. Direct inquiry would seldom reveal any felt need for education among people evidencing malnutrition, low civic participation, inadequate methods of child rearing, ill health, and family disorganization. Yet these all point up important tasks for education. Education may not always be able to alleviate the deficiency completely, but usually it can give material help.

Studying deficiencies among adults may seem to be a negative approach to program planning. Admittedly, it is related to the remedial concept which has long handicapped the full development of adult education. In an evaluation of thirteen methods of identifying need, however, the study of deficiencies ranked very high in effectiveness. It is especially useful in helping build large programs which use a variety of educational approaches. In many areas new programs attract first those who have at least moderate competence. Directors basing programs on deficiencies, however, have identified the population groups most in need of education, and they are constantly challenged to involve such groups.

A common and easy way for an inexperienced director to become acquainted with adult education is to study programs in neighboring communities. Examination of the catalogues, schedules, publicity materials, and programs of comparable institutions is a secondhand but profitable way of picking up program ideas. Although imitation always involves risk, any successful activity has presumably served a felt need in the community in which it developed, and programs soundly based upon the interests of adults may yield a high percentage of useful information. Even experienced directors are frequently stimulated by ideas found in neighboring programs. Many directors systematically interchange publicity materials as a means of keeping up with new developments. In general, the method may not be highly creative, but it results in considerable program improvement. As a method of identifying educational needs, imitation is worth using, though slightly below average in effectiveness.

Simple imitation, however, probably is seldom practiced. Ideas gleaned from other sources often lead to further local exploration and investigation, pilot studies, experimentation, and adaptation before they are adopted on a full scale. Browsing through publicity materials is most useful in discovering what services are desired and how other programs provide them.

ADVISORY COMMITTEES

Advisory committees provide one major way of involving adults in the identification of educational needs. Lay advisory groups have been used for decades and are widely praised. Many directors would not attempt to operate programs without them. Others, however, see them performing no useful function, and apparently successful programs sometimes operate without such committees. Beginning directors and administrators with conventional school backgrounds are especially likely to be skeptical of their use. Often beginners recognize the value of lay committees but feel insecure in working with them. Serious doubts expressed by nonusers show need for further evaluation of experience.

In many programs lay committees are well established. In a nationwide study [5] of 2,684 public-school adult programs, 48 per cent reported that they had some kind of advisory committee. Among 100 representative evening schools, 71 had such committees.[6] Their contribution, like that of any other approach, depends largely upon the skill with which they are utilized.

Types of Committees and Their Functions

While advisory committees vary widely in size and function, they can be classified into two types—special-area committees and general committees.

Usually the advisory committees which give the most practical help are those concerned with a limited area, course, field, need, problem, or task. This type has long been encouraged in vocational education. In trade and industrial education, an equal number of representatives from management and labor are usually appointed to develop a course or curriculum in a craft, occupation, or industry. Often they set up standards, help procure instructors, and perform related functions. Committees advising on educational programs for farmers have also proved their usefulness.[7] Such committees are likewise widely used in distributive education and to a lesser extent in homemaking and guidance programs.

Special advisory committees are becoming increasingly popular in many nonvocational fields. There is hardly a content or problem area where they are not found. Committees concerned with the development of family-life and parent education, public-affairs education, intercultural understanding, young-adult activities, community guidance services, and recreational activities are examples of broad-area groups. Committees focused on tasks of developing a preparation-for-marriage course, a radio forum, an interfaith program, a young-adult center, a testing service, or an arts and crafts program might be either more specific counterparts or subcommittees of the larger groups.

Committees of limited scope usually are of most help when they have

[5] Homer Kempfer, *Adult Education Activities of the Public Schools: Report of a Survey, 1947–48,* U.S. Office of Education Pamphlet 107, 1949, p. 18.

[6] Homer Kempfer and Grace S. Wright, *One Hundred Evening Schools,* U.S. Office of Education Bulletin 1949, no. 4, p. 41.

[7] H. M. Hamlin, *Agricultural Education in Community Schools,* The Interstate Printers & Publishers, Inc., Danville, Ill., 1949, chap. V.

a complete advisory job to do, although their field of concern may be restricted if circumstances warrant. After a committee defines its task, its most useful functions are the identification of educational need, the interpretation of findings, and the development of appropriate plans for an educational program. Identification of need may be largely an arm-chair matter if the members are intimately acquainted with the field. Otherwise it may require further data and the use of research techniques. Committees may react to and constructively criticize specific courses of study or other educational plans prepared by professional workers. They often help evaluate the activity as it progresses or after the first cycle is complete. They may assist by procuring participants and helping to screen recruits where that is necessary. They may set up qualifications for instructors and suggest personnel. Consciously or unconsciously, they help interpret the program to the public. The use of a committee primarily for publicity, however, is a practice of doubtful merit. Restricting a committee to its service as a sounding board for prepared plans is likely to insult the democratic sensitivities of its more competent members. A special advisory committee is best employed when it assists with the complete process of studying a problem, working out its solution, and evaluating the results.

Programs frequently have a number of special-area committees operating concurrently, each with its own assignment. One program in a community of 40,000 people has about 200 laymen on its several committees. The Opportunity School at Denver has about sixty committees advising on different phases of its program.

Coordination of special committees may be through the director's office or through the superintendent of schools. Often such committees work primarily with their own departments, which are administratively integrated into the total program of the agency. They may, of course, advise vertically within a field by concerning themselves with educational programs for children, youth, and adults.

Probably the most common type of lay advisory committee has responsibility for a comprehensive view of the entire adult field. While special-area committees are usually better able to identify educational needs and interests, general committees have also shown competence in this regard, especially in rural areas and small and medium-sized villages where members can be personally acquainted with many aspects of community life. The effective operation of general advisory committees in large cities requires considerable staff assistance to provide current background material.

General advisory committees must usually confine themselves to the long look, the all-inclusive view, the rough definition of needs and problems, the establishment of priorities, and broad advice on the development of areas, the over-all development of plans, and program evaluation.

Otherwise they stand in danger of shifting their characters and becoming specialized. Whereas enthusiastic special committees may develop selected areas, general committees are especially useful in initiating a more balanced program. There is much evidence to indicate that more widespread use of general advisory committees would result in improved programs.

A general committee can be set up so that it is advisory both to the school and to other operating agencies. Such committees are likely to be most successful if the agencies served participate in the original formation of the committee. Such a committee has more freedom to look at a problem in its entirety and to make recommendations to the appropriate agency.

Selection and Appointment of Advisory Committees

The selection of committees is determined by their purpose. The director must clarify in his own mind, and preferably also on paper, the purposes to be served by an advisory committee. Does he primarily want help with publicity? Does he want a sounding board? Or a rubber stamp? Or big names? Does he want yes men? Does he want the committee to be concerned only with certain aspects and specific problems? Or does he want honest-to-goodness help from laymen in identifying educational needs, in planning a comprehensive program, and in appraising results.

If identification of need, planning, and appraisal are the main purposes, then the characteristics of the people selected are most important. Whether for a general or special committee, interest and willingness to work are prime considerations. Ordinarily, interested working members are more useful than big names.

Intelligence, social vision, and leadership experience are additional assets, especially for members of general committees. On special committees intimate acquaintance with the problem of concern is highly desirable. In either case, members should constitute a balance between the practical and the ideal. They should be highly articulate and truly representative of important, although at times minority, points of view. In working with religious, labor, and ethnic groups, and sometimes with business groups, committee members must be acceptable to the group leaders. Discreet preliminary inquiry concerning a potential member's standing may help prevent errors of selection. In fact, a favorite way of building a list of potential members is by informal inquiry and solicitation of names from leaders of special groups.

Special committees working in vocational fields need both employer and employee members. Occasionally representatives of the general public may be included. Special committees in other fields usually draw from interested agencies or lay people with appropriate interests. Agency staff members are sometimes invited to sit on advisory committees. If a committee becomes loaded with them, however, it becomes more of an adult-education council than a group directly representing the interests of the adult clientele.

On an over-all committee charged with the development of a comprehensive program, representativeness is especially important. In the selection of members, the following considerations should weigh heavily:

1. The ages of members should roughly parallel the age distribution of the adult population. Young adults are often overlooked.

2. A fair balance between men and women is desirable.

3. All significant religious groups should be accounted for.

4. Nationality, ethnic, cultural, and socioeconomic groups of significant size should be represented.

5. The occupational life of the community should be reflected in proper proportion.

6. Wide community organizational contacts are desirable, although ease of operation requires that committee members act as individuals and not as representatives of such groups.

7. All major neighborhoods of the community should be included.

In these aspects, the general advisory committee should be a miniature cross section of the community. Unless care is used in systematic choice of potential members, important elements in the community are likely to be overlooked, and a lopsided committee may result. Since most boards of control come from business and professional segments of the population, selection of the advisory committee gives an excellent opportunity to involve a more representative group in planning. A perfect job of matching committee members against a seven-dimensional grid is difficult. The attempt, however, is likely to yield a better committee than one drawn from the first twenty names that come to mind.

An advisory committee should be of good working size, consisting of ten, twelve, or fifteen members. Ordinarily it should be small enough for each member to speak freely and for all members to cooperate efficiently. If it is too small, however, the production of ideas may be limited. General committees need to be large enough to represent a broad scope of community life. In some places a large committee meets occasionally, and a smaller executive committee meets more frequently. Unless there is ample staff help or a workable subcommittee system, large committees may degenerate into sounding boards or publicity panels and thus risk the danger of eventual failure.

Special committees are often smaller than over-all committees. Hamlin recommends from nine to twelve members for advisory committees in agriculture.[8] For interpreting a program to the public, gaining widespread support, and performing certain other functions, however, they may be large, provided that they can be organized for efficiency. State

[8] Hamlin, *op. cit.*, p. 126.

laws, state education department regulations, or state plans for vocational education sometimes mandate the minimum size.

No standard pattern exists for the establishment of advisory committees, but the best practice seems to favor these steps:

1. The formulation of a definite written plan which specifies the purposes of the committee, the scope of its concern, criteria for selection of members, and the relationship of the committee to the board of control, the superintendent, and to other professional staff. The plan should indicate exactly to whom the committee is advisory, with what staff members it will work, and major relational lines.

2. Approval of the plan by the board of control.

3. Canvassing of names, screening, and selection of potential committee members by the director of adult education and the superintendent, often with advice of a committee of the board.

4. Approval of committee members by the total board.

5. Invitation on behalf of the board by its secretary, the superintendent, or the director of adult education. To minimize refusals it is often wise to determine willingness to serve in advance of formal invitation.

This procedure gives the advisory committee a dignity and official status that it could not have if invited directly by the director or superintendent. It procures more responsible and considered advice and generally attracts committee members of higher caliber. The board is bound to have more respect for the advice of a committee which it established than for the opinions of an *ad hoc* group, and this procedure sets up channels through which the committee can make recommendations to the board whenever desirable. If a committee is organized according to this system, there is little chance for misunderstanding relationships.

The invitation should set forth clearly the major elements of the original plan enumerated above. The difference between advisory recommendations and legal policy determination vested in the board should likewise be in writing. Specific tasks and time limitations always need to be made clear. Advisory committees may be permanent or temporary. When a temporary committee finishes its task, it should be thanked and discharged.

The practice of appointing one or two board members to sit with the advisory committee helps strengthen communication and mutual understanding. Board members should not act as committee members, however. They should avoid leadership responsibility and always let the committee present its own recommendations to the board.

The director of adult education should sit with the general advisory committee. He or a member of his staff usually acts as secretary. It is highly desirable that the superintendent of schools also meet regularly with the committee. Where special committees are numerous, the superintendent may attend the orientation meeting of each new committee and leave subsequent detailed work to the director, department heads, and other staff members. Some directors like their administrative and supervisory staff to sit with the general advisory committee for in-service growth.

Users of advisory committees should be aware of the danger of subtle influence and control. The presence of a professional staff person or a member of the board of education, even though such persons are not technically a part of the committee, carries undue weight with most members. The ideas of an official easily acquire too much influence. It is easier for a committee to second the opinions of its creator than to do its own thinking, and it is easier for a secretary to reflect official policy in the minutes than the creative thought of the group. These facts make clear the need of leaning over backward to avoid control. If necessary, after orientation, committees might meet alone with their own secretaries. Under no circumstances, of course, should a director serve as the chairman of the advisory committee or attempt to furnish all of the agenda unless he is willing to risk a rubber-stamp response.

The Care and Feeding of Advisory Committees

After advisory committees have been selected and appointed, they must be cared for and nurtured. Beneficial results do not come automatically. Significant adult education must go on within the advisory committee itself if it is to be effective.

The orientation during the first meeting of a new advisory committee sets the stage for success, mediocrity, or failure. Special committees in the vocational field can be oriented by the director or a department head. Larger-area committees and over-all committees need a comprehensive view of their tasks. The superintendent, the director of adult education, a state education department official, or some other person of standing needs to present clearly an overview of the social, economic, and world conditions that bear on the committee's task. The orientation should include a challenging vision of the potential contribution that an adequate adult-education program can make. If this orientation is focused on the community, the committee can see that it has a very important task to perform. The group will need time to raise questions and discuss its functions. If the committee accepts the challenge—if its members individually and collectively accept the responsibility for creative planning into the uncharted areas ahead—a good start has been made.

At early meetings the committee should attempt to gain a thorough knowledge of the major adult-education activities in the community. Unless it is advisory to the total community program, the committee needs to see how the work of its agency fits into the total pattern. Subsequent meetings of general committees should carry the orientation and analysis further. Ample time should be allowed for discussion, always with such background questions as: What are the desirable conditions toward which we should work? What ought to be done about this situation? How can we best involve people in the desired learning activities? What is the role of our agency? As the broad scope of possibilities becomes outlined, priorities will suggest themselves. Some will be easy, some urgent, some long term, and some short. As priorities begin to appear, the real work of the committee begins.

Developing a Subcommittee System

Regardless of how many recommendations the professional staff may be able to carry out, an advisory committee will soon see that progress on many tasks requires the cooperation of the larger community. The educational process does not do things for people; instead, it helps people do things for themselves. A committee with an over-all view should realize that it cannot become expert in every field and that it has been organized for specialization. One way of gaining specialized understanding is by setting up a series of subcommittees such as were established by the Adult Education Advisory Committee at Niagara Falls, New York. The early subcommittees were:

1. *Public Affairs.* Because the field of public-affairs education seemed in greatest need of development, the general committee, after consulting with specialists in this field, appointed four of its members as the nucleus of a public-affairs subcommittee. This group was charged with thinking through the problem in more detail and bringing in proposals. This subcommittee invited about thirty civic-minded representatives from various organizations to join it. The group discussed the situation in three or four meetings before deciding to reorganize into three parts.

a. One part drew in several additional people and established a Sunday-afternoon radio round table, dealing primarily with local and regional issues. Each year several dozen leading personalities participate in the broadcasts. Often they represent points of view of community organizations.

b. A second group sought the help of a sizable list of community organizations in establishing a lecture-forum series. Cooperating organizations promised financial support. They often provide it by selling a block of tickets, chiefly to their own members.

c. A third group established a city-wide forum.

2. *Parent Education.* Soon after the public-affairs planning got under way, the general committee sought the help of a consultant in parent education and child development. As a result three members formed the nucleus of a new committee which called together a number of lay people interested in this field. This subcommittee, with the help of the consultant and local staff, made a study of needs, inventoried community

programs, and made proposals for serving unmet needs. The board of education accepted the recommendation that a parent-education specialist be added to the staff. A committee working with a special group in the council of social agencies developed a preparation-for-marriage course which began in the YWCA. Professional leadership was made available to mothers clubs, and training courses for volunteer leaders in this field were set up.

3. *Arts and Crafts.* Two committee members involved other interested laymen in an embryonic arts and crafts center. The center, which was set up in an unused elementary school and provided with equipment for several crafts, was built into a strong feature of the adult-education program.

4. *Young-adult Advisory Committee.* Four other members became a part of a subcommittee which was set up, not to run the young-adult activities, but to act as a liaison between the young-adult groups and the community. One activity growing out of this was a community-ambassador project which annually raises money to send selected young people to live abroad during the summer.

A subcommittee system has several advantages. It provides a natural liaison when the subcommittee includes one or more members of the general committee. Coordination and communication are easy, as all specialized groups are automatically represented at general committee meetings, and vice versa. When ready, subcommittees can formally report their thinking for full-committee consideration and action, and new instructions and redefinition of assignments can be worked out.

Another advantage of the subcommittee system is that it helps develop leadership. If the general committee is a representative group, members will have or are likely to develop specialized and diversified interests. They can usually follow their interests, specialize further, and take pride in building up their parts of the program. While a member of the general committee often serves as chairman of a subcommittee, anyone else may do so.

The close liaison inherent in this system permits subcommittees considerable freedom to develop their ideas. This arrangement encourages enthusiasm and productivity. People become involved and give freely of their energy. They tend to become not only advisers, but doers as well. Elements of the program become theirs. The creativity engendered often leads to further division of subcommittees and to cooperative relationships with other agencies. Administrators who want to keep a tight rein may find the multiplication of committees cumbersome. With the inherent provisions for intercommunication, however, the advantage of wide involvement usually outweighs niceties of formal relationship.

Advisory committees serve best if they continue to go through the educative process—problem definition, data gathering, analysis, decision, action, and evaluation. Usually, however, they cannot do all the work implied. The type of members normally chosen cannot devote more than a few marginal hours per month to committee work. They can do much of the thinking, planning, and generating of ideas. They can help identify needs, define problems, develop insight from data, and appraise results. Their work, however, basically involves judgment and differs somewhat from staff work.

Many of the data required by the committee must be fed to it by the professional staff. As new interests sprout, pertinent information must be found. Surveys may have to be made, data assembled, and research conducted. Specialists must be located and brought in at the proper stage to keep the committee and subcommittees informed, alert, and stimulated. Arrangements have to be made for members to visit other programs and see other committees in action. Some of the data must be studied, and consultant help may have to be available during the period of problem definition. Additional help may be called for at any time. Continued staff work along these lines is necessary to ensure the continuous development of advisory committees.

Action, too, is usually a staff job. Leaders, teachers, supervisors, and other professional personnel will conduct the new elements of the educational program. Volunteer help may often be utilized, but its supervision is likely to be professional. It is good when committee members become so interested in the program that they work as hard as professionals for its success, but such skilled cooperation can hardly be expected, for committees are useful more for their collective judgment than for their execution of a program.

In support of the advisory committee, there must be adequate office work—typing, duplicating, minute keeping, and correspondence. The secretariat to the advisory committee structure should be the professional and clerical staff of the adult-education department.

Seek Total Participation

Representative lay advisory committees constitute a technique for helping adult-education programs emerge from the needs and interests of the total population. Programs inspired by such groups are likely to be better in significant ways than those planned purely by the staff. The ultimate strategy, however, is to involve all the people in planning—that is, to have them participate in the educative process. Possibly no one setup achieves this ideal. A number of communities, however, have devised ways of involving the majority of the adults in certain parts of the process. Total participation seems to be most frequently approached in rural and village communities. Outside consultant help is often a stimulative factor. Methods are often fragmentary and elementary, but they point up movement in the right direction. Here are examples:

The forum-planning committee in a small Michigan town sent a reply card to every family asking it to check the most crucial problem which should be discussed. Eighty-five per cent replied and the issues selected were those of most concern to the community.

In a New York community every household was canvassed to determine its interest in and preference among community projects.

In a large community, interviewers asked a cross section of several thousand citizens how they thought the local budget should be allocated for city services. Radio and newspaper discussion before, during, and after the survey stimulated much discussion among the residents.

In Darby, Montana, a large segment of the community became participants in a drama program as a means of identifying and defining the total community problem.[9]

ADULT EDUCATION COUNCILS

In practice the term *adult-education council* is applied to a variety of organizational forms. Usually it is a formal or informal association of the major local organizations and agencies having adult-education programs. Representatives of the organizations meet periodically to discuss common concerns and promote the cause of adult education locally. Such councils often have several related purposes, although each group develops its own functions. Almost no two are alike. Among the purposes most frequently found are these:

To identify and interpret educational needs

To develop programs and stimulate agencies to serve new needs

To develop new educational approaches

To publicize and promote programs of all agencies

To cooperate on jointly sponsored projects, such as leadership training, research, forum or lecture series, and surveys

To coordinate adult-education activities

To act as a clearinghouse of information about adult-education and community activities

To increase public participation in adult education

To identify and interpret trends

To promote legislation and public interest in financial support

To represent the adult-education movement before the public

Different adult-education agencies and organizations usually serve slightly, if not completely, different clientele. Available facilities, the type of program, geographical location, and the nature of the leadership help select the participants in programs. Each agency knows adult needs from a different angle. By pooling their information and discussing it, representatives of different programs can often gain insight which will

[9] R. W. Poston, *Small Town Renaissance: A Story of the Montana Study*, Harper & Brothers, New York, 1950.

permit better service to their own clientele as well as identification of un-served community groups and unfulfilled needs. Informal meetings of leaders and joint engagement of a director are mechanisms for pooling the information. A number of medium-sized and large communities have found an organized adult-education council a more systematic approach to the identification of need. When the council members work in a co-operative spirit and abandon interagency jealousy and competition, every-one can benefit.

One major study tested the assumption that a close working relation-ship among adult agencies results in better identification of educational needs and interests of adults and a better total community program. Results showed that programs developed in closest collaboration with others attracted more participants, served more population segments, maintained a more flexible schedule, and utilized a greater number of educational approaches than did programs developed in isolation.[10]

The assumption was also tested that close cooperation with other agencies results in better identification of the educational needs and interests of adults. Among the cooperative practices listed were avoidance of identical courses, publication of a directory listing all adult-education activities in the community, interchange of instructional personnel, co-operative use of classrooms, interloan of specialized equipment, coopera-tive sponsorship of community-wide educational programs, sharing of special programs with people enrolled in programs of other agencies, and cooperative support of community projects. These cooperative prac-tices can result from the mutual understanding, the stimulation, and the intercommunication best developed within an adult-education council. The study again showed positive and significant relationships between these practices and size of program, number of population segments served, flexibility of schedule and number of approaches used.[11] In brief, it pays for an adult school to cooperate closely with other adult-educa-tion agencies in the community.

Agencies in an effective council relationship stimulate each other to a wider appreciation of the scope and meaning of adult education. It is only natural that they will see mutual benefit from joint research in identification and definition of adult needs. Some projects can be jointly planned and carried out through the member agencies. Agencies can often pool the energies of their volunteers for interview surveys. In fact, adult-education councils can work toward the development of special-ized research teams as described later in this chapter.

Research is likely to reveal some needs not served by any agencies. If so, (1) the adult school or some other existing agency may expand its program to serve the newly discovered needs, (2) a new agency may be

[10] Kempfer, *Identifying Educational Needs of Adults*, pp. 3, 8, 17–18.
[11] *Ibid.*, pp. 3, 8, 18–20.

created, or (3) in certain instances, the council itself may undertake to serve the need. As councils usually are not set up, financed, or staffed to be operating agencies, the program operation often is not a sound possibility. Some councils, however, do operate educational activities. For example, the Springfield, Massachusetts, Adult Education Council operates a public forum. More often council-sponsored activities are services to community organizations—leadership training, program planning clinics, and counseling services to adults.

STUDY-AND-ACTION GROUPS

The importance and urgency of specific community problems may result in the formation of study-action groups of interested citizens. Such groups may be set up officially to study the assigned problem and report recommendations to the appointing authority. Other groups are set up by councils of social agencies, ministerial associations, labor unions, business associations, and a range of community organizations; they may have little autonomy or considerable freedom. Some groups are entirely self-appointed. In so far as study groups are concerned with real problems, they are more or less potentially important. They can represent education at its best.

Educators frequently have the opportunity of working with study-action groups, and a few public-school programs provide educational leadership to such groups. A professionally trained staff member may be assigned, for example, to a committee concerned with housing, human relations, or juvenile delinquency. His purpose is to encourage the use of educational methods in the study of the problem under consideration. He does not present the solution to a problem; he helps others find it. He arranges for consultants and experts to meet with the group. He assembles pertinent data for committee consideration. He may do or direct essential research. In one way or another, he supplies much of the information necessary for effective problem solving. As these are essential elements of a teacher's task, the work of this professional educator with a study-action committee can be justified.

In some cases, however, the advisability of providing the services of a professional educator may be dubious. At times, groups may want to learn effective techniques for converting others to their point of view, or they may want the blessing of a person of the educator's status as an endorsement of their cause. Some groups will be committed to preconceived solutions to problems.

The primary responsibility of the educator to the study-action groups is to see that the educational process is used maximally. Without controlling the outcome, he should help the group follow a sequence of steps in problem solving. He should help it to explore the problem very thoroughly, to define it, and to obtain the necessary and pertinent data.

This work may involve the collection of available facts or it may require research—the search for new data. He should help the group use appropriate techniques in analyzing data and in reaching a decision. If the group can act, his help can extend to devising an effective plan of action. Very often this action will necessitate educating others. If it does, his professional help will be especially needed here, as it will also be in the final step, the development of proper evaluative techniques.

All this professional help can be given without the educator's assuming direct responsibility for the actions. In the education of responsible adults in a democracy, the assumption is that the group determines the action to be taken. The educator merely contributes the process which enables the group to work out a better solution than it otherwise would have.

Study-action groups contain the ingredients for the best kind of education. They start with a task—or at least a purpose which can be shaped into a specific and challenging goal. They can evolve their own plans. If they have sufficient freedom, they are in a most healthful condition to arrive at a mature solution. In such circumstances, educators should welcome the opportunity to cooperate. If the group does not enjoy or desire the required conditions for effective problem solving, the educator may want to spend his energy elsewhere.

COMMUNITY COUNCILS

Whereas the adult-education council may consist primarily of professional educators, the community council is essentially an organization of lay leaders working toward total community improvement. Educational needs are best defined when all concerned are involved in the educative process. In many situations the community-council philosophy gives most promise of involving a maximum number of people in community improvement. Community councils can set up the study-action machinery whereby communities can lift themselves by their own bootstraps. Where community councils are operating most successfully, a good proportion of the people are engaged in continuous learning.

A comprehensive community council represents the organized attempt of individuals and groups to develop cooperative ways of working together for the benefit of the whole community. Other names given to this cooperative effort are neighborhood-improvement association, citizens council, citizens association, and planning council. Recreation councils, family-life and parent-education councils, councils of churches, welfare councils, and councils of social agencies are ordinarily more specialized, although they may use many of the same ways of working together. The organizational pattern is usually designed to fit the community and often is in the process of change.

Community councils and their counterparts develop when enough people recognize that progress toward desired ends can best be made through cooperative work. Whether composed of individuals, organizations, or both, councils are usually formed in response to a felt need. This need may concern only one area of community life—recreation, agriculture, or business, for example. As the council works on the initial problem, however, it is likely to become aware of broader needs.

The community-council idea holds within itself much of the basic mechanism for a dynamic adult education. It meets many of the requirements of a comprehensive community program of lifelong learning. For instance:

It can embrace the whole community, involving all socially useful organizations and all individuals. The council can provide channels through which the total community can participate in common enterprises.

It is adaptable to communities of any size, although it seems to reach its full development more quickly in small communities having relatively simple organizational structure.

It is concerned with helping people solve their present problems; it is not focused on the past. Since it utilizes the educational approach as an inherent way of work, it can readily anticipate change and can seek to control or adapt to it.

It is democratic in that the participants control its purposes. It can be readily responsive to the will of the people without waiting for the slow processes of changing constitutions, laws, and government.

Although lack of staff and adequate financial support often restrict council activities, the community-council idea has been tried and has proved workable in hundreds of American communities.

Community councils often seek the aid of specialists to avoid working at an armchair level. Top council members may be experts in their occupational fields, but rarely are they specialists in problems of broad community study and development. Most laymen are unskilled in making sociological surveys; in determining the cause of intercultural stress, delinquency, family breakdown, housing shortages, and health hazards; in identifying trends in labor-management relations; in predicting economic trends; or in analyzing public opinion. Specialists, therefore, should be called upon.

The worth of a community council depends very largely upon how well it uses educational processes. One expert alone can give only limited help—limited by the confines of his disciplines and of his individual competence.

The solutions to many community problems do not fall within any one discipline. Family breakdown, for instance, may result from a combination of factors, and a program of strengthening family life may need to draw from sociology, economics, religion, law, and other fields.

To overcome the limitations of working with only one expert, the community council can develop a specialized educational organ—a team of specialists from different fields who can provide the expert assistance a lay council needs. Specialists are needed most often from the disciplines of cultural anthropology, social psychology, economics, mental hygiene, family life, public health, and political science—primarily from the social sciences. Broad-gauge religious leaders, scientists with social vision, experts understanding the human significance of art, and philosophers can add considerable value.

The Multidisciplinary Approach

The assembled specialists usually find that they must work together awhile before they can function as a team. It takes time to learn to talk each other's language.

While complicated, the multidisciplinary approach is a method for bringing collective, specialized intelligence to bear on a problem. Presidents, state governors, and political leaders have built up coordinated teams of specialists. Widely used in industrial research, such teams have been brought together in finance, law, military affairs, business administration, and public health. A very large and able team representing many specialties in science started with an Einstein equation, added a wealth of other knowledge, and developed the atomic bomb.

Most communities have available locally or can invite in able minds to serve on a multidisciplinary advisory team. In this situation the adult educator's function is to facilitate communication and teamwork among the specialists, and between them and the council. As a process specialist, the adult educator can help the team members break beyond the rigidities of single disciplines and focus on community problems requiring the contributions of several fields.

One major job in solving problems through the educational approach is diagnosis. The council, with the help of the specialist team, can keep searching for new insights and understandings, probing deeply into what is happening in family life, in economic life, in the relations between ethnic groups, among young people, and among the aged. The team can help interpret trends in relation to the changing forces affecting community life. Machinery can be set up to make continuing studies so that changes can be detected quickly. Machinery has long been available to keep track of economic conditions, the labor market, the real-estate situation, accident rates, and crime. The social-scientist team can develop better surveys, refinements in sociological measurement, and new methods and techniques to help the community council keep track of social trends. The council can keep its finger on the pulse of such situations as intergroup tension, conditions leading to juvenile delinquency, family breakdown, and public opinion on current affairs. A specialist team can aid the council materially by extending its sensitivity. As the use of the team continues, the council itself will be acquiring new skill, new points of view, and new competence in dealing with community problems.

Another function of the specialist team is to assist with evaluation. The team can give technical assistance in assessing the progress made, in examining the effects of the methods used, and in attempting constantly to improve them. The team can also help organizations and agencies having specialized programs to evaluate their educational activities. In these ways competence in evaluation will become more widespread.

Education has deep roots in the social sciences, although no adult-education administrator can keep abreast of the expanding boundaries of all the major social-science disciplines pertinent to his work. This situation makes it especially important that local directors work closely with social-scientist teams.

Direction for much adult education can come from insight gained as program directors from different agencies participate in council work and as community problems are identified. Close participation in team-and-council interaction will enable adult educators to keep in the forefront of community life. Program building can be more realistic because it will be on a firmer base. Many activities can be refocused on current problems, and new activities can be set up to serve the most pressing needs. New techniques and methods for helping people learn can be tried. By working with a social-scientist team, a director should become more aware of the deeper learning needs of adults and better able to design programs to serve them. Each agency can reslant its program in light of the problems diagnosed by the team and council. Within these general lines each community can experiment with its own mechanisms for ensuring continued growth.

Specialized teams can help community organizations, too, to direct their programs toward more clearly recognized purposes. In so far as citizens groups lack professional staff, they can turn to the public schools and other adult-education agencies for training and consultation on developing new approaches, methods, and ways of involving people in learning activities. In large communities a specialist from each of several areas might eventually have to be engaged on a full-time basis to serve all agencies. Each would perform a liaison service between his specialty and the community.

While the specialist team may be of most value to a community of restricted size, small communities may not be able to afford a representative team. A county, a section of a state, a region, or an entire state may be the area which can best support a specialist team. A team may be developed in a state education department, at a state university, or jointly by two or more institutions and agencies.

Council Influence

Under the community-council concept, all adult-education agencies and all organizations with educational purposes have roles to play. Through the council the community can coordinate and integrate its activities for growth and self-improvement. In most cases, however, the council does not operate educational programs. Established agencies and organizations, together with any new ones, carry on the activities.

One function of the council can be that of helping each agency and organization to do better the desirable things it wants to do. A higher purpose would be to help them see better things to do. A public library, for instance, might better fulfill its role as a distributor of books by opening branches and using bookmobiles, but it might also enlarge its role by becoming a distribution center for films. As a result of community-council deliberations, county agents, vocational homemaking and agriculture teachers, and established rural organizations might come to see their relationships in a new light. Private agencies and community organizations might see their parts in the total picture more clearly and learn to direct their efforts more wisely.

A council attempting a broad program will soon utilize committees. In a complex community these committees may well function as subcouncils, operating in such fields as family-life and parent education, recreation, industry, intercultural relations, religion, and welfare. Each specialized council, if it includes a wide representation of agencies interested in the field, can work best if it has considerable autonomy and need conform only to broad, over-all council policy.

A community council can be the clearinghouse for many types of outside assistance, but the final determination of what goes on in a community should be made by the community. In some way the community must be ensured the power of acceptance and veto. Even though state institutions of higher education, other state agencies, and Federal programs may have legal authority to extend services to localities, the local community should decide how they fit in. A similar relationship should exist with outside, nongovernmental services.

A community council is not a superboard for a community. It has only the authority granted to it by the members and only as much influence as it can earn. Its only way of work is the educative process—its only leadership is that of ideas and sound judgment. The community council is not a magic way of getting things done. It does not run itself; it requires work, staff help, and vigilance. It is merely an effective and proven way in which people can work together toward the achievement of their common goals. By building a social-scientist team, a council may be able to work more effectively. The director of adult education can help build that team.

EVALUATION OF METHOD

Success in identifying the educational needs and interests of adults shows up in a number of ways. Evidence of success in this respect is closely related to success in the total program. The following yardsticks, in order of rank, seemed to be of most use in measuring the methods used by directors of adult education in 530 public-school and community-college programs: [12]

Number of approaches used
Number of population segments served
Amount of cooperation with other adult-education organizations
Degree of coordination of progress in the community
Flexibility of schedule
Size of program (as measured by the clock-hour index)

Logic might indicate that the number of activities materializing, the percentage of groups which maintain sufficient attendance to survive, and persistence of attendance would be good yardsticks. In the study cited above, however, they failed to prove so. Daring directors who try many ideas may have a low percentage surviving; the number of activities, therefore, may be less an indication of accuracy in identifying need than of the director's imaginative leadership. Persistence of attendance does not have the same value in assessing the merits of adult programs as it has in elementary and secondary schools, where attendance is compulsory. Adults may attend until they learn what they came for, then drop out when their purpose has been accomplished. The lack of uniformity in practice and the dissimilarity with older forms of education make it a risky business to evaluate adult education by the criteria applied to other types of schools.

SELECTED REFERENCES

Begg, W. R.: *Techniques for Study Groups Concerned with Unmet Needs,* Metropolitan School Study Council, Teachers College, Columbia University, New York, 1947.
Brownell, Baker: *The Human Community,* Harper & Brothers, New York, 1950.
Dahir, J.: *Communities for Better Living,* Harper & Brothers, New York, 1950.
Deane, S. R.: "Who Seeks Adult Education and Why," *Adult Education,* 1:18–25, October, 1950.
Hamlin, H. M.: *Citizens' Committees in the Public Schools,* Interstate Printers & Publishers, Inc., Danville, Ill., 1952.
Kempfer, Homer: *Identifying Educational Needs of Adults,* U.S. Office of Education Circular 330, 1951.
Kotinsky, R.: *Adult Education Councils,* American Association for Adult Education, New York, 1940.
Myers, Eugene E., and F. E. Drake: "Keeping Pace with the Needs of the Student," *Adult Education Bulletin,* 14:144–146, June, 1950.

[12] *Ibid.,* pp. 7–23.

New York State Education Department, Bureau of Adult Education, *The Good Look: Organizing the Comprehensive Adult Education Program,* Albany, N.Y., October, 1950.

Nicholson, D. H.: "Why Adults Attend School," *Adult Education Bulletin,* 13:172–177, August, 1949.

Ogden, Jean, and Jess Ogden: *Small Communities in Action,* Harper & Brothers, New York, 1946.

Representative Advisory Committees: A Manual for School Authorities and Committee Members, U.S. Office of Education, Miscellaneous 3277, April, 1948.

Sanders, I. T.: *Making Good Communities Better,* University of Kentucky Press, Lexington, Ky., 1950.

Schacter, H. W.: *Kentucky on the March,* Harper & Brothers, New York, 1949.

Sim, R. Alex: "The Census and Community Research," *Food for Thought,* 11:23–29, February, 1951.

Smith, B. L.: "Coordinated Community Group Action Is Functional Adult Education," *Adult Education Bulletin,* 7:113–116, April, 1943.

See also General References: [13] Beals and Brody, chap. 2; Division of Adult Education Service, chap. 3; Ely, pp. 7–10, 107–125, 281–288; Essert, chaps. 6, 7, 8, 11, 12; Sheats, Jayne, and Spence, chap. 13.

[13] The General References are listed in full at the end of this book.

CHAPTER 5 *Organized Approaches to Major Areas:*
Personal Development

The approach to adult education will be via the route of situations, not
subjects. . . . Every adult person finds himself in specific situations with
respect to his work, his recreation, his family life, his community life, etc.—
situations which call for adjustments. Adult education begins at this point.
Subject matter is brought into the situation, is put to work, when needed.
(E. C. Lindeman.)

The curriculum of adult education is as broad as life itself. It includes
all adjustments, changes, and new behaviors which are necessary for
full, complete, mature, and efficient living. It includes all knowledge,
skills, habits, and attitudes which are developed throughout adult life.
However, since most learning is specific, the curriculum is usually
divided into convenient units for efficient learning.

The curriculum of adult education should arise out of the developmental tasks of adults—out of the situations which adults face. In Chapter
3 these tasks were divided into four categories: personal development
and family living, production and consumption, citizenship, and leisure
time. Activities in organized programs, however, are usually grouped by
areas or fields. While there is little standard usage among programs, their
offerings are often classified according to the type of substantive content
or subject matter brought into the learning situation. In many fields
neither courses nor curricula are rigidly organized, and often within the
same program they are in a constant state of flux.

The voluntary nature of adult education requires programs to keep
at least relatively close to the immediate concerns of people. In fact, a
flexible curriculum is essential to meet the infinite variety of adult needs.
Under these circumstances, no simple pattern of organization is likely
to be wholly satisfactory. The one proposed in the next three chapters
is thought to be as useful as any, although a small percentage of activities will still be difficult to classify. The discussion in the following three
chapters will focus largely on the most common formally organized approaches to adult education: classes, lectures, study groups, tutoring, and
correspondence study. The more informal approaches are treated elsewhere.

In personal-development areas most of the learning is concerned with acquiring specific individual skills and habits. In human-relations studies, associations, feelings, and attitudes are predominant. Habits and skills, of course, are also involved in human relations—just as attitudes and feelings are involved in the skill areas.

FOUNDATION EDUCATION

The first evening schools in America were established as private ventures to provide indentured servants with the rudiments of education—reading, writing, and ciphering. Soon other adults who had not acquired the elements of education were also attending. As commerce and industry increased, evening schools began to offer secondary and technical subjects.[1] The development of public education was accompanied by extended opportunities for adults to acquire an elementary- and high-school education.

Literacy Education

The United States, while not the most literate nation in the world, ranks among the top few (see Table 7). However, foreign visitors are

Table 7. Educational Level in Sixteen Selected States

Eight most literate states			Eight least literate states		
State	Per cent with fewer than 5 years of school completed	Median years of school completed	State	Per cent with fewer than 5 years of school completed	Median years of school completed
Iowa	3.9	9.8	Tennessee	18.3	8.4
Utah	4.3	12.0	Arkansas	19.8	8.3
Oregon	4.3	10.9	North Carolina	21.1	7.9
Idaho	4.5	11.0	Alabama	22.6	7.9
Washington	4.7	11.2	Georgia	24.2	7.8
Nebraska	4.9	10.1	Mississippi	25.2	8.1
Kansas	5.0	10.2	South Carolina	27.4	7.6
Vermont	5.5	10.0	Louisiana	28.7	7.6
United States				11.0	9.3

SOURCE: Compiled from census data for 1950.

[1] R. F. Seybolt, "The Evening Schools of Colonial New York City," *Fifteenth Annual Report of the Education Department,* University of the State of New York, Albany, N.Y., 1921, vol. 1, pp. 630–652; and R. F. Seybolt, *The Evening School in Colonial America,* University of Illinois Bulletin 24, 1925.

often surprised to learn that millions of Americans are illiterate and that additional tens of millions lack an elementary-school education. Opportunity to acquire a common-school education has presumably been a birthright of all American children for generations. Compulsory-attendance laws in the various states require from 8 to 12 years of school attendance. Indeed, for decades a high-school education has been looked upon as the privilege of American youth. Educational opportunities are actually so abundant that by 1954 the typical adult past high-school age had spent approximately 10 years in school. In 1947 the Bureau of the

Years of school completed	Number of persons included	Percent admitting illiteracy	
None	1,974,000	80.1	
1	467,000	66.6	
2	1,015,000	42.6	
3	1,764,000	19.2	
4	2,977,000	4.7	
Total			
0-4	8,197,000	34.6	

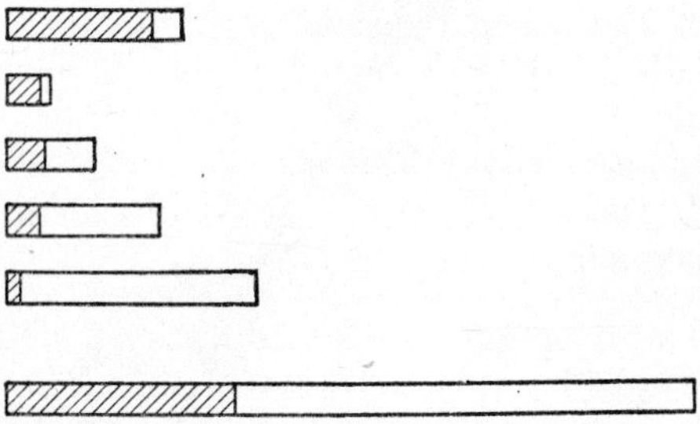

Shaded area represents proportion admitting illiteracy

FIG. 6. Relationship between illiteracy and number of years of school completed. (Source: From *Adult Literacy Education in the United States*, U.S. Office of Education Circular 324, November, 1950. Based on Census Series P-20, no. 20, Sept. 22, 1948.)

Census estimated that 2,838,000 noninstitutional civilians aged fourteen and over were illiterate—unable to read or write in any language.[2] This number represented 2.7 per cent of the adult population. Approximately one in every fifty persons is, by his own admission, illiterate. As this survey was based upon the respondent's own definition of literacy and not on any standard test, the estimate is undoubtedly low. In addition, an unknown number, literate in some other language, cannot read or write English.

Functional literacy, variously defined as ability to read a newspaper, to read and write simple sentences, or to perform at the fourth- or fifth-grade level, sets a much higher standard. The 1950 census found 9,630,000 adults, aged twenty-five and over, who had completed fewer than 5 years of schooling. This was 11 per cent of the age group—one of every nine adults. In three states, more than one-quarter of the adults fell below this level.

[2] *Current Population Reports—Population Characteristics*, ser. P-20, no. 15, U.S. Bureau of the Census, May, 1948.

During World War II registrants who tested below the fourth-grade level in reading and writing were considered unfit for military service— functionally illiterate. The equivalent of forty divisions, 716,000 men, were found to be mentally deficient.[3] Presumably, if women were subject to the draft, nearly as many would have been disqualified for the same reason. Four types of young men failed to meet the literacy requirement: [4]

1. Native-born, non-English-speaking men and those who had been in this country too short a time to master literacy skills. This group constituted about one-eighth of the illiterates inducted.

2. The mentally deficient and slow learners. The percentage mentally unable to learn to read and write is relatively small. Wartime comparison of performance of illiterate inductees with general service recruits on nonverbal intelligence tests showed only slight difference in native mental ability.

3. The mentally competent who at one time possessed literacy skills but who had lost them through disuse. During one sample month 10.7 per cent of the inductees who tested below the fourth-grade level had completed five or more years of schooling.

4. The mentally competent who had been deprived of adequate educational opportunity.

The rejection rate for educational deficiency was high again as men began to be inducted for the Korean conflict; 300,000 were rejected for this reason during the first year.[5] This is not surprising, for in spite of our tradition of free public education for all, hundreds of thousands of children of elementary-school age are not in school. Shortages of teachers, lack of buildings and equipment, and economic conditions are major factors in denying our youth their birthright.[6] Each year an estimated 150,000 functionally illiterate youth pass the compulsory attendance age.

In 1950, approximately 76 per cent of the functionally illiterate adults were white people (a minority, foreign-born), and 24 per cent were Negroes. In rural areas, 13.1 per cent had had 4 or fewer years of schooling, while in urban communities only 9.9 per cent were in this category. Inequalities in educational opportunities between Negroes and whites show up clearly. In 1950, 9.2 per cent of white persons aged twenty-five and above had fewer than 5 years of schooling, whereas 29.3 per cent of Negroes in the same age group showed this deficiency.

As might be expected in a century of expanding educational opportunity, successively higher age brackets contain increasing percentages of people with limited educations. An estimated 2.8 per cent of eighteen-

[3] Eli Ginzberg and Douglas W. Bray, *The Uneducated*, Columbia University Press, New York, 1953, p. 3.

[4] E. M. Foster, "Universal Mass Education," *School Life*, 34:27, November, 1951.

[5] Ambrose Caliver, *Literacy Education: National Statistics and Other Related Data*, U.S. Office of Education Circular 376, June, 1953, p. 2.

[6] Homer Kempfer, "Illiteracy in the Americas," *School Life*, 32:33–34, December, 1949.

Table 8. Illiteracy throughout the World

Country	Year	Per cent il-literate	Country	Year	Per cent il-literate
Africa:			Peru.................	1940	56.5
Egypt *a*.............	1937	85.2	Venezuela............	1941	56.6
Angola (Port.) *b*.......	1940	8.7	Asia:		
Mauritius (U.K.)......	1944	73.3	Ceylon *f*.............	1946	42.2
Mozambique (Port.) *b*..	1940	13.5	India................	1931	90.9
America, North:			Korea..............	1930	68.6
Canada...............	1931	3.8	Turkey..............	1935	79.1
Cuba.................	1943	22.1	Palestine *a,d*.........	1931	67.4
El Salvador *c*.........	1930	72.8	Europe:		
Guatemala *d*..........	1940	65.4	Belgium *d*...........	1930	5.6
Honduras *d*...........	1945	66.3	Bulgaria.............	1934	31.4
Mexico...............	1940	51.6	Czechoslovakia.......	1930	4.1
Newfoundland........	1945	12.0	Finland *g*.............	1930	0.9
Panama *e*.............	1940	35.6	France..............	1936	3.8
United States.........	1947	2.7	Greece..............	1928	40.8
Leeward Islands			Hungary.............	1941	6.0
(U.K.).............	1946	14.5	Italy...............	1931	21.6
Jamaica (U.K.).......	1943	23.9	Poland..............	1931	23.1
Windward Islands			Portugal............	1940	48.7
(U.K.).............	1946	28.9	Rumania *d*...........	1948	23.1
Alaska (U.S.).........	1929	20.1	Spain...............	1940	23.2
Puerto Rico (U.S.).....	1940	31.5	Sweden.............	1930	0.1
Virgin Islands (U.S.)...	1940	13.4	Yugoslavia *h*.........	1931	45.2
America, South:			Oceania:		
Brazil...............	1940	56.7	American Samoa......	1940	6.3
Chile................	1940	28.2	Guam (U.S.).........	1940	15.6
Colombia............	1938	44.2	Hawaii (U.S.)........	1930	15.1
Ecuador.............	1942	55.5			

a Excluding nomadic population.

b White or nonindigenous population only.

c 8 years and over.

d 7 years and over.

e Excluding tribal Indians.

f 5 years and over.

g 15 years and over.

h 11 years and over.

SOURCE: Compiled from data in *Statistical Yearbook—1949-50*, United Nations Statistical Office, New York, 1950. Data based on ages ten and above unless otherwise stated.

and nineteen-year-olds in 1947 had completed fewer than 5 years of schooling, whereas 21.7 per cent of those over sixty-five were in this category. At all ages women have slightly higher literacy rates than men.

The drag of illiteracy on our national strength is incalculable. In backward countries small changes in illiteracy rates may not seem to make much difference. In a highly technical culture, the penalty of illiteracy is real. Over 700,000 draftees were not educationally ready to train for technological warfare in World War II. Their peacetime contribution to production is as limited. As democracy depends upon an educated people, illiterates cannot add much strength in a crisis or at any other time. The challenge of removing illiteracy among adults is one of the most important tasks that face American education. It will continue to be a challenge as long as schools do not have the financial and personnel resources to make all children and youth literate.

Manpower requirements in World War II led the Army and Navy to establish separate training units designed to raise the educational competence of illiterate recruits to the fourth-grade level. This standard was believed to be the minimum one needed to understand written instructions, orders, signboards, and regulations. While the classification and educational program changed repeatedly during the early months, in general the program called for 18 to 21 hours of instruction per week for 12 weeks. If at the end of that time a recruit could not pass the required tests, he was discharged. Over 300,000 men were assigned to special training units after June 1, 1943, and approximately 84 per cent of them successfully completed the training. Of those who completed the training, 79 per cent did so in 60 days or less.[7]

This record has resulted in extravagant claims for Army training methods. Actually the methods and materials were based on known principles of psychology and education which can be applied when unlimited funds, compulsory attendance, and high personal motivation are available. Also, inductees had reached a state of maturity which permitted rapid learning. Reading and writing were often the only means available to the recruit for communicating with family and friends, and the desire to become a full-fledged soldier and to avoid the stigma of being sent home because of illiteracy provided added motivation. The well-regulated day with all material needs furnished gave opportunity for concentrated attention to acquirement of literacy skills. A postwar evaluation

[7] For more detail, see either of two volumes issued by the Commission on Implications of Armed Services Educational Programs, American Council on Education, Washington: *Educational Lessons from Wartime Training* (1948), chap. V; or *The Armed Services and Adult Education* (1947), chap. VIII. For a more complete report, see Samuel Goldberg, *Army Training of Illiterates in World War II*, Contribution to Education, no. 889, Teachers College, Columbia University, New York, 1951.

specified that the following additional factors also contributed to the success of the wartime literacy training programs: [8]

1. Men were carefully selected for training. Those who fell below certain scores on tests were not inducted. Assignment to instructional groups graded from total illiteracy to fourth-grade level was based on performance tests.

2. Objectives were clearly defined. Specific skills in reading, writing, and arithmetic desirable for military service were taught and tested. Much of the public-school curriculum for the first four grades was omitted.

3. Special instructional materials and training aids were used. A set of interlocking matĕrials was developed, revised, and graded by word lists and other scientific yardsticks. Films, filmstrips, charts, recordings, and other audio-visual aids were developed and used freely.

4. An integrated curriculum provided the means to develop academic and military skills, and essential instruction designed to help the men achieve personal and social adjustment was given through orientation lectures and other training sessions.

5. Performance standards were established at each grade level.

6. Instructional groups were small enough to permit individualized instruction. While the average class had about fifteen students, often only eight to twelve men were assigned to beginning groups.

7. Diversified methods were used. Lectures, demonstrations, and tutoring, as well as the use of workbooks and other practical exercises, were common.

8. Each trainee could progress at his own rate.

9. Men were tested frequently and reclassified on the basis of achievement. Recruits could complete the course at any time by passing the required tests.

10. Instructors and supervisors with training and experience suitable for this work were selected.

11. Continuous in-service training of instructors was provided. Each supervisor was responsible for only a few teachers. Additional staff members worked on preparation of materials and on testing and classification problems.

12. Results were continuously appraised through periodic inspections and the maintenance of an efficient reporting system. Competent civilian educators were brought in to help with evaluation and, as the program developed, with various other stages.

Since World War II, literacy training has been provided for certain occupation forces, and following the Korean invasion, the Armed Forces again began teaching illiterate inductees. Various unsuccessful attempts

[8] *Educational Lessons from Wartime Training,* pp. 57–58.

have been made to have Federal funds assigned to public schools, which could provide literacy education prior to induction at a minor fraction of the cost of training for men in uniform.

If a person does not learn to read and write during the years of compulsory school attendance, he is not likely to have an opportunity to do so later. In a recent year, only 351 of 3,313 public schools, in answer to a nationwide inquiry involving all communities above 2,500 population, claimed to have literacy classes for adults.[9] Very few small communities provide literacy instruction, and only one-half of the school districts in cities above 50,000 furnish such opportunity. In a follow-up study, a total of 90,000 illiterate adults were estimated to be in classes.[10] Of these, approximately 60,000 were foreign-born, and the remainder were native-born.

Practically all literacy education in schools is conducted on a class basis, although tutoring and correspondence courses are found occasionally. Most classes meet two or three evenings per week for 2 hours each. As literacy instruction is largely training in skills, classes could profitably meet more frequently if attendance could be maintained. After World War II, several states, particularly in the South, and a number of cities utilized Veterans Administration funds to support full-time schools for veterans in need of elementary education.

Teachers of literacy classes often use a combination of methods. The major discoveries in the psychology of reading are generally used in literacy classes for adults. Best results are obtained when instruction is based on the "whole," or "global," method—when the learner proceeds from the larger eye-perceptions to the small—from paragraphs and sentences to phrases and words. The majority of good teachers supplement the global approach with phonics, or a phonetic approach, in which attention is focused on syllables, sounds, accent, and spelling as a way of gaining mastery of new words.

Instruction is often centered around a particular method or set of materials. Certain states and a number of cities use Basic English almost exclusively. Nationwide, Basic English with its 850-word vocabulary is used in about 40 per cent of all literacy classes.[11] This system embodies a controlled procedure with carefully developed materials. The limited vocabulary and the accompanying structural rules make Basic English somewhat artificial for adults who are accustomed to regular English. It is, therefore, more advantageously used with foreign-born adults than with English-speaking people. A controlled experiment with Basic Eng-

---

[9] Homer Kempfer, *Adult Education Activities of the Public Schools: Report of a Survey, 1947–48,* U.S. Office of Education Pamphlet 107, 1949, pp. 12–13.

[10] Homer Kempfer, *Adult Literacy Education in the United States,* U.S. Office of Education Circular 324, November, 1950, p. 2.

[11] *Ibid.,* p. 3.

lish was conducted in New York City adult classes a few years ago with inconclusive results.[12]

Another method of literacy instruction is the Gouin theme, which was introduced from France several decades ago. It was reported in use by more than 10 per cent of the schools, but its influence probably extends to many others using the whole method.[13] The Laubach system, developed with the phonetic languages of the East Indies, is admittedly difficult to use with English. A few schools use it, although in general it runs counter to accepted psychological principles by starting with the alphabet and advancing through syllables to words and sentences. The Fernald visual-kinesthetic method, the read-write-spell contract plan, and several other systems that are usually described in the introductions of texts or workbooks all have their devotees.

Fully three-fourths of all adult literacy instruction is based on texts written for adults. Material prepared for children is objectionable primarily because of its lack of interest for adults. A few teachers use the literacy series of the *Federal Textbook in Citizenship* with native-born adults, although it was written for candidates for naturalization.

With any method, texts and workbooks are often supplemented by newspapers, digest and picture magazines, wall charts, flash cards, pictures, dramatization, objects, and blackboard sketches. Appeal is made to sight, hearing, and other senses. Filmstrips and films, records, catalogues, maps, posters, scrapbook materials, signs, and tape and wire recorders are used by fewer teachers. Much of the supplementary text, worksheet, and visual material is teacher-made and duplicated.

Illiterates do not respond readily to promotional practices which fill other classes. Many a director of adult education has publicized courses in beginning reading and writing only to have them ignored at registration time. The psychological resistance and limited educational experience of illiterates make it difficult for them to begin attending classes. They find practices strange which better-educated adults take in their stride.

There are, however, motives which can be tapped and incentives which can be used to encourage more illiterates to seek education. Sympathetic assistance, competent teaching, and an efficient program resulting in visible progress will be of great help. Where a broad cross section of adults participate in a variety of educational activities, illiterates can often be induced to enter groups in which the chief outcome for them is improvement in literacy skills. Instruction in such cases may be slanted to civil defense, nutrition, occupational training, or other activities having

[12] Perry L. Schneider, "An Experiment in Basic English for Foreign-born Adults," *Adult Education Bulletin*, 9:73–74, February, 1945.
[13] Kempfer, *Adult Literacy Education in the United States*, p. 3.

current prestige and appeal. In communities with many illiterates, an "everybody's going" attitude sometimes can be built up to lead to concerted attendance in literacy classes. The need for occupational advancement or a desire to be able to write to children, to read a newspaper, to study the Bible, or to handle accounts can be capitalized upon. Enrollment usually increases if religious leaders, employers, and neighborhood leaders encourage illiterates to learn to read and write. One evening-school principal found that calling a course in elementary education a "pre-high school program" induced many more adults to enroll than had done so previously, when the course had a title with less prestige. These and many other devices can be used by a director who takes time to become acquainted with the drives and interests of the uneducated. Autonomous-group approaches, discussed in Chapter 9, should offer other productive ways of involving illiterates.

Any comparison of literacy instruction in the Armed Forces and in civilian schools leaves the impression that the latter is much inferior, chiefly because of limited resources. Large classes (averaging thirty-three students in the survey mentioned), limited instructional aids, ill-suited materials, inaccurate classification of enrollees and the lack of homogeneous grouping, inadequately trained and supervised teachers, and the lack of an intensive program often combine to yield results which discourage the illiterate.

Elementary Education

Many adult schools conducting literacy classes also provide elementary education for adults, although the percentage of overlap is by no means complete. About one-fourth of the cities reporting literacy classes in 1950 offered adults an opportunity to earn an eighth-grade diploma. Others sometimes arrange to grant an elementary diploma based upon a special examination. Literacy education is commonly equivalent to the lower two to four grades, whereas elementary education presumably covers the entire 6- or 8-year period of the elementary school. The 1947–1948 survey found 323 schools claiming to provide elementary education for adults.[14] This was only 12 per cent of all public schools having adult programs.

Only 27 of 100 evening schools surveyed in 1949 reported having elementary education for adults. In 1952 an NEA study [15] found 64 per cent of the cities in its sample offering Americanization and elementary education, although it made no breakdown between the two. Aside from the full-time veteran-training programs in the South, other adult schools

---

[14] Kempfer, *Adult Education Activities of the Public Schools,* p. 12.
[15] Division of Adult Education Service of the NEA, *A Study of Urban Public School Adult Education Programs of the United States,* National Education Association, Washington, 1952, p. 10.

issued an estimated 3,500 eighth-grade diplomas in 1949. Over one-half of these were granted in Chicago and New York City. Numbers enrolled are hard to estimate, for many foreign-born who need only English instruction are usually included.

The typical elementary course of study for adults includes the traditional subjects. Aside from reading and writing skills, instruction in arithmetic, spelling, English usage, geography, health, history, selections from literature, and other subjects is usually given during each session by one teacher with only such integration as he may care to develop. Above the literacy level, texts written for children are often used since, except in citizenship and English, few have been written at the intermediate level for adults.[16] A number of cities have developed their own courses of study, although in many cases courses for children have been adapted. In recent years the New York City evening elementary schools have developed a unified program which, in addition to offering courses in English, treats the social studies under seven areas of living, providing instruction in each area at four educational levels.[17]

Area One—Preparing for American Citizenship
Area Two—Being an American Citizen
Area Three—Getting and Holding a Job
Area Four—Establishing and Maintaining a Home
Area Five—Maintaining Health and Safety
Area Six—Establishing and Maintaining Human and Intergroup Relations
Area Seven—Promoting Recreational and Leisure Time Activities

Usually no standard period of study is required for adults seeking an eighth-grade diploma. The time-serving concept has been largely abandoned in favor of competence demonstrated on achievement tests. A great many illiterate adults in New York City evening elementary schools in 4 years of 100 nights each, 2 hours per night, are able to learn enough to qualify for the eighth-grade diploma. These 800 clock-hours compare favorably with the 216 to 252 hours allowed by the Armed Forces for achieving the equivalent of a fourth-grade education, especially when difference in class size is considered; and they are, of course, only a small fraction of the 6,400 to 8,000 clock-hours usually spent by children in the first eight grades.

Fundamental Education

The concept of fundamental education as developed by UNESCO for the great uneducated and underprivileged areas of the world is not widespread in the United States. Fundamental education is concerned

---

[16] Homer Kempfer, "Simpler Reading Materials Needed for 50,000,000 Adults," *School Life*, 32:115, May, 1950.

[17] *Manual for Teachers of Adult Elementary Classes*, Curriculum Bulletin 1949–50, ser. 2, Board of Education, Brooklyn, N.Y.

with the development of functional knowledge in the masses of un-developed people. It attempts to make the findings of elementary science usable to all. The aim is improved agricultural production, better health and sanitation, more adequate buildings, conservation of natural and human resources, and the development of home arts and local industries. Literacy as such is not the paramount concern, although it may be an important tool whereby knowledge to raise the level of life may be gained. Cultural missions, demonstrations, local experiments, moving pictures, radio broadcasts received on home sets or made available through street-corner loud-speakers, posters, and literacy campaigns are among the methods and approaches used to diffuse knowledge among undeveloped peoples.

UNESCO is either sponsoring or collaborating with scores of demon-stration projects in dozens of undeveloped countries around the world. More information is available on them in *The Courier, Fundamental and Adult Education, Education Abstracts,* and other periodicals and mono-graphs issued by this international agency.

One example of fundamental education is the community-education program in Puerto Rico. More than a score of carefully trained leaders show films and lead discussions with rural audiences. Jeeps carry a power plant, projector, films, posters, and inexpensive illustrated booklets for distribution to country areas. Films on the economic geography of the island, family life, agricultural practices, sanitation, homemaking, and similar subjects set the stage for discussion. The development of local initiative toward neighborhood and community self-improvement is a primary objective.

Such community-education approaches would be very useful among our own economically depressed groups. The level of life of the Spanish-speaking people and the Indians in the Southwest could be lifted ma-terially by giving them ideas on how to solve the problems of economic opportunity, medical service, and adequate housing. Sharecroppers, slum dwellers, and migratory laborers are often caught in a vicious circle of low education and low income.

High-school Education

The five largest public high schools in the United States are evening high schools.[18] An estimated 800 to 900 public-school districts offer adults the opportunity to earn secondary-school credit, and possibly a third of all school adult-education programs offer high-school subjects. A high-school dropout has a much better chance of finding opportunity to finish the twelfth grade than an elementary school dropout has of finding a place to earn his eighth-grade diploma.

[18] "Statistics of Public High Schools, 1945–46," *Biennial Survey of Education, 1944–46,* U.S. Office of Education, chap. V, p. 6.

Traditional regulations requiring completion of courses of a standard length are still widespread in evening high schools, although required attendance is usually lower than in the day school. The need of many World War II veterans to complete high school rapidly helped break the academic lockstep in recent years. Accelerated programs for veterans became widespread and many were opened to other out-of-school youth and adults with satisfactory results. Such courses, designed to cover the essentials at a faster rate, depend more upon outside preparation than upon detailed teaching. Most accelerated programs permit the student to progress as rapidly as his time and abilities permit.

In accelerated programs, credit and diplomas are usually based on achievement tests. In 1949, veterans and servicemen could obtain high-school equivalency certificates based upon General Educational Development Tests in thirty-three states. Twenty states permitted the high school to issue such certificates directly. Twenty issued equivalency certificates to nonveterans, and five others permitted local schools to do so.[19] A majority of state education departments recommend that local schools grant credit based on examinations given under the auspices of the U.S. Armed Forces Institute.

In Small Communities

Foundation education in small communities is often neglected because too few adults demand instruction. Actually the typical community of 500 persons has enough illiterate adults to form a class if they could be induced to attend. Many rural neighborhoods of 100 people could produce a roomful of illiterates. The number lacking an eighth-grade or a high-school education runs much higher and represents a deficiency in nearly all communities.

Small-group and individual approaches can be used where there are too few adults to fill a class. Tutoring of small groups can be a practical method resulting in rapid progress, and it is not too expensive where volunteer helpers can be enlisted. At times, neighbors, employers, a spouse, or a grown son or daughter can be taught to assist the adult student. In such cases the professional teacher may spend only 10 or 20 per cent as much time with the adult as he otherwise might. With the helper and the pupil both present, the tutor can arrange for, or approve, suitable instructional materials, check on progress, demonstrate additional techniques, and give general supervision and encouragement. Correspondence instructional materials are often used in tutoring situations, as they are usually more self-teaching than texts prepared for class use. Extensive use of home-study courses at the secondary, elementary, and

[19] *Accreditation Policies of State Departments of Education for the Evaluation of Service Experiences and USAFI Examinations,* American Council on Education, Washington, 1949.

literacy levels is another practical way of caring for needs which cannot be served by group instruction. (Further information on correspondence study is given in Chapter 10.)

Evaluation

Both the external and the internal effectiveness of the foundation-education program should be evaluated. The former can be measured by comparing the numbers of illiterates, elementary-school dropouts, and high-school dropouts served by the program with the numbers in each of these categories in the community. What proportion of recent high-school and elementary-school dropouts are induced to participate? The percentages brought into the program are a good index of its general worth.

Internal effectiveness can be determined by tests of individual and group progress. Success on standardized achievement tests, General Educational Development Tests, and similar measuring instruments that are periodically used can serve as a criterion in judging the merit of methods. A comparison of the achievement in control and experimental groups can help select the better methods, techniques, and procedures.

Possibly a better way of evaluating a program is by answering questions such as these: To what does the instruction lead? To what extent are lives enriched? How many adults either continue their formal education or acquire the habit of lifelong learning? How many participate more broadly in other adult-education activities and in the life of the community? Evidence of success along these lines should be more conclusive than scores on a test.

FAMILY-LIFE AND PARENT EDUCATION

The basic trouble in human relations is our not having been happy and really loved as children. My experience of nearly 30 years with college boys corroborates this. The past is not water over the dam. It is water behind the dam, pushing way down deep . . . if the colleges do not accept responsibility for disseminating the things we now know to the student—*all* of the students— we *now* have, what of the future? [20]

Professor Magown's conclusion applies equally well to educational programs for children, youth, and adults.

Purpose and Content

Family-life education enriches the experience of living in families. It emphasizes the values, principles, and practices of our most intimate relationships. In so doing, it provides the roots for everything else we

[20] Alexander Magown of the Massachusetts Institute of Technology at the Northwestern Conference on Higher Education, Corvallis, Oreg., 1946.

hold dear in life, including our ability to understand and accept the responsibilities of democracy. Competence in making independent decisions and initiating responsible action is prerequisite to responsible citizenship. This ability or the lack of it develops early, and nothing short of intensive, extensive, and exceedingly expensive psychotherapy can change the pattern formed. Once initiative and self-reliance have been killed by improper home and school handling, they can be revived only with difficulty, if at all.

We are steadily acquiring more scientific understanding of how homes may nourish, protect, encourage, and enrich the personalities of their members, how they can lead toward emotional maturity and well-rounded development. Family-life education in the modern age calls for a synthesis of knowledge from a variety of fields. All the sciences and arts of human development can make contributions to this area of living. Appropriate findings from such fields as biology, genetics, medicine, health, nutrition, psychology, psychiatry, sociology, and cultural anthropology can be channeled to improve family living. In addition, religion, philosophy, and the humanities have important contributions to make.

Family-life education is for all ages and both sexes. It is a broad tent covering many activities, each with its specific purpose: marriage education, prenatal and infant care, child development through adolescence, and marital adjustment during maturity and old age. Aimed at building strong and satisfying family relationships, it builds attitudes that carry over into community life. It tends to reduce delinquency, crime, and social disorganization, and to increase the personal and social satisfactions that accompany ever-developing and happy personalities.

Successive stages of the parent-education phase of family-life education are concerned with learning the fundamentals of infant care, child development through the pre- and in-school years, and adolescent development. During these years emphasis is on helping parents learn how to raise their children to happy, mature adulthood. Parents need to become acquainted with the standards or normal behavior and learn how to arrange conditions for the best development of their children. Eventually parents must provide for a shrinking family as youth find mates and establish homes of their own.

Preparation for marriage include group and individual teaching and counseling activities during youth and young adulthood. Such activities may begin with adolescent boy-girl relationships and carry through the courtship stage to marriage. Marriage counseling may be concerned both with preparation for marriage, which may be provided during the courtship years, and with assistance on problems of adjustment after marriage.

Family relations are obviously one part of human relations. As new homes are established and children are born, an ever-changing set of relationships comes into existence: husband-wife, parent-child, grand-parent-parent-child, and in-law. Grandparent education has been set up in some communities to help parents of young couples adjust to their new roles.

As a field of human relations, education for family living is emerging as a synthesis of several older areas. Certain aspects of family-life education have grown out of home economics as this field has changed from the earlier cooking-and-sewing stages to include a broader concern for family living. A good share of family-life education deals with family relationships and social-emotional growth, to which homemaking skills and knowledge are handmaidens. The fields of applied social science, mental health, group development, and biology also make significant contributions.

Agencies

A great many community agencies, both public and private, are concerned with family-life education. The home-school-church triad has inescapable responsibilities. No doubt the family itself, by exerting an early and constant influence, is the most powerful agency for setting patterns of family living. The school, *in loco parentis* for a significant part of every young person's life, has a supplementary function. The school and play coteries provide the face-to-face groups of contemporaries so potent in building personality and character. Ultimate ideals and standards of family life, of course, come largely from philosophy and religion. Clergymen and religious educators often provide marriage counseling. Family-service agencies, marriage-counseling bureaus, and other social agencies offer supplemental services, often of educational character. County home-demonstration agents of the cooperative Extension Service usually promote activities in this field. A great many voluntary community organizations likewise have significant interest in family improvement and often sponsor activities related to it. Clarification of ideals and improvement of the practice of human relations in the family, however, are educational tasks, regardless of aegis or agency.

While education for better family living can be influential at nearly any age, improvement in the younger generation is an uphill fight unless it is accompanied by education for adults. Most progress is made, of course, if education is employed with all ages simultaneously. For this reason some communities set up machinery to coordinate their efforts toward the improvement of family life.

In a recent survey [21] covering primarily communities of 2,500 population and above, only 414 schools of 2,684 districts reported family-life and parent-education activities for out-of-school youth and adults, although 925 reported homemaking for adults. Only 117 schools reported

[21] Kempfer, *Adult Education Activities of the Public Schools*, p. 12.

activities which prepare specifically for marriage. A later NEA study,[22] based on a sample of communities of essentially the same size, found 32 per cent having one or more groups in family-life and parent education, while homemaking was reported by 80 per cent. The same study showed a growth in enrollment of 51 per cent during the preceding 4 years. Obviously the family-life field is one in which many schools have not yet assumed responsibility, although the role of the school seems to be increasing.

Where a field is shared by many agencies, each should define its role and clientele in relation to the others. The particular aims of family-life education and the clientele served by various agencies differ somewhat among communities. From the practical point of view, every local director of adult education has to face issues in the family-life field. In any community, public, private, and religious agencies would do well to form a family-life education council consisting of all organizations and agencies interested in this field. Such a council can provide the mechanism for exploring the field and reaching agreement on the type of service to be rendered by each agency.

In many communities the major portion of the organized educational program can be carried on by public agencies. In theory, public agencies can, and possibly should, feel free to cover all content areas not reserved by religious groups.

Family-life councils, either as independent groups or as branches of community or adult-education councils, can provide good ways of planning integrated programs in this field. They can survey need, assess resources, conduct or advise on research, project plans, consult with existing agencies, or stimulate the formation of new ones to serve new functions.

Approaches

In relatively static societies, the knowledge, skills, habits, attitudes, and ideals in family life are passed to successive generations without much change. Where neither children nor adults have systematic educational opportunities in this area, the young must learn how to rear children and how to get along with the family group chiefly from folklore.

The basic approach to parent education is the study group in which parents with children of similar ages discuss their common problems and do related reading. The approach dates back about 60 years, when small groups of mothers with leisure time and superior education began to seek advice on child development, to read books on the subject, and to discuss their common problems. Hundreds of groups were formed throughout the country. In the early days, study clubs depended largely upon the

[22] Division of Adult Education Service of the NEA, *A Study of Urban Public School Adult Education Programs of the United States*, p. 10.

dissemination of information by experienced lay persons and specialists.

Various phases of this movement led to the formation of the Child Study Association of America, the National Congress of Parents and Teachers, the National Committee on Parent Education, and other national and local organizations. The American Association of University Women was active early in bringing the contributions of various sciences to bear upon child development and the family. Three White House conferences, held at approximately 10-year intervals beginning in 1930, were focused on children and family life.

The study-group movement took a new turn when grants from the Laura Spelman Rockefeller Memorial were made in the 1920s. A survey of the programs, problems, resources, and needs of the field led to establishment of the National Council of Parent Education, which became a clearinghouse and coordinating agency. Several grants were made to universities to establish programs for training professional leaders to work in state education departments, school systems, and voluntary agencies. Usually, in order to extend services and to involve many more parents, the professionals started training lay leaders, often using itinerant trainers for this purpose. Emphasis was placed on the development of study groups concerned with the problems and interests of parents. Lay workers trained in discussion and leadership processes were looked upon as organizers and leaders of local groups rather than as dispensers of authentic information. Volunteers were not expected to acquire truly professional knowledge and competence. The trained-amateur status often led to greater group participation and improved learning situations. Through reading, observation, and discussion, the participants themselves were expected to provide much of the content.

Usually 2 to 4 years of biweekly or monthly meetings are required to train competent lay leaders. The task is (1) to identify people who demonstrate potential group leadership, (2) to improve their discussion-leadership techniques, and (3) to add a knowledge of resources. Problems of organization and training have led to a high mortality rate among volunteer workers, but there are compensations. For instance, studies of lay leaders show that their development often follows this pattern: A mother with a narrow interest in the development of her child joins a study group, where she becomes aware that her problems are similar to those of other mothers. As her interest in the social and physical environment of the neighborhood and community grows, she becomes concerned with how the school and community meet the needs of her child and of other children. She assumes some degree of leadership. Broader horizons continue developing until she sees the relationship between her family, the nation, and the whole world. Training in parent-education leadership, then, actually becomes training in community leadership.

A number of school systems use the study-group approach led by lay leaders who are trained by professional staff members. Groups may be affiliated with a larger organization—such as a PTA, church, settlement house, or social agency—or they may be independent mothers' clubs. Some elementary-school principals encourage the formation of parent groups at each grade level. A room-mothers group led jointly by a teacher and lay leader can develop significant insights into the problems of a specific age level. The efforts of the school and home can be closely integrated in this way. In rural areas a parent-education specialist working out of the county superintendent's office can train lay leaders in small villages. Newer approaches tie these activities in with those of the school psychologist and the school nurse and with the specialized services of various local agencies.

As cases brought up by group members may have heavy emotional connotations, discussions in recent years have tended to start with a common objective experience. Group observations, a film, a panel discussion, role playing, and puppets can give common immediate background and are good springboard devices for starting discussion. Weekly discussions are supplemented with selected reading materials, films, recordings, individual counseling, and talks by the school psychologist and other specialists.

Groups studying infant care are popular if they can be scheduled at times when mothers and fathers are free or under circumstances that allow them to bring their babies. Discussion groups on infant care and family relationships for fathers and mothers to be can supplement the individual guidance of physicians.

At the kindergarten and nursery-school level, guided observation is a common prelude to discussion. Observation of the children for an hour or two is followed by discussion and related reading. Much of the purpose is to develop adequate concepts of normal behavior. Where mothers assist a few hours each week in cooperative nursery schools and play groups, discussion groups can be a natural outgrowth. Fathers can participate if discussions are held at night.

Study and discussion groups for parents of adolescents are much less widespread than they are for parents of younger children. Groups in which both parents and youth participate can provide a good way to develop mutual understanding. Youth-parent panels, committees, and discussion groups can work out well if the opinions of young people are given adequate weight.

Sex education represents an important problem. Although at one time it was treated as a separate topic or course, the best practice today, both in schools and in parent groups, considers this subject as an integral part of personality and character development. Nonetheless, a number of adult-education programs offer a short series on sex education for parents who desire such help.

Lectures, forums, classes, institutes, conferences, and similar organized activities in parent education and family relations are among the conventional formal approaches which are still popular. Although large group meetings cannot in themselves constitute a well-rounded program, in conjunction with other approaches they can have important functions. In the main, formal instruction has the same strengths and weaknesses in this field as in other areas. The lecture and other authoritative approaches disseminate information quickly but often fail to change behavior. In many communities people are so hungry for education in child development, parent education, and family relations, that considerable numbers will attend lectures and institutes led by recognized authorities. Short courses often maintain good attendance. Semester or year-length courses are usually too long to attract sizable numbers of adults. A favorite system is to run a course of four, six, or eight weekly sessions and then to start another short course a few weeks later. The willingness to undertake a few sessions in the foreseeable future, the specificity of instruction, and the sense of completion give an appeal difficult to obtain in a longer course.

One- or two-day institutes frequently highlight the year's activity in family-life education, especially where an extensive discussion program has been in operation. Such events once or twice yearly can make good use of outstanding authorities and can provide an opportunity for all family-life organizations in the community to evaluate their work, to gain inspiration, and to lay groundwork for integrated planning of further activity. Institutes normally have greatest value as an in-service training experience for lay leaders, although they may be designed to stimulate interest among segments of the community not yet participating in more intensive activities.

City health departments and family-welfare agencies frequently operate child-development centers and well-baby clinics where new mothers and parents of small children can seek advice on their individual problems in health, psychological and social development, and personality adjustment. In such cases the school usually has no operating responsibility but does have opportunity to relate its work to clinic activities. Close cooperation helps the school keep abreast of need, indicates desirable changes in instructional content and materials, and often results in an expanded enrollment from the clinic's clientele.

As the physical, social, and psychological environments in which children grow are all-important, parents can learn much by engaging in activities designed to improve these surroundings. The school and community organizations together can provide ways for parents to participate in community building. Such activities include cooperative studies; surveys of need, programs, facilities, and opinion; social-action projects;

community-interest forums; workshops on curriculum; and similar projects. Several examples are listed below.

1. Volunteer service in policy making and in operation of cooperative nursery schools, play groups, and tot lots.

2. Leadership in child and youth groups and activities sponsored by the school and other community organizations: Boys and Girl Scouts, Campfire Girls, Brownies, church-school groups, arts and crafts groups, trips, and teen-canteens. Much of the learning comes from training as leaders for these activities and from carrying them out under supervision.

3. Participation in block-mother activities and discussions, which lead to common understanding and cooperative supervision of play.

4. Cooperation with school activities, such as instructional units in social living, holiday observances, noon-hour supervision, school-lunch programs, safety patrols, school publicity, equipping a playground, library activities, visual aids, and a school-exchange service of common equipment.

5. Service on monitoring committees for television, radio, and movie programs.

6. Service on youth-parent committees to arrive at community standards on such matters as desirable conduct, allowances, budgets, homework, boy-girl relationships, use of automobiles, part-time work, social and recreational activities, radio and television listening, and baby sitting.

7. Participation in an annual health roundup and other family-related drives.

8. Studying the causes and developing remedies for juvenile delinquency.

9. Participation in family activities: father-son and mother-daughter classes, family shop nights, family kitchen classes, family fun nights, family stay-at-home nights, parent-child study groups, camping experiences, gardening, etc.

10. Participation in three-generation discussions, panels, and round tables on problems of standards and expectations.

Over 200 communities have marriage-counseling centers or bureaus which provide individual advice to married couples or to those approaching marriage. Usually such centers are sponsored by social agencies and supported in part by the community chest. A growing number of schools, however, provide service in this field, which is often given by the supervisor of family-life education, but occasionally by the school psychologist or guidance counselor. In a few cases a marriage counselor, engaged by the school, arranges office hours for counseling, and county or city mental-hygiene specialists can sometimes be induced to offer their services on a regular schedule at the adult school.

Group counseling on marital problems and adjustment is sometimes provided by the same professional people. Tests of psychological fitness for marriage and of psychological compatibility between couples may be a part of the service to groups. Preparation-for-marriage groups are likely to be sponsored by churches, YWCAs, and other social agencies. Particularly in the absence of other adequate counseling, the school has the opportunity to provide group counsel on matters on which the major religious faiths do not differ. Preparation-for-marriage courses usually can deal with many of the financial, legal, medical, sociological, and psychological aspects of marriage, leaving to churches and private organizations the building of attitudes on such matters as the spiritual meaning of marriage, sex education, and divorce. As the whole field of preparation for marriage is a community responsibility, the important thing is that the community organize to do the job. An alert adult school will assume initiative in this field and define its role in the community setting.

Evaluation

Family-life and parent education is succeeding when family living becomes richer for all members. This success is a more fundamental basis for evaluation than are parents' expressions of satisfaction, which may be based on popularity of leadership. The best yardsticks are probably long term: the reduction of juvenile delinquency, the reduction of divorce and family disorganization, the development of mentally healthy personalities, the reduction of insanity, the maintenance of social activity in the older years, the reduction of intergroup tensions, the increase in well-matched couples, and the building of communities in which mature and healthy personalities can develop.

As an intermediate evaluation, a local director of adult education or a supervisor of family-life education may want to seek evidence of change in child-rearing practices, in the number and use of family councils, in the amount of whole-family recreation, in the participation of fathers in child study, and in the interest shown by parents in community projects bearing on child and family welfare.

The ultimate evaluation of family-life education is the increase both in the personal happiness of all family members and in their effectiveness in all phases of life.

EDUCATION FOR LEISURE TIME

Leisure is what you make it. It may be your greatest blessing or your greatest curse. You determine its quality, and its quality also determines you. In the old era, the job determined the worker. In the new era, leisure determines the man. (Walter B. Pitkin.)

The quality of a civilization is known by the recreation of its people. (Lord Lytton.)

As the amount of leisure time grows, it becomes more important both to individual development and to the community. Aside from the recreational possibilities and the chance for pure enjoyment it offers, leisure provides great opportunities for personal growth, cultural development, and the maintenance of mental health. Man has fought human and physical enemies from time immemorial to achieve wealth, security, and freedom from persistent drudgery—to achieve leisure time. Yet, never has a highly developed civilization survived long when it had an abundance of leisure. Only primitive cultures have been able to exist for long periods with plenty of free time. The implication is that if we cannot learn to use our leisure wisely, constructively, and creatively, our civilization, too, may decline. Without doubt, this concept is related to the challenge-response theory developed by Toynbee.[23]

Our civilization, however, differs from all others in three ways:

1. Our leisure is the property of all people regardless of occupation. We have no substantial leisured class as conceived by Veblen.

2. We have more energy to devote to leisure activities. Better health, laborsaving machines, and shorter hours result in ample energy to accompany the leisure time.

3. We have a more equitable distribution of education than any other civilization has had. Our people have a better opportunity to make wiser choices.

The case can be made that education for leisure is as important as education for labor—that avocational education is as important as vocational education. This may be especially true as the labor-leisure ratio comes more into balance.

The values of leisure-time activities are widely recognized, but the idea of spending public money to help adults learn to use leisure wisely raises doubts in many minds. Even though more school districts conduct adult-education activities in recreation than in any other field,[24] the recreational phase of leisure-time activities is not universally accepted as a responsibility of public schools. The leisure-time field is second only to public affairs as a source of controversy in adult education. The conflict may arise in part from differing ideas about what constitutes desirable and proper recreational activities. The public willingly pays taxes to support leisure-time activities offered in the name of recreation, but often hesitates to do so when they are considered a part of education. Badminton, social dancing, parties, bridge playing, fly casting, and stamp collecting are acceptable recreational activities in many communities, but instruction in these by the public schools is taboo. Even instruction in arts and crafts, golf, the study of antiques, dramatics, and music are suspect in some quarters. The wise director knows the temper of his

[23] A. J. Toynbee, *A Study of History*, Oxford University Press, New York, 1947.
[24] Kempfer, *Adult Education Activities of the Public Schools*, p. 12.

community and builds his program accordingly. Three considerations enter into program decisions in this field.

1. State education departments, particularly where financial aid is available, usually have established regulations concerning education for leisure-time activities. Such regulations attempt to draw the line between what is legitimate education as a state-aided activity and what is not. Often the regulation approves education in the activity, but not mere participation. Thus, as long as a group is taught the rules and fundamentals and is given controlled and supervised practice in an activity, it may be defined as education and reimbursed as such. After participants have gained reasonable facility and are merely enjoying the activity without significant further learning, it may be declared recreation and, *ipso facto,* educationally off limits. Splitting hairs further, in some cases a town team receiving instruction in basketball may be considered a class in physical education and, therefore, possibly entitled to public funds; but competition with another team is classified as a recreational activity. The proper source of information on public-school policy on these matters and its interpretation is the state education department.

2. Presumably policies governing the use of public money are based on public sentiment. Even so, the policies of the state education department may be too liberal for some local communities, and the local directors may have to organize more conservative programs. Or, if local sentiment permits and the board authorizes, a local school may exceed the state regulations by conducting activities without the use of state funds. The public in one community may wish to pay for recreation directly and keep it under voluntary or private auspices. In another, full cooperative purchasing of recreation through taxation may be desired.

3. State and local provisions for recreation have a direct bearing on the leisure-time activities sponsored by the schools. Schools in a community having a strong recreation department with diversified activities for all ages must limit their own work in this field. Their task calls for cooperation and coordination with the recreation department, which may want to provide its own instruction and do its own leadership training. The school may have little to do. Sometimes, however, the school can instruct in leisure-time activities while the recreation department provides facilities and supervision. In any case, such relationships must be worked out amicably.

Schools in Pennsylvania are authorized by law to conduct recreation for youth and adults, both in and out of school, and many do so. Yet, even under such authorization, schools need to reach an understanding with recreation departments wherever they exist. Where there are no recreation departments, leisure-time activities may fall to the school by default. Certainly in many rural areas, community schools can do a great deal in recreation which, in urban areas, is done by specialized agencies.

Areas and Approaches

Interest and participation patterns in leisure-time activities change with age.[25] While interests can develop at any age, most older people have no new leisure-time interests beyond those developed in childhood and youth. Since many interests decline with age, elementary and secondary schools, as well as youth-serving agencies, should do all they can to generate many broad and deep interests which will carry on through maturity and retirement, a period often blighted by an inadequacy of interests.

In school, youth enjoy a plethora of group activity, much of it under institutional sponsorship. The same benefits of inexpensive and abundant activities can be made available throughout life. Homemakers and work-ingmen, without help, have little time for elaborate planning of recreational activities, and older people characteristically need encouragement. The school can do much, both directly and in cooperation with community organizations, to educate for creative use of leisure. Leisure represents the growing time of life—the time when mind, body, and spirit refresh themselves and take new steps forward.

Group sports and athletic activities often hold interest after the school years. Physical-education activities for adults were listed by 20 per cent of the schools reporting to the Office of Education in 1948. In after-school years, activities in which both individuals and couples can take part grow in popularity. Often competition gives way to group participation. Archery, badminton, golf, riflery, swimming, and tennis are among the activities which may be taught. Red Cross lifesaving classes, first aid, square dancing, ballroom dancing, fly casting, tumbling, and trapeze work interest their share of adults. Women in the thirties and forties often fill classes in gymnastics as a method of weight control, under such captions as "Reducing to Music" or "Rhythm and Relaxation."

Classes in arts, crafts, and hobbies are usually easy to fill. In the 1948 U.S. Office of Education survey, 28 per cent of the schools reported instruction for adults and out-of-school youth in this field. The diversity of the field offers materials and media for self-expression to every adult who develops an interest.

Courses in the arts, including study of and performance in the several kinds of painting, sketching, designing, and sculpturing, succeed largely according to their leadership. A teacher insisting on high standards of performance may produce a few talented students. Another leader may use a more popular approach to build interest and appreciation in more average performers.

In the arts and crafts, ceramics is very popular, although the expense

[25] E. K. Strong, *Change of Interest with Age*, Stanford University Press, Stanford, Calif., 1931.

of a kiln, wheels, and other equipment often slows its development. The shop crafts, such as upholstering, woodworking, furniture repair and refinishing, metal art, jewelry making, and lapidary work, often have waiting lists unless equipment and instruction are plentiful. Where storage is no problem, staggered shifts permit service to more people when equipment is limited. Weaving, however, is an exception because one class ties up the looms. Photography, lampshade making, printing, leatherwork, plastics, block printing, silk-screen printing, commercial art, stenciling, etching, textile painting, china painting, flower arrangement, hooked rugs, knitting, needlework, beadcraft, and chair caning are other possibilities.

Usually these activities are taught purely for their appreciational values and the opportunity they afford for self-expression. In some cases, however, native materials and the developing skills provide the basis for a local industry. Mountain arts and crafts, crafts for retired people, and Indian arts are examples of economic enterprise developed out of this field. Where sale of goods becomes a significant objective, production and marketing usually are handled through cooperatives or other outlets independent of the school.

Few communities are too small to have the three basic kinds of musical activities—a community orchestra, community singing, and listening groups. Mixed choruses, men's choruses, women's choruses, choirs, glee clubs, quartettes, bands, orchestras, symphonies, drum-and-bugle corps, and appreciational groups are a part of many adult-education programs. In the 1948 U.S. Office of Education survey, 20 per cent of the schools reported music-education activities for adults and out-of-school youth. Large vocal groups are usually open to all interested in singing. In addition to weekly instruction and practice, such groups often put on special events, such as the *Messiah,* and supply music for patriotic exercises, religious holidays, community programs, and regular summer concerts. In instrumental groups a minimum competence on an appropriate instrument is required. Where high-school students can graduate into a community band or orchestra, special beginning instructional groups for adults are not likely to be found. If the adult band is too mature for the average high-school player, an intermediate, junior, or young-adult group may help the transition. Aside from classes in piano and violin, instruction in single instruments is not very widespread on a public basis.

In addition to direct sponsorship of music instruction, the school can provide leadership for much community music. Music in such groups as religious societies, men's and women's clubs, parent organizations, foreign-language societies, patriotic societies, and lodges can be developed with the aid of public-school personnel, if they are made available under appropriate policies. In fact, if the average man is again to participate in vocal music as he did in the Middle Ages, it will probably be through developing music in the organizations to which he belongs.

Appreciation can come to groups through instruction, enjoyable study of music, supervised and directed listening, exposure to good music, and performance in music organizations. General instruction by means of tape or disk recordings and specific preparation for opera and concert programs help build listening groups. A number of libraries have collections of records which may be used at the library or borrowed.

Drama, like music and art, has a significant part in shaping both individuals and groups. The educative influence of the noncommercial theater has long been recognized, although some uninformed people classify it merely as entertainment. Even aside from the therapeutic values of drama, the behavior changes induced through both participation and observation are real.

The little theater is probably the most common approach to drama. In 1948, such theaters for adults were reported to the U.S. Office of Education by 20 per cent of the school systems. Whether through the cooperative efforts of a few village volunteers or through the full-time leadership of an organization such as the Cleveland Play House, the theater offers extensive opportunity for different levels of participation. For every part in the main drama there can be a dozen related parts, all contributing to and benefiting from the visible product. Product quality, of course, may not be as important as the process itself, where popular drama is concerned. Play selection, casting, acting, staging, and technical services can involve literally hundreds in dramatic activity, even in relatively small communities.

Audience education can be effected in several ways. Play selection and high quality of production can raise standards of expectation and appreciation. Presentation of social and economic problems can stimulate thinking and serve as a basis for discussion in organized or autonomous groups. Audience questionnaires, lectures, study groups, play-reading groups, and other devices can build appreciation of good drama.

One of the best educative experiences that a community can undertake is the development of its own community drama, based upon its own peculiar history and folklore. Such a project usually starts with a study group which traces the historic influences that shaped the development of the community. This activity corresponds essentially to the data-gathering stage of the educative process. When the group has become saturated with the history and folklore of the community, a sequence of locally written and produced dramatic episodes constitute an excellent way of presenting the story to the public. A good share of the community, of course, will be involved in the planning, writing, and production. If successively larger groups of the community are involved, the project can become a significant problem-solving activity. Under these circumstances, the drama itself can be an immensely expressive experience.[26] Even if the outcome does not include solving a community problem, the building of local pride and understanding is worth the effort. Community drama can arise out of the hearts of people in a way that leaves the little theater a vicarious experience.

Serious formal study of the great ethical issues which mankind has faced down through the ages attracts a significant, though often small, percentage of adults. Classes and discussions in philosophy would appeal to more adults if leaders could treat the subject more popularly than some of them seem able to do.

Under the stimulation of the Great Books Foundation, a number of libraries and schools sponsor Great Books Discussions. The Great Books embody the most significant ideas developed by mankind and provide the content for the very heart of a liberal education. Groups of twenty or more meet for 2-hour sessions biweekly, usually with two volunteer coleaders who have been through at least a year of discussion and a training course given by representatives of the foundation. Participants are expected to have read the assignment. The Socratic method is used in discussion, with the leaders asking a chain of penetrating questions designed to induce rigorous thinking. About eighteen meetings are held annually, and sequences of 5, 6, or more years of reading and discussion are available to those who wish to continue. While it was originally hoped that the discussions would attract the more literate two-thirds of the population, experience has shown that the appeal is primarily to the more intelligent and thinking minority. Typical groups, however, often include a broad economic, vocational, and educational level. No doubt an abundance of competent leadership could popularize the discussions further.

Noncredit literature courses have some appeal for adults. A number of schools have book-review groups, concerned with both current fiction and nonfiction; poetry clubs; classes in feature writing and short-story writing; play-reading groups, semantics classes, and great-films showings. Occasionally a course in the French novel, Chinese literature, or Old Testament literature attracts a group.

Classes and discussions in gardening, landscaping, flower growing, and flower arrangement are popular in some communities. The school can often cosponsor these with some other agency.

Travel is a persistent interest of all ages. Some adult schools conduct courses which constitute preparation for a trip. The trip is taken, usually by bus, and followed by discussions and a review of films and colored

---

[26] See B. Brownell, "The Community Drama in Adult Education," *Teachers College Journal*, 18:26, November, 1946; and R. E. Gard, "A Drama Plan for Wisconsin," *Adult Education Bulletin*, 11:137–139, June, 1947.

slides. Pictures are usually left for succeeding groups to view. They are supplemented by pictures taken by world travelers, explorers, geologists, geographers, and naturalists. Travel ties in well with a study of local history, geography, or geology. With a little planning and ingenuity, a great deal of education can be worked into a program which might otherwise consist only of a travelogue film or lecture.

Social activities provide opportunity for much informal education, especially for newcomers to a community. Some people, for a variety of reasons, seem not to have learned a repertory of social skills in their youth. Consequently, courses in contract bridge, social dancing, home entertaining, party giving, the arts of conversation and listening, magic, etiquette, and similar subjects often fill to overflowing.

Community Programs

Most leisure-time activities provide opportunity for integrated, community-wide programs involving all ages. A whole network of activity can often be developed in dramatics, music, art, arts and crafts, and athletics. A few communities have state-wide and even national reputations for vocal music, instrumental music, painting, craftwork, or little-theater activity. Holland, Michigan, puts on a tulip festival every year. One community presents Handel's *Messiah* annually. Another may develop a cantata, an oratorio, a massed chorus, or other musical program. Christmas, Easter, and the summer season provide opportunity for much cooperative music activity among the churches, bands, orchestras, and music clubs. A few communities hold extensive art exhibits around which much of the art activity during the year is centered. A dramatic festival, a pageant, or a season of dramatized local history may climax a year's activity. Through persistent leadership over a long period, high excellence may be built up to a culminating public display of some kind.

Behind a top activity often is the participation of a whole community. Numerous groups, both public and private, do the understudy work to provide the voices, the competent players, and the artists. In an atmosphere of high morale, they are chosen for positions in the hierarchy, much as the actors for the Passion Play are selected at Oberammergau. Schools, community centers, recreation centers, and many community organizations contribute their space, facilities, and leadership to the total community enterprise. Art, music, or acting becomes popular as everybody participates. A committee or council usually does the necessary over-all planning.

Leader Training

Adult-education programs often can make a major contribution to recreation programs by training leaders even though recreation as such may be a responsibility of other agencies. Much recreation is led by volunteer amateurs. The school can often join together with other appropriate agencies in training tot-lot supervisors, playground leaders, camp counselors, arts and crafts instructors, hobby leaders, boy- and girl-club leaders, scout masters, Great Books Discussion leaders, song leaders, storytellers, referees, square-dance callers, and leaders of a dozen other kinds. Many leadership skills are relatively simple and can be acquired without much difficulty by competent participants. In fact, since some recreation-leadership skill is needed by nearly everyone, the school can offer training in this field to all.

GUIDANCE SERVICES

We need guidance when we feel that we cannot make a personal decision or adjustment alone. We may also need guidance without recognizing the fact. Guidance is the educational process applied to a personal problem so that an individual may better direct his life toward desirable objectives.

As an educational service, guidance for adults is not new, although it is not yet widely available in public-school programs. In 1952 over 17 per cent of the public secondary schools in the United States reported employing counselors, with an average of two per school reporting,[27] and only 12 per cent of all public-school adult-education programs in 1948 claimed to provide guidance services for adults.[28] Further inquiry revealed that some of this service was only over-the-counter registration counseling.[29] Even so, adult-guidance services utilizing special personnel are growing rapidly in both public and private agencies. This growth stems partially from the stimulus of the veterans guidance services that became available at Veterans Administration offices and university centers following World War II. Basically, the growth is in response to the demand of the adult public, which is gaining an understanding of the values of psychological testing, evaluation of work experience, and counseling.

Types of Guidance

Nearly every adult-education program provides advisory service of some kind at registration time. This may be given by instructors, counselors, or members of the administrative staff. Sometimes, however, registration clerks are the primary source of information about courses. This type of counseling is usually limited to a description of the content and the level of difficulty of the course. Dropout studies frequently reflect on

[27] Arthur J. Jones and Leonard M. Miller, "The National Picture of Pupil Personnel and Guidance Services in 1953," *The Bulletin of the National Association of Secondary-school Principals,* 38:105–159, February, 1954.

[28] Kempfer, *Adult Education Activities of the Public Schools,* p. 8.

[29] Homer Kempfer and S. V. Cheskie, "Adult Guidance Services in Public Schools," *Occupations,* 29:324–327, February, 1951.

the adequacy of counseling at registration. In a professional sense, dispensing information on courses over the counter is not guidance, although it is not always easy to differentiate such assistance from more intensive service.

For nearly a half century, vocational guidance has been concerned primarily with helping young people select, prepare for, enter upon, and progress in an occupation. It has usually been assumed that once a person is climbing the vocational ladder, he is safely on the road to success and will need little further help; but this is becoming less and less true. As old occupations die and new ones are created, more and more adults are having to change their line of work in middle life and later. This means that vocational-guidance services should be available throughout life.

The process of retirement demands guidance possibly as much as the period of youth. The rewards, both personal and social, may be almost as great. Successful retirement from full-time employment to a part-time occupation or to some other suitable activity requires planning and sound judgment. While vocational adjustment is only a part of the total reorientation needed, it is often the key to maintaining personality integration. As maturity is relative, many adults approaching the chronological age for retirement are unable to assess their situations accurately and make sound plans unaided.

Vocational guidance of mature adults usually follows the general pattern applicable to young people, with characteristics due to greater maturity taken into account. After age twenty-five, for instance, adults are likely to have more stable interests than they had as adolescent youth. Other personal characteristics are also likely to be more fixed. Work experience gives their goals a reality that they may not have had earlier.

Most vocational guidance is an individual matter. Information on a detailed personal inventory is often supplemented with other systematic information including records of work experience, education, and scholarship. Additional data may include results on standardized inventories, tests, and rating scales of mental ability, aptitude, achievement, interests, and other personality dimensions. In some areas satisfactory tests for adult use have not been developed. Since many of the available tests have been standardized on high-school or college populations, appropriate forms for the general adult ages may not exist. In such cases interpretation of results must be unusually cautious.

An occupational information service is useful to adults, especially young adults, if kept up to date. A system of directed visiting and interviews with workers in an occupation can be a basic service provided that it is supplemented with systematic information.

Schools vary widely in the amount and quality of the placement service they provide. Apparently the majority of public-school adult programs have no aggressive placement policy whatever. Private schools often handle this phase of guidance much better than do public schools. A number of public-education programs, however, have gained a reputation with employers for their attempt to place their graduates selectively. Placement is a phase of guidance that can well afford to be strengthened. If business courses in public schools, for instance, were organized into a unified sequence and adequate placement service were given, public adult schools could offer more competition to proprietary business schools.

Few adult schools with vocational-guidance services make follow-up studies, and those that do are most often concerned with the success, failure, and shortcomings of the guidance and training provided young adults who enter the labor force. Relatively few studies are made of middle-aged or older adults. The potential values leading toward program improvement warrant many more follow-up studies. Personal follow-up, without regard to systematic study, can extend the influence of the school far into the occupational life of the adult. It is a major means of maintaining an educational connection throughout life with adults once served.

A few adult-guidance departments provide special services for the community. Business firms and industries without adequate technical assistance sometimes call upon the school to provide testing, psychological services, and counseling. Schools may provide such service to clinics, medical centers, mental hospitals, the Red Cross, or other educational and social agencies. They may also screen apprentices for labor unions and test applicants for employment or civil-service positions. They may screen cases before referring them to more specialized agencies. As proficiency certificates often lose their value with the lapse of time, one worthwhile service which can be provided by the school is an assessment, whenever desirable, of the competence of specific individuals. Since diplomas and degrees depreciate as indicators of competence in mature adults, employers may desire more of this type of assessment.

Educational guidance is the type of counseling most frequently provided by public adult schools. Young people who have had their education interrupted are particularly in need of this service. However, adults of any age facing significant training may also need to have their backgrounds analyzed objectively, their interests probed, and their abilities reassessed. Returning servicemen, middle-aged women without salable skills or recent work experience, adults who have been squeezed out of their occupations early, and mature people desiring to reorient their lives through education are also among the candidates for educational guidance.

In addition to its other services, educational guidance includes information and orientation, educational planning, and help in adjustment to new situations. As the educational level of adults may range from illiteracy to completion of college, the adult counselor should be familiar with the entire scope of educational institutions in the area—public schools, colleges, technical schools, correspondence schools, and private opportunities. Catalogues, bulletins, and related informational materials should be on file.

When an adult wishes to resume his education after interruption, he often requires long-range educational planning. He may have a clear objective or only some hazy plans. Counseling should help clarify the educational objective and relate immediate objectives to a long-range sequence. While specific goals may be laid out, the adult should be led to realize that education is a lifelong process. A well-rounded educational program should be mapped out.

Various kinds of educational adjustment problems will face the counselor. Some adults will seek to have their unattainable ambitions supported. In light of their abilities, age, family situations, and competition within the occupation, they should be shown the advantages of more modest programs. Diagnostic, achievement, and performance tests may sometimes confirm or reveal inadequate basic preparation which must be remedied before further progress can be made. Educational tests can help build security and confidence in adults who have had little formal education. Adults with motivation lower than their ability can be helped toward more worthy goals. Observation, interviews, and conferences with teachers may reveal weak study habits which can be improved by counseling and special instruction. A few adults may need help in transferring from the compulsory atmosphere of the formal school to the permissive atmosphere of an adult school.

Educational guidance can be provided most easily if educational and work-experience records of the individual are available. A few schools accumulate significant personnel information before a child enters school, add to it while he is in the elementary and secondary grades, and carry it on into the post-high-school years of his adult life. For persons who remain in one community, such records are invaluable, although they may have to be supplemented with new information as new problems arise. Since no adequate provision has been made for transferring such records (except scholastic and related information to higher institutions) to other communities, the system breaks down for the mobile parts of our population. Personnel records within a large corporation, civil-service records in the Federal government, and service records in the Armed Forces, however, often do follow the person and are useful for guidance purposes.

One primary by-product of educational guidance is the information gathered for reorientation of the curriculum. While one major objective of guidance is to help the individual select the most appropriate course and curriculum, the counterpart is to help shape the curriculum to the needs of adults. Few persons are in a better position than the counselor to know what adults need. The guidance office, then, should be directly related to the curriculum-improvement and program-making process. Findings of the guidance office may result in new courses, new curricula, or changes in existing courses that make them better able to meet the needs and interests of adults.

Helping the individual to achieve the greatest possible personal development and to make the greatest contribution to society may involve additional guidance. Not all problems are vocational or educational. Some concern the development of a philosophy of life, personality development, home and family relationships, the use of leisure time, the development of leadership potential, social-civic areas, or the maintenance of mental balance and integrity. Problems related to choice of a mate, adjustment to one's spouse, naturalization and immigration, and human relations may also call for personal attention.

Guidance in most of these areas depends on the same general techniques as are used in educational and vocational fields, but with somewhat more emphasis on psychological counseling and follow-up and less on formal testing. Often the case calls for an adjustment of the person to situations beyond his control. Workers in this field must take care to assess each situation and refer the persons concerned to more competent specialists whenever necessary. Cases may call for psychological and psychiatric aid that the adult counselor cannot give. Large communities usually have specialized agencies to deal with many personal problems. In small communities the school may be the most competent agency to serve a variety of needs.

Group Approaches

Most guidance is individual. Group approaches, however, are being used increasingly with adults. At best, work with groups is a time- and energy-saving supplement to individual counseling.

Group approaches have several uses. One is to disseminate information about educational opportunities and occupations. Several adults with similar problems can be oriented to adult education at the same time. Analysis of study habits can begin in a group. Orientation to ways of studying career opportunities can be given here. Much information-giving through films, printed materials, and oral presentation can be done in groups, as can certain follow-up studies and evaluations.

The group approach is also suited to making individuals aware of values, expectations, and needs. Adults often have erroneous impressions of guidance services and expect quick or miraculous results. False ideas can be corrected in group situations, and self-evaluation can begin there.

The use of tests can be explained to groups, and many of them can be given in groups.

A group offers many opportunities for counseling. In fact, many classes in any comprehensive program will serve this purpose. Instruction may occupy a minor role in such areas as child care, family relations, psychology, public speaking, mental hygiene, and human relations, for it may be given largely on a counseling basis. Child study and adolescent psychology, for example, often provide a means of counseling with parents. From these studies, integrated guidance services may develop to help both parents and children make desirable behavior changes. Counseling in groups also has therapeutic values. Often perspective can be maintained better in a group than in an individual situation. Knowing that others have similar problems often has some value in itself.

In most cases group counseling should be supplemented with individual counseling. For example, while a general understanding of tests can be imparted to groups, individual interpretation and application are necessary. In so far as each person presents a special problem, individual attention should be available. Where group approaches are used, the time and number of interviews required for individual counseling usually are materially reduced.

Organization for Guidance

As adult education develops, one problem which will face every community is how to organize its guidance services. While nonschool agencies sometimes provide certain services, no comprehensive guidance service exists in many communities. In fact, until after World War II one could look in vain for vocational guidance open to the public in certain large cities. Guidance is becoming increasingly available, however. Services established for veterans in many colleges have been continued for adults. Adult-school guidance services are expanding, and other agencies, both governmental and private, are providing service in this field.

A few adult-education programs are now equipped to provide most of the guidance service needed in the community. A number of directors readily realize that adequate publicity would engender such public interest that their staffs would be swamped. Frequently, however, programs are limited to services traditionally expected of the school. While schools seldom try to provide the total community service, they often establish informal cooperative relationships with other agencies. Staff members may work out informal arrangements with the Veterans Administration, the Office of Vocational Rehabilitation, and the United States Employment Service. Community agencies, other governmental departments, and private employers frequently call upon the school for testing services. Family-service bureaus and other social agencies may seek specialized types of assistance from the school. The school in turn refers many cases to these specialized agencies.

Some communities, stimulated by the flood of returning servicemen after World War II, established guidance centers. These often developed into community service centers operating with advisory committees and supported by community-chest funds. At times, the several major agencies concerned with guidance in the community pooled their resources. Some of them have remained active and now open their services to all adults. The idea of a community guidance center, of course, is not new. The St. Louis Red Cross, over a quarter century ago, established a Vocational Counseling Service. While the school usually plays a major role in such counseling centers, incorporation of other community organizations on the governing committee and in the active operation of the center gains broader community support. Certain County Boards of Vocational and Extension Education in New York State provide one or more guidance specialists to serve either the entire county or districts contracting for the service. Itinerant guidance specialists are operating in other states.

The majority of schools having guidance services limit them to those enrolled or about to be enrolled in other adult-education activities. Fewer than one-half offer services to the general public. Most schools serve veterans, and a number pay special attention to out-of-school youth and the foreign-born. Special guidance services for the aging are not yet widespread. Schools in one survey reported that only 30 per cent of the adults who need guidance receive it.[30]

Guidance for adults seems to be underpromoted. A number of schools do not publicize it at all, probably because of their inability to handle the anticipated load. In many instances, additional promotion has resulted in dramatic increases in case load. Often the availability of counseling service is publicized only in the general announcement of the adult program.

Guidance services are staffed from a number of sources. A counselor qualified to work with high-school youth ordinarily needs considerable maturity and a great deal of experience in the adult world before he will make a good counselor for adults. A number of graduate training programs have recognized the difference between counseling youth and adults and offer special courses in counseling adults and out-of-school youth. Some schools draw counselors from outside the day-school ranks, much as they do teachers of adults. Personnel managers, psychologists, and others from business and industry are frequently engaged to counsel adults.

Usually there is a close relationship between the day guidance program and that of the adult school. While administratively the direction of adult guidance is under the director of adult-education and evening-

[30] Kempfer and Cheskie, *op. cit.*

school principals, supervisory staff services are often provided by the guidance department of the school. The same staff members in the Bureau of Guidance, Placement, and Adult Education in the Springfield, Massachusetts, school system supervise guidance at all grade levels and provide an integrated education and guidance service for adults.

Among adult schools with specialized guidance services, over three-fourths of the administrators engage directly in counseling. Most of them supplement their own activities with those of other professional helpers—counselors, advisers, and psychologists. Only a few schools have full-time adult-guidance specialists, although a number have the services of half-time or nearly full-time people. Engagement for evening work only is the usual pattern.

The cost of providing individual guidance service undoubtedly is a major handicap to its more widespread development. While cost data often are not comparable, the true costs are higher than individuals usually are willing to pay. The cost per client in the Veterans Guidance Center at Stanford University was $21.[31] Nearly three-fourths of the schools surveyed by Kempfer and Cheskie charge no special fees. The services are supported by funds provided by the board of education, supplemented by state aid in the majority of cases. At the time of the survey, Veterans Administration funds were a factor in about one-third of the schools. About one-fourth of the schools charge fees, which are most often used for testing and special services.

Trends

1. More schools are adding counseling services for adults. Staffs are expanding.

2. Guidance services for adults are expanding in scope. Schools are adding testing services, vocational guidance, educational guidance, counseling in personal and family-life problems, and follow-up programs.

3. Guidance is being integrated into other educational activities and planned for special groups, such as the unemployed, the parents of nursery-center children, and the aging. Predropout interviews, the development of individual folders for all new cases, and the transfer of folders for permanent residents of the community are new services.

Evaluation

Exact evaluation of the results of adult-guidance services is difficult, if not impossible. However, sufficient clues often can be obtained to point up places for improvement.

As dropout studies frequently show poor registration procedures, a reduction in dropout rate may reveal better educational counseling dur-

---

[31] G. D. Barshal, *Converting a Veterans Guidance Center,* Stanford University Press, Stanford, Calif., 1950, p. 57.

ing and before the registration period. Likewise, if guidance helps change the curriculum, the results may include better retention of students and better satisfaction on the part of all concerned. Interviews with or even questionnaires to recipients of guidance service often can reveal points of strength and weakness—and places for improvement. As only a fraction of those enrolled in an adult school are likely to have received specialized guidance service, experimental and control groups can be used to make comparative studies of dropouts, satisfaction, persistence of attendance, and similar factors. Interviews to assess the opinions of the service received probably give more valid results if carried on by personnel not directly associated with counseling. Barshal reports moderately high reliability among raters using a permissive-interview approach.[32]

Informal evaluation is easier and often as satisfactory, although it may not result in the proof sometimes demanded by the holders of purse strings. Discussion of cases with faculty members, growth of the demand for service, visiting teams from other adult programs, and anecdotal records all are a help in evaluation.

SELECTED REFERENCES

Foundation Education

Caliver, Ambrose: "Illiteracy and Manpower Mobilization," *School Life,* 33:131–133, June, 1951.
———: *Literacy Education: National Statistics and Other Related Data,* U.S. Office of Education Circular 376, June, 1953.
Cass, A. W.: "Reading Materials for Adults," *Adult Education,* 1:26–31, October, 1950.
Ginzberg, Eli, and Douglas W. Bray: *The Uneducated,* Columbia University Press, New York, 1953.
Goldberg, Samuel: *Army Training of Illiterates in World War II,* Contributions to Education, no. 966, Teachers College, Columbia University, New York, 1951.
Grace, Alonzo G.: *Educational Lessons from Wartime Training,* American Council on Education, Washington, 1948, chap. V.
Houle, Cyril O., et al.: *The Armed Services and Adult Education,* American Council on Education, Washington, 1947, chap. VIII.
Kempfer, Homer: "Manpower through Literacy Education: State School Systems Can Create It," *School Life,* 34:1–2, October, 1951.
Kotinsky, R.: *Elementary Education for Adults,* American Association for Adult Education, New York, 1941.
United Nations Educational, Scientific, and Cultural Organization, *Progress of Literacy in Various Countries,* Monographs on Fundamental Education, no. 6, Paris, 1953.
UNESCO Clearing House: *Inter-American Seminar on Illiteracy and Adult Education,* Occasional Papers in Education, no. 1, Paris, 1949.
———: *Literacy Education: Selected Bibliography,* Occasional Papers in Education, no. 5, Paris, 1950.

[32] *Ibid.,* p. 51.

Witty, Paul: "Principles of Learning Derived from the Results of the Army's Program for Illiterate and Non-English-speaking Men," *Adult Education Bulletin,* 11:131–136, June, 1947.

Wood, W. R.: "Community Responsibility for Literacy Education," *School Life,* 34:23, 26, November, 1951.

Family-life and Parent Education

Brown, Muriel W.: *With Focus on Family Living: The Story of Four Experiments in Community Organization for Family Life Education,* U.S. Office of Education, Division of Vocational Education Bulletin 249, 1953.

The Family Today: Education for Home and Family Living, Superintendent of Public Instruction Bulletin 350, Lansing, Mich., 1948.

Gabbard, Hazel F.: *Working with Parents: A Handbook,* U.S. Office of Education Bulletin 1948, no. 7.

Grossman, Jean S.: *Ways and Means of Reaching Parents,* Play Schools Association, Inc., New York, 1946.

Gruenberg, Sidonie M.: "Parent Education and Child Development," *Social Work Year Book,* Russell Sage Foundation, New York, 1947.

Houdek, P. K.: "How to Develop a Community Family Life Institute," *Journal of Social Hygiene,* 37:346–355, November, 1951.

Lyle, Mary S.: *Adult Education for Democracy in Family Life,* Collegiate Press, Inc., of Iowa State College, Ames, Iowa, 1944.

McClusky, H. Y.: "Dissemination of Child Development Information through a Program of Adult Education and Community Action," *Child Development,* 19:40–51, March, 1948.

McHose, E.: *Family Life Education in School and Community,* Teachers College, Columbia University, New York, 1952.

Moller, E. F.: *Parents Participate,* The Woman's Press, Whiteside, Inc., New York, 1945.

Nebraska Council on Children and Youth: *Family Living: A Handbook for Nebraska Communities,* Lincoln, Nebr., 1952.

"The Parent-Nursery School Program in Berkeley," *California Journal of Elementary Education,* 20:176–192, February, 1952.

Riner, Elizabeth: *Frontiers in Homemaking Education: Programs for Adults,* U.S. Office of Education, Division of Vocational Education Bulletin 239, 1949.

Whiteside-Taylor, K.: "Cooperative Nursery Schools Educate Families," *Teachers College Record,* 54:332–339, March, 1953.

Education for Leisure Time

Butler, George D.: *Introduction to Community Recreation,* McGraw-Hill Book Company, Inc., New York, 1949.

Carter, Jean, and Jess Ogden: *Everyman's Drama,* American Association for Adult Education, New York, 1938.

Division of Adult Education Service of the NEA: *The Educational Theatre in Adult Education,* National Education Association, Washington, 1951.

Meyer, H. D., and C. K. Brightbill: *Community Recreation: A Guide to Its Organization and Administration,* D. C. Heath and Company, Boston, 1948.

Miller, Paul A.: *Community Health Action,* Michigan State College, East Lansing, Mich., 1953.

Nash, J. B.: *Physical Education: Interpretations and Objectives,* A. S. Barnes and Company, New York, 1948.

Van de Wall, Willem: *The Music of the People,* American Association for Adult Education, New York, 1939.

Williams, J. F., and C. L. Brownell: *Administration of Health and Physical Education,* W. B. Saunders Company, Philadelphia, 1946.

Guidance Services

Cartwright, M. A., and G. Burch: *Adult Adjustment,* Teachers College, Columbia University, New York, 1945.

Coates, R. H.: "Adult Counseling in the Philadelphia Public Adult Evening Schools," *Adult Education Bulletin,* 12:152–155, June, 1948.

Jager, Harry A., and Franklin R. Zeran: "Community Adult Counseling Centers: Some Illustrative Experiences in Organization," *Occupations,* 23:261–308, February, 1945.

Kempfer, Homer, and S. V. Cheskie: "Adult Guidance Services in Public Schools," *Occupations,* 29:324–327, February, 1951.

Klein, Paul E., and Ruth E. Moffitt: *Counseling Techniques in Adult Education,* McGraw-Hill Book Company, Inc., New York, 1946.

Lockwood, W. V.: "Adult Counseling for Better Adjustment to Problems of Aging," *Teachers College Record,* 55:183–190, January, 1954.

———: "Adult Guidance: A Community Responsibility," *Adult Education,* 3:79–83, February, 1953.

Logie, I. M. R., and M. R. Ballin: "Group Guidance for Adults: An Evaluation," *Occupations,* 30:530–533, April, 1952.

Vocational Education in the Years Ahead, U.S. Office of Education, Division of Vocational Education Bulletin 234, 1945, pp. 300–320.

Ward, Roswell: *Out-of-school Vocational Guidance,* Harper & Brothers, New York, 1949.

See also General References: [33] Beals and Brody, pp. 130–158, 363–383; Ely, pp. 83–95, 159–175; Essert, chap. 13; and Kempfer.

[33] The General References are listed in full at the end of this book.

CHAPTER 6

Organized Approaches to Major Areas: Citizenship

PUBLIC AFFAIRS EDUCATION

In a democracy, education for citizenship deserves the highest priority. One widely accepted principle holds that the primary interest of the state in education is to ensure its own perpetuation.[1] Because the making of public policy is a continuous process, public-affairs education, or citizenship education, cannot be confined to childhood and youth.

Citizenship education is important for adults in two respects:

1. In a democracy, everyone has an obligation to assist in making public policy. A basic assumption is that participation by everyone results in the best possible decisions for all. Presumably, through sufficiently widespread and intelligent participation, we can not only adjust to our ever-changing relationships with our fellow men but solve our public problems as they develop. Indeed, an earmark of the civic sophistication of a people is their ability to detect incipient problems, define them, and solve them as they arise instead of months or years after they have become acute.

2. Education in citizenship is also essential in helping man achieve his full personal dignity. Man grows and develops as he has a part in determining the policies which affect him. Only by working with others on his civic problems and having a hand in shaping his own destiny can an individual acquire mankind's most priceless possession—the full feeling of freedom and dignity.

Levels of Public Affairs and Their Relationships

Public affairs cannot be precisely defined. In general they comprise the public relationships and common responsibilities of all or most residents of a community. Problems requiring policy decisions arise among people in communities of all sizes—from the smallest face-to-face groups to the world community.

---

[1] T. H. Briggs, *The Great Investment*, Harvard University Press, Cambridge, Mass., 1930.

Many problems affecting public interest arise in neighborhoods. Usually these can be solved informally or by general agreement. For instance, neighbors may cooperatively repair a road, protect children at crossings, build a shelter for waiting bus passengers, set up a first-aid station, or establish a tot lot.

Community affairs embrace problems of the schools, recreation, transportation, traffic, safety, housing, health, public utilities, welfare and social services, economic development, and cultural growth. Village, town, or county governments provide channels for the development of many of these services, although many more are matters of nongovernmental action. A great deal of extralegal public activity goes on in most communities. Often official and unofficial groups work closely together. One index of healthy interest in public affairs is the amount and level of spontaneously organized discussion of public problems. Although community organization, community development, and community-planning movements started many years ago, they received a great impetus during World War II. At that time war councils, civil-defense councils, and postwar planning councils represented comprehensive organized attempts at total community planning. In fact, the whole community-council movement has grown out of the need for a more coordinated approach to common problems.

Public affairs at the state level are largely concerned with the wider aspects of community affairs. Because most state boundaries are artificial, public concerns at this level often are governmental. A number of voluntary organizations are organized on a state basis, although others operate regionally along economic or geographic lines. The responsibilities of regions, substates, port authorities, drainage and irrigation districts, and other specialized governmental agencies are roughly similar to those of the state.

National and international affairs constitute a major area of concern which holds the public limelight partly by virtue of the mass media of communication. Domestic policy covering economic development, wages and labor relations, the Armed Forces, atomic energy, internal security, taxation, and conservation is sometimes overshadowed by foreign policy regarding war and peace, trade, aid to underdeveloped areas of the world, cooperative defense, population movements, world government, and human rights. Voluntary organizations solve some national problems, although much of their energy is ultimately intended to influence official policy.

Public affairs at all levels are interrelated. The various parts of government are so interwoven that specialists in law, legislation, and public administration work full time to maintain an understanding of the wheels within wheels. Division and delegation of authority, checks and balances, and political parties operating at all levels present a complex maze to the average citizen. In fact, except at the simplest community level, the complexity of civic relationship requires a system of elected officials whose responsibility it is to study and formulate policy. Even so, ultimately every citizen, at his level of competence, also has a responsibility for public policy. Only a selected few can become specialists, but we must all acquire general knowledge about the major public issues and problems if we are to discharge our responsibility for eternal viligance, for final review of the work of our elected representatives.

In recent decades, world events, expansion of the Federal government, and the development of new mass media of communication have focused attention on activities in Washington, often to the neglect of the statehouse, the courthouse, and the city hall. There is valid reason to believe that a nation can be no stronger than its communities, for healthy civic intelligence and local activity are the foundation of a healthy state and nation.

Neighborhood and community activities during World War II showed anew that adults have enough ability to solve their local problems and will do so when adequate stimulation and assistance are available. Civil-defense councils, block-leader organizations, and similar activities under a wartime dynamic demonstrated a healthy, inherent vigor. This demonstration of vigor has significant meaning for the public-affairs educator. It should give him hope, as well as clues to better educational activities.

Several characteristics of modern civilization make the task of adult citizenship education more difficult than it was in the days of the New England town meeting. Full recognition of present-day conditions may help reveal the dimensions of the problem.

Urbanization, with its accompanying specialization of labor, compartmentalization, anonymity, and socioeconomic stratification, keeps people apart. The bigness, remoteness, and complexity of government bring feelings of frustration to citizens who find it hard to know how to influence policy and who may even feel that elections are of slight use. Citizens often sense little connection with elected representatives and even less with appointed officials. Complex government operates slowly, and citizens often find it difficult and time-consuming to get to the officials they want and to make their voices heard. People easily come to feel that they cannot influence the forces that control them.

Immediate day-to-day pressures of making a living, of family responsibilities, of business competition, and other demands on time keep most people too busy to give much attention to public problems.

Much of the structure of government is a patchwork of antiquated form which makes little sense to people used to the streamlined operation of competitive business.

People, especially in cities, bombarded with sensational headlines, blatant advertising, hundreds of personal contacts per day, and numerous other invasions of privacy, in sheer self-protection develop a psychological shell often difficult to penetrate.

The conflict of values bothers a great many: individualism and collective action, cooperation and competition, selfishness and altruism, religious teachings and worldly behavior. Concepts of right and wrong learned in childhood are put to severe tests.

These and other circumstances of modern life militate against participation in public affairs. Yet research, experimentation, and accumulated experience are beginning to reveal ways of involving more adults in citizenship activity. These ways are based on the fact that people want to cooperate in the solution of their common problems. They will do so if they see evidence that their activity makes a difference.

In order to participate more effectively in public affairs, people need knowledge about public problems, issues, and tension areas. They need to know present official policy. They need better understandings and appreciations of various points of view and of cultures and conditions giving rise to them. They need better means of getting information. Most of all, they need to learn ways of making their efforts count.

Basic to all this is the principle that people learn effective citizenship best in the local community. The community is a microcosm duplicating in many respects problems of the larger world. Until people learn to live justly and democratically in neighborhoods and communities, they can hardly expect to build a peaceful, free, and united world. Education-through-action programs at the community level can build in people the necessary know-how for working on broader problems. Such programs must be built on needs as the people themselves feel them, not as outsiders or even professional educators view them.

Objectives

The primary purpose of public-affairs education in a democracy is to increase the quantity and quality of participation of the citizenry in the solution of their common problems. This broad purpose may be broken down into three objectives:

1. *Stimulating Concern with Public Issues and Problems.* An assassination in Sarajevo, racial discrimination at a local plant, a bribe at city hall, a low primary vote in Georgia, the closing of a refinery in the Near East, a revolution in Central America, and the crossing of a parallel in Korea, may have varying degrees of importance to any one individual, but they all affect everyone. The first task of public-affairs education, therefore, is to help every person become aware of the changes that scientific developments in communication, transportation, and war-making potential have made in our relationship with other countries and peoples and the impact that events everywhere have on our lives.

This realization does not come easily. We are most aware of what personally affects ourselves, our families, our friends, and the others whom we see and know. Beyond sight, beyond personal experience, awareness is difficult to build. Pictures, newspapers, radio, and television build secondhand awareness. A reported flood or drought across the continent means only a fraction as much as it would if it were in the next community. The same event in Asia is hardly noticed. People find remote events difficult to visualize and understand.

The public-affairs educator must be conscious of this difficulty as he strives to help people see early the significance of conditions, trends, issues, and problems. Timeliness is the key. During and after a war or an economic upheaval, it is easy for people to see the effects of military, economic, social, political, or moral forces. Understanding at such a date, however, is too late to prevent or modify the situation. If people are ever to live up fully to the democratic ideal, they must become aware of social, economic, and political forces early enough to modify them and make them serve the desired ends. We have developed sufficient understanding in science to predict quite accurately the results of certain actions. We must seek to apply this same kind of thinking to public affairs. Through seeing the favorable results of their actions, people must develop faith that early sensitivity and attention to public affairs will pay dividends. Therefore, the first task of a public-affairs educator is to build sensitivity in adults which will ensure further study and action.

2. *Building an Enlightened and Informed Citizenry.* The founders of our republic realized that an educated citizenry is its best insurance of success. If citizens are invested with the final authority and responsibility for formulating public policy, then they must have ample opportunity to become informed and enlightened.

The manner in which this widespread information and enlightenment comes about is crucial. It raises two related questions: First, to what extent should the government, having a high stake in its own perpetuation, provide education for its citizens? Second, and more important, what kind of education in public affairs should it provide?

Nondemocratic governments often use education as one of the forces to maintain themselves. Less danger exists under our democratic tradition. Most educational agencies in America operate in an atmosphere of relative freedom from political interference. Such interference as exists is as likely to be concerned with personnel as with curricula. Schools and colleges must keep eternally alert to forces which would restrict freedom of inquiry and teaching. Usually, however, such interference is not aimed at the support of one political party over another. Instead, it is more often concerned with foreign ideologies.

Danger from government-disseminated propaganda is further reduced by the freedom given to nongovernmental agencies to engage in educational activities. At the adult level, a great deal of education in public affairs is conducted by voluntary organizations, private agencies, mass-media agencies, and other organizations in no way connected with official government. The activities of private agencies ensure a healthy counter-balance to information handed out by governmental agencies.

Assuming that it has an interest in education rather than in propaganda, a government or agency can take a position at either of two extremes, or anywhere in between, in regard to public-affairs education. On the one hand, it can passively open public records to all who care to inspect them; on the other, it can aggressively reveal and interpret its information so that the public can easily acquire all the pertinent facts bearing on public problems. Actually, a very high proportion of all the facts needed to make intelligent decisions on public policies are available in print. Only a few people, however, have time to search out and study the *Congressional Record,* surveys, official reports, research data, statistical tables, and similar documents. Even by one who had the necessary research skills, full time would be required to keep up with a single field. Under these circumstances government agencies can do much to facilitate the education of the public (1) by abstracting the most important data from the total, (2) by presenting information in an attractive manner, and (3) by issuing information in a style easily read by the average person. In this way they would serve educational purposes. In so far as governmental agencies do not take such action (and they cannot do the complete job), public and voluntary educational agencies should do it.

Selecting, preparing, and making available readable information is only one step in building an enlightened citizenry, however. Educational agencies should also help citizens develop skills in the following areas:

1. In finding information on a problem and in tracing out further information

2. In evaluating information according to source, substantive fact, and relevance of fact

3. In differentiating between information and propaganda

4. In detecting what further facts are needed

5. In seeing wider relationships so that enlightenment will be of a broad, social type rather than narrow self-interest

While these skills may be taught at earlier educational levels, they need constant improvement during the adult years.

3. *Leading People to Act in the Light of the Best Interests of All.* Being concerned and informed is not enough. Citizens must act in the public interest. A major task of public-affairs education is to help people learn the many things that they can do. Voting is usually the first, and with many almost the only, act of citizenship that comes to mind. Voting is important—yet there are literally hundreds of other ways of civic expression which contribute to policy making. Hundreds more con-

tribute to the general welfare, but most people are largely unaware of them. These activities need to be sharpened and made attractive; their contribution needs to be made clear. Citizens need to learn the skills required to perform them competently. These are tasks for education.

Even voting needs to be built up as a civic act. It is embarrassing to compare our voting rate with that of foreign democracies. Even countries of high illiteracy have made impressive voting records. Voter turnout in other literate democracies is consistently higher than in the United States, as is shown in the following list:

Country	Date	Per cent of potential voting population who cast ballots
Italy.............	1948	92
Holland...........	1950	87
Britain...........	1951	83
Sweden...........	1948	83
Norway...........	1949	82
Denmark..........	1950	82
France...........	1951	76
Finland...........	1950	75
Canada...........	1949	74
United States......	1948	52
United States......	1950	41
United States......	1952	63

The three primary objectives of public-affairs education are interest, information, and action. Concern alone is not enough. Neither is knowledge enough unless it leads to action toward the social good. The merit of all educational approaches and methods must be evaluated against these three criteria.

Forum Meetings

Some ways of developing an interested, informed, and active adult citizenry have come down to us from colonial times. Others have been developed during the intervening decades. A few are quite new. The following pages discuss the more common approaches and indicate some of the promising new ones.

Until recent decades public educational agencies have assumed little responsibility for adult civic education. Historically, most of it has been conducted by voluntary organizations. Only within the past 25 years have the schools shown much activity in this field. In fact, public schools have not yet wholeheartedly embraced responsibility for public-affairs education for adults. In 1948 only 8 per cent of the public schools reporting adult-education activities claimed to have civic and public-affairs education.[2] At least seventeen other fields or subjects were mentioned more frequently. In 1951, however, an NEA study[3] found that 30 per cent of the cities reporting had activities in civic and public-affairs forums, informal classes, and other groups. The same study showed an increase of 428 per cent in enrollment in this area during the previous 4 years.

The *lecture*, one of the oldest approaches to education, is still one of the most widely used. It has roots in European universities, and it often follows the academic pattern. In the 1948 survey, only 318 among 2,684 public schools (12 per cent) claimed to have lecture series for adults, usually in public affairs.

The lecture is useful in informing and inspiring large numbers. A great deal of information can be disseminated quickly. Mass media of communication can extend the lecture to a wide audience. The lecture, however, provides only a one-way flow of information. Although it may be factually well-balanced and may fairly present all sides of an issue, without opportunity for questions, the audience has little chance to test balance and fairness. Propaganda may be difficult to detect. In many situations the lecture is relatively ineffective in changing behavior.

In formal *debate*, two sides of controversial questions are presented systematically. If the participants are of equal competence, opposed ideas may receive critical examination. Propaganda can be challenged, and the element of conflict helps attract listeners. The inherent weakness of this approach lies in the perversion of purpose. Debaters often are less interested in seeking the truth than in defeating the opposition. Each debater may use combinations of personal charm and legalistic tricks to win his case, and the average listener finds it easier to affiliate with personalities than to consider the merits of an argument. Relatively few adults will go away with a changed mind. Instead, their previous impressions will be reinforced, for most people, in reading or listening, unconsciously select and remember primarily the material that fits their preconceived notions. In most quarters the formal debate has given way to more useful problem-solving approaches or has been supplemented with other devices.

A *forum* is "any meeting of individuals gathered to hear the presentation of any subject in which opportunity is given for questions and discussion from the floor."[4] The forum is a basic approach to public-affairs

---

[2] Homer Kempfer, *Adult Education Activities of the Public Schools: Report of a Survey, 1947–48*, U.S. Office of Education Pamphlet 107, 1949, pp. 12–13.

[3] Division of Adult Education Service of the NEA, *A Study of Urban Public School Adult Education Programs in the United States*, National Education Association, Washington, 1952, p. 10.

[4] J. W. Studebaker and C. S. Williams, *Education for Democracy*, U.S. Office of Education Bulletin 1935, no. 17, p. 46.

education. It has all the advantages of a lecture plus the advantages of audience participation. If the process is largely one of questions and answers, the education may consist primarily of dissemination of information. A skilled educator, however, after a systematic presentation of a problem, situation, or issue will induce the audience to explore further for solutions. While the forum alone is not an action group, convictions and plans may develop which sometimes lead to action. Ordinarily the formal presentation occupies more than half of a 90- or 120-minute session, although good leaders with a shorter talk may stimulate a longer period of discussion.

The typical forum consists of a lecture followed by questions and discussion. Variations include the *forum-dialogue,* in which two experts or an expert and a chairman engage in conversation on a given subject, and the *symposium,* in which each of three or more representatives of different points of view gives a short address. A similar group under the leadership of a chairman discussing a matter informally among themselves without fixed speeches constitutes a *panel.* A *lecture-panel* consists of a lecture which is discussed by a panel. In a *debate-panel* two or more debaters argue on opposite sides of an issue and then discuss it as a panel. Thus the "Town Hall of the Air" assumes a debate-panel form. In each case the formal presentation and discussion by the leaders are followed by questions and discussion from the audience.

The well-managed educational forum aims to develop in the audience a clear understanding of the subject being discussed. Free and open inquiry must be the cardinal rule. A chairman skilled at helping speakers clarify their points is an invaluable asset to any forum. He must be able to state and enforce a simple set of rules for the discussion period and to handle with fairness, firmness, and good humor the variety of personalities found in public audiences.

In a forum program there should be a balanced presentation of all significant viewpoints. If one speaker cannot treat all these fairly, representatives of different sides should be included on the program. Care in selecting spokesmen of different points of view will help assure balance. The use of panels and symposia helps avoid the charge of partiality. If a meeting should turn out to support one side of an issue too strongly or unfairly, early opportunity should be arranged for the other side to present its case. Impartiality can be gained by consulting with a representative advisory committee and by including the audience in the planning process. In fact, if the forum is attended by a representative cross section, the advisory committee may come from its ranks.

Forums have limitations, however, which should challenge the community to use other ways of building an enlightened citizenry. Forums inform and sensitize only those originally interested enough to attend. They do little to train for action. They appeal primarily to the upper

socioeconomic and educational groups. After a 5-year experimental program at Des Moines under a Carnegie Foundation grant, a questionnaire
returned by 1,349 forum-goers showed that 64 per cent had some college
education, whereas only 5 per cent had less than an eighth-grade education.[5] The majority were from the professional, semiprofessional, and
skilled-labor occupations. Very few were unskilled. At four Federal
forum centers, nearly 20 per cent of those attending were grammar-school
people, and about 40 per cent had a college education.[6] Over one-half
of those attending forums in Springfield, Massachusetts, had more than
a high-school education.[7] Old people, single persons, women, the white-
collar occupations, and upper socioeconomic levels were more often represented in forum audiences than were young people, men, married persons, manual laborers, and the lower socioeconomic groups. The main
reasons given for nonattendance were lack of interest, lack of time, lack
of awareness of the forums, and inconvenience. Such experiences are
common.

Forums appeal to only a small proportion of the total population. In
the nineteen Federal forum areas the cumulative attendance in forums
which ran from 5 to 15 months was usually less than 40 per cent of the
total adult population. As most participants attended forums monthly
or more often, it is estimated that only 5 per cent of the adults in the
Federal demonstration communities attended a forum during a typical
month. Even in Des Moines, forums at their peak seldom drew more
than 10 per cent of the adult population of the city during any one month.
After 7 years of free public forums in Springfield, Massachusetts, only
10 per cent of a large sample of adults from fourteen selected areas of
the city reported attendance during the preceding year, when twelve
meetings were held.[8] A combination of excellent direction, top talent,
and good publicity is required to induce more than a small number of
adults to attend forums. This is true even when they are decentralized
into neighborhoods.

Forum discussion is indigenous to this country. New England town
meetings were, and still are, local forums for discussion and formulation
of public policy. The Lyceum movement and the traveling Chautauquas
of the past century used the forum approach with large audiences. Much
of the structure for public discussion of this type disintegrated during
World War I, however, and not until the 1930s did it re-form as the
public-forum movement. The Des Moines public-school forum experi-

---

[5] *Choosing Our Way: A Study of America's Forums,* U.S. Office of Education
Bulletin 1937, Miscellaneous, no. 1, p. 110.

[6] *Ibid.,* p. 70.

[7] A. A. Kaplan, *Socio-economic Circumstances and Adult Participation in Certain
Cultural and Educational Activities,* Bureau of Publications, Teachers College,
Columbia University, New York, 1943, pp. 36–93.

[8] *Ibid.,* p. 36.

ment excited imagination which led to the Federal forum demonstrations in 1936–1937.

A few public schools have conducted adult forums for decades, but most of them, while open to the public, are not sponsored by public educational institutions. A survey finished in 1937 developed a list of nearly 1,500 forums, 431 of which were studied.[9] Sponsorship of these was distributed as follows:

Sponsor	No. of forums sponsored
Religious organizations, including churches and religious societies	119
Civic or educational organizations, such as service clubs, parent-teachers associations, veterans groups, adult-education councils, the League of Women Voters, and branches of the Foreign Policy Association	109
Citizens committees	75
Public schools	53
Universities and colleges	28
Individual directors and private sponsors	22
Public libraries	7
Political parties and associations	7
Miscellaneous	12
Total	431

Two-thirds of the forums studied in 1937 had not been started before 1929, and the majority of these had been in existence only since 1933. The forum is the most common approach to public-affairs education in public schools; 331 school districts reported forums for adults in 1948.[10] This appears to be a substantial gain in 11 years, but the data are not wholly comparable. An unknown number in the 1948 study may have dealt with subjects other than public affairs. Even so, only one of every eight schools with an adult-education program in 1948 operated a forum of any kind. A large part of the growth in public-school forums prior to World War II, no doubt, was due to the leadership of the U.S. Office of Education and its forum-demonstration program.

Public-school forums are usually organized with a director, who may be the director of adult education, an evening-school principal, or other administrator who can give full or part time to the task. He identifies issues of interest, arranges the schedule, engages and orients forum leaders or resource persons, devises ways of obtaining maximum participation, and promotes attendance. He usually serves as chairman of forum meetings although occasionally the superintendent of schools or some other person performs this function. General forum policy is usu-

[9] *Choosing Our Way: A Study of America's Forums*, pp. 17–19.
[10] Kempfer, *op. cit.*, Table 2, pp. 6–7.

ally approved by the board of education. Policies may be formulated and much of the detailed planning done, however, by a representative advisory committee.

Free forums are usually financed by the local board of education, state aid, foundation grants, or contributions from business and community organizations. In Springfield, Massachusetts, membership dues from a large adult-education council underwrite a forum free to the public. In many other communities enough individual and family season tickets are sold to support the forum. Even small communities sometimes sell enough low-priced tickets to raise a budget which will bring in top talent. Support by fees not only limits attendance but depends upon headline speakers. A system of free forums is less dependent upon big names; other competent leaders, including good local talent, can be used.

Most school-sponsored forums are community-wide except in large cities. In addition to large central meetings, the Des Moines and Federal forums developed sectional meetings with medium-sized audiences and neighborhood meetings attracting 25 to 50 or 100 people. Elementary schools usually provide the neighborhood centers, while sectional forums are held in junior- or senior-high-school auditoriums. While central forums often use a big-name leader for only one meeting, leaders for sectional or neighborhood forums can be engaged for an itinerary of a week or longer. This procedure usually reduces the cost materially. Under such circumstances a leader may be scheduled to return repeatedly to the same neighborhood and thus be able to develop more continuity of group thinking than is possible with separate leaders. Rural and small-village areas can make economical use of itinerant leaders serving on a master schedule. While most forums are held in the evening, additional people can be reached if breakfast, luncheon, afternoon, and dinner forums are scheduled. Leaders may appear before junior forums in high schools or before young-adult groups, women's clubs, service clubs, community radio forums, and forums conducted by voluntary organizations.

Effective directors often relate a number of other educational activities to forums. The following are illustrative:

1. Librarians, if informed early, will often compile special reading lists and arrange exhibits at the library and provide book displays for the rear of the forum hall. Books and pamphlets may be examined, sold, or checked out, and reading lists distributed at forum time.

2. The library can take the leadership in promotion of reading-circle work, especially in rural areas.

3. Larger forums often issue publications which announce forthcoming meetings, review pertinent books, list related reading, and provide study-guide questions for follow-up groups.

4. Many volunteer organizations can be induced to discuss forum

topics both in advance and after the meeting. Numerous study clubs, too, are willing to read and discuss forum issues.

5. Institutes of 1 to 3 days or weekend conferences can be arranged for those desiring to study a problem more intensively.

6. Visiting leaders may meet at dinner for informal discussion with ten to twenty community leaders before the evening meeting.

7. If the speaker is suitable for a high-school assembly, his appearance before the youth may increase attendance at the evening meeting.

8. Informal groups may hold a preforum discussion a week early; the same groups may discuss the issues in one or two subsequent meetings. Voluntary reading and discussion in advance of the forum raise participation to a significantly higher level. In a few communities most of the regular forum audience meet a week early in small groups and again meet to discuss the topic a week after the main forum. If groups are well organized and led, this procedure can result in weekly meetings centered around a large forum that is scheduled every third or fourth week. A variation is to alternate biweekly forums with informal discussions.

9. Informal groups can meet at dinner or an hour before the main meeting to think about the problem and develop questions.

10. The main forum meetings can be broadcast as a local "town hall of the air."

11. Disk, tape, or wire recordings of the main presentation can be made for use in neighborhood forums, voluntary organizations, and study groups.

12. Tie-ins with newspaper editorial columns, letters to the editor, roving reporters, opinion polls, and features can be arranged.

Aside from lectures and forums, numerous other large assemblies, such as conferences, conventions, luncheons and dinners, public hearings, and political conclaves, provide educational opportunity. For most people listening to a lecture or forum is a relatively passive activity, which violates the principle that active participation with a purpose is the key to learning. Several techniques can be used to induce most, and sometimes all, members of a large meeting to participate:

1. The Phillips 66 technique is a very flexible method which can be used to involve everyone in formulating agenda, main problems, questions, points of view, plans, and in testing decisions.[11] By this technique the entire audience is quickly divided into groups of six people, each of which simultaneously spends 6 minutes discussing an assigned matter in a way announced by the chairman. Within limits the number of participants and the length of time are flexible. Each small group selects a spokesman to report its consolidated thinking to the whole meeting.

[11] J. Donald Phillips, "Report on Discussion 66," *Adult Education Journal*, 7:181–182, October, 1948.

2. The audience can be divided into listening teams, each to judge a presentation critically in the light of assigned purposes. Through Phillips 66 groups or through buzz sessions within each team, group conclusions and opinions can be developed and reported by spokesmen.

3. Role-playing scenes can be introduced with the audience divided into sections, each asked to observe particular aspects critically or to identify with specific characters. Either in discussion groups or in buzz sessions, members can agree upon the important observations.

4. After a problem and supplemental facts are presented by a leader, by film, television, or radio, groups of ten to fifteen can retire to assigned rooms, discuss the problem, and attempt to reach a solution. In doing so, considerable group and personal commitment is likely to develop. As proposed solutions are reported to the whole meeting, feelings of commitment may be reinforced.

5. Brief written answers to specific questions from the total membership can encourage commitment, test consensus, and give opportunity to make suggestions for improvement of future meetings.

6. The audience, through buzz sessions or other techniques, can propose questions to be answered by the resource people. This gives the audience control of the content and encourages participation.

7. Panels of spokesmen can be drawn from different audience groups to question speakers, react to questions raised by other groups, or present the thinking of their groups.

8. All who wish to speak can be invited to public hearings on specific issues.

Often these and similar techniques can be used in combination and sequence as the purposes of the meeting require.

Discussion Programs

Small groups permitting extensive participation of members appeal to significant numbers of adults. In the 1948 survey, 308 schools (11.5 per cent) claimed to have civic-education discussion groups; the variety of groups in this category is almost infinite. In addition to classes for college or high-school credit, a number of schools operate non-credit classes entitled, for example, Current Events, World Background, World Affairs, Behind the Headlines, Our Government, City Government, or Taxation—the possibilities go on ad infinitum. These may be quite informal discussions with the content determined by the group or the leader, or they may follow a study guide. Often they meet weekly and use a news magazine or a daily newspaper for common background. A series of pamphlets may form the reading core, with magazines, books, and radio or television programs used as supplemental information. Government officials, reporters, and other experts may be brought in as resource people.

Schools may provide various types of discussion leadership. Social-studies teachers may meet with groups all over the community, or the school may train volunteer discussion leaders who go back to work in their groups. Several schools have organized staffs for the improvement of the quality of lay discussion leadership through training, provision of suggested study and discussion guides, consultative services, and stimulation of more community discussion.

Radio and television programs on controversial issues are sometimes used to provide a common base for discussion. In the 1948 study only thirty-eight schools claimed to have radio-listening discussion groups. In these groups the first part of the period is spent in listening to a major round table or other regular broadcast in some home, club, or other convenient place. The latter portion is spent in discussing the content and issues, either with or without a study guide previously sent out by a central organization. The Canadian Farm Forum has an effective system of collecting the opinions developed in an extensive network of discussion groups and broadcasting a summary of them the following week. Attempts at building a network of listener groups in this country have largely been abandoned.

The Farm Bureau in Ohio and other states has developed hundreds of discussion groups. Some groups are advisory committees. The League of Women Voters and a number of other organizations promote systematic discussion as a means of public-affairs education. In a recent campaign the Republican party stimulated a network of Republican forums. As discussion groups under voluntary auspices are widespread, schools may extend their services greatly by serving them as suggested in Chapter 8.

The effectiveness of the discussion-group approach varies widely. It is strong in building enlightenment through sharing of information and attitudes. As groups move from one topic to another, they build sensitivity and increase concern about public problems among their own members. Their success in spreading this sensitivity to other segments of the population depends chiefly on their ability to bring in new members. When well organized and promoted on a neighborhood basis, they may involve many new people, including some who take little part in other discussions. If the sponsoring framework permits action, thereby resulting in adequate psychological satisfactions, discussion groups may gain a virility and importance often lacking in those satisfied with academic approaches.

Discussion, of course, is a basic method in adult education. Face-to-face discussion is the quickest way for minds to meet and attack their common problems. Most of the steps in problem solving depend heavily upon discussion. The public-affairs educator cannot stress too strongly the building of certain skills in everyone—namely, those needed for defining the nature of public problems, for gathering pertinent data through pooling information in discussion and otherwise, for analyzing information, for deciding democratically, for acting in harmony, and for evaluating the results. Teaching the skills of group leadership is without doubt a major task for the public-affairs educator.

Community Surveys and Action Programs

Surveys based on a sample or a complete census have long been used in gathering sociological data. In recent years, however, neighborhood and community surveys using the personal interview have become recognized as an important educational approach. While the process of involving adults in the acquisition and analysis of firsthand data is useful in many fields, it is especially effective in public-affairs education.

A primary virtue of the survey as an educational approach is that for many kinds of problems it can involve a number of people in assembling the most realistic and accurate data upon which decisions can be made. Newspaper reporters, commentators, political-party leaders, elected officials, and community leaders of all sorts often claim to know the trend of public opinion concerning housing conditions, discrimination, economic trends, unemployment, health, and other matters of public concern. Except where systematic data are gathered recurringly, however, such opinions are often unreliable. For this reason, surveys which gather facts contribute more to sound education than do discussions of the "pooled ignorance" type. Those who engage in the process of gathering the facts will benefit most from the experience.

Local surveys or inquiries are often the only way to get facts about communities and neighborhoods, inasmuch as data gathered by the census and other national, state, and city agencies (1) are often not reported for subareas and (2) usually consist of relatively standardized statistical information. More detailed and discriminating data may be needed. Illustrative of questions which may call for local surveys are these:

1. How many old people are in our community and what are their needs (in health service, education, occupational training, guidance services, companionship, financial support, etc.)?

2. Why do not more people of the different age levels vote? join civic organizations?

3. What do the people want from their schools?

4. What are the standards of behavior that parents expect of their children?

5. For what services, if any, are people willing to pay more taxes?

6. Does the public want adult education to be paid for through taxes or by fees from participants?

7. To what extent are racial segregation and discrimination practiced?

These are general questions likely to arise in any community meeting. They would need to be broken down and refined before they could be used in a survey.

Such a survey might operate in this way. A corps of interested citizens, desiring the answer to question 3, might first study their present school set-up: curriculum, outcomes, objectives, and general methods. Basing inquiry on this factual information, they could then set out to learn what the remainder of the community expected of the school. The survey itself might be a sampling or a complete census, a formal inquiry or a set of informal conversations, individual interviews or small-group discussions. The statistical reliability of the data gathered would depend upon many factors, such as representativeness of the persons included, objectivity, and comparability of methods used by the different surveyors.

The first assessment of public opinion about the kind of schools desired may reveal much hazy thinking, indifference, lack of information, and misinformation. Survey results can then provide the base line to educational activities designed to stimulate more community thinking on school matters. Interviewers could become discussion leaders, block leaders for individual work, or informed resource people, and help the community organize its thinking about the kind of results it desires from the school. At the same time, parent-teacher committees could work on curriculum and other aspects of the program. Pupils and nonparents could be included in other educational activities. Study and discussion could carry forward the educational process until it increased local interest, information, and action in regard to building a better school which most people would support with pride and understanding. A later evaluative survey could show the growth which took place, not only among the original interested corps of surveyors, but throughout the community.

This survey-education process has almost limitless application. Facts can be gathered as a basis for action toward improving conditions and solving public problems. If the level of public information on a matter is too low to permit sound policy making, the survey should lead into further educational activity until a stable and wise decision can be made. In this way a democracy, through the educational process, can build intelligence as it applies it to the solution of its practical problems. The Citizenship Education Project of Teachers College, Columbia University, the "Back of the Yards" movement in Chicago, the Committee for Kentucky, the Citizens Councils of New York State, the world-affairs program in Cleveland, episodes reported by "The People Act," the work of the Kansas Commission for UNESCO, activities of the University of Virginia Extension Division, and many more such experiences reinforce the fact that citizenship education becomes most effective if it combines knowledge with action. Adults can best grow in civic stature by working on practical projects which will make their communities better places in which to live. The community provides the laboratory, and educators can provide much of the supervision for the learning experience.

Opinion Polls

Nationwide public-opinion polls based on personal interviews started only a few years ago. Several states and a number of cities are already using a similar approach, often in connection with newspapers. Such surveys are in addition to the "roving-reporter" features of hundreds of papers, which have great human interest and readership but little scientific reliability.

Continuous public-opinion polls are a specialized type of survey which have tremendous implications for democracy. In a country where government is based upon public opinion, it is important to know what people think. Many nongovernmental public affairs likewise depend upon the opinions of people. Opinion polls based on a representative cross section can often reflect the feelings of the total adult population more truly than do many elections, pressure groups, and letters of an articulate minority.

Community public-opinion polls can have these educational values:

1. Results of opinion polls reported in newspapers and over the air build up information and stimulate interest in public affairs.

2. Polls illuminate issues in which action groups are interested. They stimulate action among both individuals and groups who are for or against proposals, thereby increasing the general interest in public affairs.

3. Through opinion surveys, congressmen, councilmen, legislators, school-board members, and other policy makers can keep in touch with public attitudes and thus better represent their constituencies. Polls educate the policy makers. In so far as they think the public is uninformed or misinformed, they can take steps to exercise an educational leadership.

4. Participation in polling operations is an excellent educational experience. Almost unanimously, interviewers report deepened insight into the thinking of people on public issues and into the reasons underlying attitudes. The dozens of volunteers necessary to take a poll of opinion at minimum cost will gain an invaluable understanding of the problem of involving people in civic participation.

Opinion polling involves eight steps:

1. Development of a representative cross section of the adult population of adequate size to keep within the desired margin of error. Decisions on size of sample, methods of sampling, location of sampling points, and related technical matters are tasks for an expert. However, the sample design developed may be used repeatedly with alternation of persons interviewed, until population shifts or other factors require a

new sample. A carefully constructed sample of 500 to 600 interviews in a community will ordinarily yield results as reliable as those obtained in national polls, if no analysis of subgroups is desired.

2. Preparation of a set of questions designed to stimulate a response from the maximum number of people. These questions need repeated field trial and revision until they are clear and neutral. The techniques are similar to those used in building and evaluating good objective test items.

3. Training of interviewers through instruction, demonstration, role-playing, and supervised field experience.

4. Assignment of interviewers to their respondents—an administrative task.

5. Personal interviewing in the field under supervision. Policy on call-backs and substitutions should be settled by experts in the light of sampling requirements, size of interview force, and time schedule.

6. Tabulation of results under supervision—and office task.

7. Analysis and interpretation of results.

8. Reporting of results to the public and to policy makers.

The whole operation should be supervised by a person competent in sampling design and experienced in polling procedures. A local director can acquire these skills by reading and course work in a university center devoted to social-science research work. As designing an adequate sample is the most difficult part, he may want to work this out with someone having the necessary competence.

Volunteers from organizations interested in public-affairs education make good interviewers and can return benefits to their organizations. As their pay is the education they receive, all stages of the polling operation should be explained to them. Volunteers benefit most from a preliminary tryout of questions and an analysis and interpretation of results. When eight to ten questions are used, a corps of thirty can cover a sample of 500 provided that each volunteer spends 4 or 5 hours interviewing. This assumes easily accessible respondents.

If a community poll is conducted monthly, certain questions may be repeated periodically to establish trends. Periodic polling also permits detection of points of ignorance in the population and assessment of the effects of specific educational programs. Opinion pollers, of course, must be strictly objective and honest in their methods and treatment of results. Polling is not a task for propagandists. Once the polling organization is established, it can collect data and opinions of value to such community organizations as the community chest, the council of social agencies, and governmental agencies.

Public-affairs Councils

If responsibility for civic education is shared by the whole community, a cooperative relationship involving the school and other organizations is most useful. Programs operate most efficiently and smoothly if four principles are accepted and understood:

1. A major problem in public-affairs education revolves around the role of the school in controversial issues. If the board of education and the administration establish the principle that the school should facilitate free, fair, and open study and discussion of controversial matters without advocating any preconceived solution, the problem is largely settled. No issue should be too hot to be discussed. This is the application of the principle of free and responsible speech in a democracy. From committee meetings to the U.S. Senate, full and open discussion is an accepted part of the process of policy making. Those opposing this principle can be suspected of being unsympathetic to democratic ideals. In the struggle to establish public education, partisan politics and special interests have been largely weeded out. The schools serve the whole community and not special segments of it. It is out of character for the public school to advocate any position on controversial public issues by aligning with any one interest group. An educational agency must permit individuals to examine all information fairly and objectively and to express an opinion on its meaning, but the school should not assume responsibility for the opinions expressed.[12]

2. Every community organization and agency interested in public affairs should have a part in the total community program of public-affairs education.

3. Organizations and agencies cannot do the job that needs to be done if they operate independently. The need is greater than can be served by existing programs. New patterns of community organization in the field of public-affairs education must be developed—patterns which will use the resources of existing organizations and involve more citizens.

4. The involvement of more citizens in effective education requires new and creative approaches. Conventional academic classroom approaches do not ensure intelligent civic behavior. Action programs are necessary. Involvement of adults in community study and action in real-life situations will build information, maintain interest, and lead to continued action—and eternal vigilance.

The planning of an effective and comprehensive program of citizenship education for adults requires some kind of cooperative machinery, such as may be provided by public-affairs councils, world-affairs coun-

---

[12] For a full discussion on handling controversial issues, see *Adult Leadership,* 21:1–31, November, 1953.

cils, U.N. associations, UNESCO commissions, or foreign-policy councils. Business and taxpayer organizations, church and affiliated organizations, the council of social agencies, current-events clubs, foreign-language societies, labor unions, the League of Women Voters, libraries, luncheon and service clubs, management and professional societies, men's and women's clubs, patriotic societies, planning boards, veterans' associations, and governmental agencies are usually included in such councils. Political parties are usually omitted.

As the community agency vested with responsibility for education, the school can call together representatives of community organizations to survey the need, make an inventory of their resources, seek agreement on objectives and principles of operation, and begin the planning of comprehensive public-affairs education services for the whole community. A number of meetings will be required to develop the mutual confidence, a common view, and a broad understanding of the situation. The operation of these councils will not be far different from that of a community council. After broad outlines of the total community program are laid out, an executive committee and other operating committees may carry some of the detailed load.

A public-affairs council representing the combined civic educational forces in the community can give adequate sponsorship to such activities as block discussions, a block-leader plan, the community opinion poll, other community surveys, the system of public forums, a discussion-leadership training program, and an extensive discussion program throughout the community. Many of its services, of course, will be of benefit to voluntary agencies desiring help. Such a council can make a continuous evaluation of the effects of programs and can conduct research helpful to all organizations. It can keep an alert eye on the horizon to anticipate problems far enough in advance to permit adequate preparation of materials and leadership. It can facilitate the expression and flow of public opinion from the people to public officials. It can establish committees or divisions to give special attention to the foreign-born, college and university students, economic development, local government, intercultural relations, international affairs, state affairs, women's interests, and young adults. Staff and office services for these many activities can well be supplied by many agencies; the program that evolves must be a community program. Directors of adult education in local schools and community colleges often play important roles in forming and servicing public-affairs councils.

Through a public-affairs council the community can experiment with ways of interesting large numbers of citizens. Member agencies can facilitate the flow of information to citizens. They, in turn, through their voluntary organizations and official channels, can build the kind of community they want.

EDUCATION FOR THE FOREIGN-BORN

Until two generations ago little educational assistance was given to immigrants who settled in the United States. Most immigrants prior to 1890 came from the countries of Northern and Western Europe which had educational systems and cultural heritages similar to those of early America. Such differences as existed caused little concern in a country with a rapidly expanding frontier.

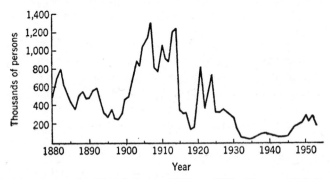

Fig. 7. Immigration to the United States, 1880 to 1953. (Source: U.S. Immigration and Naturalization Service, *Annual Reports*.)

About two generations ago sources of immigration shifted to Eastern and Southern Europe. Educational opportunities in these areas were extremely limited; a high proportion of the newcomers could not read or write. So many illiterates came that Congress, in 1917, established a literacy requirement. The flow of immigration was highest after the turn of the century, continuing to increase until it was checked following the first World War.

World War I, the literacy requirement, the quota laws of 1921 and 1924, the economic difficulties of the 1930s, and World War II have reduced immigration severely (see Figure 7). The problem of immigrant education may never be as large as it was a generation ago. However, barring changes in law, economic disaster, and general war, the influx of aliens probably will continue at the rate of 150,000 to 200,000 annually. The present quota alone authorizes the entrance of approximately 154,000 immigrants yearly. The education of our foreign-born is a reasonably specific adult-education task which is likely to be with us for some time.

The Melting Pot versus Cultural Pluralism

As the geographic frontier closed, the newcomers settled in industrial centers. Some large cities began early to provide English and citizenship instruction for foreign-born adults. Not until World War I, however, did the public generally become aroused—in fact, alarmed—about the great numbers of unassimilated immigrants. Americanization programs, designed to teach American ways, spread to many smaller communities and to all states having significant numbers of foreign-born. In fact, the bureaus of adult education in several state education departments and the adult divisions of many school systems have their origins in the Americanization work which developed during the decade centered around World War I. Americanization programs became so large that they often overshadowed other adult-education activities. In the minds of many adult education became synonymous with Americanization, and even today some people think of adult education primarily as the education of immigrants.

While there were many exceptions among the leaders in the Americanization movement, public attitude regarding the assimilation of the foreign-born in general was that presented in a play by Israel Zangwill, *The Melting Pot,* which appeared first in 1908.[13] This philosophy held that America was "God's Crucible . . . where all the races of Europe were melting and reforming." In essence, it held that everything American is good and that all immigrants should seek as rapidly as possible to abandon their native language and culture and adopt American ways. In extreme form it asked the melting down of cultural differences and ignored the values in other heritages. Cultural change was to be a one-way process achieved as rapidly as possible.

The melting-pot theory made popular drama, but it is based on weak psychological and sociological assumptions. Cultural assimilation is essentially a slow process. It usually cannot be achieved quickly by superficial, or even intensive, programs of Americanization. Native languages, mores, folkways, customs, political concepts, and modes of behavior cannot be abandoned and forgotten quickly. Even under favorable circumstances, generations are usually required to erase just the more obvious cultural characteristics. This is especially true where the foreign-born live in ghettos in large cities. The dangers of developing psychological insecurity by attempting to make fundamental changes within one generation are considerable. One culture cannot be absorbed quickly into another, even when willingness is mutual.

While the melting-pot theory has been largely discredited by sociologists, cultural anthropologists, and psychologists, it still retains considerable influence. Gradually, however, the newer concept of cultural pluralism has developed, although it is far from being universally accepted. Cultural pluralism recognizes cultural diversity and capitalizes upon it. It seeks acceptance of the essential political conditions under which different groups can live together in peace. Beyond that, it does not press for cultural uniformity. It does not assume that all that is American is perfect and that everything foreign is inferior. It encourages the

---

[13] Israel Zangwill, *The Melting Pot,* The Macmillan Company, New York, 1923.

retention of elements of foreign culture that do not handicap participation in or conflict with our own. Immigrants are encouraged to retain and feel secure in their own language, cultural values, and other national characteristics as long as they wish.

Cultural pluralism denies that there is one American culture which was fixed in detail by our forefathers. It realizes that our culture is dynamic, that it has a mosaic pattern, and that all cultural groups can contribute, and have contributed, to its richness. Actually, one has only to review the latest casualty list, local honor roll, or ball-team roster or to think of his favorite dishes, dances, and music to see the varied national backgrounds represented. Cultural pluralism is cultural democracy; it assumes that the foreign and the native culture will be mutually enriched by their contact with one another. By placing value on the contribution which the foreign-born can make, cultural pluralism helps maintain the psychological security and personality integration which are so important in preventing severe first- and second-generation problems. Where the different ethnic and cultural groups have common political ideals and aspirations and social equality, cultural pluralism has proved itself workable in many parts of the world. This experience has affected the way in which a program of immigrant education is conducted. At its best, immigrant education under cultural pluralism becomes a phase of intercultural education.

Identification of Educational Needs

While immigrants to our shores have always sought freedom and opportunity, the nature of immigration shifts rapidly enough to require continuous study of particular educational needs. Within two decades regular immigration has been supplemented by waves of political refugees from Europe, by overseas brides, and by displaced persons. Each group has somewhat different characteristics. In addition, there remains a sizable backlog of older aliens who still need help. Many of these came prior to World War I, and a number remain who entered before 1900.

Once the foreign-born have settled in a community, they are not always easy to find. Foreign language and accent are telltale marks, although some learn American English well enough to pass as natives. While noncitizens are required by law to keep the U.S. Department of Justice informed of their correct addresses, these data are not available to the general public. Some schools make initial acquaintance with many aliens, however, by publicly offering to help them fill out the form required in the annual registration.

Where names and addresses are not available, experienced directors and teachers of the foreign-born can locate immigrants in a variety of ways. Apartment-house managers, clergymen, policemen, school principals, settlement-house workers, and visiting nurses can often help them.

The aid of leaders of foreign neighborhoods, foreign-language societies, and the foreign-language press is also valuable. These leaders can often open channels of communication, disseminate information, and encourage cooperation, even if individual names are not produced. Likewise, such leaders are able to help clarify certain educational needs, although they may be unaware of others. School officials can sometimes obtain names and addresses of applicants for citizenship from the clerk of the naturalization court. As the candidate is likely to be called for examination only a few weeks after filing his petition, this period permits little more than an intensive review. Many local offices of the Immigration and Naturalization Service of the U.S. Department of Justice refer applicants for citizenship to the schools. This is especially true of petitioners who have failed the naturalization examination.

Locating incoming immigrants is easier. For some years the Immigration and Naturalization Service has cooperated with local and state school authorities by supplying names and addresses of new arrivals destined for specific communities. This gives the educator an opportunity to establish acquaintance with newcomers within a month or two after their arrival.

The problems of the foreign-born can best be identified through close personal acquaintance with them. Home visiting and interviewing at school or agency headquarters are favored, systematic methods. Association with the foreign-born in their own informal groups likewise helps the educator gain insight into their problems. Whether used by teachers, social workers, or sincere and neighborly volunteers, these approaches permit early identification of adjustment problems faced by the newcomer. The home visitor or staff member, if well acquainted with community resources, can help the newcomer establish connections with church, social organizations, congenial neighborhood groups, and the adult school. Personal visits pave the way for long educational association and effective integration.[14] If direct contact cannot be established with all newcomers, valuable assistance in identification of need is often available from organizations and agencies having firsthand acquaintance with newly arrived foreign-born.

Orientation

An early need of most immigrants is general orientation into American life. Prior understanding of America often is based on the Hollywood version, tales from immigrants returning to their native lands, observations of American tourists, and other one-sided pictures. Need for a truer understanding may vary, but usually it calls for specific and immediate experience with such matters as our monetary system, banking and postal

[14] See Homer Kempfer, "New Approach to Americanization," *American School Board Journal*, 112:17–18, June, 1946.

services, public utilities, shopping practices, employee-employer relations, traffic regulations, transit facilities, social customs, the social roles of men and women, community and governmental services, and American family and household routines. Some newcomers have relatives who may help with these matters. Voluntary agencies can also aid greatly in orientation. Schools which take small groups of newcomers on educational trips, arrange for cooperative dinner parties in homes, show films of typical Americana, and plan visits to meetings of community organizations find that a high proportion of them continue to depend upon the school for other educational assistance in later years. One director who took groups of war brides on weekly tours of city departments and points of community interest found most of them in adult classes that fall.

Many problems of the foreign-born may not be educational, and these may properly be referred to social agencies, recreation departments, churches, and immigrant-aid organizations. Where such agencies do not exist, however, many of the orienting experiences can be undertaken by volunteers under the instruction and supervision of the school.

More intensive orientation can be given by classes, film forums, and discussion groups in child care, family living, American customs, laws for newcomers, American music and recreation, intercultural understanding, and consumer buying. Where newcomers are numerous enough, activities may be slanted directly to them. Otherwise, the foreign-born may be induced into regular adult activities along these lines. The secret of good orientation is to find out what the newcomers want and what they need to know and then to help them learn through concrete experiences.

Occasionally a community has opportunity to provide orientation experiences for temporary residents from other countries. Laborers from Mexico under special agreement during World War II were an example. Many communities ignored them and assumed no responsibility for their education. A few schools, however, made an effort to orient them to American customs, taught them simple English, and provided suitable recreation. One can imagine the improvement in international understanding if tens of thousands of temporary visitors could return to their homeland able to interpret properly the wholesome friendliness, helpfulness, and hospitality experienced among Americans. The reduction of fear and mutual distrust alone is probably worth the cost of such orientation programs. In the Southwestern states a sizable number of Mexican laborers, often illegal entrants, return home seasonally.[15] Currently tens of thousands of Puerto Ricans, although citizens, return home annually after a few months of seasonal labor in the States. Their ties to the rest

[15] See *Migratory Labor in American Agriculture*, Report of the President's Commission on Migratory Labor, 1951.

of the country could be strengthened materially by planned educational programs.

In so far as social agencies have, or can assume, a responsibility for orienting the foreign-born and serving their other needs, the adult-education programs have a responsibility for training volunteer personnel. Social agencies should be able to depend upon the primary adult-education agencies of the community to train their volunteer teachers, home visitors, and other nonprofessional service workers. This type of service requires a much closer integration of schools and other social agencies than has often existed in the past.

Orientation, while an early need, should continue for some months, if not years. A diversity of experiences is desirable to prevent the early formation of stereotyped concepts of American life. Well-selected films showing a variety of types of home life, community activities, agricultural and industrial scenes, sections of the country, and customs of people are quite useful.

English

As almost all present-day immigrants want to become integrated into American life, English instruction is a prime need among most of them. The well-educated European is likely to have learned British English rather than American English. Conversational English is usually the greatest need, although silent reading and letter writing also rank high.

The foreign-born are usually assigned to instructional groups according to their ability to use English. Determination of the appropriate group is not easy as the diverse skills of understanding, speaking, reading, and writing must be assessed. Grouping can be done according to the predominant purpose. Grouping within a class or regrouping for different classes is possible for instruction in the different skills, although personal attachment to one instructor usually makes frequent transfer inadvisable.

Assignment to groups may be based on informal judgment or on home-made or standardized tests.[16] No one test seems to fit a wide range of conditions.

A working knowledge of English in practical situations is the first objective of instruction. The direct method of teaching is most useful for

---

[16] Among such tests are those of the English Language Institute of the University of Michigan; the Inter-American Tests by H. T. Manuel, available through the Cooperative Test Division, Educational Testing Service; and the Villareal Test of Aural Comprehension for native speakers of Spanish. See also R. Lado, "Survey of Tests in English as a Foreign Language," *Language Learning*, vol. III, nos. 1–2, 1950; and R. Lado, "A Practical English Language Test for Foreign Students," *News Bulletin of the Institute of International Education*, April, 1951. Registration cards give information important in grouping. Three class levels are common: beginners, intermediate, and advanced. Large numbers may permit division into low and high subsections within each level. Well-educated foreign-born persons acquainted with formal language structure may constitute a special group.

both beginning and advanced classes. In addition to being psychologically less sound, the translation method of teaching is impossible in the usual class, which may contain persons from a dozen countries. Instructors should be well versed in methods of language teaching. Beyond the lowest beginning levels, diversified content is highly desirable in so far as easy-to-read materials can be found.

Three or more class sessions per week are necessary to yield maximum results. Frequent repetition, review, spaced practice, and similar principles from the psychology of language learning can be put into effective use. Formal instruction should be supplemented with ample opportunity to hear and practice English in informal groups. If the newcomer is not normally in an English-speaking environment during several hours each day, special arrangements should be made, if possible, to give him additional practice in English conversation.

Immigrants of advanced years and long residence in this country present a different and difficult problem. If they have had little prior experience with English, facility will come slowly. Many of them believe that they are too old to learn. With a few hours of instruction per week they may make only limited headway if they continue to live in a foreign-language environment. They must have a strong desire to learn English and voluntarily join English-speaking groups for practice several hours per week if they are to make satisfactory progress. As the naturalization examination relieves many older immigrants from English requirements, pressures to learn English may be less than they were formerly. However, a desire to qualify for better employment, a need to communicate with family members, and other conditions may give the necessary motivation to many.

Naturalization and Citizenship

Recent immigrants admitted for permanent residence almost unanimously desire naturalization. They ordinarily can qualify for citizenship after 5 years of residence, or in less time if married to a citizen. Sometime during this period many of them can be induced to make educational preparation for the naturalization examination.

Petitioners for citizenship must be able to demonstrate an understanding of English, including an ability to read, write, and speak words in ordinary usage, and to answer moderately simple questions on the history of the United States and on the principles and form of our government. The examination on history and government includes the principal historical facts concerning the development of the United States as a republic; the organization of local, state, and federal government; the Constitution of the United States; the relationship of the individual to government; and the rights, privileges, duties, and responsibilities of citizens.

Public schools can obtain free textbooks covering these requirements from the Immigration and Naturalization Service of the U.S. Department of Justice. Correspondence-instruction materials written at three levels of difficulty are likewise available. The Federal government does not supervise or service the home-study arrangements, although a number of university extension divisions, state education departments, and adult divisions of city school systems do so, either without cost or for a small fee.

The Immigration and Naturalization Service is responsible for examining petitioners—whether or not they have attended school. If the naturalization court concerned approves, the Service may accept a school certificate as evidence of meeting the educational requirements. This approval does not waive the right of the Service or of the court to examine further, but usually it means that only a cursory examination, if any, is given. Because of the advantages its certificate holders will have, a school should seek approval of its course of study and standards.[17] A school offering an approved certificate gives the alien an added reason to attend. The certificate need not show ratings or marks. It should cover both language requirements and knowledge of history and government, but it should not vouch for loyalty or attachment to the Constitution. While good schools attempt to develop desirable attitudes in prospective citizens, examination for loyalty remains wholly a responsibility of the Service.

Courses preparing for the naturalization examination are organized in two major ways, and evidence does not clearly prove the superiority of either. Many schools have one course for the foreign-born in which English and citizenship are combined. This course usually runs through beginning, intermediate, and advanced terms or in a four- or five-step sequence. Most time is given to English, with enough citizenship content included to ensure passing the naturalization examination.

The other way is to have a special course in citizenship which includes the history and government necessary to pass the examination. This course assumes enough command of English to profit from class instruction. Aliens from English-speaking countries are often grouped together. Now that certain older aliens need not show competence in English, instruction in history and government can legally be given in a foreign language. It is doubtful, however, that any public agency will want to do this. Churches and social agencies serving primarily a single language group might well provide such instruction for certain older residents who still need to pass the examination in history and government.

The better-educated refugees, displaced persons, war brides, and other immigrants arriving in recent years with full intention of remaining here are more receptive to broad citizenship education than were many in

---

[17] Homer Kempfer, "Certification for Citizenship: Relationships between the Public Schools and Naturalization Officials," *Adult Education*, 2:74–77, December, 1951.

generations past. While many earlier immigrants became citizens, it was sometimes difficult to induce them to participate in broad public-affairs education activities, particularly after passing the naturalization examination. Usually only a small minority did so and then often because of personal loyalty to a teacher who urged them to do this.

There is a growing feeling that preparation for naturalization is only a small part of citizenship education for the foreign-born—only an intermediate step to further learning in which new citizens should engage. Broad instruction will not only go more deeply into the phases of government and history needed for naturalization but will include many additional aspects of everyday life in America. Some specific tasks which an adult school can undertake in this connection are:

1. Stress intercultural education to develop understanding and appreciation of contributions of various nationalities, religious faiths, and races to the American dream and reality. Teach the intercultural ideals toward which we are still striving.

2. Induct each succeeding group into an Americans-all club, a new-citizens club, or a naturalized-citizens association with monthly programs of civic-education content—forums, discussions, intercultural banquets, films, and educational tours. Such activities should, however, lead toward broader programs of participation.

3. Intensify the social atmosphere and convert each class into a club which can later meet on a biweekly or monthly basis with a less formal program of citizenship content.

4. Capitalize on holidays by utilizing the above groups in observing Citizenship Day and other major holidays.

5. Organize former students into a system of block leaders to locate newcomers and induce other foreign-born to participate in special activities.

6. Organize trips to historical spots, utilizing them both as incentives to study and as follow-up activities.

7. Introduce the foreign-born, while still under full instruction, into neighborhood and community groups having civic-education activities. Take them to forums, hearings, public meetings, and other activities of civic groups until they form the habit of participating.

8. Set up special post-naturalization classes leading to further citizenship competence. Where educational qualifications for voting are higher, or different from those for naturalization, aim at voting as a next step.

9. Make the foreign-born aware of a variety of other adult-education activities, some of which are related to citizenship. Help them acquire the habit of lifelong learning.

In all these activities, citizenship should be stressed as a process of continuous growth—not as a static achievement reached when the oath of citizenship is taken. In a broad sense, citizenship education for the foreign-born is a responsibility of the entire community and of the individual residents and organizations composing it. The total task is nothing less than the integration of the foreign and native cultures to their mutual enrichment. Ideally, special orientation and citizenship education for the foreign-born is no longer necessary when they are sufficiently competent and interested to participate in the community and civic-education activities of our normal population.

INTERCULTURAL EDUCATION

Intercultural relations is one aspect of the whole frontier of human relations. In the last decade we have become intensely aware of the need for broadening human sympathies and understanding among members of different nationality, language, social, religious and socioeconomic groups. As technical advances in transportation and communication bring about closer intermingling of people of different backgrounds, intergroup or intercultural education becomes necessary. Isolated homogeneous groups may feel superior without endangering social stability. When such groups intermingle, they must learn to get along with one another, or tensions and conflict will result. As our population becomes more diversified and the intermingling of its various segments increases, concepts of cultural democracy need to be expanded.

A wide range of evidence points to the need for intergroup understanding—the rise and defeat of Hitlerian fascism based on a theory of racial superiority; an occasional race riot; the throwing off of colonial yokes by the colored races; the intensified struggle of Negroes for civil rights; discrimination in this country against the Spanish-speaking, Orientals, Jews, and foreign-born; removal of FAO headquarters from Washington to Rome by a close vote, largely because of the discrimination experienced by representatives of colored nations; Ku Klux Klan activities; tensions and violence in South Africa. These and many other developments illustrate the issue that is being fought out all over the world. State Department officials with international conference experience report that our treatment of minority groups is a negative influence several time more potent than most Americans think. Many of the ideals of our Declaration of Independence, our Constitution, and our democracy still need to be achieved. The Universal Declaration of Human Rights invites changes among us as well as among other peoples. Any permanent peace must be based upon adequate understanding among the different peoples of the world. Mere tolerance is not enough. Dynamic understanding, appreciation, and acceptance of the basic equality among all people are required. In the rising tide of people demanding equality, old relationships will not suffice. A major world-wide social revolution is under way—one which calls for new and basic learnings.

Intergroup relationships have several sides, three of which are the

interfaith, intercultural, and interracial aspects. Changes are usually required in attitudes and ideals, although new knowledge, skills, and habits
are also necessary.

Specifically, such learnings as these are desirable outcomes of intergroup education:

1. The recognition that the range in differences among individuals
within a group is likely to be much greater than that between groups.
The concept of the dignity of man is based on the psychological and
physical uniqueness of the individual.

2. The habit of judging, thinking about, and dealing with people as
individuals instead of as members of groups.

3. The recognition of the essential biological similarity among all people and their ability to develop culturally.

4. An understanding of the sense and nonsense about race; an abolition
of ideas of racial superiority.

5. The recognition that the culture in which people live is responsible
for much of their behavior. Concepts of God, patterns of family relationships, food and dress, music and art forms, and many more cultural
elements are the product of the nurturing culture.

6. An appreciation of the contributions of many religious, racial, and
nationality groups to American life and to the world.

Here in America intercultural education in behavior terms aims to
help people behave acceptably toward members of groups other than
their own, to ensure basic economic and civil rights to all, and to free
all citizens to participate fully in our common life.

Approaches

Many people believe that the best way to extend civil rights, reduce
discrimination in employment, eliminate bigotry, ensure religious freedom, and extend cultural democracy is through legislation and enforce-
ment of law. Others are convinced that education is the only way. Experience in the employment field supports the educational approach. Best
results are achieved when education and law work hand in hand. The
law can be the club behind the door, which—because it is there—seldom,
if ever, needs to be used. The New York State Commission against Discrimination began early to use education. It depends upon law enforce-
ment only as a last resort. In New Jersey the Division against Discrimination is located in the State Department of Education. Most other state
fair-employment agencies emphasize fact finding and educational approaches.

Classes, lectures, and formal instruction can provide the necessary
background information from cultural anthropology, psychology, sociology, biology, comparative religion, economics, and other disciplines.
Since, however, only people with special interests in such matters or

those who possess unusual intellectual curiosity will seek such knowledge of their own accord, such methods have limited usefulness.

Informational programs using mass media may stir up concern with intergroup problems but often do little to change behavior. Knowledge, of course, should be provided to as many people as possible through both group instruction and mass media. Even though there is definitely a relationship between knowledge and behavior toward members of outgroups, one cannot depend heavily upon changing attitudes and behavior merely by presenting facts.

An approach through the intercultural workshop is popular, although its value may be limited.[18] Such workshops most often appeal to teachers and others seeking credit. Shared experiences in group living, plus a common concern with both content and professional skills, enhance the value of workshops.

The best intercultural relations seem to develop where members of different groups work together on common projects. Under the stress of achieving a common goal, differences are forgotten and every person can be judged by the contribution he makes. Friendships, mutual respect, and desirable attitudes grow as a by-product of association on common undertakings of value to all participants.

There is no doubt that this key approach produces good results at both the neighborhood and the international level. The chief difficulty is in getting different groups to begin working together. If there is much mutual antagonism, two or more groups are likely to cooperate only under emergency conditions demanding combined efforts for survival. Although these conditions are usually not planned, a wise community leader or director of adult education can identify many opportunities for Negroes and whites, Mexicans and native whites, foreign-born and natives, Protestants, Catholics, and Jews, and different socioeconomic groups to cooperate on block, neighborhood, or community-wide projects of importance to all concerned. Projects aimed at better housing, political action, economic betterment, civil defense, safety, or a dozen other types of community improvement can often use the combined energies of all interested people. With this approach, improved intergroup understanding is never the primary purpose of the cooperative activity, but it is always a concomitant.

A social invention which facilitates the association of members of different groups is the neighborhood-home festival developed by Rachel Davis DuBois.[19] This approach, which has many possible variations, is based on the idea that problems of prejudice will be solved in thousands of small, emotionally satisfying face-to-face meetings of mixed groups of

[18] D. J. Levinson and R. A. Schermerhorn, "Emotional-attitudinal Effects of an Intergroup Relations Workshop on its Members," *Journal of Psychology*, 31:243–256, April, 1951.

[19] Rachel Davis DuBois, *Neighbors in Action*, Harper & Brothers, New York, 1950.

neighbors. Starting some particular holiday season, neighbors of different cultural backgrounds can discuss with each other the significance of the season in their respective homelands. This beginning can be expanded to include singing, home-art festivals, dinners, folk dancing, pictures, and other sharing of folk culture. Psychologically, the approach is sound in that all cultural heritages are given the limelight, all egos are enhanced, and the experiences are emotionally satisfying to all. In a few places city-wide fiestas and festivals with pageantry, dramatics, music, fairs, exhibits, and mass-participation events climax a year of increasing activity.

Both labor unions and employers sometimes hesitate to establish policies more favorable to minority groups, but considerable experience shows that minority-group members can be integrated into the labor force without trouble if this is done properly. Although preliminary inquiry among other employees might yield a vote of rejection, actual, matter-of-course hiring or promoting of minority-group members tends to remove the matter from the verbal and controversial level. After a newcomer works alongside other workers for a while, he is usually accepted. Attitudes become neutral and, in time, positive. The approach is made easier if the first persons to be integrated are outstandingly competent and likable personalities.

Integration can be applied in nearly any group situation. If a community leader, organization officer, or director of adult education invites members of minority groups to serve on committee affairs, they will eventually be accepted as a matter of course.

Schools can help with integration by providing educational programs to those having a key action relationship to minority groups. For instance, labor leaders and personnel directors can learn how to integrate minority-group members into unions and plants and still maintain good feeling. Policemen can learn how to deal constructively with their minority-group problems. Bus drivers can learn how to handle routine conflicts. Housing and real-estate officials can be led to understand successful programs that do not discriminate. In these and other cases information can be drawn upon, not for its own sake, but as a guide to action and the solution of problems.

In recent years a number of interracial, interfaith, intercultural, race-relations, human-relations, and unity committees have been organized to help achieve greater cooperation and harmony among community groups. In several cities the mayors or city councils have established such committees. In other instances councils of social agencies or councils of churches have taken the lead. Sometimes such committees are self-appointed. School representatives often participate.

These committees may focus on civil rights, fair employment practices, reduction of tensions, and trouble shooting, although education and research often receive major attention. Their educational activities follow no standard pattern. They may make surveys of fact or opinion, conduct intercultural clinics, set up study groups, seek specific changes in employment practices and housing regulations, or promote the use of public facilities more favorable to minority groups. Often they disseminate information through printed materials and a speakers bureau, arrange all-nations festivals, conduct radio and television programs, and promote exhibits. Usually they work with and through existing community organizations.

The effectiveness of committees of this nature depends largely upon their use of the educational process. If they depend largely upon the brotherhood-week approach or use hortatory methods, they may disseminate information but may bring about little change in the community. A number of such committees, however, can point to significant changes in attitudes and overt behavior which are the results of their work. Certainly, where such committees are more than political window dressing, they have the opportunity of providing adult education at its best.

In the documentary or fact-finding method, which is similar to a community survey, participants search for truth through firsthand investigation of some phase of the intercultural situation. Personal interviews and personal experiences are primary methods; reading is secondary. The fact finders usually discuss and evaluate their experience and data before reporting to the community through drama, mass media, public hearings, or panels.

The best strategy in intercultural education is the whole-community approach. Intercultural relations cannot be treated as a subject to be taught on schedule. Intercultural education is essentially a concern with attitudes and actions which permeate the entire life of the community. If community leaders and educators are aware of the significance of extending our democratic ideals to all parts of the population, they will be able to integrate intercultural learning with many community processes. A multiple approach is necessary. Many agencies and community organizations, many methods, and many media must be used. If civilization is a function of numbers, there must be opportunity, planned if necessary, for people of many different backgrounds to meet, know, understand, and appreciate one another.

Watson [20] has identified seven patterns of action used by agencies working to improve community relations:

1. *Exhortation* to good will is a frequently used method that has some value but tends to be ineffective, evades conflicts, reaches chiefly the saved, and salves the conscience.

2. Long and thorough *education* of the informational type is effective,

[20] Goodwin Watson, *Action for Unity*, Harper & Brothers, New York, 1947.

especially if it reaches people who do not ordinarily hear lectures or read serious matter. Programs of emotional reeducation are particularly useful.

3. *Participation* programs in which people of different cultural backgrounds get acquainted, work on common projects, and live together as neighbors can integrate education and living.

4. *Revelation* of conditions through surveys and other fact-finding approaches has inherent dangers but often succeeds in disturbing complacency, thus creating a condition conducive to change of attitude.

5. *Negotiation* uses compromise and represents a balancing of forces which may or may not pave the way for new social advance.

6. *Contention* is a fighting way to change. Although it is unpleasant, fighting often results in equalizing opportunity in education, social services, commerce, the labor force, and housing, in removing segregation, and in overcoming political anti-Semitism.

7. Agencies employing *prevention* use measures for predicting areas of potential conflict, introduce prophylactic action, train public employees, encourage self-discipline, and remove sources of frustration. Prevention is a useful element in the strategy of improving community interrelations.

Evaluation

Much well-intentioned energy is spent in intercultural education without hardheaded appraisal of results. Admittedly evaluation is especially difficult in this field. Appraisal is a major challenge, particularly as new approaches and methods are developed. In so far as program evaluation is concerned with changes in attitude and behavior of the whole community, surveys and indexes of discrimination may reveal progress.

Changes in attitude among the clientele of a particular agency may be studied by some of the better attitude tests and social-distance scales. Any change, of course, can be shown only if such tests are administered early and again at a later time. As such verbal tests are always subject to bias caused by insincerity, direct observational techniques are preferred. Informal evaluation is always possible, but systematic observation of "incidents," behavior samples, and other expression of attitudes gives more valid evidence.

SELECTED REFERENCES

Public-affairs Education

Adam, Thomas R.: *Education for International Understanding*, Institute of Adult Education, Teachers College, Columbia University, New York, 1948.

Crabtree, A. P.: "Adults Keep Up with the Times," *NEA Journal*, 43:94–95, February, 1954.

Dagliesh, W. Harold: *Community Education in Foreign Affairs: A Report on Activities in Nineteen American Cities*, Council on Foreign Relations, New York, 1946.

Essert, P. L., and C. Verner: "Education for Active Adult Citizenship," *Teachers College Record,* 53:16–31, October, 1951.

Garland, J. V.: *Discussion Methods: Explained and Illustrated,* The H. W. Wilson Company, New York, 1951.

Hallenbeck, W. C.: "Participation in Public Affairs: A Diagnosis of the Problem," *Adult Education,* 2:8–17, October, 1951.

"Handling Controversial Issues," *Adult Leadership,* 2:9–28, November, 1953.

Heathers, G. L.: *Young People and World Citizenship,* Association Press, New York, 1950.

Herring, J. W.: "Adult Education: Senior Partner to Democracy," *Adult Education,* 3:2–10, November, 1952.

Horn, Francis H.: "International Understanding: The Lament of a Discouraged Adult Educator," *Adult Education Journal,* 9:109–118, July, 1950.

International Congress on Mental Health, *Mental Health and World Citizenship,* National Committee for Mental Health, New York, 1948.

Kempfer, Homer: "Public Affairs Education: The Community Approach," *American School Board Journal,* 111:21–23, November, 1945.

Ogle, M. B.: *Public Opinion and Political Dynamics,* Houghton Mifflin Company, Boston, 1950.

Parten, Mildred: *Surveys, Polls, and Samples,* Harper & Brothers, New York, 1950.

Sillars, R.: "Education for International Understanding," *Adult Education Journal,* 8:91–98, April, 1949.

Stensland, Per, and Carol Stensland: "Community Education for International Understanding," *Adult Education,* 2:17–23, October, 1951, and 2:89–97, February, 1952.

Strauss, Bert, and Frances Strauss: *New Ways to Better Meetings,* The Viking Press, Inc., New York, 1951.

Studebaker, John W., and Chester S. Williams: *Forum Planning Handbook,* U.S. Office of Education, Washington, 1939.

Education for the Foreign-born

Brown, M. G., and Jane M. Russell: *A Bibliography of Materials for the Teaching of English to Foreigners,* U.S. Office of Education Bulletin 1946, no. 20.

Committee on Refugee Education: *Teachers' Manual: Guide for Teaching English to the Foreign-born,* New York, 1949.

DuBois, Rachel D.: "Group Conversation Methods Used in English Classes for Newcomers," *Adult Education Bulletin,* 12:199–203, October, 1948.

Kempfer, Homer: "Civic Education among the Bozos," *Adult Education Bulletin,* 8:103–105, April, 1944.

———: *Eight Measures for Evaluating Educational Programs for the Foreign Born,* U.S. Office of Education Circular 357, 1952.

Kiser, C. V.: "Cultural Pluralism," *The Annals of the American Academy of Political and Social Science,* 262:117–130, March, 1949.

Maaske, Roben J.: "Stimulating Students to Study after Naturalization," *Adult Education Bulletin,* 12:167–169, August, 1948.

New Jersey Department of Education, Division of Adult Education: *Standards for Issuance of Citizenship Course Certificates,* Trenton, N.J., 1951.

"Reappraising Our Immigration Policy: Assimilation of the Foreign Born," *The Annals of the American Academy of Political and Social Science,* 262:117–165, March, 1949.

Roucek, J. S., et al.: *The Immigrant in Fiction and Biography,* Bureau for Intercultural Education, New York, 1945.

U.S. Senate Committee on the Judiciary: *The Immigration and Naturalization Systems of the United States,* 81st Cong., 2d Sess., S. Rept. 1515, 1950.

U.S. Department of Justice, Immigration and Naturalization Service: *Annual Report,* latest issue.

Whipple, Caroline A.: *Education for Citizenship,* New York State Education Department, Albany, N.Y., 1953.

Intercultural Education

Arndt, C. O., and S. Everett: *Education for a World Society: Promising Practices Today,* Harper & Brothers, New York, 1951.

Brickman, W. W.: "Education for Intergroup Relations," *School and Society,* 77:70–76, Jan. 31, 1953.

Clincy, E. R.: *Intergroup Relations Centers,* Farrar, Strauss & Young, Inc., New York, 1949.

Cook, L. A.: "Intergroup Education," *Review of Educational Research,* 17:266–278, October, 1947.

Jennings, H. H.: *Sociometry in Group Relations,* American Council on Education, Washington, 1948.

The Journal of Education Sociology, special issue on Labor Education in Intergroup Relations, February, 1952.

Kilpatrick, W. H., and W. Van Til (eds.): *Intercultural Attitudes in the Making,* Harper & Brothers, New York, 1947.

Lewin, Kurt: *Resolving Social Conflicts,* Harper & Brothers, New York, 1948.

Lippitt, R.: *Training in Community Relations,* Harper & Brothers, New York, 1949.

Redden, J. D., and F. A. Ryan: *Intercultural Education,* The Bruce Publishing Company, Milwaukee, 1951.

Snyder, H. E.: *When Peoples Speak to Peoples,* American Council on Education, Washington, 1953.

Taba, H.: "Workshop in Intergroup Education," *The Journal of Educational Sociology,* special issue, 18:513–572, May, 1946.

Van Til, William, and G. W. Denemark: "Intercultural Education," *Review of Educational Research,* 20:274–286, October, 1950.

Vickery, William E., and S. G. Cole: *Intercultural Education in American Schools,* Harper & Brothers, New York, 1943.

Watson, Goodwin: *Action for Unity,* Harper & Brothers, New York, 1947.

Williams, R. M., Jr.: *The Reduction of Intergroup Tensions,* Social Science Research Council, New York, 1947.

See also General References: [21] Beals and Brody, pp. 232–240; Division of Adult Education Service, chap. 4; Ely, pp. 46–59, 101–106, 126–132; Essert, chap. 9, and Kempfer.

[21] The General References are listed in full at the end of this book.

CHAPTER 7

Organized Approaches to Major Areas: Production and Consumption

EDUCATION FOR PRODUCTION AND SERVICE

Vocational education [1] is the most highly organized and widely developed phase of adult education in the United States today. The high regard that Americans hold for occupational competence stimulated vocational education early and has given it a consistently high place among the broad areas of study.

Until recent generations most systematic occupational training was on an apprenticeship basis. Well over a century ago, however, colleges and universities began developing specialized professional curricula. State universities in particular extended their curricula to include vocations other than the learned professions. Concurrently, polytechnic institutes developed to teach the application of science to economic enterprise. Paralleling the rise of the academy, the private trade school was established to give systematic occupational training of less than college grade. Private trade schools still provide an important part of vocational education in this country.

Vocational education in public schools began slowly, developing largely during the past two generations. Public-school educators long restricted their functions primarily to preparing youth for college and providing general education. As the need for skilled craftsmen multiplied, however, curricula were revised to make them more practical and less academic. Manual training and industrial arts were introduced and taught for decades as preparation for those who wished to enter the mechanical trades. Good though such training was, it eventually became recognized as a part of general education, largely because it taught skills which all people should have. Finally, after the turn of the century, public schools began introducing trade and industrial education on a vocational basis. Homemaking education and the public commercial high school devel-

[1] In this book *occupational training* refers to preparation for and improving competence in any occupation; *vocational education,* as commonly used, refers more to the federally aided programs in agriculture, homemaking, trades and industries, and distributive education.

171

oped at about the same time. The first successful agricultural high school started in Minnesota in 1888.[2]

The need for occupational training stems primarily from the great changes brought on by the industrial revolution. The subsequent economic development began to accelerate about a century ago. The increasingly complex social order discussed earlier is based on an evolving science and technology. A complex industrial society requires trained people to keep it functioning. This training is the task of occupational education.

Before our society became so complex, most nonapprentice occupational training was confined largely to the professions. The rise of technology called for skilled mechanics and craftsmen. As technology increases, many more occupations require special training. This fact, coupled with the necessary social and economic adjustment, has brought a demand that all workers be better trained. Whether in peace or in war, a constantly higher percentage of workers must be specialists. Thus, the schools face the task of training a great many workers for their occupations. More and more, public sentiment demands that occupational training be available to all as a right.

For most people personal development into adulthood requires the choice of an occupation, training for it, entrance into it, and progress to higher levels of efficiency. In spite of widespread vocational guidance and occupational training programs in secondary schools, for most people these steps are not made until early adult life. A fair percentage of youth make vocational choices while in school, but such early choices are relatively unstable. Great numbers leave high school and college without any occupational training. The rise in general educational level, child-labor laws, minimum wages, and the increased maturity required by more complex occupational processes have pushed upward the years of occupational training. For many this period is after high school—in the young-adult and adult years.

Occupational training is growing in importance throughout adult life. Inventions, technical advances, and other improvements often require retraining at intervals during the working years. Even in peacetime the birth and death rates among occupations are so great that a growing number of adults must leave old occupations and enter new ones. In changing from a peacetime to a wartime economy, or vice versa, tens of millions of adults may not only change employment but learn totally new occupations.

In line with the American dream, our people for generations have accepted the idea that man can make his world a better place in which to live if he will but develop his intelligence and apply it to his problems.

[2] Arthur B. Mays, *Principles and Practices of Vocational Education*, McGraw-Hill Book Company, Inc., New York, 1948, pp. 28–37.

This fits in perfectly with the concept of occupational training as intelligence applied to work. In the trades and industries vocational education results in better production. In fact, economists have estimated that the normal rate of improved productivity per man is currently as much as 3 per cent per year.

While vocational education began first in agricultural, homemaking, commercial, and trade and industrial fields, in recent years it has spread to the social services. Strong movements have arisen to provide adequate occupational training for nurses, religious workers, social workers, recreation directors, personnel managers, and workers in related fields promoting physical, mental, and moral development.

Adult Vocational Education in Public Schools

Public schools now widely recognize a responsibility for providing education which leads to gainful employment. They provide a great deal of organized occupational training both for young people and for adults and out-of-school youth. Schools still need to develop much more occupational training for adults. Although the principle of providing vocational education at public expense has become widely accepted, especially since Federal money has been made available for certain defined fields, schools conduct a large amount of occupational training aside from that stimulated by Federal funds.

A combination of forces led Congress, in 1917, to pass the Federal Vocational-Education Act. This, the Smith-Hughes Act, provides for Federal aid to states for vocational education of less than college grade in agriculture, homemaking, and trades and industry. Other acts supplementing and extending the original were replaced by the George-Barden Act of 1946, which added distributive education. Federal monies distributed under these acts may be spent for salaries and travel expenses of teachers, supervisors, directors, and teacher-trainers and, at times, for equipment and supplies. In addition, states and localities provide buildings and pay all other costs of supplementary training necessary to constitute a well-rounded education.

The U.S. Office of Education, while responsible for ensuring that plans conform to the provisions of the acts, has no responsibility for program operation. The Office cooperates closely with the staffs of state boards in identifying instructional needs of individuals and communities; in planning, organizing, supervising, and administering programs; in developing instructional materials and standards; in selecting and training professional personnel; in improving instructional and guidance procedures; and in evaluating vocational education.

The primary purpose of federally aided vocational education is to fit individuals for useful employment. This involves training in skills, work habits, understanding, attitudes, and appreciation. It calls for providing the knowledge and information needed by workers to enter upon and progress in productive employment. Such education must meet the needs of those employed in specific fields or preparing to enter them. Training opportunities are available only to persons fourteen years of age and older. Many who do not participate in vocational education during their years of full-time schooling, enroll for instruction as out-of-school youth or older adults. Instruction is open, of course, as long as the participant can benefit from it for vocational purposes.

Public-school vocational education for adults relies heavily upon a combination of group and individual approaches. The development of skill and the teaching of related technical knowledge require somewhat different methods. Explanation and demonstration with audio-visual aids in classroom, laboratory, shop, home, store, factory, or on the farm, with opportunity for imitation and repetition, develop skill—although only through practice under a wide range of typical conditions can one become a master craftsman. While the school cannot provide many operating conditions, it can extend experience through supervised practice, field work, and educational trips. Adults training in their own occupations often have convenient opportunity for broad experience. Related technical knowledge is taught through lecture, discussion, and personal explanation combined with visual and auditory aids.

The project method is a favorite in vocational education, partly because it maintains a high interest and provides an experience around which much learning of skill, knowledge, and attitude can be integrated. It combines theory with practice. Often it needs to be supplemented with exercises to develop skill and with extra lessons on related knowledge. With adults, the best procedures often are (1) to let the person face his most crucial problem demanding a solution, (2) to provide the necessary data or teach the necessary skills, and (3) to let him use his knowledge or skill in solving the problem. This, in short, is an application of the educational process outlined earlier. It uses a self-selected project. When the adult is in a setting in which he has a vital and personal interest, supervised practice has the best opportunity to induce learning.

Vocational curricula are best developed from occupational surveys and analyses which should be made on a continuing or a frequently recurring basis. Curricula preparing for or extending competence in one occupation are often broken down into a sequence of short units, completion of which marks definite progress. Rapid learning occurs when instruction is closely related to work on the job. For this reason cooperative part-time training programs, apprenticeship arrangements, on-the-farm training, training within industry, and similar programs provide the best possible approaches in vocational education. Craft committees, apprenticeship committees, area committees, and other types of advisory groups are widely used to help keep instruction close to the needs of the occupation.

Agricultural Education

Nearly 10,000 schools have vocational agriculture departments and an estimated 60 per cent of them conduct classes for adults. Part-time and evening teachers of agriculture number nearly 8,000. Through financial incentives, supervision, and in-service training programs, state boards of vocational education are encouraging the expansion of adult programs. While adult enrollment in agriculture increased 72 per cent in a recent decade (see Table 9), in cities with a population above 2,500 there is

Table 9. Enrollment in Federally Aided Vocational Classes for Adults and Out-of-school Youth, by Type of Program, 1943 and 1953

Field	1943	1953	Per cent of change
Agriculture (evening and part-time)...........	187,299	322,943	72.4
Homemaking (evening and part-time).........	330,851	544,793	64.7
Trade and industry..........................	422,038	585,143	38.6
Distributive.................................	283,020	178,352	−37.0
Total.................................	1,223,208	1,631,231	33.4

SOURCE: Based on data derived from *Digest of Annual Reports of State Boards for Vocational Education to the U.S. Office of Education*, 1943 and 1953.

evidence that enrollment more than doubled from 1947 to 1951.[3] Adults and out-of-school youth now constitute nearly one-half of the total enrollment in agriculture, and the number of adult classes is increasing rapidly. In some states nearly all vocational agriculture departments conduct classes for adults. In a nationwide survey,[4] agricultural education for adults was recently reported by more communities of 2,500 and above than was any other field except recreation. Every rural community, of course, can make good use of agricultural education for adults.

A comprehensive agricultural curriculum for adults, in order to serve all the farm groups in the community, must be fitted to the types of farming carried on. Young men who are becoming established in farming have different problems and needs from those of experienced owner-operators. Owner-operators, cash tenants, sharecroppers, part-time farmers, salaried farm workers, retiring farmers, and absentee owners all have

[3] Division of Adult Education Service of the NEA, *A Study of Urban Public School Programs,* National Education Association, Washington, 1952, p. 13.
[4] Homer Kempfer, *Adult Education Activities of the Public Schools: Report of a Survey, 1947–48,* U.S. Office of Education Pamphlet 107, 1949, pp. 12–13.

specific training needs requiring special consideration. Production courses dealing with livestock and crop enterprises are popular. Courses in marketing, farm economics, farm accounting and business management, insect control, farm-machinery repair, use of fertilizers, and repair of farm buildings are examples of specialized courses. Most of these are taught on a seasonal basis and organized around the problems of those enrolled. Many of the best agriculture teachers use advisory committees, make extensive advance inquiries among their potential group, or inventory problems early in the year as a basis for course planning. Many courses, such as farm-machinery repair, soil conservation, and food conservation, are organized and conducted on a workshop or participation basis.

In recent years a significant development has been the enrollment of out-of-school young men for systematic instruction in agriculture designed to help them become established in farming. While emphasis is always on instruction concerning problems faced by beginning farmers, the young men often organize as local units of the Young Farmers of America to develop leadership skills.

The institutional on-the-farm training program for veterans after World War II reached its peak enrollment of 361,987 in the spring of 1950. This program consisted of supervised practice supported by a specified amount of related group and individual on-the-farm instruction. Evaluations of this program reveal a number of features which are applicable to the regular adult program.

School-community food conservation centers, which grew rapidly during World War II, are still in existence in a number of states. While actual food processing is the major activity, instruction in food production, preservation, and utilization is an integral part of the program.

Agricultural education for adults is undergoing change. In accordance with the trend toward democratic vocational education, classes and programs are being set up to reach effectively all ages and types of farm workers. New research findings, new market conditions, and a changing economy are making it necessary for farmers to continue their learning throughout life. Adult and out-of-school youth programs in agriculture are growing faster than are day programs for farm youth. Supervised practice, as exemplified in all-day classes for youth and institutional on-the-farm programs for young adults, is the heart of the agricultural education program for adults. The close relationship between instruction and long-time, on-going farm enterprises gives a direct means of evaluation. If the projects involved succeed, the instruction has been successful; if the projects fail, the agricultural education has failed.

Homemaking Education

Nearly 9,000 evening and part-time teachers of homemaking are paid in part by Federal funds. Table 9 shows that enrollment of men and women in vocational homemaking classes increased by nearly two-thirds in 10 years. Since vocational homemaking departments are widespread in both cities and rural areas, adult homemaking courses undoubtedly enroll more adults than do courses in any other field, vocational or general. Schools provide a great amount of homemaking education, either occupationally slanted or intended as general education, apart from the federally aided program.

Vocational homemaking has evolved from the cooking-and-sewing type of domestic science of two generations ago. Modern homemaking education is based on a much broader concept which includes the total range of problems in the home as well as specialized related occupations outside the home. Homemaking education includes the following major areas of instruction: clothing and textiles; food and nutrition; housing, home furnishings, and home equipment; child development; family health; family economics and home management; and family and community relationships. In two generations, homemaking education has broadened from household arts and skills to include much of the field of human relations.

A little thought about the major instructional areas shows how many are primarily concerns of adult life. In-school adolescents often have only limited interest in such subjects as housing, home furnishings, home equipment, child care, and family economics. Their psychological readiness to learn certain aspects of homemaking will be keener in late courtship and after marriage. In fact, one major group served by homemaking education consists of young men and women planning to establish homes. Experienced housewives needing to keep up with new developments and working women who are part-time homemakers also need special attention.

The primary approach to adult homemaking education is through short-unit courses given in evening, afternoon, or morning hours. Part-time classes for youth who have left regular school are successful in some communities during the school year or summer. More than two-thirds of all day-school homemaking teachers are employed from 1 to 3 months beyond the regular school term. The percentage is growing steadily. During this time they can work more intensively with out-of-school youth and adult groups. In addition to laboratory work and discussion, instruction often includes home visits, directed observation, demonstrations, clinics, and consultation on individual or group problems. Family-life institutes, parent-education discussion groups, and joint activities with community organizations interested in homemaking are growing.

The preparation of women, and to some extent men, for wage-earning jobs in home economics is of growing importance, although training for such occupations is properly a concern of trade and industrial education. Short, intensive courses may prepare women for waitress work. Both pre-employment and upgrading courses are useful to salespeople and fitters in clothing stores. Employees in food and housekeeping positions in hotels, clubs, and restaurants can benefit from pre-employment training, supervised on-the-job training, and part-time short courses. A number of semiprofessional occupations requiring knowledge and skills in child care, health, dietetics, clothing, and textiles require post-high-school training, which can be offered to young people or older adults on a full- or part-time basis. These vocational courses should be based on continuing occupational surveys and job analyses and taught by persons who have had practical and successful experience in the field.

The vocational homemaking and agriculture departments in some rural communities jointly provide programs in farm-family living for young adults and more mature men and women. Whole families are included in a unified farm-life educational program in a few instances.

Another trend resulting in increased enrollments is the selection of teachers of adults with broad backgrounds of experience. Coupled with this is a real effort to base the curriculum upon the needs of adults and to provide learning experiences in practical home and community settings. Teachers with an academic and theoretical approach are seldom able to hold the interest of homemakers.

The extension of homemaking training to adults of all ages, educational levels, and economic circumstances is another significant trend. Increasingly adult education is accepting responsibility for providing continuous learning for the millions who have dropped out of school without adequate training in homemaking. Likewise, the scientific and technical advances which have significant bearings on home life make educational programs in homemaking advisable for great numbers of people. Related to this is the trend toward including men in homemaking classes. While it started in high school, this movement is extending upward to include young men approaching marriage and those already married. The number of men in part-time and evening homemaking classes has more than doubled within the past decade.[5]

Trade and Industrial Education

Trade and industrial education is intended to train in "any occupation which directly functions in the designing, producing, processing, assembling, maintaining, servicing, or repairing of any manufactured product; and any public or other service trades or occupations which are not classified as agricultural, commercial, professional, or homemaking."[6] The field has undergone a number of significant changes in the past generation, one of which is the growth in number of occupations. From

[5] *Digest of Annual Reports of State Boards for Vocational Education to the U.S. Office of Education,* 1952, p. 27.

[6] *Statement of Policies for Administration of Vocational Education,* U.S. Office of Education, Division of Vocational Education Bulletin 2, 1937.

1923 to 1944 the number of occupations in which T-and-I education received Federal aid grew from 50 to 85.[7] Wartime programs and demobilization brought about radical changes in size of enrollment, although currently it has stabilized. T-and-I education for adults and out-of-school youth embraces the following types of programs:

1. *Trade preparatory* classes, which provide instruction in both manipulative skills and related and technical subjects. Instruction covers skills, related subjects, industrial relations, and worker attitudes. Classes are usually filled with out-of-school youth and young adults, although older people may enroll. Instruction may be given in intensive all-day classes often of a few weeks' duration. In times of rapid industrial expansion, military mobilization, and other major occupational shifts, all-day preparatory programs are intensified to train a sizable influx of mature adults. Ordinary part-time trade preparatory classes serve employed adults who are working in some other occupation.

2. *General continuation* classes intended to increase the civic, social, and vocational intelligence of young workers who left school before the final school-leaving age. Continuation classes often operate under compulsory-attendance laws and usually require 4 to 8 hours of instruction per week. While continuation classes reached their peak enrollments nearly a generation ago, they are still an important part of vocational education in several states.

3. *Trade extension* classes, which provide training supplementary to the daily employment of apprentices, journeymen, and other workers in trade and industrial occupations. Instruction is intended to develop the skill and extend the knowledge of these workers in regard to their particular occupation. Most instruction is part-time, chiefly in the evening. It appeals especially to ambitious young adults, although workers of any age desiring to brush up or extend their skills and knowledge are found in trade extension classes.

In times of rapid industrial expansion *foreman training* and supervisory training become especially important. Inasmuch as most foremen are promoted from the ranks, they may have the required technical competence. Their greatest need ordinarily is in the area of human relations—learning how to teach and handle employees. The conference method, which calls for a few weeks of intensive training, has given good results. The trainer acts as chairman of a series of planned discussions dealing with the problems of foremen, especially personnel problems. The leader may be an officer of the company or an instructor especially engaged by the public school. Through proper training of foremen, supervisors, and conference leaders, the stage is set for effective on-the-job training of semiskilled and unskilled workers in the industry.

[7] *Vocational Education in the Years Ahead,* U.S. Office of Education, Division of Vocational Education Bulletin 234, General Series, no. 7, 1945, p. 256.

In recent years, industry has come to recognize the value of training unskilled workers. Unskilled and semiskilled workers are employed in great numbers for work requiring endurance, often dexterity, and sometimes judgment. Most work, however, no matter how simple, can be done in ways which save time and energy. Many workers never learn the best ways unless shown. In addition, factory regulations, safety rules, and other elements of efficiency can be taught. Such training reduces accidents, builds morale, and saves time, material, and energy. Teaching may require only a few minutes or a few hours on the first day of work, or it may require extended incidental training on the job. In this area, the school can help best by training supervisors how to orient and teach their workers.

Semiskilled workers, such as machine operators, require only a few special skills and a little knowledge to perform their tasks. A short breaking-in period supplies the necessary instruction and practice. Often the new worker is placed beside an experienced operator in hopes that the newcomer will pick up the required skills with occasional help from the experienced worker. Sometimes the arrangement is not too successful; new workers may become discouraged without training. A foreman skilled in teaching can do much to save the situation, but in some cases a short, well-conducted course has proved much better. In a few hours or days of instruction the new worker can learn not only the required skills and technical facts but also general plant regulations, safety rules, company policies, and the economic importance of his work. If the instructor has had ample production-room experience and knows how to teach, the vestibule training may be more thorough than that given by a foreman. It has proved itself by reducing job turnover and improving the production and morale of new workers. Again, the school can help chiefly by training job instructors and supervisors and consulting with them on setting up training courses.

In an age in which most production is done by automatic or semiautomatic machines, *skilled workers* are responsible for assembling, adjusting, and repairing the tools of production. Toolmakers, electricians, millwrights, steamfitters, power-plant engineers, and others must spend years learning their highly skilled occupations. The building-repair and construction trades account for many more skilled occupations.

Apprenticeship is the historic approach to learning a skilled trade, although in recent years this arrangement has been supplemental. Short courses may prove effective. Often a helper is employed for a few years and at the end of that time admitted to journeyman status. Increasingly, however, apprenticeship agreements call for a specific number of hours of job experience coupled with a fixed amount of related training. Where a progression of work experience and related training is carefully worked out and adhered to, the training can be of high quality. The related training and work experience, however, must be closely coordinated to be of maximum value. Related training is usually given in part-time trade extension classes.

Trade schools also prepare for the skilled occupations by providing full-time curricula covering 2 or 3 years, or evening courses extending over a longer period. A combined program of study and work can turn out well-grounded mechanics.

Corporation schools conducted by industrial plants also train skilled mechanics. The technical training is closely related to the work done. While effective from the plant standpoint, sometimes the curriculum becomes somewhat circumscribed.

Vocational-technical training for industrial occupations came into prominence during World War II, although its origin was much earlier. Junior engineers and technical workers of less than engineering grade rank above the skilled mechanic, but below the professional engineer, in general education and technical training. In this grade are draftsmen, inspectors, estimators, laboratory assistants, and installation experts. In these occupations manipulative skill is secondary to technical knowledge. Some technicians are promoted from the ranks, but technical schools provide many more. The general education, science, and technical training are best given on a post-high-school basis by technical schools, junior colleges, and community colleges. Well-equipped institutions can offer evening courses for adults which add up to the equivalent of the 1-, 2-, or 3-year curricula for youth. Technical institutes, area vocational schools, university extension programs, training-within-industry programs, home-study schools, and cooperative vocational-technical curricula also offer training of this character to adults. During World War II, the Engineering, Science, and Management War Training Program was of this level.

Public-service training has become a differentiated field in recent years. It includes the training of public employees such as firemen, policemen, sanitary inspectors, custodial workers, school-bus drivers, safety inspectors, water and sewage plant operators, guards, and of late a wide range of paid and volunteer civil-defense workers.

Related to this area are a number of *service occupations,* in which the worker sells his services rather than works on materials to produce consumer goods. Typical service areas in which training has grown materially in recent years are practical nursing, hospital work, food services, hotel work, building maintenance, cosmetology, and rural electrification.

Changes in our industrial economy have a material effect on trade and industrial education. Obvious trends are the continued expansion of adult enrollments, the increase in part-time programs for mature people, and the inclusion of many more production and service occupations. With rapid technological changes, more adults are returning for part-time courses. In fact, vocational educators can look forward to the time when—instead of the few who now intermittently seek to further their occupational education—a great majority of workers will voluntarily maintain a continuous part-time relationship with training programs. Through continuous learning they can maintain their employability.

Any rapid increase in the labor force, as in times of national emergency, must necessarily be supplied by women and old people. With increased longevity, more older people are seeking training for occupations which they can follow after retirement from their original work. More out-of-school girls and middle-aged women are likewise turning to trade and industrial programs for training.

Another trend is the development of cooperative training programs in which labor, industry, and the school are jointly responsible for the training function. This is typified by the newer training-within-industry programs. Industry provides the job, the school provides the instruction, and labor provides the learner and ensures his faithful participation.

Business Education

Business education includes office training, distributive occupational training, and basic business courses of a general-education nature. In the public schools, office training, which consists of courses in typing, shorthand, bookkeeping, business arithmetic, office-machine operation, filing, office practice, business law, business economics, business English, and business organization, is supported largely by state and local funds. The distributive phase of business education receives financial assistance from Federal funds which became available first in 1936 with the passage of the George-Deen Act (later superseded by the George-Barden Act). Federally aided distributive occupational training is limited to those employed or preparing for employment in "merchandising activities, or in contact with buyers and sellers when: (1) distributing to consumers, retailers, wholesalers, and others the products of farm and industry, or selling services, (2) managing, operating, or conducting a retail, wholesale, or service business." [8]

Three types of vocational business education are generally recognized:

1. *Pre-employment training,* which develops marketable skills, knowledge, understanding, and attitudes which enable a person to enter employment in a business occupation. In the past, this type of training has served largely secondary-school youth. However, as out-of-school youth, men and women leaving the service, and older adults may want to enter business occupations for the first time, it is necessary to upgrade and expand pre-employment business training to the post-high-school, junior-college, and community-college level. Courses at this level should be geared to employment needs and opportunities and built upon job

[8] *Administration of Vocation Education,* U.S. Office of Education, Division of Vocational Education Bulletin 1, 1948, p. 45.

analyses; they should hold to job requirements and use occupationally competent teachers.

2. *Cooperative part-time training,* which combines specific work experience with vocational instruction. It prepares part-time workers, out-of-school youth, and more mature adults for full-time employment. More of it should be developed on the post-high-school and community-college levels. When instruction and work are closely coordinated, this type of training is very effective.

3. *Adult extension training,* which improves the efficiency of the employed business worker. It also builds additional occupational competence which may lead to positions of greater responsibility. Adult extension training in office occupations has not been either well or extensively developed. Typewriting, shorthand, and bookkeeping are widely taught in public evening schools, but a great majority of schools offer no other office training.[9] That which is offered too often duplicates the objectives and content of the preparatory courses in the all-day school. With the perennial shortage of competent stenographers and other office workers, there is a continuing need for supplementary training. A series of short-unit courses could be set up in such areas as filing, special phases of business arithmetic, and business communication. Trainees in typing, secretarial practice, and accounting could be tested and grouped for graded short courses. Some evening schools have instructional units and exercises worked out for each office machine so that an employed worker can come in at any time and learn to operate any machine he may need to master. Short, intensive refresher courses in a great variety of business subjects may also be needed for unemployed adults.

There is no reason why the larger public evening schools cannot establish well-rounded office curricula to provide pre-employment training, cooperative part-time training, and adult extension training. If adequate guidance and placement services were made available, and if local advisory committees were used, these larger schools could offer all the essential training services required by the business community.

As many problems faced by every adult are of an economic and business nature, business training of a nonvocational type should be made available to those for whom faulty business methods, poor judgment, and unwise decisions may be disastrous. Short-unit evening courses in such subjects as personal finance, the use of credit, insurance, investments, bookkeeping, buying and selling, everyday business law, and practical economics can contribute significantly to economic literacy and business competency.

The need for adult extension training in the distributive occupations increases with the number, variety, and importance of these occupations.

[9] Homer Kempfer and Grace S. Wright, *100 Evening Schools,* U.S. Office of Education Bulletin 1949, no. 4.

Instructional content in distributive occupations, as in any other vocational subject, must be based upon job requirements and coordinated
with work experience. Textbook teachers and teachers inexperienced in
merchandising are less effective than occupationally competent instructors
using materials arising out of the problems of the class. Classroom discussion, projects, illustrations, conferences, and demonstrations are most
effective when based upon the realities of job situations. Advisory committees are widely used in distributive education to give reality to the
instruction.

A number of changes are occurring in distributive occupational training. Generalized courses in salesmanship or merchandising are being
replaced with courses for specific occupational groups. Classes with large
enrollment are giving way to smaller instructional and discussion groups.
Sanitation courses for restaurant workers, institutes for secretaries of
trade associations, and well-planned curricula for adults which lead to
a retail diploma are among the newer developments. Management and
supervisory courses packaged as human-relations training or job-instruc-
tion training are more and more often supplemented by longer courses
in management and in store operation and control. Functional training
programs provided by adult schools can aid materially in reducing
failures in small-business ownership, provided that they are led by experienced and successful businessmen who can teach. Increasingly,
schools and business firms are developing long-range integrated distributive programs for adults. In this way instruction will have the greatest
opportunity for fitting directly into business occupations. This holds true
especially for retail training, which can help upgrade retail workers at
the same time that it is meeting the needs of business.

Cooperative Extension Service

The cooperative agricultural and home-economics Extension Service,
which originated in the Smith-Lever Act of 1914, is probably the largest
adult-education program in the world. Nearly 7 million families are influenced by some phase of this extension work.[10] Local directors of adult
education, especially in rural areas, almost inevitably will have occasion
to cooperate with the Extension Service.

Cooperative extension work is a Federal-state-county system of education designed to develop adults and young people through learning by
doing. While it serves primarily rural and village people, in some states
it also provides homemaking education in urban areas.

The county agent is the backbone of extension work. Nearly every
county in the United States has at least one specialist in agriculture—the
agricultural agent—who does educational work among farmers. Over

[10] *Extension Activities and Accomplishments, 1950,* U.S. Department of Agriculture
Extension Service Circular 473, June, 1951.

86 per cent of all counties have one or more home-demonstration agents, who conduct educational activities among housewives. About 28 per cent of all counties also have a 4-H club agent who works with youth.[11] Many counties have assistant agricultural and home-demonstration agents.

A state extension director in each state heads the Extension Service as a department of the state agricultural college. He is coordinate with the director of the agricultural experiment station and dean of resident instruction. He is responsible to the dean of agriculture or to the president of the college. Assisting the state director is a group consisting of an administrative and supervisory staff, subject-matter specialists, editors, publicity agents, clerical helpers, and the county agents, who are the field agents of the state staff. Supervisors facilitate communication between the state office and the field workers. Subject-matter specialists and editors help translate findings of research into a form suitable for use among lay people.

The Extension Service of the U.S. Department of Agriculture is the administrative and service agency through which the other divisions of the Department channel educational materials and information to the field. Its Washington office, with approximately 100 professional workers, is divided into six divisions: Extension Information, Field Studies and Training, Field Coordination, Subject Matter, Agricultural Economics, and Business Administration. The Federal office interprets national policies affecting agriculture, requires state reports, reviews the plans and budgets of state offices, and works with state colleges of agriculture in developing and improving the Extension Service.

Extension work is financed by a combination of Federal, state, county, and individual funds. Under several basic acts Congress appropriates money to the states according to rural and farm populations. While less than one-half of the Federal money must be matched, ordinarily state and local funds outweigh the Federal. In 1948 the amounts allocated for cooperative extension work were:

Source	Amount
Federal	$27,367,660
State and college	17,174,963
County	12,268,128
Farm organizations	1,563,605
Total	$58,374,356

SOURCE: *Federal Legislation, Regulations and Rulings Affecting Cooperative Extension Work in Agriculture and Home Economics*, U.S. Department of Agriculture Miscellaneous Publication 385, 1948.

Most state funds are granted to the agricultural colleges. Private funds may come from business, industry, and from farm organizations. Salaries

[11] *Ibid.,* p. 47.

of county agents may be paid entirely through the state extension office, in which case county funds are deposited with the state, or paid partly by the county and partly by the state.

In local communities Federal agencies work most smoothly when they define their respective fields and methods of operation. At the Federal level, the Extension Service touches upon the work of such agencies as the Bureau of Reclamation, the Grazing Service, the Fish and Wildlife Service, the Indian Service, the Veterans Administration, the Public Health Service, and the Office of Education. On several occasions, as problems arose, the Office of Education and the Extension Service have studied their relationships and have reached agreements. In essence, since they both deal with agricultural education for youth and adults, they have divided the field to reduce overlapping. Schools, in general, provide organized classes while the Extension Service avoids organizing classes and utilizes other approaches. In the youth field, the Extension Service works through 4-H clubs, while the schools sponsor Future Farmer groups. This is illustrative of agreements existing between this Service and a number of agencies.

At the state level, similar relationships must be worked out between the Extension Service and departments of agriculture, forestry, education, conservation, and health. The Extension Service, for example, takes the findings of research conducted by Federal and state agencies and experiment stations and makes them available to farmers; it refers the problems of rural people back to the research agencies.

The major local and state problem in establishing satisfactory relationships with other organizations concerns the farm bureaus, which are private, voluntary organizations originally formed to cooperate with county agents in their educational work. In its early days the Extension Service promoted the development of farm bureaus, but they soon began to support legislation, operate cooperatives, and engage in a number of other noneducational activities. The Extension Service, which has repeatedly asserted its independence from the American Farm Bureau Federation, insists that the extension staff not solicit memberships, receive dues, or take any other active part in bureau affairs outside their duties as educators. While the problem of relationship still comes up occasionally, it is clear (1) that a logical organization to assist the county agent in his educational work is desirable, (2) that such an organization should confine its work to education, and (3) that the entire support of the Extension Service should come from tax sources. In recent years the proportion of private contributions have been declining.

Programs and Methods of the Cooperative Extension Service

The Extension Service, which is concerned with changing human behavior, measures its results by counting the changes in agricultural and home practices. Its aim is to induce farm men, women, and youth to do their work better. The percentage of time spent by county agents in 1949 in each of the major lines of work is shown below: [12]

Type of work	Per cent of time spent
Extension organization and planning	21.3
Farm crops	12.9
Soil and water	3.5
Fruits	1.5
Dairy cattle	5.1
Poultry	2.7
Animal husbandry	8.0
Forestry	1.1
Agricultural economics	3.9
Agricultural engineering	2.0
Marketing	3.3
The house, furnishings, and surroundings	5.3
Home production of family food supply	2.6
Food preservation and storage	2.2
Food selection and preparation	3.6
Other health and safety work	1.5
Home management and family economics	1.8
Clothing and textiles	5.7
Family relationships and child development	1.1
Recreation and community life	4.9
Miscellaneous	6.0
Total	100.0

The original emphasis on production has broadened to include more comprehensive phases of rural life, family relations, agricultural economics, public affairs, leisure-time activities, and community life. Except in periods of emergency, the Federal office exerts relatively little influence on the program. For the most part, program planning is a county and state function.

Program planning goes on in a number of ways. In most counties numerous planning, advisory, and operational committees are at work. They may be called program-development committees, educational committees, commodity committees, home-economics councils, project committees, special-interest committees, 4-H councils, or other names. The important fact is that literally scores and hundreds of farm families are involved in planning—an educational activity of the deepest significance, and one which school directors of adult education do well to remember. In a direct way county agents and their neighborhood leaders keep in close touch with the problems of farm families through innumerable meetings, individual conferences, office calls, telephone calls, farm and home visits, and correspondence.

[12] *Extension Activities and Accomplishments*, p. 47.

The Extension Service uses many approaches and methods without depending upon classroom instruction as such. Experience has shown that people are influenced to change their farm and home practices in proportion to the number of methods used. Multiple methods are a part of the extension design. Personal- and group-contact methods are many times more effective than are mass approaches. Personal- and group-contact methods include:

1. Method demonstrations in which a process is shown step by step
2. Result demonstrations in which the application of a proven fact or principal is shown
3. Discussion groups and meetings—organization meetings, planning meetings, training meetings, special-interest groups, and large meetings
4. Office calls
5. Correspondence
6. Telephone calls
7. Farm and home visits

Agent-to-person methods induce less than one-fifth of the changes, while group methods account for one-quarter of all changed practices. Mass media, which include newspapers, circular letters, radio, television, motion pictures, talks, exhibits, bulletins, and posters, provide nearly two-fifths of the influence. Visiting, informal talking between neighbors, observation of practices, and similar indirect influences bring about one-fifth of the changes.

Vocational Rehabilitation

Disabled and handicapped adults of employable age can often procure occupational training through the state-Federal system of vocational rehabilitation which started in 1920. Disabled veterans are usually eligible for rehabilitation services under other legislation. Federal funds pay approximately 70 per cent of the costs of a rehabilitation service, which in most states is operated, supervised, and controlled by state boards of vocational education. Most states maintain several regional offices.

Nine services are provided: (1) medical examination to determine the extent of disability and potential work capacity; (2) individual counseling and guidance; (3) medical, surgical, psychiatric, and hospital care needed to remove or reduce the disability; (4) artificial appliances; (5) training for the selected occupation in schools, colleges, or universities, on the job, by tutor, through home-study courses, or otherwise; (6) maintenance and transportation of the person, if necessary, during his treatment and training; (7) occupational tools, equipment and licenses; (8) job placement; and (9) follow-up to ensure that the rehabilitated person and the employer are satisfied with each other. The individual pays for services (3), (4), (6), and (7) above in so far as his financial ability permits.

Approximately 60,000 people, one-fourth of whom are women, are rehabilitated each year. Nearly a quarter-million adults are seriously disabled by injury, illness, or congenital causes each year. The backlog of men and women who could benefit from rehabilitation is estimated at 2 million. Three-fourths of the cases are unemployed and nearly one-half have dependents when they start the rehabilitation process at the median age of thirty-four. Persons of working age who have a substantial mental or physical handicap interfering with employment are usually eligible provided that there is a reasonable chance of their rejoining the labor force. Training is usually provided on a contractual or payment-of-cost basis with a training institution. In addition to the personal values accruing to the individual, the rehabilitants have many years of service to contribute to the economy. The program saves many millions of dollars in public and private assistance. As rehabilitation usually costs less than 1 year of public assistance, local directors of adult education can perform a valuable personal and public service by encouraging the eligible disabled to seek the help of vocational rehabilitation offices.

EDUCATION FOR CONSUMPTION

Objectives and Point of View

Consumer education is the converse of occupational training. In our schools we have stressed preparation for earning a living, but often we have done little to teach the individual how to spend the income earned. Education for consumption aims to increase satisfactions in using the goods and services made available by our productive economy. It is concerned with the whole art of getting the most out of life—of the improvement of living through wise selection and use of resources. The objective of consumer education for adults is to help them learn how to obtain a richer and fuller living for their expenditure of money, time, and energy.

Consumer education as an organized movement is less than 30 years old, most of its growth having occurred since 1930. The need for consumer education became apparent slowly—long after the need for vocational education was recognized. The constant expansion of our economic system and the advance of technology intensify the need for consumer education. With the multiplication of goods and services, the creation of new brands, the intensification of advertising, and the development of attractive packages, the task of spending money, time, and energy wisely has become a complex process. Monopoly and imperfect competition, wide differences in income, unwise expenditures among the low-income and undereducated groups, unemployment, depression, price control, and rationing point up additional needs. Some of the needs arise from the enterprises of a free economy, which in developing the highest standard of living, also present the most diversified opportunities for spending money.

Consumer exploitation likewise shows the need for a public educated in intelligent purchasing. Much of the interest in consumer education arose from the revelations of fraud, dishonesty, and exploitation in unregulated areas of the economy a generation ago. Certainly before an economic field is either self-disciplined or regulated by government, malpractice is likely to exist. Consumer education was an outgrowth of early nostrums and quackery in medicine, excesses in the security markets before Federal regulation, and flamboyant advertising. As both government regulations in the public interest and self-discipline are likely to develop more slowly than exploitative practices, helping the public to acquire prudence, wisdom, and understanding in consumption becomes necessary.

During the past two decades emphasis has changed in consumer education. In the early 1930s, after the exposés of business malpractices, most instruction attempted to develop competence in buying. This was facilitated by a need for personal thrift. This period gave way to an analysis era, in which emphasis was on product testing. Consumers' Research, Inc., and Consumers Union, organizations which tested, analyzed, and reported on products, flourished. The emphasis grew to a concern with consumer protection. In 1938, a revised Federal Pure Food, Drug, and Cosmetic Act was passed, and the Federal Trade Commission was given additional powers to deal with unfair commercial practices.

Today consumer education still includes the best of the former emphases, but it is now concerned with the whole of individual living as a consumer. Attempts to serve the selfish interests of the consumer are now supplemented by study of his relationships with other important economic and social factors. Consequently, the goals of consumer education may be stated as follows: [13]

1. The consumer should learn to make intelligent choices.
2. The consumer should learn to be an effective buyer.
3. The consumer should be an efficient user of goods and services.
4. The consumer should learn to manage his personal financial affairs.
5. The consumer should be conscious of his wider social and economic responsibilities.

Or, as the Educational Policies Commission states the task, efficiency in consumption may be divided into four parts: [14]

[13] National Association of Secondary-school Principals, *The Relation of Business to Consumer Education*, National Education Association, Washington, 1945, pp. 5–7.
[14] Educational Policies Commission, *The Purposes of Education in American Democracy*, National Education Association, Washington, 1938, p. 90.

1. Personal economics. The educated consumer plans the economics of his own life.

2. Consumer judgment. The educated consumer develops standards for guiding his expenditures.

3. Efficiency in buying. The educated consumer is an informed and skillful buyer.

4. Consumer protection. The educated consumer takes appropriate measures to safeguard his interests.

Areas

Whereas vocational education is primarily a concern of the working years, consumer education is for all ages. Everyone is a consumer. Historically, home economics contributed a great deal to the education of consumers. As the movement grow beyond purchasing of goods for family consumption, it drew from economics, business education, science, social studies, mathematics, and other disciplines. Indeed, the Consumer Education Study sponsored by the National Association of Secondary-school Principals related the movement to most of the fields of study in high schools.

For the most part, consumer education is a part of general education in that it deals with a common body of learnings which all or most people should experience. Whether to treat it as a new emphasis in all courses, as a part of a core curriculum, or as another course is still an issue in secondary schools. At the adult level, however, most successful education of the consumer starts with his problems rather than with systematic treatment of subject matter. In the main, consumer education for adults, while seldom set up in courses of this nature, is concerned with such problems as these:

1. The selection, purchase, preparation, utilization, and conservation of food: Study of food values, grade-labeling, methods of preparation and preservation

2. The selection, purchase, care and repair of clothing and accessories: Study of style, quality, fabrics, labels, advertising, cleaning and care of clothing, making and remaking clothing

3. The procurement and maintenance of adequate housing: Purchase versus renting, building versus buying, building operation and maintenance, cooperative housing, location and zoning, financing, architectural services, modernization, prefabrication

4. The building of adequate security: Understanding budgeting, banking services, consumer credit, life insurance, social security, pension and retirement plans, savings plans, credit unions, and other investments

5. The procurement of adequate medical, dental, and other health services: Physical examinations, health and accident insurance, early detection of chronic conditions and ill health, maintenance of mental health, selecting a doctor, safety at home, in traffic, and on the job

6. Self-improvement and recreation: Development of personality, selection of leisure-time activities, lifelong learning, travel, vacations, development of friendships and of good human relations

7. Transportation services: Automobile purchase, maintenance, insurance; common carriers

Approaches

Dissemination of information through lecture and class instruction are favorite approaches in consumer education. Very often outside specialists are brought in to supply the substantive content while the educator arranges the learning situation. Occasionally a comprehensive course is offered adults in consumer education or consumer buying. More often short courses of four to eight weekly sessions serve specific needs and interests. Typical of such courses are these:

Law for the Layman, in which one or a series of lawyers explains what the ordinary citizen most needs to know about such things as wills, property transfer, accident liability, buyer-seller relationships, tenant-landlord relationships, and contracts

Investments, with a broker explaining the operation of the stock markets, stocks, bonds, mutual funds, savings plans, annuities, mortgages, and the commodity markets

Housing Problems, with a realtor, a builder, and other specialists discussing location, landscaping, architect's plans, selecting a contractor, building problems, economics, and financing

Health for Middle and Later Life, in which a series of physicians answer questions on cancer, hypertension, diabetes, prostatic diseases, arthritis, weight control, exercise, arteriosclerosis, hyperthyroidism, and rheumatic heart disease

Feeding the Family, in which a nutritionist or home economist discusses the nutritional values, the grading, the purchase, and the preparation of food and supplements instruction with practical shopping experiences

Life Insurance, with a broker leading a series of discussions on social security, different kinds of insurance, costs, purposes, etc.

Consumer Economics, utilizing film forums, lectures, or discussions dealing with advertising, grade-labeling, tests for quality, installment buying, and the timing of purchases

Group instruction is facilitated by demonstration, laboratory tests, study of printed materials, examination of consumer goods, and exhibits, which commercial firms are often willing to provide. Reports of results by the consumer testing organizations provide effective study materials, especially when test methods are explained. Such study can lead to better care of equipment and better utilization of goods. Field trips, committee projects, clubs, liberal use of visual aids, and forums are other approaches and methods used in direct instruction.

In this field numerous timely short courses and single demonstrations can be arranged in cooperation with utility companies, appliance stores, trade associations, and manufacturers. If the advertising is not too objectionable and does not arouse ill feeling among competitors, this approach can be useful in keeping consumers abreast of the newest gadgets.

Large audiences are practical for some types of consumer education. To avoid having specialists deal with the fine points of their hobbies, the curriculum for each session can be determined by questions of common interest formulated by buzz groups.

Intensive 1- or 2-day annual or seasonal institutes focused on new developments are held in some communities. Special sections dealing with new fabrics, new findings in nutrition, and new housing ideas serve special interests. Commercially sponsored auto shows, home shows, and garden shows also serve consumer-education purposes.

Consumers are the largest unorganized population group in the country. Compared with the production, trade, and occupation groups of our economy, relatively few groups speak directly for the consumer. True, the Home Bureau, the AAUW, the YWCA, the national PTA, the General Federation of Women's Clubs, the League of Women Voters, the American Home Economics Association, certain religious bodies, labor unions, and other national organizations represent consumer interests, but for most of them, giving a voice to the consumer is a secondary reason for existence. As we learn best by doing, organized consumer action is the preferred means of educating consumers.

Consumer cooperatives organized along the Rochdale principles constitute the oldest consumer-action movement of significance today. Their programs include collective purchasing and distribution combined with consumer and economic education. Both local cooperatives and their national organizations usually involve significant numbers of people in educational activities. Local cooperative educational programs are often intended to acquaint the public with such consumer information as quality goods and government grading of foods. This information is disseminated through nontechnical demonstrations before community groups, store demonstrations, exhibits, and radio and television broadcasts. Customer advisory committees not only learn about commodities but help identify the kinds of goods the public desires. Regional institutes and local lecture series help acquaint volunteer leaders and others with the history and present work of various kinds of cooperatives.

In many sizable communities Better Business Bureaus represent a potent influence on behalf of the consumer. Their acts are largely protective—the elimination of fraud, the improvement of quality in advertising, and the raising of standards of business ethics. Nationally, their work in part supplements that of the Federal Trade Commission; within states and localities, the bureaus have a greater role to play. Committees associated with such bureaus are essentially educational in nature.

A number of consumers councils, study groups, and other consumer-action groups have organized under the stimulus of depression or war. Most of them have been local organizations concerned with price-quality relationships, maintenance of price ceilings in wartime, driving out black markets, promotion of union labels, support of consumer testing agencies, promotion of consumer protective legislation, operation of consumer-information centers, support of government agencies serving consumer interests, and education of the consumer through mass media. Those which have joined together in national organizations have, with certain exceptions, been loosely organized and have not demonstrated great strength over long periods. Potentially, however, the consumer movement could be even stronger than the labor-union movement. In certain European countries, it equals labor unions in influence.

Consumer education has a number of community aspects. Housing, health, sanitation, recreation, and education are not only individual concerns but also matters for community study, planning, and action. Intelligent activity toward the improvement of conditions in any of these fields is likely to be educational. In fact, one important facet of consumer education is examination of the values received for the tax dollar. The collective buying, through taxes, of roads, fire and police protection, health, and a host of other services needs constant reexamination.

SELECTED REFERENCES

Education for Production and Service

Administration of Vocational Education, U.S. Office of Education, Division of Vocational Education Bulletin 1, 1948.

Brunner, E. deS., and E. H. P. Yang: *Rural America and the Extension Service*, Bureau of Publications, Teachers College, Columbia University, New York, 1949.

Haas, Kenneth B.: *Distributive Education Organization and Administration*, Gregg Publishing Division, McGraw-Hill Book Company, Inc., New York, 1941.

Hamlin, H. M.: *Agricultural Education in Community Schools*, The Interstate Printers & Publishers, Inc., Danville, Ill., 1949.

Hawkins, L. S., et al.: *Development of Vocational Education*, American Technical Society, Chicago, 1951.

Keller, F. J.: *Principles of Vocational Education: The Primacy of the Person*, D. C. Heath and Company, Boston, 1948.

Kelsey, L. D., and C. C. Hearne: *Cooperative Extension Work*, Comstock Publishing Associates, Inc., Ithaca, N.Y., 1949.

Kerrison, I. L. H.: *Workers' Education at the University Level*, Rutgers University Press, New Brunswick, N.J., 1951.

Loomis, W. P.: *The Operation of a Local Program of Trade and Industrial Education with Emphasis on Improving Instruction through Supervision*, U.S. Office of Education, Division of Vocational Education Bulletin 250, 1953.

Mays, Arthur B.: *Principles and Practices of Vocational Education*, McGraw-Hill Book Company, Inc., New York, 1948.

McCarthy, John: *Vocational Education: America's Greatest Resource*, American Technical Society, Chicago, 1951.

Pollard, L. B.: *Adult Education in Homemaking*, John Wiley & Sons, Inc., New York, 1946.

Prosser, C. A., and M. R. Bass: *Evening Industrial Schools*, American Technical Society, Chicago, 1951.

—— and T. H. Quigley: *Vocational Education in a Democracy*, American Technical Society, Chicago, 1949.

River, E.: *Frontiers in Homemaking Education*, U.S. Office of Education, Division of Vocational Education Bulletin 239, Home Economics Series, no. 26, 1949.

Selvidge, R. W., and V. C. Fryklund: *Principles of Trade and Industrial Teaching*, rev. ed., Chas. A. Bennett Company, Inc., Peoria, Ill., 1946.

Soden, W. H.: *Rehabilitation of the Handicapped*, The Ronald Press Company, New York, 1950.

Vocational Education in the Years Ahead, U.S. Office of Education, Division of Vocational Education Bulletin 234, 1945.

Vocational-Technical Training for Industrial Occupations, U.S. Office of Education, Division of Vocational Education Bulletin 228, 1944.

Education for Consumption

Ambrose, W. L.: "A Project in Consumer Education: Buying a Home," *Industrial Arts and Vocational Education*, 39:267, September, 1950.

Lifson, S. S.: "Health Departments in Adult Education," *Adult Education Journal*, 8:21–24, January, 1949.

Mendenhall, J. E., and Henry Harap: *Consumer Education*, Appleton-Century-Crofts, Inc., New York, 1943.

National Association of Secondary-school Principals: *Consumer Education in Your School: A Handbook for Teachers and Administrators*, Consumer Education Study, National Education Association, Washington, 1947.

Troelstrip, A. W.: "Consumer Problems in General Education," *Junior College Journal*, 21:283–288, January, 1951.

See also General References: [15] Beals and Brody, pp. 168–176, 273–284; Ely, pp. 11–45, 96–100; Kempfer; Sheats, Jayne, and Spence, chap. 5.

[15] The General References are listed in full at the end of this book.

CHAPTER 8

Program Services
to Community Organizations

"The state is our campus." So said the president of a well-developed state university who organized an extension division to carry the resources of his institution to people throughout the state. A dynamic public-school adult-education program extends education throughout its community in much the same way. Within its service area it develops appropriate tactics for involving a maximum number of adults in learning activities. The adult-education program is the extension division of the public school.

Formal group instruction in schoolrooms is the most conventional approach to organized adult education. Directors who depend solely upon this approach, however, greatly limit their clientele. Historically, only a small proportion of adults have ever enrolled in evening classes at any one time. Only a minority in the typical community have ever attended an adult school even for a year or two. While this number is increasing, as yet relatively few people continue systematic study throughout life. Few pull away from other interesting and pressing activities to join new groups for serious study.

These observations have led many people to conclude erroneously that adult education will always be a small enterprise of limited general interest. This may be true when new groups must be formed for every educational purpose. Directors who work with and through the organized life of their communities, however, can multiply their educational activities several-fold because community organizations provide ready-made groups. The presence of these groups simplifies enormously the task of involving large numbers of adults in organized learning.

COMMUNITY ORGANIZATIONS

Prevalence of Groups

"This community is overorganized." This oft-heard remark emphasizes the American habit of voluntarily associating in innumerable organized groups. An amazing number of groups with regularly elected officers, membership lists, scheduled meetings, and planned programs exist in every community. Eighty organized groups with officers have been identified in one rural village of 1,000 people. One community of 800,000 people has an estimated minimum of 2,500 groups concerned with some phase of public affairs alone. A director of adult education in a community of 100,000 identified 1,100 groups—all meeting on some schedule for some purpose involving interaction of personalities—a primary opportunity for bringing about change in people. Surely anyone even superficially studying the organized life of communities could easily conclude that, if not too many, there are at least enough organizations to enable everyone to belong to several.

Close examination of participation patterns, however, usually shows that certain people, rather than whole communities, are overorganized. A few persons may participate in so many groups that conflicts in personal schedules develop. Usually, however, in a representative sampling, only a small percentage of those who take part in organizations are active in more than one. A few active leaders may be too heavily involved; communities, however, are not overorganized as long as great numbers of adults do not take part in any organized group.

Studies of membership and participation in organizations show considerable variation among communities according to economic level, educational level, location in a rural, urban, or suburban area, local traditions, and other sociological characteristics. Results of several such studies are summarized in this chapter. While membership, attendance, participation, and leadership in organizations are different concepts, and studies of these characteristics are seldom directly comparable, gross generalizations can be made. In many communities roughly one-half of the adult population belongs to formally organized groups having officers and regularly scheduled meetings. The most frequently named organization is a church, and the major activity is the regular church service. Where attendance at church services is not counted, although membership in church-connected organizations is retained, the number is much lower. Under special leadership or other favorable conditions, membership and participation may run higher. The majority of studies show 40 to 70 per cent nominal membership in organizations; participation usually runs considerably lower. Nearly all studies show a sizable proportion of the population which can be reached through organizations.

Community groups differ considerably in composition. Middle-aged and older people usually predominate. Sampling studies show that often only 10 to 30 per cent of the young-adult group (eighteen to thirty years old) belong to organized groups. Young people are busy courting, establishing homes, starting families, and gaining occupational footholds; presumably they have little time for organizational activities. While many of them have been in high-school organizations, they often lack the skills of membership and leadership for effective participation in adult

Studies of Organizational Membership and Participation

Source	Findings
A Report to the People, Morningside-Manhattanville Redevelopment, New York, 1951, p. 10.	Of all adults in this urban area, 69 per cent belong to community organizations.
W. A. Anderson, "Family Social Participation and Social Status Self-ratings," *American Sociological Review*, 11:253–258, June, 1946.	In self-ratings of 344 farm *families*, 69 per cent claimed little or no participation in leadership in community affairs; 59 per cent, little or no participation in formal organizations; and 26 per cent, little or no participation in informal social affairs.
W. A. Anderson, *Farm Families in the Grange*, Department of Rural Sociology, Cornell University Agricultural Experimentation Station Bulletin 7, March, 1943, pp. 19–29.	Per cent of 788 Cortland County and 390 Ostego County farmers and their wives belonging to organizations is reported as follows:

No. of organizations	Farmers		Farm wives	
	Cortland County	Ostego County	Cortland County	Ostego County
None	21	13	32	21
1	20	19	25	31
2	17	27	17	17
3	14	19	10	11
4	11	9	7	11
5	7	7	5	6
6	4	4	2	3
7 or more	6	2	2	
Total.....	100	100	100	100

Of the above, 17 per cent of the men and 15 per cent of the women held one or more offices.

Source	Findings
W. A. Anderson, *The Membership of Farmers in New York Organizations*, Cornell University Agricultural Experiment Station Bulletin 695, April, 1938.	Of 2,925 farmers 79 per cent belonged to one or more organizations; 66.1 per cent belonged to 1 or more organizations besides church.

Studies of Organizational Membership and Participation (*Continued*)

Source	Findings
D. G. Hay, "The Social Participation of Households in Selected Rural Communities of the Northeast," *Rural Sociology*, 15:141–148, June, 1950.	In 93.4 per cent of all *households* 1 or more members participated in some formal organization.
R. B. Hudson, *Radburn: A Plan of Living*, American Association for Adult Education, New York, 1934.	In this planned New Jersey village, where a program of activities was definitely promoted, participation of adults in "community activities" was as follows in 1931–1933:

Participated in—	Per cent	
	Men	Women
At least 1 community activity....	97.5	94.5
At least 2 community activities...	91.6	87.4
At least 3 community activities...	83.1	79.0
At least 1		
Citizenship activity...........	53.7	56.6
Religious activity.............	30.3	46.7
Educational activity...........	62.2	77.3
Recreational activity..........	90.3	77.9

	Women accounted for 54.4 per cent of all organizational participation, 51 per cent of citizenship participation, 70.8 per cent of religious participation, 78.6 per cent of educational participation, and 39 per cent of recreational participation.
Mirra Komarovsky, "A Comparative Study of Voluntary Organizations of Two Suburban Communities," *Publications of the American Sociological Society*, 27:83–93, 1932.	In an upper middle-class homogeneous residential community, 40 per cent of the adults were members of one or more organizations, while 36 per cent were organization members in a middle-class heterogeneous suburb of similar size.
C. P. Loomis and D. Davidson, "Social Agencies in the Planned Rural Communities," *Sociometry*, 2:24-42, July, 1939.	Prior to resettlement 41.5 per cent attended religious meetings each year; 30.6 per cent attended at time of survey (range: 22.8 per cent to 62.9 per cent). Before resettlement 5.3 per cent attended nonreligious meetings each year; after, 8.3 per cent. Above report based on average of 7 communities.

Studies of Organizational Membership and Participation (*Continued*)

Source	Findings
W. M. Smith, Jr., "The Social Participation of Rural Young Married Couples," Cornell University Agricultural Experimental Station Bulletin 812, July, 1944.	Of 50 married adults between ages 21 and 35, 29 were *members* of some organizations. Of all organizational connections, 39 per cent were religious. One-half of the young married people did not *participate* in any organization.
Springfield, Massachusetts, Looks at Adult Education, Springfield, Massachusetts, Adult Education Council, 1951, p. 19.	Of a sample of 380 adults in 4 census tracts, 66 per cent belonged to one or more organizations.
F. A. Stewart, *A Study of the Leadership Structure in Selected Astoria and Sunnyside Blocks,* mimeographed, 1947.	Sampling survey showed 55 per cent of the adults belonged to no organization; 25 per cent, to 1 organization; 11 per cent, to 2 organizations; and 5 per cent, to 3 or more. Unreported, 4 per cent.
Washington [State] Public Opinion Laboratory Reports, poll no. 9, March, 1949.	Of a representative sample 51 per cent belonged to "social, fraternal, civic, or church clubs." In 1948, 25 per cent attended no meetings; 17 per cent, 1 to 10 meetings; 28 per cent, 11 or more meetings. Unreported, 30 per cent.

groups. In the Springfield study of twenty-nine young adults below age twenty-five, not one held office in a community organization, and only one held a committee membership. Differences in viewpoint and social needs are barriers to the intermingling of age groups. Young people seldom feel at home in organizations of middle-aged adults, and groups of older people in turn are often unable to make younger adults feel comfortable. Full group acceptance, interpersonal ties, and skills of leadership in an organization are usually results of years of participation. Lack of young-adult participation indicates, in part, weak transition from highly organized high-school life to the organized groups of the middle-adult years. While there are explanations for this phenomenon, the fact that people often wait 10 to 15 years after finishing high school before they join community organizations is a major handicap to many phases of education.

Adults of upper socioeconomic and educational levels participate most in community organizations. The educator working with community organizations must realize that he is reaching relatively few in the lower educational and economic brackets.

The value to individuals of participating in organizations can hardly be overestimated. Participation in groups helps one to maintain personal integration and to achieve a number of basic satisfactions. Personalities often become most effective and reach their highest integration within groups. There is every reason to believe that taking part in both formally organized and informal groups contributes materially to mental health. In fact, the mental-health values alone are so great that adult schools and social agencies should aim to help as many adults as possible to establish and maintain congenial associations in a variety of groups throughout life.

In the modern world, participation in community organizations is also a social virtue. Within broad limits the more one associates with others in groups, the more likely he is to become aware of social problems and contribute to their solution. The influence of the unaffiliated person is weak, even if he wants to carry his social responsibility. Interstimulation within groups helps members keep abreast of the times. Members learn from each other. In the Springfield study group members more often voted, held library cards, and wanted to continue their education. The social isolates—those who neither belonged to nor participated in any organization—were most bigoted, ignorant, and least contributive to their culture.

The fact that a sizable proportion of adults in the typical community belong to established organizations is a highly significant fact for directors of adult education. Organizations usually claim purposes considered worthy by a number of people. The ability of organized groups to stimulate members to contribute to the solution of their problems of living depends greatly upon the quality of programs and the richness of human relationships developed. Adult education can extend its social worth mightily if it can help a wide range of organizations either to achieve their purposes better or to develop more worthwhile goals.

Educational Emphasis of Groups

Many volunteer organizations exist chiefly for educational purposes. The emphasis on education may vary greatly among local units of the same name, general type, or national affiliation. Likewise, emphasis within the same organization may change from time to time. These facts make any classification by purpose arbitrary and less useful than close study of the activities of specific groups. Nonetheless, a crude listing can be made.

Illustrative of local organizations (or national associations with local units) which often have education as a primary function are these:

American Association of University Women
Art societies

Botanical and zoological societies
Business and Professional Women's Clubs
Church-connected organizations
Civic forums
Health associations (heart, cancer, tuberculosis, polio, etc.)
League of Women Voters
Literary societies, book-review clubs, reading circles, and study clubs
Little-theater and other dramatic groups
Mothers clubs
Museums
Music clubs, community bands, orchestras, vocal groups
Parent-Teacher Associations
Professional associations
Public-affairs organizations
Religious and interfaith groups

Most organizations do not claim education as their primary purpose. They may exist primarily for fellowship, maintenance of the status quo, propaganda, recreation, self-protection, social action, social activity, social service, or some other purpose. Many of them, however, recognize education as a secondary, and sometimes as a coordinate, purpose. While the director of adult education usually spends his energy with organizations primarily concerned with education, a significant fraction of his time can well be spent in helping groups that have only a secondary interest in education and in increasing the educational interests of the marginal groups.

Some of the organizations that usually include education among their purposes are these:

American Automobile Association
Chamber of Commerce
Farm and Home Bureau
Grange
Junior Chamber of Commerce
Junior League
Labor unions
National Council of Jewish Women
Red Cross
Service clubs (Altrusa, Exchange, Kiwanis, Lions, Rotary, Zonta)
Settlement houses and neighborhood centers
Trade associations
Veterans organizations
YMCA, YMHA, YWCA, YWHA

Names of local organizations can be found in the classified section of the telephone directory and in the local city directory. Many national organizations with local units are listed in the *Handbook of Adult Education* (see General References), and in the *Service Directory of National Organizations.*[1]

Councils or federations of agencies and voluntary associations having similar purposes but different membership or clientele often provide the best entree for the director of adult education. Personal acquaintance with federation officers can open the way to educational planning with a network of similar groups. Often local units will cooperate much better if a service, program, or person has been endorsed by their central organization. Among councils which often include clusters of similar organizations are these:

Central labor council	Intercultural council
Consumers council	Interfaith council
Council of churches	Interfraternity council
Council on problems of the aging	Parent-teachers association council
Council of social agencies	Rural-life council
Family-life council	Recreation council
Farm Bureau Federation	Safety council
Federation of citizens associations	Veterans council
Film council	Welfare council
Federation of women's clubs	World-affairs council
Group-work council	Young-adult council
Health council	

The educational activities of groups may be directed toward their own members or toward the public. That is, they may exist for self-improvement or for bringing about change in others. Most organizations with educational purposes fall somewhere along an education-propaganda scale. Some organizations, believing that they already possess a part or all of the truth on a given subject, may be more interested in persuading others to accept their solutions to problems than in helping in the search for ever-better solutions.

Adult education at its best is concerned primarily with process. Groups having educational purposes, by definition, will be more interested in helping people go through educative processes than in inducing them to accept a preconceived solution. This concept is basic to education in a democracy. Propaganda seeks conformity. Democratic education asks that everyone, through the educational process, find his own workable solutions.

Opportunities for Service

Many organized groups with officers, regularly scheduled meetings, and planned programs devote considerable time to educational activities.

[1] National Social Welfare Assembly, New York, 1950.

An estimated 25 per cent of the program time of 140 organizations in Springfield, Massachusetts, was given to educational activities (see Table 28). The amount of program time ranged from 0 to nearly 100 per cent. Eighty-eight Springfield organizations with educational activities provided over 46,000 man-hours of educational activities each year. Educational activities are rarely given much time in fraternal, veterans, and recreational groups which exist primarily for other purposes. Professional societies, parent organizations, men's and women's clubs, church groups, hobby clubs, and cultural organizations, usually have much more educational activity. If sufficiently attractive educational activities were available as an alternative to business meetings, social activities, and entertainment, people might allocate more time to education. The desires for social activity and entertainment need not be slighted if educational activities are designed to satisfy those desires. Conceivably, organizations now having no educational activities could be induced to include attractive educational features in their programs.

Well over 100 public-school districts reported in 1948 that they provided program services to community organizations.[2] PTAs and other parent groups expect a great deal of assistance from the school staff. To a lesser extent, business, trade, and industrial associations; hobby and interest groups; luncheon and service clubs; public-affairs groups; and literacy societies and study clubs, in that order, also seek the help of the schools. Organizations which are not yet adequately served include veteran and patriotic associations, church groups, fraternities and lodges, labor unions, nationality and foreign-language clubs, farm organizations, and government departments.

The number of groups served depends partly upon the size of the community. A few schools in communities of 100,000 or more people serve from 100 to 500 groups a year. Work with ten to thirty organizations is more common. Probably no school yet provides services to one-half of the community organizations it has identified.

A variety of program services can be provided to organized groups. Increasingly, directors of adult education and their staffs are working out long-term cooperative programs of service to such groups. Local directors can assist organization officers with their program planning and can help discover and procure resources both within and without the community. They can provide instruction and group leadership directly. They can help develop leadership within groups. They can help plan joint educational undertakings and can make facilities and equipment available to groups. The possibilities are almost endless.

The provision of these and other services to organizations can be justified by the public school on four grounds:

[2] Homer Kempfer, *Adult Education Activities of the Public Schools: Report of a Survey, 1947–48,* U.S. Office of Education Pamphlet 107, 1949, pp. 6–7.

1. If the school is adequately supported, the public and constituent organizations have a right to expect extended educational services. Most state laws expressly, by implication, or by absence of prohibition permit a range of community services. A number of state education departments encourage such community services through financial aid, liberal regulations, provision of consultation services, and other benefits. If public sentiment favors community use of the school plant, equipment, and staff, the way is open to help the community engage in lifelong learning through organizations.

2. In all communities, except a few college and university centers, the public schools represent the largest concentration of educational competence. On the school staff presumably are the people having specialized training and experience in educational methods, techniques, instructional materials, and training aids. They, of all people in the community, should know how to help people learn with maximum efficiency. By capitalizing upon the educational competence of its staff, a school can increase that competence and can build a reputation for giving worthwhile educational assistance. Where this is not done, the school may be embarrassed by having other organizations, sometimes noneducational agencies, called upon for aid with educational projects.

3. Education can be provided to a large segment of the community at little cost for housing, promotion, and similar overhead. Most educational activities of community organizations take place in space which they provide. Likewise they furnish the groups ready-made. Little promotion is needed.

4. If the school directly and competently serves a large segment of the public, that segment will come to know the quality of the school firsthand. The general attitude toward the school will be strengthened. Long-term benefits will accrue to childhood and youth education as well as to adult education.

Principles of Service to Groups

Work with community organizations requires more imagination, versatility, and resourcefulness than is usually demanded in other evening-school work. The specific types of professional competence needed are not always found in the training or background of public-school staff members. Five principles derived from the experience of schools working with community organizations are suggested as guides to successful work:

1. *Providing Service.* The primary attitude requisite for success with organizations is that they, not the school, set the pace. The school is not in a situation to sell a standard bill of goods. Organizations must feel free to ask for any type of service for which they feel a need. Desired assistance may be in the field of recreation, entertainment, housing, health, or

social service. If the adult school cannot supply the need directly, it should help fill the request by turning to the proper resource in the community in full expectation that credit will go to the agency performing the service.

Under these circumstances an adult school may soon find that its reservoir of educational skill is not as extensive as it ought to be. It may have to expand its resources in the field of social group work, social casework, community organization, or recreation. New staff members with special competencies can be added, or the present staff can learn to operate in new ways. In providing services, that adult school is fortunate that is free to acquire staff help without regard to the rigid academic standards set up for day-school positions.

2. *Respecting the Autonomy of the Group.* Every group has a fundamental right to its own independence, its own purposes, and its own direction. Its privilege to accept or reject any proffered aid should be respected. The skilled consultant, however, can help the organization to rethink and reinterpret its purpose. The relationship between the consultant and the group or its leaders must be adult and democratic. A consultant must be skilled in winning the confidence of the group and must help its leaders maintain their security. The educator is not present to take over the group, to exercise any arbitrary control, or to persuade the group against its wishes. The only rightful approach he has is the educative one.

3. *Starting Where the Group Is.* Groups not used to educational leadership may have ideas that strike an educator as primitive. Many activities which are called educational may have little value. Such is the lecture, which is likely to be the most widely encountered and accepted educational approach in community groups. New approaches may irritate, disturb, and so upset the group tradition that the educator may not be invited back.

The services of the educator need to be adapted to the needs of each group. Needs of independent groups can never be anticipated as accurately as those of a class; they require different techniques of identification. These needs may not be obvious either to the group or to an outsider. Careful work over a period of time and considerable trained insight may be necessary to define the basic needs of a group or of the individuals composing it.

Planning must be done in cooperation with the group, at its own level of operation. An outside leader must maintain great patience, take the long view, and stay with a group long enough to obtain maximum results, even though this may take many months, if not years.

4. *Offering Education—not Propaganda.* Adult educators offering their services to community groups are occasionally expected to apply their

skills to the promotion of preconceived solutions to problems. If such situations arise, as they sometimes do, with religious, political-action, labor, management, and veterans groups, the adult educator, as a matter of ethics, should stick to education. He should insist upon free and full use of the educational process by all concerned, including the group holding the preconceived answers. The process does not allow for perversion. If the organization is not willing to search for the best answer no matter where it may be found, the adult educator should withdraw. Certainly the procedures and techniques of adult education should not be used to promulgate blind acceptance of any predetermined line of thinking.

5. *Staying in the Background.* Volunteer leaders are paid in credit, recognition, applause, and praise from their group. In working with community organizations, paid professional educators can afford to stay out of the limelight. Among the skills of an adult educator should be that of inducing others to act, to experience, to change, to lead, and to teach so as to stimulate changes in behavior.

An adult-education program operated on these principles, along the lines discussed in the following sections, will be on the road to a significant expansion. Directors who work persistently along these lines over a period of years find their programs growing in stature, influence, and favor throughout their communities.

CLEARINGHOUSE FUNCTIONS

The school adult-education office should know what adult education is going on in the community. It should be an adult-education headquarters—not a control hub, but a source of information on what is happening educationally in the community. This center should be aware of adult-education activities at two stages:

1. The planning stage. If every organization and agency would report its adult-education program proposals to the school adult-education office at an early date, the information could be shared with other community organizations upon request.

2. The materializing stage. If the same information were provided as programs materialized, any organization or any individual could turn to the central headquarters for information on available activities.

The latter practice would permit the development of an information and counseling service for all persons desiring to participate in adult-education activities. It could facilitate more widespread promotion of all activities through joint publicity.

An educational headquarters probably serves best when it provides staff services for and operates under policies developed by an adult-education council, coordinating council, or community council. Such a headquarters can collect information on educational activities, publicize it, and provide counseling for individual inquirers. This staff service frees the adult-education council for planning research on current needs and integrating the program.

If the educational exchange center, as it is sometimes called, maintains information of both types, it can help keep the total community aware of the local activities of the university extension division, the YMCA, the state college, and other agencies. Out-of-community agencies especially, to prevent embarrassment and duplication, should check with the center before developing local programs. If problems or conflicting purposes arise, the local adult-education council should be the arbiter, on the ground that coordination at the local level should be a local function.

Especially in communities under 10,000, a master central calendar should be maintained, primarily to help organizations avoid conflicting dates. Even in larger communities a master calendar usually is worth keeping, although it may have to be organized on both a city-wide and a neighborhood basis. Where the school works closely with community organizations, the adult-education office is the logical place for such a calendar.

A school working closely with community organizations will want to identify as many groups as possible within its range of interests. If the building and maintenance of a list of clubs are projects of an adult-education or community council, organizations may be more inclined to share the necessary information than if the school alone were responsible. Lists can be used for cooperative publicity and for distributing a community calendar. The controlling agency will need to set policies regarding the use of the list. A number of councils issue directories with information running to a paragraph or a page for each organization.

The minimum information desired is the name of the organization and the name, address, and telephone number of the chief officer. Additional data often collected are addresses of officers; number of members; meeting times, dates, and places; average attendance; range and median age of members; purpose of the group; types of meetings held; and nature of educational activities. This information can be kept most conveniently on Keysort cards and quickly sorted by meeting day, time of day meetings are held, age and sex of members, average attendance, purpose or type of group, and any similar item desired. With Keysort, one can, for instance, identify groups which might be interested in sharing a noted speaker during a given day or week.

In small communities names of organizations are easily listed, and compiling additional data may require merely a few telephone calls. Collecting the desired information becomes more difficult as the size of community increases. Inquiry at the headquarters of federations and councils of organizations will yield much pertinent information. Chambers of commerce, libraries, and newspapers may have and may share considerable data. Constant perusal of newspapers and inquiry among neighborhood leaders are necessary to list 80 to 90 per cent of all groups. Lists can be kept up to date by an annual inquiry to the last known officers. Such inquiries bring best results if mailed after the annual election of each group.

Resource Personnel

Every sizable community needs an office to which program planners can turn for information on available resource people. Libraries, chambers of commerce, and other agencies sometimes provide this service; more often no agency does. The information often remains scattered. There are few better places to centralize it than the adult-education office. Local directors who assemble these data find that they have invaluable information for their own use. With adequate promotion of such a list, many program directors will turn to the school for suggestions about discussion leaders, lecturers, and other experts. The list can be built up by starting with the special competencies of the school and adult staff. The staff can recommend others of special ability. Community leaders can name other competent authorities in the region. Evaluations of particular experts by organization leaders who have had experience with them are useful, especially in choosing paid speakers. The card file is of maximum value if it is cross-referenced by name of expert, type of participation preferred, and field of interest.

A related service is that of arranging for program chairmen to see and evaluate potential program resource people. If a dozen or more speakers are each invited to make 3- to 5-minute presentations of their specialties before the assembled chairmen, each leader can decide for himself whether or not any of them would suit his group. A social hour permits further acquaintance. Leaders can arrange directly for desired services. This device works best with paid speakers; competent volunteers may be reluctant to cooperate in such an exhibit of their talents.

CONSULTATION SERVICES

Probably the least time-consuming way for an adult-education staff to serve community organizations is to provide consultation services on program planning. A director of adult education or an assistant who knows the community and the resources available can often help raise the educational level of an organization's program for a whole year through an hour's conference with the planning committee. Even a few minutes with a key person may set in motion a chain of thinking that will ensure an improved program. As community leaders receive competent help by consulting with the adult-education staff, more of them will seek assistance. A few adult-education departments have built up this type of service to the point of assigning one or more staff members to consultation. In communities with well-developed services, hundreds of organization leaders seek advice every year.

Assistance on the content and procedures of projected programs is the heart of consultation service. Advice is also given on organizing meetings and conferences, gaining participation of members, organizing for action, planning publicity and promotion, selecting and briefing resource persons, and using prepared materials, mass media, and exhibits. Occasionally counsel is also given on conducting of surveys for educational purposes. Sometimes a group will want to know whether or not it should organize, how to build an effective organization, or how to resurrect an old one.

Advice is usually given by the program consultant directly to one person or to a committee in one session, although more time may be required. Often, however, referral is made to other sources of help. Most consultation is provided in the office, where information is convenient, although it is increasingly offered by field workers.

TRAINING SERVICES

An adult-education staff able to do more than offer consultation services should give high priority to the training of group leaders. A primary way to improve adult learning opportunities is through developing community leadership. Less than 5 per cent of the schools reporting in a recent survey claimed to provide training for community leadership, but the number is undoubtedly growing.[3]

A high percentage of each year's crop of organization officers is relatively inexperienced in the arts and skills of democratic leadership. Frequent turnover makes tenure too short for incumbents to benefit much from experience, unless they progress through a hierarchy of positions. Most of them may have picked up enough skill in handling a meeting to get along in a congenial group, but any serious issue challenges their parliamentary and discussion-leadership skills. For suggestions on organization and administration they often depend on manuals issued by the national or state office. They serve their terms to the best of their ability and are replaced by others of similar background. It is amazing that organizations get along as well as they do. Actually membership mortality is relatively high. In fact, inefficiency is so widespread that often only a small proportion of the members of an organization attend regularly or are active in any way. One wonders how many nonmembers of organizations are former members who dropped out because of poor leadership. Conversely, how much more could be accomplished if leaders were competent?

Few organizations either singly or in federation with others provide systematic training for their potential leaders or ensure progressive ex-

---

[3] Kempfer, *Adult Education Activities of the Public Schools*, p. 8.

perience. A continuous training need exists which is a challenge to the alert director of adult education. The skills needed cover a wide range. Some are common to all offices, and others are specialized. Officers of certain groups could benefit from parliamentary procedure.[4] Chairmen ought to know how to permit full discussion without prejudice, how to facilitate and summarize discussion, and how to conduct other parts of group meetings. More important than these may be the out-of-meeting work of organizing and administering the affairs of their groups and appointing and supervising committees. The technical offices, too, call for specific skills. Secretaries need to know efficient and accurate methods of keeping minutes and records. Treasurers need simple and accurate ways of keeping financial accounts.

Program chairmen, vice-presidents in charge of programs, and executive committee members are key people responsible for whatever educational activities the organization may have. The poverty or richness of the program comes from their planning. Consultation and observation of committee work should help reveal needs for further training. All predetermination of the needs of leaders and program planners, however, should be checked against the problems raised when the group assembles for training. In a 2-day program-planners workshop sponsored by the Adult Education Council of Denver, the following problems were discovered:

I. PLANNING PROGRAMS TO MEET INTERESTS AND NEEDS

How to: a. plan a wide range of programs for a wide range of ages and interests
b. interest people of different interests
c. get to the level of all the people in the group
d. stimulate an awareness of needs through programs and meet real needs without over-emphasizing problems
e. remedy lack of understanding of objectives of programming
f. stimulate interest to sustain program
g. overcome prejudice without offending the prejudiced
h. relate national problems to local needs
i. encourage world-mindedness and concern for more serious problems than entertainment
j. meet needs of mixed racial groups

II. WAYS TO ENCOURAGE PARTICIPATION OF MEMBERS

How to: get full participation
a. discover hidden talents of non-participants
b. deal with monopolizers
c. establish individual dependability and group responsibility

[4] For example, see F. G. Stevenson, "A Course in Parliamentary Procedure as an Approach to Leadership Training for Adults," *School and Society*, 69:315–316, Apr. 30, 1949.

    d. get the group to accept experience and how to follow through

    e. stimulate group ideas for programs and topics

    f. develop leadership training to define objectives and train leaders to have poise, confidence, inspiration, originality, personality and a sense of humor

III. MECHANICS OF PLANNING

How to: a. plan for the right people in the right place at the right time

        b. time program—music, talks, discussion

        c. assure good physical arrangements for meeting

        d. make the best use of a speaker

        e. integrate each program into a year's program

IV. MATERIALS FOR GOOD PROGRAMS

How to: a. locate materials within the budget

        b. stimulate use of library

        c. recognize need for outside sources of information

V. WAYS TO INSURE ATTENDANCE AT MEETINGS

How to: a. remedy lack of attendance

        b. cut attendance to fit program

        c. attract new people

        d. attract youth

        e. start a new group

        f. get proper publicity

VI. HOW TO OBTAIN VARIETY IN PROGRAMS

VII. HOW TO EVALUATE PROBLEMS

Various approaches can be used to help leaders improve in their roles. Some of the necessary learning can be through formal instruction. A single session may be sufficient for simpler skills. Courses in psychology and parliamentary procedure may have some value, although courses tailored more directly to club administration, the work of organization presidents, discussion leadership, and committee work usually yield greater benefits. Sometimes the adult department cooperates with the library or the adult-education council in organizing a 1- to 3-day institute for club officers or program planners. Such an institute may meet once or twice a year. Sectional meetings serve specialized interests. Intermittent instruction and practice may be necessary for the more complex tasks. In fact, a good share of the leader-training program can well consist of demonstration, observation, and supervised practice. Occasional clinics with outside experts dealing with specific problems may benefit all, with the experienced leaders gaining most.

Courses, institutes, previews, displays of material, workshops, clinics, and demonstrations for a miscellaneous assortment of organization leaders have value, but it is intensified if enough leaders in similar groups can train as a special class. At least in the elementary stages, a group of in-experienced and holdover PTA program chairmen or new farm bureau chairmen can grow most by meeting with their own kind. Problems of intercommunication will be few; the leaders will meet on common ground. Before the season starts, a few experienced leaders can project programs and promotional ideas for discussion and improvement by the rest of the group. Under a trained leader newcomers can pick up many practical ideas. If such a group can meet monthly as a leader-training group, it can mix a variety of activities with observation, demonstration, trial back home, and evaluation. Such training groups are important enough to warrant use of outside help as necessary to train in special skills and conduct special clinics. The growth possibilities are so great in training groups facing similar problems that many councils could well afford to turn most of their meetings into in-service training experiences. As leaders gain experience and maturity, participation in training meetings involving representatives from different organizations is likely to be most stimulating.

Training Discussion Leaders

Democracy depends heavily upon group discussion—the interstimulation of thought, the sharing of ideas, the weighing of suggestions on their merits, and consensus freely arrived at. The number of leaders skilled in democratic discussion processes, however, is rather limited. As a result, our democracy suffers severely. The domineering discussion leader, the leader who insists on stating his ideas first, the one who must have his way, the leader who cannot arrange for the group to discipline the persistent speaker, the leader who shows personal preferences, the leader who does not encourage the timid, the directionless leader, the leader unable to summarize or to follow any sequence of thought—all these and many more undesirable types are well known and too numerous. Volunteer leaders in civic-affairs groups, parent groups, and many other organizations often succumb to the urge to propose solutions rather than to develop the educative process as a group activity. As leaders they can think, but often they are unaware that under proper management the group as a whole can think better than any individual. Some of this tendency to do thinking for the group is deeply imbedded in our culture. Through family life, government, economic relations, and church, we have inherited sizable strains of authoritarianism from our European roots. Our opinion polls reveal that a strong, though minor, fraction of our adult population does not believe fundamentally in freedom of speech —for the other fellow. A great deal of inept leadership in discussion, however, is the result of ignorance. Many leaders would like to do better, but they do not know how.

Discussion leadership is more than a series of tricks that can be learned by observing a smooth operator. Good discussion leadership depends upon a philosophy of human relations, upon subtle skills, and—in finished form—upon years of experience. Given the desire for it, democratic discussion leadership can be taught through demonstration, directed observation, supervised practice, group analysis and self-criticism, role playing, and similar methods. Extension divisions of universities have been training discussion leaders for a generation. Modern schools are putting more emphasis on democratic discussion within the classroom than was common under the authoritarian methods of the past. As many adults need skill in democratic discussion, either as leaders or discussants, the adult-education agencies can well afford to develop programs for training in discussion.

Not all discussion has exactly the same purposes, of course. They may call for variations in training procedures. Great Books Discussion leadership, if it follows the original pattern, will emphasize the Socratic approach to thinking and discussion. The development of sensitivity to interpersonal feelings within a group is a primary aim of the group-dynamics approach. Discussion for foremen, supervisors, and business executives may aim to focus the best knowledge and thinking of the group on the problem at hand in a disciplined way. Other discussion may be designed to stimulate creative thinking—to "brainstorm" a problem.

Training Group Workers

Slightly different in some respects and quite different in others from discussion leadership is the work of scoutmasters, Sunday-school teachers, recreation leaders, camp counselors, and a whole range of workers with adult and youth groups. Every community has dozens, if not thousands, of them—either paid or volunteer. Many of these leaders are trained by their own agencies or organizations. Others, however, receive little or no training. In many cases their organizations will appreciate help from professional educators. The central organization or agency may provide the content, instructional materials, and the group, but the local unit can benefit from the instructional and planning skills of the educator. If the adult staff participates widely in community organizations, it probably has a member who is already familiar with the instructional content. This opens the way to an integrative and cooperative school-community relationship of the most desirable type.

Integrated Training through Participation

A staff that has program service as a major objective is in an excellent position to induce community organizations to incorporate the educational viewpoint into their activities. By serving on community councils and problem-solving groups, educators can train community leaders to inject educational approaches and methods at every appropriate opportunity. A great many community problems can be solved through educational means. Just as it is a physician's responsibility to relieve physical suffering, so it is the educator's responsibility to see that educational processes are used whenever they can offer benefits. Many people of different backgrounds will not readily understand the value of the educational process. Other ways may seem to be more efficient or to offer a quicker solution. It is the educator's responsibility, however, to try to gain acceptance for as much of the educational approach as is appropriate. He should explain the operation and value of his proposals as necessary.

When used in working on community problems, the educative approach will often require a maximum number of people to change their habits, skills, knowledges, and attitudes. Civil defense, for instance, is less a matter of authoritatively ordering people around than it is of developing understanding, attitudes, and skills in the total population. The adult educator, by participating in councils and on boards, should consciously help community leaders to use educational methods and to develop situations in which a maximum number of people can grow through solving their individual and group problems. A council, for example, is a major mechanism whereby a community can improve its total life through educational processes which lead to action and evaluation. A community council involving 100 people in thinking through their mutual problems is a more potent force, under the democratic philosophy, than a committee of 10 deciding an issue. The involvement of 1,000 would be still more powerful.

The Stephenson, Michigan, Community School Service Project is an example of this integrative process at work.[5] A community coordinating council was organized in 1946 with representatives of every social, civic, economic, and religious organization in the area. Committees were set up to study community problems: religious life, community services, health, home and family living, trade and industry, farm and land use, and education. Educators, by serving on these committees, were able to see that a great deal of the educational process was incorporated into the thinking of the groups. Literally hundreds of committee members learned better ways of solving community problems. Educators did not often give answers to these problems, but they helped establish processes and procedures which enabled the committee to find the best answers. This type of leadership is adult education at its best.

[5] Information taken from *Third Annual Report of the Community Coordinating Council,* Stephenson, Mich., 1949.

EXTENSION OF LEADERSHIP AND FACILITIES

A simple way of encouraging educational activities throughout the community is by extending the personnel and material resources of both the day school and the adult program directly to organizations.[6] If the idea is accepted that the school should serve the total community, the staff needs to acquire few new skills except those of working with adult groups. Staff members must believe that their work with adult groups is as important as their classroom assignments.

Direct Provision of Leadership

If the adult school has on tap the resource personnel discussed earlier, it is in a position to provide considerable direct leadership to community groups. Both subject experts and group leaders can be furnished.

Direct leadership may be provided under any of several arrangements. Initial assignment of staff members may include specified amounts of service to community groups. For instance, the new assignment of a mature homemaking teacher competent in family-life education may include work with community organizations. As the demand for service increases, additional staff members may be released from a part of their normal load to work with organizations. Such work may be in lieu of day-school extracurricular activities. Occasionally the work is voluntary, especially where the task carries considerable prestige. It may be paid for as part-time instruction and at comparable rates. Outside leaders, especially if they can be certificated for part-time work, often can be engaged to carry a part of the load.

Personnel services to community organizations sometimes may be supported as a part of the regular adult-education budget. State regulations may or may not permit meetings of community groups enrolled under school auspices to be reported for state aid. Occasionally a series of such meetings can qualify for aid if the members are registered and attend as members of a class with an organized course of study. A few other requirements concerning number and length of meetings may have to be met. Community organizations, of course, may be charged fees for personnel services.

Facilities, Equipment, and Materials

The lighted schoolhouse teeming with people at night has long been an ideal in America. However, shortage of tax funds, of professional and custodial staff, and especially of vision still keep many buildings dark. The little use to which some public-school buildings are put is poor

---

[6] The University of Minnesota provides office facilities, fiscal services, research assistance, and consultation help to several state-wide education-action organizations. See *Higher Education*, 6:200, May 1, 1950.

economy to say the least. As the tide of adult education rises, more intensive use must be made of these buildings. While the 24-hour-a-day schedule on which some vocational schools operated during World War II may not be necessary in peacetime, an afternoon and evening schedule for out-of-school youth and adults is good public economy.

Use of school buildings by outside organizations should also be encouraged. While state laws and regulations usually specify the uses to which school buildings may be put, seldom do the rules hamper any legitimate educational activity. Even where buildings are crowded in the daytime, heated and lighted building space is usually available at night for qualifying groups, on either a free or a rental basis. An alert adult-education program will promote the extensive use of the school plant among educational groups whether or not it provides any other service to them.

Only a few public-school buildings have been built primarily for adult use, although several colleges and universities have such buildings. While adult groups can use a fair proportion of space in typical high-school buildings, they often can use only a few rooms in elementary buildings. More schools are being built with flexible features which permit their adaptation to adult use.[7] Provision for adults is gradually entering into the thinking of school architects.

As daytime adult activities grow, the number of buildings exclusively for adult use will increase. Occasionally these buildings are new. More often they are remodeled elementary or high-school buildings in areas having a declining day-school enrollment. Large houses sometimes can be made suitable for adult-education activities. Rooms can usually be adapted to craft and homemaking activities, parent education, informal discussion, and academic subjects. At least one large city with an extensive adult program is considering the purchase of a number of houses scattered in residential neighborhoods to serve the demand for more daytime facilities, permit an extension of the family-life and parent-education program, and make adult education conveniently available to more people. If nursery-school children, kindergartners, and possibly first and second graders could each have a room in the same building, certain phases of the parent-education program could be integrated much more closely into the life of the school. Such an arrangement could also relieve overcrowding in many elementary schools.

Most schools have educational equipment which could be used by community groups without interfering with the program of the day school. Schools with extensive program services available to outside groups, however, often have additional equipment. Community organizations often need movie, mimeographing, or duplicating equipment; a filmstrip or slide projector; a disk, wire, or tape recorder; a record player;

[7] See articles by Edward H. Redford in *The American School Board Journal,* September and November, 1949, and January, 1950.

or some other piece of audio-visual equipment. If such items were conveniently available, the educational quality of more organizational programs would be higher. Either the community adult school or the public library is a logical provider of such equipment.

The lending of equipment for outside use requires some regulation and some insurance of proper handling. Adequate transportation must be provided. Often a trained operator must accompany the equipment. In some cases he may be a trained and reliable high-school student. If the operator is a professional educator, he can often double as a discussion leader, demonstrator, film-forum leader, or moderator.

A wealth of educational material is available for programs of community organizations. Excellent books, films, filmstrips, magazines, pamphlets, recordings, and slides are constantly being issued. In fact, there is so much from so many sources that the task of collecting, classifying, evaluating, and promoting the use of materials is larger than most local voluntary organizations can undertake even for their own purposes. In a great many communities a materials center could perform worthwhile service by keeping up with these resources. The recent Public Library Inquiry encourages libraries to become centers for mass media of communication.[8] The school, however, is also likely to have some materials, such as films. Where the library does not have an extensive collection of audio-visual materials, the adult school might want to build one. Probably the best service develops where an adult-education council or a film council faces the problem and advises on the development of the materials center for use of all organizations. It should be housed by the agency which can best provide the desired related services.

Related services include (1) facilities for distributing and promoting materials, (2) opportunities for community leaders to examine materials and preview films and filmstrips, (3) maximum office hours to receive requests, (4) provision for repair and maintenance of materials, and (5) personnel to train borrowers in the use of the material. Materials centers often compile information about instructional and study aids and distribute it by mail to officers of community organizations. Several adult schools, university extension divisions, and adult-education councils issue monthly bulletins carrying information on the new materials available, new radio and TV programs, new community resources, and suggestions for programs.[9] An annual guide to materials and program services available in the community is prepared in other adult-education offices. Brief,

[8] Robert D. Leigh, *The Public Library in the United States,* Columbia University Press, New York, 1950.
[9] Among these are *Program Notes,* University of Wisconsin Extension Division; *Tips and Topics,* Adult Education Department, Schenectady, N.Y., Public Schools; *Live and Learn,* Adult Education Council of Metropolitan Cincinnati; *Bulletin of the New York Adult Education Council; The Monitor,* Adult Education Council of Denver.

popularly written leaflets on the use of films, filmstrips, and other aids help extend materials to new users.

Several of the larger adult-education programs develop study guides, study kits, exhibits, reading courses, book lists, and demonstration materials for use by community organizations. This may be a cooperative venture of the school, the library, and possibly other interested groups working with the advice of an adult-education council. The study materials can be geared to local resources and related to other local problems. People who develop them often can be leaders in their use or can serve as resource people. A primary advantage is that they can be prepared quickly and be used while still timely. Often materials from national headquarters are not available until a problem is acute or half solved. Likewise, local issues and problems can be set up for study, whereas discussion guides from outside the community usually deal only with broader concerns.

Community-center Activities

Adult-education programs of schools, community centers, and settlement houses have much in common. Objectives often coincide although methods may differ at times. Nonetheless, it is incumbent upon the director of adult education and the executives of community centers and settlements to work out mutually satisfactory relationships. If the center or settlement has insufficient staff to do all it would like, maybe the adult program can provide certain instructors and group leaders. Equipment and materials can be loaned. Certain projects and programs can be operated jointly with shared leadership.

COSPONSORSHIP

As concepts of adult education have broadened beyond the evening school, a number of patterns of working with and in the community have evolved. More school-sponsored adult activities are carried on outside the school walls. More staff is drawn from outside regular school personnel. More effective educational approaches are being used, and new ways of working together toward common ends have emerged. The advisory committee, the adult-education council, and the community council are examples of these new developments.

Cosponsorship is a simple and yet flexible method of collaboration which, although not new, is growing in popularity. In such a cooperative arrangement two or more educational agencies or organizations assume responsibility for separate parts of an educational activity. Instead of working independently, organizations having similar objectives join forces to do a more effective job, to reach more people, or to save energy. For example, both the adult school and the League of Women Voters may be interested in setting up a public-affairs discussion program. They may decide to supplement each other by cosponsoring discussion groups in which the league might furnish neighborhood locations, publicity, and study material; and the school might furnish discussion leaders, resource personnel, supplementary materials, and audio-visual equipment.

For maximum success each organization should (1) do what it can best do, (2) clearly understand what the other is going to do, and (3) understand the operating policies in regard to publicity about sponsorship, study versus action, and credit. Voluntary organizations can often contribute interested groups, study materials, and a certain amount of leadership. The adult school can furnish leaders or help train them. It can provide equipment and educational techniques that will enrich the whole enterprise. In simple arrangements publicity can show a joint sponsorship. Usually there can be enough credit to satisfy everyone. The voluntary organization can count the enterprise as one of its activities, and sometimes the school can count the activity as its own. A clear understanding of relationships is the key to harmony in cosponsorship.

Most cosponsorship agreements involve two organizations. The plan can work in any field in which community groups are interested. Cosponsorship may be arranged by departments of government; by educational agencies, such as the library and the school; by an institution and a voluntary group; or by lay groups. For instance, the health department and the schools may cooperate in a health-education program. A public-affairs group and the Foreign Policy Association may join forces in a project designed largely for the public at large.

Frequently more than two organizations join together in an educational enterprise, thereby creating multiple sponsorship. In one community the hotel- and restaurant-owners association and the labor union jointly encouraged attendance of their workers in a food-sanitation course, the city and state health departments furnished the instructional materials and the course of study, the school provided the instructional personnel, and the city council provided the certificates of completion. A high percentage of the food-trade workers went through the short course. If the school alone had publicized the course, very few would have enrolled. In another community the safety council, the police department, the local university, and the schools cooperated in a community-wide traffic-safety campaign. In still another community approximately eighty organizations participated in planning a driver-training program, and a number of them contributed directly to its success. Occasional multiple sponsorship involves more than 100 organizations. Such wide involvement, if more than nominal, ensures the success of the enterprise. Community-wide discussion programs, family-life education activities, Citizenship Day celebrations, new-voter preparation schemes, intercultural festivals, community-council projects, civil-defense drills, forums, health and safety campaigns, fire-prevention drives, and literacy campaigns are examples of educational activities in which multiple sponsorship can be profitable.

While cosponsorship has existed in some form for many years, it has spread considerably in recent years. In general, adult departments in big city schools are more likely to engage in cosponsorship than are departments in smaller places. Of 369 schools reporting cosponsored activities, the percentages cosponsoring with various types of organizations were as follows:

Types of institutions or organizations with which schools cosponsored activities	Per cent * of schools giving assistance
Business and industry	36.9
Labor unions	29.3
Parent-teachers associations	23.8
Colleges and universities	14.4
Welfare agencies	14.4
Public recreation departments	13.0
Public libraries	9.5
Luncheon (civic) clubs	7.9
Other organizations and community groups	5.7
Fraternal societies	4.6
Museums	1.9
Other institutions (farm bureau, VA, YMCA, etc.).	3.8

* Percentages add to more than 100 because some schools cosponsored several activities with several different organizations.

SOURCE: Data are from pages 48–49 of the NEA study listed in the General References.

SCHOOL-SPONSORED ORGANIZATIONS FOR ADULTS

The educational values of clubs have long been recognized in elementary schools, high schools, and colleges. In a study in 1948, however, only 6 per cent of all public-school districts reporting adult education claimed to have school-sponsored adult clubs.[10] Many voluntary organizations start through the stimulation and assistance of parent institutions, such as churches and social agencies. Since the habit of voluntary association is a deep-rooted characteristic of our people, it is entirely in order for the adult-education program to encourage the formation of clubs having educational purposes and activities. In fact, in a highly industrialized and urban civilization where neighbors may seldom know each other, the adult school can contribute to social integration by facilitating the formation of such groups.

Studies of reasons for attending adult-education activities often show that a desire for congenial companionship is an important motive. While many voluntary groups already exist, membership in them is often closed to outsiders. They are not always adept at recruiting new members. Potential members likewise are often unskilled in finding their ways into congenial groups. Often would-be members are unacquainted with

[10] Kempfer, *Adult Education Activities of the Public Schools*, p. 8.

groups into which they might well fit. Still others have not had their interest sufficiently aroused to realize the benefits of belonging to organized groups.

To facilitate social integration, to encourage personal growth, to contribute to mental health, and for a variety of other similar reasons, adult schools should accept as a prime responsibility the encouragement of people to associate in groups. Many adults belonging to only one or two organizations can be persuaded to join more. Those who have no group associations can be helped to join and participate. In a highly fragmented society the reintegration of the individual into the total group is a function of growing importance. If civilization is a function of numbers of human contacts, as certain sociologists claim, then adult education should seek to multiply the number of civilizing associations. Sponsorship, promotion, and support of organized groups are important ways of accomplishing this objective.

Two population groups which educational programs have special opportunity for serving through clubs are young adults and people past middle life.

Young Adult Groups and Councils

Two to two and one-half million young people leave full-time school each year. For the most part they drop from a well-organized environment having numerous school clubs and classes into an organizational vacuum. The YMCAs, YWCAs, 4-H clubs, certain church and lodge groups, a handful of "junior" organizations, and a few others include only a small percentage of the total young-adult population. Yet, as pointed out in an earlier chapter, during the young-adult years people have more need for functional learning than at any other period in life.

Young people respond enthusiastically to suitable educational approaches. They constitute the biggest single age group in day and evening classes for adults. Their interest in learning and their need for it are so great that sizable numbers seek out organized educational opportunities. They fill vocational classes to prepare for and upgrade themselves in occupations. On a part-time basis, they complete high-school, junior-college, and college requirements. Short courses with specific objectives in preparation for marriage, family living, homemaking skills for the newly married, home buying, home management, and hobbies also attract. Significant numbers, however, must be involved through informal and noninstitutional approaches if they are to be brought within the influence of the adult-education program.

In working with young adults, the educators who have had most success with informal approaches have operated on a different set of principles from those used in traditional evening schools. Young-adult councils, which have been most highly developed in New York State, provide a good example. In this approach no attempt is made to involve young people in classes. Instead, the school, through its young-adult counselor, encourages the young-adult group to form and to establish its own direction. Usually the council begins as a small group. Members may or may not have connections with other organizations. As they begin to assess their interests and define the needs of young people, the group grows.

Often these young men and women feel a need for better recreation which may call for new programs and more suitable facilities. They set about solving the problem. They also face and work on other needs as they arise. Interest groups may begin working in such separate fields as dramatics, music, public affairs, and family living; they may want to establish community forums or any other activity which they think they themselves need or the community should have. This thinking often develops into projects. In one community the young-adult council assumed leadership in developing a coordinated program of guidance services for returning veterans and other adults. Another council brought new industry into a rural village. In several communities these councils have been instrumental in bringing about changes in local government. In one case the young adults organized a campaign and elected a new village council. Starting with their own interests, they eventually work on projects of value to the whole community.

Freedom to write their own ticket is the key characteristic of successful young-adult groups. Nothing is imposed from the school. The counselor does not direct young-adult activities. He is an adviser—an older brother —one who helps the young adults accomplish the goals they set. He and an advisory council help the young adults maintain liaison with older members of the community and help community groups incorporate young adults and young leadership into their organizations.

In its early stages the council may be largely an operating group; in small places it may remain so. Where many activities develop, it is likely to focus more on coordination and over-all planning. Ideally, it will be concerned with encouraging the several young-adult organizations to extend their programs and membership. It will facilitate activities which appeal to the great majority of young people. There is danger, of course, in developing young-adult activities separate from those involving the rest of the community. With proper consulting leadership, adequate articulation with both full-time schools and older-adult groups can be developed, while special energy can begin to fill a nearly empty field with activities organized by young-adults.

While a young-adult council may start with a specific project and then become involved in a number of others, its approach is essentially an integrated one. That is, it meets several of the needs of young people— the need for associating together informally while working on common problems, the need to develop leadership and group-participation skills, the need for group recreation, and the need for growth in citizenship. Some of these needs may not be put into words. A direct approach to serving them would not attract many young people. They are by-products of situations in which young people establish their own curriculum. In the task of finding a satisfactory mate, council activities supplement the more fortuitous associations of informal and autonomous groups. Students in a coeducational college may enjoy several years of extensive opportunity for meeting other young people of both sexes. Stay-at-homes often continue associations formed chiefly in high school. A well-developed program of young-adult activities can provide extensive and systematic opportunity to meet others under favorable conditions.

Leadership skills, too, may deteriorate after high-school days. Development of leadership in young people may cease as they leave full-time school. They often feel unable to tie into adult groups and find that their former groups have disintegrated. An alert adult-education director can help high-school associations to continue by offering them leadership, sympathetic consultation, and facilities. Schools which provide a smooth transition from high school into adult life are most likely to find their services sought whenever learning at later stages is needed.

The basic operating principles of young-adult councils are not new. They have been applied for generations by a number of social agencies. They offer the public schools a way of involving many more young people in educational activities than are likely to come into a formal program. The education they receive will be closely integrated with life. Its content will be determined largely by the learner. While the pattern and results may not fit the academic mold, a good many young people will be maintaining social integration during a period when many of them would otherwise begin to lose contact with organized groups.

Councils and Clubs for Senior Citizens

Progress in health sciences and health education has caused a dramatic growth in the number and percentage of older adults in our population. Relative to the rest of the population the number over sixty-five increased 88 per cent between 1900 and 1950.[11] Many complex social, political, economic, and personal problems accompanied this population shift. Powerful social forces are at work creating problems and issues which must be solved. Some of them may be posed as questions:

1. With improved vigor and longevity in our people, what changes will be made in the retirement age and retirement practices?

2. Will criteria other than chronological age be developed as a basis for retirement? What are they?

[11] *Forecasts of the Population of the United States, 1945–75*, U.S. Bureau of the Census, Mar. 15, 1948.

3. How much of the social-security load will the working force carry? Will the years of productivity be lengthened?

4. What contribution will women past the child-rearing ages be expected to make to our economy?

5. What is the best use that can be made of the potential contributions of older people to our common life?

Whatever answers may be determined by research and by re-formation of public policy, three educational tasks present themselves: (1) to change the attitude of our total population toward older people, their status, and their roles; (2) to develop appropriate expectations and behavior in all aging persons; and (3) to retrain older persons for social usefulness in line with their changing capabilities.

What are the problems in regard to the developmental tasks of aging people? Problems of changing family relationship, of community status, of financial security, of health, of unemployment, of rehabilitation, of housing and living arangements, of leisure activities, and of religious feeling are among the major ones. Education has an important role to play in helping people solve these problems, in helping them make the necessary adjustments. At this stage, authoritative instruction is absurd. Old people themselves must solve their problems. Only they can work through the educative process to arrive at the necessary changes.

Many community agencies besides the schools, however, have resources to offer. Health and recreation departments, libraries, employment and rehabilitation offices, welfare and family-service agencies, housing groups, churches, nursing services, convalescent homes, homes for the aged, and a range of other community agencies have services for the aging. While the adult-education program has a great deal to offer, one of its roles is that of providing the educational ingredient in the activities of other social agencies.

Possibly the most important role of the school, which it shares with a few other agencies, is to stimulate the formation of groups and councils of aging people who are concerned about their own problems. The assignment of a sympathetic counselor to work with groups of older residents is probably the best first step. Without imposing a program, such a counselor can advise, help discover resources, interpret the needs and potential to the school, and help set up educational activities desired by the older people. The counselor is a "friend in court" who opens channels of communication to all agencies and programs having educational services to offer. Golden-age clubs and other groups of older people can turn to such a counselor for help in approaching their problems through the educational process.

Ways of Working with Clubs

School-sponsored organizations start in two primary ways. First, the school may take the initiative in forming a club. This can come about through various approaches:

1. The teacher or leader of an adult group may purposely mold the original assortment of strangers in a class into a congenial group. On occasion he may plant an idea of continuing the group beyond the scheduled closing date or he may encourage such an idea if suggested by someone else. If bonds among group members have grown strong enough, the group may organize into a permanent club. This is most likely to happen with discussion groups, foreign-born groups studying English and citizenship, vocal music classes, language-study groups, and groups which have had a unique experience or have enjoyed an unusual teacher.

2. A staff member may go into a community deliberately to organize a group of people who face the same developmental task. Brides to be, new homemakers, overseas brides, new homeowners, mothers of kindergartners or first graders, parent-education groups, young farmers, and music clubs are examples of groups having common interests which might be melted into a school-sponsored club.

3. Community groups can be developed from high-school organizations and interests. Members of high-school clubs can continue meeting after graduation. They can set their own policies about taking in other age groups.

4. Special young-adult interest groups may provide clubs into which dropouts or graduates can move. High-school band members can transfer into a young-adult band and eventually into the regular community band. Interest can easily be carried over from high-school choral groups, science clubs, language classes, athletic teams, hobby groups, and dramatic clubs into the out-of-school years. The age range can be several years or as long as members want to stay. To smooth transition, some out-of-school groups take in high-school seniors.

5. Especially in smaller communities high-school alumni can be induced to return periodically for a combination of educational and social activities. These alumni-education programs can consist, in part, of film discussions, forums, discussions of new developments affecting the school, and explanations of new educational opportunities. A counselor should see that such groups are not turned into alumni fund raisers.

School sponsorship may also result when previously formed groups, on their own initiative or by invitation, seek some form of affiliation. Occasionally, a group will want to enroll as a unit in some educational activity, or it may request other professional help—continuing consultation service, use of facilities, or training services.

It is always wise for the school and the club to understand their relationship clearly, even though it may be a changing one. Ordinarily, a school-sponsored club has a closer relationship to an educational program than is occasioned merely by the club's use of a school building or equipment. Often the only school leadership desired by the club is instruction on specific phases of a project. A staff member—maybe the original teacher of the group—may meet regularly with the club and, perhaps, also with a planning or executive committee. In fact, program planning and assistance in procuring resources are usually the chief services performed by the school.

Control of membership must be clear. Some groups are tightly knit units and are careful about accepting newcomers; others welcome anyone. Some public schools will not serve closed groups. In such cases, school-sponsored clubs must remain open to all possessing the desired qualifications or having the necessary prerequisites.

The degree to which the club is willing to be treated as a class may determine whether or not state aid can be claimed. Often, however, certain portions of the meeting time can be scheduled to fit school regulations, while other time can be devoted to club activities with regular officers in charge.

Groups vary widely in viability and vitality. Some die after a few meetings, even when they have had competent professional help. Others last for years and often grow stronger. Death, departure of members, the coming of families, and change of occupation contribute to group mortality. Unless groups have strong internal cohesion, they may disintegrate when a leader or consultant drops out. If a group starts from one class, sometimes it is difficult for its members to integrate with the next class, even though both were taught by the same teacher. In such cases, it is sometimes better to form a succession of groups and encourage them to federate loosely. As associated groups they can share joint activities, such as forums, lectures, panels, large social activities, holiday observances, and similar mass activities.

The educator sometimes may be troubled by the lack of serious educational interest in clubs. He must not expect the same standards as exist in a class. A class that has met weekly may want to meet only monthly as a club. A portion of the time may be devoted to business meetings, recreation, entertainment, and social activity, as is true in other clubs. In short, standards should be those applied to a voluntary organization and not those applicable to a class. This, however, should not deter the educator from injecting as much educational experience into the schedule as possible.

EVALUATION

The extent of program services is measured by such yardsticks as the number of programs improved, the number of organizations helped, the number of leaders trained, and the number of people ultimately affected. All of these should be compared with the total size of the job to be done.

Quality indexes, of course, though more difficult to devise and apply, are truer measures of worth. At present most indexes of effectiveness are very subjective and impressionistic. Rating scales and observation by teams of qualified outsiders are not very refined ways of assessing the stage of leadership development, but few better and widely applicable ways have been devised. Ability of leaders to handle meetings, effectiveness in human-relations skills, competence in parliamentary procedure, the educational emphasis in programs, the availability and use of materials, the use of supplementary learning aids, the use of educational rather than propaganda methods, and the competence displayed in discussion meetings are elements to be observed. If a base line is determined, program services are provided, and a later assessment is taken, maybe some evidence of growth can be gathered.

SELECTED REFERENCES

Annals of the American Academy of Political and Social Science, special issue on Social Contribution by the Aging, vol. 279, January, 1952.

Biddle, William W.: *The Cultivation of Community Leaders,* Harper & Brothers, New York, 1953.

Bradford, L. P., and S. M. Corey: "Improving Large Group Meetings," *Adult Education,* 1:122–138, April, 1951.

Colcord, J. C.: *Your Community,* Russell Sage Foundation, New York, 1947.

Donahue, W. T.: "Experiments in the Education of Older Adults," *Adult Education,* 2:49–59, December, 1951.

"The Dynamics of Work Groups," *Adult Leadership,* 2:8–28, December, 1953.

Essert, Paul L., et al.: "Preparation for a Constructive Approach to Later Maturity," *Teachers College Record,* 53:70–76, November, 1951.

Hunter, Floyd: *The Community Power Structure,* The University of North Carolina Press, Chapel Hill, N.C., 1953.

Iowa State Department of Public Instruction: *Educational Needs: Iowa's Young Adults,* Des Moines, Iowa, 1951.

Kempfer, Homer: *Education for a Long and Useful Life,* U.S. Office of Education Bulletin 1950, no. 6.

————: *Selected Approaches to Adult Education,* U.S. Office of Education Bulletin 1950, no. 16.

Man and His Years: An Account of the First National Conference on Aging, sponsored by the Federal Security Agency, Health Publications Institute, Inc., Raleigh, N.C., 1951.

New York State Joint Legislative Committee on Problems of the Aging, Legislative Documents: *Birthdays Don't Count,* no. 61 (1948); *Young at Any Age,* no. 12 (1950); *No Time to Grow Old,* no. 12 (1951); *Age Is No Barrier,* no. 35 (1952).

Olsen, E. G.: *School and Community Programs,* Prentice-Hall, Inc., New York, 1949.

Parsons, Harriet: *Where and Why? A Study of the Distribution of Program Materials,* Canadian Association for Adult Education, Toronto, October, 1952.

"Personal Growth through Group Experience," *Adult Leadership,* 2:11–26, February, 1954.

Rich, Kathryn: "In Adult Education, It's Mass Media Tools," *School Executive,* 73:82–83, September, 1953.

See also General References: [12] Beals and Brody, pp. 228–232; Division of Adult Education Service, chaps. 9, 16, 18; Ely, pp. 133–142; Essert, chap. 5; Knowles, chaps. 6, 7; Sheats, Jayne, and Spence, chap 8.

[12] The General References are listed in full at the end of this book.

CHAPTER 9 *Working with Unorganized*
Autonomous Groups

If an adult school were to provide services to all formally organized groups expressing an interest in education, roughly one-half of the adults in the typical community would be reached. The other half would be unaffected because they ordinarily do not participate in groups having officers and regular programs which provide systematic stimulation to learning. Their stimulation to learning comes largely from coworkers, at the store or church, over the back fence or on the front porch, from the corner bar, from family members, and from the radio, the press, movies, and television. Most adult programs, including those aiming at organized groups, are ineffective in reaching this other half of the population. An educator seriously interested in helping all adults learn throughout life must look to sociology and anthropology for leads on approaches to people whose motivations drive them neither to conventional classes nor into organized groups.

As seen in Chapter 8, studies of membership and participation in community organization show that the size of the unorganized segment varies widely from place to place. In a very few communities practically all adults are members of organized groups. In Radburn, New Jersey, nearly 96 per cent of all adults participated in community activities.[1] This, however, was a model-village housing development in which special encouragement was given to organized activities. In isolated rural and village areas, organizational membership may run as low as 10 or 20 per cent, exclusive of church membership but inclusive of church-connected groups. While participation in organized groups varies widely, a sizable portion of any community remains outside of all but the most informal of groups.

Groups differ in the degree to which they are formally organized. Some, like lodges and patriotic associations, have many officers, minutely assigned responsibilities and relationships, definite committee structures, formal routines, and regular meeting times and places. Others, such as certain literary societies, mothers clubs, women's clubs, hobby and in-

[1] R. B. Hudson, *Radburn: A Plan of Living*, American Association for Adult Education, New York, 1943.

terest groups, and study groups, may have fewer officers or only one leader. Many others have no formal program or officers except leaders who emerge and are recognized because of their natural ability. Groups

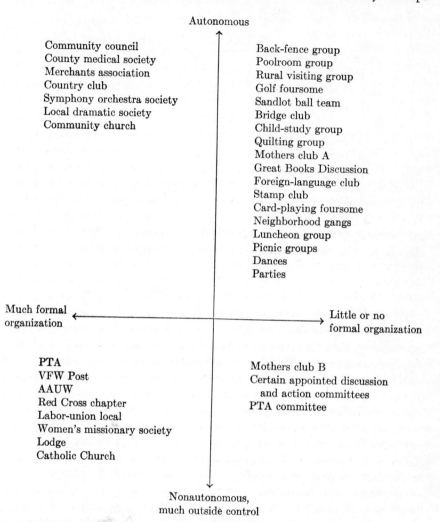

Autonomous

Community council
County medical society
Merchants association
Country club
Symphony orchestra society
Local dramatic society
Community church

Back-fence group
Poolroom group
Rural visiting group
Golf foursome
Sandlot ball team
Bridge club
Child-study group
Quilting group
Mothers club A
Great Books Discussion
Foreign-language club
Stamp club
Card-playing foursome
Neighborhood gangs
Luncheon group
Picnic groups
Dances
Parties

Much formal
organization ←   → Little or no
formal organization

PTA
VFW Post
AAUW
Red Cross chapter
Labor-union local
Women's missionary society
Lodge
Catholic Church

Mothers club B
Certain appointed discussion
    and action committees
PTA committee

Nonautonomous,
much outside control

Fig. 8. Relationship between degree of organization and autonomy of various groups.

can be arranged along a scale of formal organization from the highly organized to the unorganized. The position of a group on that scale may change from time to time, moving upward or downward, although growing groups usually tend to move toward more complex organization.

Groups also differ widely in their degree of autonomy. By definition, an autonomous group is independent and self-governing with no outside allegiance or relationship. An American Legion Post, a Knights of Columbus unit, a labor local, an affiliated PTA, and an Elks Lodge are not autonomous groups. A Great Books Discussion group may be relatively autonomous and self-directing, although a locally formed book-discussion group is likely to be more so. An independent block-mothers club or a local association of professional workers may be completely autonomous. Such groups usually begin to lose their autonomy as they affiliate and strengthen their relationships with other similar groups. Autonomous groups may be formally organized to achieve announced purposes, although a great many more are held together only by the personal attraction of their members.

The degree of formal organization and the degree of autonomy are separate variables, although they tend to be related. That is, a great many organized groups are nonautonomous while simple and informally organized groups tend to be autonomous. A few sample groups are roughly classified in regard to each scale in Figure 8. Few groups can claim to be in the lower right corner—low in both organization and autonomy. While it is not strictly in accord with the dictionary definition, the term *autonomous groups* is widely applied to groups which fall primarily in the upper right quadrant of Figure 8.[2] This chapter is concerned with such groups.

NATURE AND IMPORTANCE OF AUTONOMOUS GROUPS

People can be classified in two basic ways. For generations sociologists have devoted much time to studying people classified by categories, and grouping by categories—often with a single characteristic as the criterion—is the common way. People are Democrats, laborers, civil servants, parents, foreign-born, Negroes, Methodists, white, Anglo-Saxon, Gentiles, veterans, women. With the exception of the common characteristic, the spread of individual differences within any category is usually as great as among the whole population. On most matters, aside from those directly involving the attribute they share, members of such groups may feel little or no desire to work together or associate in common enterprise.

The other way of classifying people is by their natural groupings. Common observation throughout history has revealed that people associate together according to their liking for one another. The basic nuclear units of social organization are the small, informal, intimate, face-to-face groups which form spontaneously in response to personal affinities. The family, which in our culture usually starts with two people having a very close affinity, is one type of natural group, but many other less institutionalized groups exist which are not the result of blood kinship. Sociolo-

---

[2] An *autonomous group* is "the web of relationships binding a number of individuals in an intimate group whose members are spontaneously attracted to each other, in which aims and interests are congenial and the group is free to carry on out of motivations intrinsic to the interaction between members." From an annual program announcement of the Committee on Autonomous Groups.

gists have long studied the family, but until recent decades they have given little attention to the nonkinship natural groups.

As far back as 40 years ago, a few sociologists began pointing out the importance of these primary face-to-face groups in providing the psychological environment out of which the ideas, attitudes, opinions, and social natures of individuals grow.[3] In a common-sense way, of course, their importance in forming individual personality has been recognized from time immemorial. Their importance in the structure and functioning of organized social life, however, has not always been clearly understood, although politicians, able administrators, truly effective teachers, and many other leaders who deal successfully with people have a practical understanding of the operation of natural groups. Certainly, successful social organization is based upon the facts of natural groupings and natural affinities between people. In fact, the degree to which any human enterprise is successful depends very largely upon the degree to which the expected cooperation can be based upon natural groupings.

Characteristics

Exactly why one person feels spontaneous affinity toward another, is neutral toward a second, and is repulsed by a third is not too well understood. The spontaneous attraction-repulsion pattern around an individual constitutes a social atom which, when social science has discovered as much about it as is known about the physical atom, will probably have effects as far-reaching as the release of atomic energy. Interlocking social atoms constitute a network. Pairs, triangles, chains, and stars are common network patterns, whereas isolates are attracted to no one. Feeling projected through the network is the *tele*.[4]

A natural group forms because members like one another. Pleasure in meeting together is their prime motivation. Congeniality among acquaintances is the dominant attraction and cohesive force. Educators of adults must become accustomed to this primary fact because they are usually most familiar with groups which form because the activity is the center of interest. In the latter type of group, individuals are seldom acquainted with the others in the beginning. Spontaneous attraction usually causes natural groups to form within the activity group, although usually little use is made of them.

A very high percentage of all people belong to autonomous groups. Only hermits and a few other psychological deviates seem to get along with a minimum of human contact. They apparently are unable or unwilling to maintain the necessary psychological interaction with others.

Many natural groups are long-lived. Occasionally groups last from the

[3] C. H. Cooley, *Social Organization*, Charles Scribner's Sons, New York, 1912.
[4] J. G. Franz, "Survey of Sociometric Techniques," *Sociometry*, 2:76–92, October, 1939.

childhood to the death of their members, although lasting groups are more often formed during adolescence or later. They can form at any age above infancy. Many groups begin to form the instant two people meet, on almost a love-at-first-sight basis, although circumstances prevent the great majority of personal attractions from developing into social atoms. While individuals vary widely in their potentialities for attraction, there may be definite limits beyond which any individual cannot multiply effective natural-group relationships.

Other groups form more slowly. The internal loyalty of members to one another and to the group as a whole depends upon such factors as the length of life of the group, the closeness of association, and the amount of common activity. Members of natural groups are highly interested in one another's activities and in the activities of the group. On the whole, loyalty of members is much higher than among groups initially formed on the basis of activity. Seldom are other activities permitted to interfere with attendance at group meetings.

Functions

In natural groups of long standing the members get to know one another extremely well. Timidity is overcome, and security of response is achieved. One belongs. Members develop intercommunication to a point where a deep understanding of one another's opinions, personalities, points of view, prejudices, and personal strengths and weaknesses is achieved. Indeed, it is in such understanding that growth and development of personality take place. Likewise, from a psychiatric point of view, it is largely in such groups that mental balance is maintained. Kinship and nonkinship natural groups can satisfy practically all the need for affection, much of the need for response and recognition, and some of the need for adventure and innovation. Persons who are continuously rejected and never become members of socially acceptable natural groups are the outcasts, the delinquents, and the misfits of society.

The influence of these primary groups on both the formation and maintenance of personality can hardly be overestimated. The heaviest influence during the early formative years comes from the interpersonal relationships of the family. The early influence of play groups grows rapidly. During late childhood the influence of contemporary age-mates begins to equal that of the family. During adolescence and throughout adult life the interpersonal relationships in intimate groups of peers essentially determine the degree of social adjustment of the individual. The social structure in free societies is based very largely upon the family and the nonkinship groups.

Social organization, too, has its roots deep in natural groups. There is mounting evidence to show that natural groups are more important in the formation of public opinion and in the development of community attitudes than are all the mass media combined. The shrewdness, basic attitudes, and outlook of people gained and anchored in their personal relationships are so stable that all the winds of propaganda change human behavior only slightly, even with great effort.

Dangers and Opportunities

The social stability inherent in long-enduring natural groups carries with it a danger. As pointed out in Chapter 1, the development of science and technology makes it highly desirable that whole cultures learn fast— that they make numerous and great changes in their behavior and thought. In a politically unstable world this need for rapid learning becomes imperative. Whenever natural groups hold onto institutional traditions that have long ceased to serve a functional purpose or that are in direct conflict with deeper values, changes through learning should take place. To overcome the tendency to stagnate, both cultures and natural groups within them need to acquire a tradition of change and to develop an expectancy of change and a pride in their ability to change. Alert natural groups can provide a basic security and social milieu out of which innovations and change can come. Natural groups should encourage deviation and development of new ideas stimulated by gifted persons even at the risk of loss of members and disintegration of the groups themselves.

The tendency toward stability in natural groups challenges the professional skill of educators. Many of the methods and approaches developed in formal education have relatively little effect in changing the attitudes, beliefs, and basic behavior of people. As American education developed, it became concerned largely with methods of helping people acquire skills and knowledge of a limited sort. Reading, writing, rote-learned knowledge, and vocational skills can be taught by systematic instruction in formal classes. Usually, however, the instructor in day schools is outside the peer group and can effect only limited changes in the group's culture—its deep-seated behavior patterns, beliefs, ideals, and attitudes. The same limitation applies to adult groups in so far as the traditional teacher-pupil relationship is maintained. Educators who would maximally affect the behavior and beliefs of adults need to develop ways of working with autonomous groups and serving them. But first, such groups must be recognized.

Identification of Autonomous Groups and Leaders

Names, officers, meeting places, and activity schedules of organized groups can be assembled through inquiry. Sometimes a school or other community agency will attempt to keep an up-to-date list of organizations for its own use. Identification of natural groups, however, requires different approaches. Some of the simpler ones can be used by anyone; others are more difficult.

Proximity of residence, work, or play; association in organized groups; ease of meeting; common background; and similarity of age and interests all facilitate the formation of natural groups. One expects to find groups which have formed under these circumstances.

Family visiting patterns reveal the coteries in village and rural areas. Borrowing of equipment and exchange-of-work patterns at harvest, threshing, butchering, and silo-filling times show them, as do marketing and buying trips. Play association of children and family grouping for recreation—hunting, fishing, horseback riding, and ball games—reveal others. Rural ministers, teachers, county nurses and extension agents, local politicians, bookmobile drivers, farm-club leaders, and officers of other formal groups often are aware of natural groups and can identify their members and leaders. Inquiry of these key people is a way of identifying groups which can be reached through contact with one member and learning of the activities shared by these groups.[5] Friendship ties in a community are usually weakest and fewest among newly married couples, among families with few or no children, and among newcomers.[6] This generally is true in both rural and urban areas.

Identification of natural groups in cities requires more systematic effort. Some visiting patterns, especially in neighborhoods of low economic level, are obvious, but many others are not. Friends may be scattered. Direct inquiry of a person may be necessary to discover who his most intimate associates are and the type of activity they share. Close observation, however, can reveal many natural groupings. Natural groups can be identified where leisure time is spent—street corners, bars, drugstores, parks, playgrounds and gymnasiums, club rooms, social settlement houses, front porches, backyards, and other loafing places. Librarians may be aware of autonomous groups through reading interests. Social workers know some of them, especially those connected with group-work agencies. As many natural groups originate from associations within formal organizations and carry on both inside and outside of these groups, leaders of organizations can usually identify a number of coteries. In-

---

[5] For examples of systematic study in village and rural communities, see these articles in *Sociometry:* C. P. Loomis, "Informal Grouping in a Spanish-American Village," 4:36–51, February, 1941; C. P. Loomis, "Informal Social Participation in the Planned Rural Communities," 2:1–37, October, 1939; C. P. Loomis and D. Davidson, "Sociometrics and the Study of New Rural Communities," 2:56–76, January, 1939; G. A. Lundberg and M. Steele, "Some Attraction Patterns in a Village," 1:375–419, January–April, 1938; H. F. Infield, "A Veterans' Cooperative Land Settlement and Its Sociometric Structure," 10:50–70, February, 1947; and H. F. Kaufman, "Defining Prestige Rank in a Rural Community," 8:199–207, May, 1945.

[6] A. P. Hare and R. T. Hare, "Family Friendship within the Community," *Sociometry,* 11:329–334, November, 1948.

sight into the social stratification of the community simplifies understanding the composition of natural groups.[7]

The most systematic ways of identifying affinities among people, and thus their natural groupings, have come from the sociometrists. While sociometric techniques can be most easily used in a classroom, a fraternity, or other closely associated face-to-face group, some of them have application to neighborhoods and communities.

The sociometric test and the spontaneity test are the two techniques most useful in identifying social atoms and other interpersonal relationships. In a sociometric test each person selects or rejects other members of a group according to a specific criterion. Questions such as these are usually asked: "With whom would you like to exchange work?" "Who are your best friends in the neighborhood?" "Whom do you wish to have as a neighbor?" "Whom would you like to have on your committee?"

Questions are most meaningful if the choices made can be granted. Repulsion patterns are discovered by asking with whom the respondent would rather not work, neighbor, play, or associate. Usually three choices are requested. When results are plotted as a sociogram, they show visually the pattern of attraction-repulsion relationships which may be used as a basis for sociometric assignment or spontaneity training.[8] *Sociometric assignment* is the practice of assigning people to groups according to their attractions and repulsions for such purposes as interesting isolated individuals or breaking up harmful combinations. *Spontaneity training* is helping them develop satisfactory behavior in assigned groups. The assignment and training together make up *psychodrama.*

When a complete picture of relationships is desired, all adults in the group, neighborhood, or community should be queried, either in a paper-and-pencil test or by interview. When an understanding of only the leadership structure or power structure is desired, testing can be on a sampling basis.[9] In either case, a follow-up interview can probe deeper for reasons for choices.

A *spontaneity test* is an arranged "standard life situation" in which attraction-repulsion patterns can be explored further. Observation of emotions displayed, words spoken, and duration of the association gives deeper insight into the social atom. Ordinarily this method is not fre-

[7] C. Sower, "Social Stratification of Suburban Communities," *Sociometry*, 11:235–243, August, 1948.

[8] Franz, *op. cit.* See also the following by J. L. Moreno: "Foundations of Sociometry," *Sociometry*, 4:15–35, February, 1941; and *Spontaneity Test and Spontaneity Training*, Psychodrama Monographs, no. 4, Beacon House, Inc., New York, 1944.

[9] See the following articles in *Sociometry* by Frank A. Stewart: "A Sociometric Study of Influence in Southtown, I," 10:11–31, February, 1947; "A Sociometric Study of Influence in Southtown, II," 10:273–286, August, 1947; "Sociometric Testing at the Adult Level," 9:147–148, May–August, 1946; and "Some Sampling Problems in Sociometric Surveys," 11:301–307, November, 1948.

quently used in identifying natural groups, although it may be used to study them. The acquaintance volume of a person can be determined by an acquaintance test in which one is asked to list the number of persons within a group with whom he is acquainted.

Sociometric techniques are time-saving. They enable a relative stranger to find out quickly what a keen observer finds out by long association as a member of the group. If time is not an important consideration, close personal acquaintance is an excellent and simple way to identify natural groups.

SERVICES TO AUTONOMOUS GROUPS

Work with autonomous groups offers a fertile field for educators of adults who use their imaginations unfettered by rigid ideas of what education should be. Directors who have come up through the formal school tradition, especially, will find that successful approaches with informal groups vary considerably from conventional patterns. County agricultural and home-demonstration agents, group workers, a few librarians, and certain other professional educators have been using methods which work with and through natural groups and their leaders. The following illustrations begin to show the range of approaches, the variety of ways that unorganized people can be incorporated into learning situations. Illustrations from foreign lands magnify cultural elements the counterparts of which in our own culture may otherwise be overlooked.

Autonomous Groups in a Balkan Village [10]

In a Bulgarian village with a population of 1,600 the mayor's courier made a house-to-house announcement of a meeting at the schoolhouse on the morrow for expectant mothers. The public-health nurse from Sofia was coming to instruct them in prenatal and postnatal care—a subject which outside observers would have agreed was needed. By nightfall the pregnant women, sensitive about becoming a public spectacle, had decided among themselves not to attend. Only a bare handful, women whose families were under obligation to the mayor, showed up. The mayor and nurse were disappointed in the turnout but went ahead with the demonstration. After leaving the meeting, the bewildered women told their friends, "We couldn't buy all the stuff she told us to buy, even if we should want to do everything she suggested." Educational results— zero.

This type of incident occurred frequently. The mayor and his assistants were well-intentioned, but the system of bringing in outside lecturers made little if any change in the life of the villagers. It was reported that "what was supposed to be an extension of the new really became an

[10] For the complete account, see I. T. Sanders, "The Folk Approach in Extension Work," *Applied Anthropology*, 2:1–4, September, 1943.

extinction of the new before it had time to take root." The uplifters failed to utilize the accustomed local ways that women had of getting together. Formal meetings in the schoolhouse, where they were on the receiving end of instruction, seemed unnatural. The women were used to meeting informally in their homes.

According to a folk custom, the village women meet occasionally in *sedenki*, or "sittings," to help one of their number card wool or spin. A *sedenka* is similar to the rural American "quilting." The accompanying gossip, singing, and food give the *sedenka* important recreational and social values. In addition to certain customary invitational procedures, dishes, time schedules, and social activities, these *sedenki* provide autonomous group relationships in the truest sense. Any hostess will select her guests carefully, inviting those who owe her work or those from whom she wants an invitation. She invites women congenial to one another and to herself. Troublemakers and other unacceptable personalities are not asked. At these *sedenki*, especially in villages with few highly organized groups, news and information are spread and opinions are formed.

Outside specialists who work adroitly through *sedenki* can make real progress in helping women learn better ways of doing things. Friends meeting in a familiar place avoid the strangeness and distractions of a new environment. No interpersonal exploratory period is necessary as it would be with strangers. Personalities distracting to the group have been weeded out. Fortunately, most incompatibles fit in some other group. *Sedenka* members know how their remarks and questions will be received. There is no excessive timidity. In the home setting, a demonstrator can use the equipment that is at hand and that is likely to be found in other homes. Demonstrators can discuss the improvement in present practices possible through the use of available equipment rather than some remote ideal. Local leadership acceptable to the group can be recognized and used. Seldom is a mayor, club president, or teacher a leader in every respect. A great many people are leaders in specific matters. *Sedenki* can let different leadership talents be used. By skillful questioning, the mayor or outside specialist can identify neighborhood leaders, induce them to understand the nature and worth of an activity, have them call a *sedenka* at a convenient time, and let them assume an important role in the demonstration. This same general home-demonstration or party idea has been commercially exploited in this country by distributors of cosmetics, aluminum wear, and similar household products.

In such close work between the specialist and the local group leader, new techniques can be accompanied by a satisfactory ideology. *Sedenka* members can acquire ready explanations and answers for a skeptical husband, mother-in-law, or neighbor. If the outsider is unaware of details of local customs, beliefs, or values, close work with the local leaders will reveal them. In the Bulgarian village, superstition prevents sewing and the preparation of layettes in advance of birth by a pregnant woman. Advance preparation presumes the baby will live, and women must expect the worst, which often happens. Labeling the superstition silly does not help. Such attitudes can be got around, however. Soap, clean cloths, and other equipment can be prepared. Mothers to be can be taught in advance about the construction of simple garments which they are free to make after delivery. Some mothers-in-law can be induced to make clothes in advance. Sharp breaks with tradition can be avoided, and social changes can occur without the people feeling that their mores are threatened.

The *sedenka* approach may not satisfy educators of adults who want a big attendance or those who confuse numbers with educational effect. Also, as the *sedenka* approach involves accepting many of the local patterns, some conventional leaders will feel somewhat insecure because they cannot operate within a familiar tradition. Likewise, individuals with dominant personalities might have difficulty in yielding leadership to a local group member. This probably can be remedied by proper selection of leaders and adequate training. An informal group demands greater adaptability and personal resources of a specialist than does a formal one. For those adaptable enough to work through meetings of women in homes, the folk approach to education has much to offer. It starts where the people are and leads them along familiar paths to better ways of living.

The Peckham Experiment [11]

In 1926, two London physicians started a health center with a new set of assumptions about health and how it is attained. They assumed that health, both mental and physical, was an active and positive thing. Health, they thought, would not be improved much by further research into sickness. It can be gained best where the total environment provides the conditions necessary for healthy minds and bodies to grow.

The central idea was to give families, not merely individuals, a thorough physical examination annually. Work began in a small house, the Pioneer Health Centre, in a neighborhood inhabited by a wide range of middle-class people. The part of the house not needed for examining rooms was converted into a neighborhood club for a variety of free-time activities.

Early findings revealed that many families welcomed the annual examination as a practical way of maintaining their health. Under careful medical scrutiny the general vitality was found to be low, much lower

[11] See I. H. Pearse and Lucy H. Crocker, *The Peckham Experiment: A Study in the Living Structure of Society,* George Allen & Unwin, Ltd., London, 1943; and M. B. Palmer, "Experiment in Health," *Harper's Magazine,* 194:427–432, May, 1947.

than should be expected, although few complained of actual illness. The examinations revealed disorders long before definite diseases became apparent to the individual. When discovered early, these disorders could usually be cleared up easily. The doctors found, however, that the disorders often came back when the individual returned to the environment from which the disorder had sprung. Malnutrition and underdevelopment were prevalent, even though ample food, which the families could afford, and adequate exercise facilities were available. By probing below the surface, the doctors came to feel that the isolation and friendlessness of the city resulted in living patterns which were keeping vitality low.

Using money from many sources, the doctors planned a new building of glass and concrete to serve as a community center. Large enough to accommodate 2,000 families and complete with swimming pool, gymnasium, cafeteria, theater, library, game rooms, and nurseries, it was intended to provide a special kind of environment in which people, moving freely about in unorganized fashion, could find many and varied opportunities for action. Stimulation of possibilities for action opened the way for physical and mental health to develop spontaneously. The idea utilized the "global" approach. Physicians assessed the capacity of facilities in regard to group plans and gave information, but they did not treat groups in a remedial way or organize activity. In fact, no permanent organization was permitted to maintain headquarters in the center. The doctors observed how health expresses itself. From this observation they hoped to discover the guiding principles for cultivation of health.

Membership was open to any family in the neighborhood upon payment of a weekly fee of about 40 cents. This covered the periodic medical examination and free use of the building, except for certain activities that required payment of a small fee. Examinations were made on a family basis. When results were ready, children were discussed first. They left when the parents' health was considered.

The permissive atmosphere pervading the building and the building structure itself induced friendliness. Glass partitions and roof sections not only let in sunlight and made observation of activities easier, but reduced isolation. With facilities readily available, many people, old and young alike, developed social and recreational skills without formal instruction. They learned by trial or with the help of their friends. When billiard tables, pools, card tables, phonographs, dart boards, books, and workrooms were convenient, even the timid, in the congenial company of their natural groups, offered little resistance to new activities. The sight of activity, especially when engaged in by those of little skill, was an incentive to action. No socially approved standards of competence existed to keep anyone from trying something new. Numerous checks showed that new members having very few recreational skills upon arrival gained several new ones within a few months. The repertory of interests visibly grew. "The release from social loneliness, and with it the increase in physical, mental, and emotional energy, was tremendous. This shift towards health and vitality was reflected in the findings at the yearly recurring overhaul of the family." [12]

The fact that no leaders were provided, no organizations existed, and no age segregation was encouraged opened the way to mental and social health. The environment provided opportunities for people to express themselves without artificiality. Many people who resist propaganda, avoid organized activities, and refuse to join educational groups will respond freely to facts and information that they feel are useful. The Centre demonstrated that many people will take advantage of opportunities and use knowledge voluntarily, provided that they are freely available. The specific gains in health as revealed by periodic-examination records over the years were marked.

The significance for adult education of the Peckham demonstration is very great in that two types of autonomous groups were at the heart of it—the family and the nonkinship group. No formal adult education existed, not even formally organized groups—yet the amount of learning was considerable. To be sure, not all phases of learning were included in the experiment, but in those that were, learning and living were almost completely integrated. The public school and other educational agencies can afford to study the lessons of Peckham. Among other things, the entire experiment points up the desirability of providing education for all on a free or inexpensive basis. Amidst the fragmentizing influences of urban life on both health and happiness, the Peckham experiment demonstrates a practical way of helping families reestablish the psychological bonds of integrated community living. This may well be its greatest contribution.

Infiltration in Harlem Gangs

Neither ordinary social work nor police watchfulness had been able to overcome the extreme antisocial activities of tough teen-age and young-adult gangs in Harlem. These well-organized gangs spent their time in bull sessions at their hangouts. Their members stole, smoked marijuana, carried weapons, engaged in gang warfare, and were habitual truants.

For a 3-year period the Welfare Council of New York City assigned four young social workers to the worst gangs. The social workers—

began by loafing near gang hangouts, gradually drawing the boys into conversations, playing the jukebox with them, letting them cadge occasional cigarettes. As distrust faded, the council men identified themselves, proved that they were not cops and not out to nag, report the gang members or break their gangs. On the contrary, they were available for advice, an occa-

[12] The Secretary, *The Pioneer Health Centre,* Hyde Park Mansions, London, p. 6.

sional two-bit loan, or help in arranging for the use of a gym or a place to hold a dance.[13]

In time, the social workers were able to steer the groups toward socially constructive activities. They induced the gangs to organize basketball games, picnics, and hikes. The social workers maintained a nonauthoritarian attitude and started with no fixed program. Eventually, one gang found that it could share the same gymnasium with another without trouble. In 3 years the social workers became well integrated into the gangs, stopped gang warfare among the four groups, and reduced sex offenses and stealing. Some truants returned to school. Dozens of boys were helped in obtaining jobs. The general behavior of group members changed materially through the influence of young men, who—while retaining stable and socially approved values—were able to become accepted as members of the gang and to start from there.

VD Education in Taverns [14]

Taverns, corner bars, pool halls, and similar recreation places usually have a following of patrons showing up rather regularly—autonomous groups. During World War II local social-hygiene committees arranged to show venereal disease films in such places. By emphasizing the free and voluntary aspects of this project and the contribution to the manpower situation, a committee member would prearrange with a proprietor to show a film. As a minimum, the projectionist would drop into a dimly lighted place, set up his machine, show the film on the wall, and depart. Usually, however, the proprietor would encourage a short question-and-answer period which the projectionist was prepared to handle. Well-selected leaflets were sometimes distributed. Short preliminary films to attract attention and brief talks were used in some cases.

Proprietors who received appreciative letters from the committee recognizing their public-spiritedness stimulated other owners to follow suit. Response was good. Owners often cooperated by disconnecting the juke box, switching off the lights, and inviting their patrons to pay attention. While the health films were never advertised, one poolroom proprietor brought in a pocket-billiard expert, advertised his appearance, and thus drew a sizable crowd on the night the film was to be shown.

This approach permits extension. Films can be shown between floor shows at night clubs, before a favorite television program, and at the busiest times at bars. Similar arrangements can be made to spread information on tuberculosis, cancer, or certain other health subjects. If care-

[13] *Time*, 59:40–43, Dec. 4, 1950. For a full report, see Paul L. Crawford, D. I. Malamud, and J. R. Dumpson, *Working with Teen-age Gangs*, Welfare Council of New York City, 1950.

[14] H. G. Williams, "Reaching the People in 'Unorganized Groups,'" *Journal of Social Hygiene*, 34:22–25, January, 1948.

fully selected, educational films in other fields might also be shown in this way. This approach reaches people otherwise hard to reach—groups which provide few members for organized clubs and still fewer for formal classes.

Backwoods Folk in Modern Homes

Hundreds of families from underprivileged Southern rural and mountain areas moved into a Northern city low-rent housing development during World War II. Nothing in their background gave them skills and knowledge in the use of modern plumbing, gas stoves, refrigerators, electrical appliances, and similar household equipment. Trouble soon multiplied. The migrants were not attracted by the normal range of homemaking classes offered by the school. A demonstrator cultivated the acquaintance of a few women at midafternoon neighborhood-center movies and made the rounds to show each one and her invited friends how to make the best use of their new equipment.

Group Reading and Discussion in Brooklyn [15]

In 1929 the Peoples Guild in Brooklyn, an organization concerned with the constructive use of leisure time, started to work with women's groups interested in reading and discussion. The guild staff had worked in neighborhood and school centers for years and knew well the shortcomings of conventional adult-education programs. Housewives with children, especially, were unable to take part in most of the available educational activities.

One day a guild staff member discussed the idea of an informal afternoon meeting for reading and discussion with a group of fifteen women who had been associated with a neighborhood center. Out of this grew a pattern of afternoon meetings of congenial groups of women to read and discuss books. They met in their own homes, the natural centers of comfort and sociability. The guild supplied a discussion leader, but the women set the time schedule and selected the topics and content of their reading.

By word-of-mouth other groups sought guild assistance. The idea was not actively promoted, but more requests for help came than could be serviced. Even when foundation funds were received for additional staff, and cooperative relationships were developed with the public library, all requests could not be filled. In each case the new groups came as coteries of women who already knew one another. Sometimes they had associated together for years. When groups obviously were too small to result in good discussion, members recruited additional women from

[15] See Seymour Barnard, "A Community Recruits Itself," *Journal of Educational Sociology*, 19:562–570, May, 1946; and "After the Fact," *Journal of Adult Education*, 9:74–79, April, 1950.

among their close friends. The friendship pattern within the group was a prime characteristic; no group ever included strangers.

Leaders did not go to new groups with a preconceived plan. Most group members had little desire to assume responsibility for discussion leadership, but the guild leader had to become an acceptable member of the group and contribute as one of them without any attempt to dominate or dictate. At the same time she had to utilize her professional skills of discussion leadership, of drawing out the timid, of holding the bold in check, of helping all to see the worth of new ideas expressed, of leading wandering discussion back on the track, and of advising on reading materials.

Intellectually, the leaders found their function to be complicated. First, they had to achieve genuine objectivity in their own thinking. This meant being interested in seeing that all possible points of view were raised and successfully avoiding the temptation to be carried away with any one point of view. Thus, often, they played "the devil's advocate." Second, the leader had to set an example of restraint in presenting her own points of view, both in making them concise and in refraining from talking more than other members. Yet the leader was expected to be quite frank about her own opinions and risked loss of the confidence of the group by any attempt to conceal her own views. Third, she had to help members to *listen* to what others said and to try to understand what a speaker meant by what she was saying. Fourth, she had to help the members achieve objectivity in stating their own points of view. Fifth, and extremely important, she had to set an example of ease and good humor in discussion.[16]

The evaluation of these groups during the 20-year experiment shows that several significant things happened to the members. In the beginning reading was varied—magazines, articles, fiction, and scattered chapters from books which individual women liked. Novels, however, soon gave way to more serious reading, which in time became centered around major themes. These themes, although they provided the subject matter for a few weeks, months, or a year, never became crystallized into a course of reading; they were always flexible and subject to change. The leader contributed only a member's viewpoint in determining the interests and content of reading and never tried to upgrade it unduly.

Oral reading around the circle was an early practice which gradually gave way to discussion. Reading became homework, so that more time could be available for discussion. The purposes of the participants changed somewhat as the months added into years. Women began to think of the discussion groups as something more than a pleasant way of spending leisure time. They became enthusiastic about reading for more serious purposes—to understand the causes of a social movement, to gain

[16] See Maria Rogers, "Summary: Report of the History of the Experiment," *Autonomous Groups Bulletin*, 5:9–24, Autumn, 1949.

deeper insight into human frailty, to grasp the background of a national problem. Reading was done seriously, for each woman came to feel a personal responsibility for her contribution to the group. At this stage, when a new member was sought to replace one who had moved away, new qualifications for membership were considered—background and potential contribution. Women with narrow prejudices and a few intellectual interests were sometimes rejected even though they met the criterion of congeniality.

The periodic discussion based on common reading strengthened immeasurably the personal relationships among members. After years of sharing thoughts, members of a group came to know each other in ways impossible at the end of a semester or term. The personal rewards were so great that the groups ran on for years, a number past the decade mark. In fact, most of them were still carrying on by themselves in 1953, since the guild disbanded in 1949. The community feeling is high. Social cohesion is probably as great as it is in any well-knit village or rural neighborhood. Out of a sprawling city has come a way to recapture the values of the frontier village—through the sharing of exciting ideas instead of common dangers. The basic ingredients in this demonstration seem to be freedom of choice of associates, convenience of meeting time and place, absence of academic requirements, joint group-leader assumption of responsibility, self-selection of subject matter, and flexibility in dealing with it.[17]

Other Examples

Change takes place in a great many other autonomous groups which are subject to purposeful organization and guidance. As discussed later, the cooperative Extension Service of the Department of Agriculture does a great deal of work with autonomous groups. Community organization workers are able to help rural areas and small towns to lift themselves by their own bootstraps through helping community councils and other autonomous groups to define their problems and plan intelligently for their solution.[18] The whole art and science of group work among social agencies is based upon autonomous-group relationships. Approaches developed in these and related fields offer fruitful study to the director interested in broadening the base of participation.

Many study groups likewise become most effective as they take on the characteristics of autonomous groups. The original Junto, established in Philadelphia in 1727 by Benjamin Franklin, was an autonomous reading and discussion group made up largely of craftsmen and shopkeepers.

[17] For a more comprehensive history and evaluation of these groups, see *Autonomous Groups Bulletin*, vol. 5.

[18] See Jean Ogden and Jess Ogden, *These Things We Tried*, University of Virginia, Extension Division, Charlottesville, Va., 1948; and *Small Communities in Action*, Harper & Brothers, New York, 1946.

From Franklin's *Autobiography,* one realizes that the members made real progress toward self-improvement in their Friday-evening meetings.

Initially, Great Books Discussions, which are treated in Chapter 5, may be concerned with applying a specific method to selected content under trained leadership. Often, however, incompatible members drop out, leaving a congenial group of associates fully able to carry on as an autonomous group even after the original leader has gone.

Group study and discussion of selected books as conducted in San Francisco, Washington, and other places usually develop along autonomous-group lines.[19] Clublike groups developed by David Mackaye, public-school director of adult education at San Jose, California, are another variation of the same method. "The essence of this group is its permanence, the relation of its subject matter to the members' 'continuing dynamic interest,' and the solidarity of group feeling among the members which arises on a high intellectual level." [20]

General Principles—Working with Groups

Fixed ways of working with autonomous groups are established at the risk of freezing patterns that are useful for only limited purposes. Several fundamental principles, however, can be stated for educational workers and agencies.

1. Accept the group as it is with its own self-selected interests, functions, membership, and leadership. Do not attempt to make it over directly. The group's acceptance of outside aid is voluntary. There can be no pushing around. Remember that cohesion within the group is stronger than any influence an outsider can bring to bear. One must start where the group is.

2. Seek sincerely to become integrated into the group. One wishing to influence an autonomous group must become personally liked by its members. The influence of a newcomer depends upon the degree of acceptance that he can gain within the group. A common ethnic background, language, experience, occupation, and other cultural similarities make acceptance easier.

3. Identify the basic needs of the group and select objectives in harmony with those deeper needs. An educator's task is to recognize those needs and to help the group discover better ways of satisfying them. One who would cause change must visualize his objectives clearly and must discuss them only in ways that the group can understand.

4. Introduce steps in a sequence which leads most rapidly to the objectives. These steps, however, must be well within the abilities of the

[19] See John W. Powell, *Education for Maturity,* Hermitage House, Inc., New York, 1949; and Helen T. Steinbarger, "Group Reading under Leadership," *Adult Education Journal,* 4:149–152, October, 1945.

[20] Quoted from personal correspondence between Mr. Mackaye and the author.

members and must not violate too drastically or too suddenly the established habits, customs, and ways of doing things.

5. Work closely with the natural leaders. Involve them deeply in teaching and learning processes. Leaders and members make changes in proportion to their voluntary participation in the new.

6. Provide services which the group wants or is willing to accept, even though they may not be what the agency, institution, or educator is prepared to give. Autonomous groups must be met on their own ground —not in terms of institutional standards or expectations. Unwillingness to adapt official institutional purposes and methods to the group accounts for the limited numbers influenced by the traditional evening schools and colleges, libraries, and churches. An agency must be willing to provide any socially desirable aid or service requested by an autonomous group, or else it must lose its place in the life of the group.

7. Lead group members toward extending their associations outside their own autonomous group. Help them keep their security while making other individual and group contacts. The breadth of human sympathy in a highly interdependent world depends largely upon the number and variety of associations which can be developed.[21]

Most of the services discussed in Chapter 8 can be made available to autonomous groups. Space, equipment, facilities, and resource personnel are especially likely to be desired. Extensions of acceptable leadership present a challenge, particularly to institutionalized educational agencies. Teachers are likely to carry over preconceived notions about formal learning from their academic experience. Leaders with group-work training and experience are more often likely to be successful in establishing and maintaining satisfactory relationships with autonomous groups. In Pennsylvania, and in certain other states, schools are authorized to engage in broad recreational and social services which can include informal activities with autonomous groups. In some cases full-time and often part-time personnel can be employed for this service.

Where schools are unable to provide all the services which autonomous groups may need, they can usually cooperate with other community agencies. Schools can help plan and conduct surveys designed to identify autonomous groups and their needs and aspirations. Schools can help train volunteer or paid leaders to work with autonomous groups. In many cases the school can act as an information center about activities of community groups, as a center for community study, as a sponsor or cosponsor of a neighborhood-leader system, and as a working partner in an effort to gain greater participation of autonomous-group members in organized activities. Finally, if there are local or state restrictions on

---

[21] For an extended list of principles based upon experience, see F. L. W. Richardson, Jr., "First Principles of Rural Rehabilitation," *Applied Anthropology*, 4:16–31, Summer, 1945. See also H. B. Allen, *Come Over into Macedonia*, Rutgers University Press, New Brunswick, N.J., 1943; and Crawford et al., *op. cit.*, pp. 127–138.

the activities of the school, it can seek to have policy changed to permit greater participation of the school in total community life.[22]

VOLUNTEER SERVICES: NEIGHBORHOOD AND BLOCK-LEADER SYSTEMS

Volunteers play extremely important roles in American life. In fact, much of our national and community strength lies in the voluntary participation of citizens in work necessary to the common welfare. In both war and peace, on battle lines and the home front, in emergencies and the long pull, on national councils and neighborhood committees, volunteers have rendered priceless service. In national emergencies millions of people give time and energy to the protective services, to bond drives, to salvage campaigns, to surveys, and to other service activities. While the motivations in wartime and in emergencies are not identical to those operating in peacetime, many people—year in and year out—give freely of their energy and time to the satisfaction of broad human needs.[23] Volunteer firemen and rescue squads in thousands of communities provide a dramatic example of the value of voluntary community service.

Volunteers are important in adult education. Indeed, a primary characteristic of adult education as a movement in a democracy is its voluntary nature. Significant adult education can take place with paid leadership but, in the end, it is what people do and learn for themselves that counts. The agency or program that fails to utilize the freely available energies of adults is accepting an unnecessary limitation.

Use of Volunteer Leaders

A wide variety of educational, health, recreational, religious, social service, and welfare agencies use volunteers extensively. Annually a million volunteers solicit funds for community chests and other causes. Volunteers serve as Gray Ladies, hospital hostesses, home visitors, nurses aides, nursery assistants, naturalization aides, office workers, publicity agents, receptionists, recreation assistants, scoutmasters, telephoners, travelers aides, and welfare workers. Aging volunteers visit infirm old people and provide companionship and communication with the outside world. The need for volunteers and the numbers available have grown so in recent years that in hundreds of communities volunteer bureaus have been established to assist with the recruitment, training, and general organization of volunteers.[24] These bureaus are often sponsored by a

[22] For other suggestions, see Walter Pettit, "Education and the Autonomous Group," *The Journal of Educational Sociology*, 19:529–533, May, 1946.

[23] Clarice Pennock and Marion Robinson, "Why We Volunteer," *The Survey Midmonthly*, 84:273–276, September, 1948.

[24] See *A Handbook on the Organization and Operation of a Volunteer Service Bureau*, Community Chest and Councils, Inc., Volunteer Service Department, New York, 1946; and *Handbook on Volunteers*, Federation of Protestant Welfare Agencies, Inc., New York, 1949.

council of social agencies, although in some instances they are independent or under other auspices.

Much work of volunteers is educational, but often it is combined with other social service. Most religious instruction is given by volunteer church-school teachers. Much of the formal and informal instruction provided in boys clubs, mothers clubs, nationality societies, the Red Cross, and scout organizations is volunteer. Local educational work stimulated by national health organizations concerned with cancer, diabetes, heart disease, tuberculosis, and other diseases is done largely by volunteers who spread information through films, printed matter, and short talks. In addition, volunteers serve as book reviewers, discussion leaders, hospital library aides, instructors in arts and crafts, teachers of the foreign-born, kindergarten assistants, recreation group directors, and settlement-house group workers.

Most organizations concerned with education in civic affairs likewise depend heavily upon volunteers. Community councils, chambers of commerce, citizens associations, business and trade associations, the PTA, and luncheon clubs often are essentially organized ways for volunteers to work effectively toward common ends. The success of most community campaigns depends directly upon the number of volunteers involved and the amount of work they do. The educational work of the League of Women Voters and other groups interested in civic and political issues is largely volunteer. The activities of labor unions, political parties, and farm organizations—in fact, of a great many nongovernmental groups—depend greatly upon the unpaid work of participants, from board members to clerks.

The formal-school tradition of using paid staff gives little impetus to working with volunteers. In recent years, however, more work has been done through volunteer leadership. Progress is being made especially in family-life and parent-education study groups. Lay leaders are trained in discussion methods by specialists on the school staff. Leaders then meet with parent groups for discussion. Some public-affairs, radio-listening, and TV-viewing groups have been similarly formed. A few schools use volunteers to interview newly arrived foreign-born, to give naturalization assistance, to serve as instructors in English and citizenship, and to act as helpers with correspondence courses. Without infringing upon the duties of paid personnel, many more schools could expand greatly the use of volunteers.

Since its inception in 1914, the extension work of the cooperative Extension Service of the U.S. Department of Agriculture has been based on a decentralized pattern of local volunteer leadership assisted by county agricultural, home-demonstration, and 4-H club agents. Prior to World War II, 700,000 neighborhood leaders were active. When transportation difficulties prohibited mass attendance at county or district meetings, an additional 500,000 wartime leaders were organized to supplement the regular ones. More than 1 million unpaid men and women currently serve as neighborhood leaders, each giving, on the average, about 3 weeks of time per year.[25] Local patterns vary to suit geographical and sociological conditions.

Usually rural areas are broken up into neighborhoods of five to twenty-five families, each served by a neighborhood leader. This decentralized system of leadership, which began nearly 40 years ago, built to a peak during wartime and, still continuing, provides the volunteer backbone of the largest adult-education program in the world. The small core of paid workers consists of a few thousand county agents and their office help, a professional staff at land-grant colleges, researchers at experiment stations, and specialists in the Department of Agriculture in Washington. Neighborhood leaders, providing the liaison between county committees and farm men and women, can furnish specific information on a face-to-face basis. Essential information or promotional programs can be carried from the national to the local level quickly—within a few days.[26] Neighborhood leaders can also keep county, state, and Federal officials informed of local needs, sentiment, and cooperation. This two-way communication is an important feature of any adult-education program in a democracy.[27]

Much direct instruction in skills is also provided to farm people by volunteers. The educational content of a field can be divided into small segments, each of which can be taught to a group of leaders who can take it back to their neighbors. In this way food-preservation processes, insect-control methods, lamp-shade making, and a thousand other skills can be spread. Information on marketing, economic conditions, world trade, and other matters affecting rural people can be disseminated and discussed. No one leader is asked to do too much or to become skilled in everything. Instead, leadership is shared and spread.

This system is useful, too, in closing the time gap between the de-

[25] *Report of Cooperative Extension Work in Agriculture and Home Economics, 1950,* U.S. Department of Agriculture Extension Service, p. 16.

[26] See M. L. Wilson, "Agricultural Extension in an Industrial Society," *Adult Education Journal,* 2:85–89, April, 1943.

[27] For more detail on neighborhood leaders in rural areas, see the following U.S. Department of Agriculture Extension Service Circulars: *Highlights of the Neighborhood Leader Conference,* no. 402, March, 1943; *Second National Neighborhood Leader Conference,* no. 404, April, 1943; and *A Second Nation-wide Status Inventory of Neighborhood-leader Work,* no. 415, February, 1944. For more general information on the work of the Extension Service, see L. D. Kelsey and C. C. Hearne, *Cooperative Extension Work,* Comstock Publishing Associates, Inc., Ithaca, N.Y., 1949; and E. deS. Brunner and E. H. P. Yang, *Rural America and the Extension Service,* Bureau of Publications, Teachers College, Columbia University, New York, 1949.

velopment of new knowledge through research at experiment stations and its general application on farms. Whereas the average American school lags nearly a generation behind best practice,[28] in agriculture—largely through the work of the Extension Service—this lag has been cut to a very few years—often less than 5.

Organizational Principles and Problems

Systems of block leaders, as they are often called in urban areas, have many characteristics in common with neighborhood leaders in rural areas. Either may be organized for educational purposes by a community council, a school, a citizens committee, a defense council, or a similar group. They can be organized for a single campaign or a specific purpose —publicizing certain events, interpreting a campaign, stimulating attendance at specific meetings, soliciting funds for a community chest, making surveys of fact or opinion, welcoming newcomers, getting out the vote, disseminating health information, or obtaining compliance with a rule. They may use interviewers, block wardens, block mothers, block solicitors, or discussion leaders. Energy is saved, however, if a good organization is built up to serve many purposes, as has been done by the cooperative Extension Service and a few other agencies. In a few communities a general block organization operates on a permanent basis ready to go into action on any approved project.

A block-leader system is essentially a set of informal human relationships which have been organized enough to assure responsible and systematic face-to-face communication. Often, as during World War II, this flow of communication is predominantly downward. This is especially true in the protective services, in which organization and discipline are usually somewhat along military lines. Save-the-fat, share-the-meat, and salvage campaigns were designed to spread information and enlist support. They supplement mass media by presenting information in a more personal, and thus more effective, way.[29]

In a democracy the upward flow of information is of equal importance. Surveys of housing accommodations, recreation needs, and candidates for nurses' training no doubt provided useful information during the war. The possibilities for gathering and reporting information and opinion useful for policy making are great and, with few exceptions, have hardly

[28] See two books by Paul R. Mort and Francis G. Cornell, *Adaptability of Public School Systems* (1939), and *American Schools in Transition* (1941), Bureau of Publications, Teachers College, Columbia University, New York.

[29] See the following U.S. Department of Agriculture Extension Service Circulars: *Evaluation Study of the Neighborhood Leader System, Berkshire and Essex Counties, Massachusetts*, no. 386, July, 1942; *Orange and Lee Counties, North Carolina, Demonstrate How Neighborhood Leaders Can Help in Securing Participation of Rural Families in Agriculture's Wartime Programs*, no. 387, June, 1942; *Influence of Neighborhood Leaders in Waldo County, Maine*, no. 389, September, 1942; and *Evaluating Your Neighborhood Leadership*, no. 414, 1943.

been tapped. If a two-way flow of information can be maintained, democratic participation, with its morale-building values, can be materially strengthened.

The ideal block-leader organization provides a personal connecting link between the total population and the organized governmental and nongovernmental life of the community. Block leaders interpret the activities, programs, problems, and purposes of community organizations, service agencies, and governmental divisions to the rank and file. In reverse, leaders interpret the needs, interests, opinions, and aspirations of people to officials in these agencies. The primary educational function of leaders is to develop understanding—both ways.

Careful selection of block leaders pays. They serve best if they are looked upon as leaders by their groups, or at least are liked. Ready acceptance of all who volunteer is not likely to result in the best choice. Isolates, maladjusted individuals, and people with axes to grind readily volunteer but may give endless trouble. Natural leaders are likely to be busy and may not readily volunteer. Better potential leaders can be identified by using sociometric techniques.[30] Simple sociometric surveys including all or most of the people in a large building or small neighborhood will usually reveal the bonds of acquaintance and affinity which can be the basis of leader choice. Sociograms will reveal the lines of influence and liking. A popular leader may not be able to accept responsibility for all who chose him. Isolates may have to be assigned to some leader if everyone is to be included. A sociometric approach at least will avoid some of the misassignments and personality rejections which are likely to occur when leaders are assigned arbitrarily. In addition, sociometric assignment is democratic in that, within limits, it permits people to select their own leaders.

Aside from being personally acceptable to those in the block, qualities desired in a leader are reasonably good intelligence, better-than-average social awareness, tact in human relations, and enough spare time to engage in the necessary field work.

Block leaders need to be oriented to the general nature of their work and its importance. The field of activity, the methods of work, and the major policies must be clearly defined. Leaders should have opportunity early to understand the general and specific purposes to which they are asked to give time. The fact that busy people ordinarily will not volunteer unless they clearly understand the purposes of the project helps assure competent initial orientation. The training devices, in addition

[30] For details on methods, see these articles in *Sociometry*: G. A. Lundberg and Mary Steele, "Social Attraction Patterns in a Village," 1:375–419, January–April, 1938; I. T. Sanders, "The Use of Block Leaders in Effective Community Mobilization," 12:265–275, November, 1949; and R. W. Wakeley, "Selecting Leaders for Agriculture Programs," 10:384–395, November, 1947.

to group meetings, are individual home instruction, handbooks, leaflets, and circulars.

Attitudes and traditions of community service must be built into the corps of leaders. Loyalty to total community welfare and to the principles of democratic human relations and sound education must be placed above interest in a church, ethnic group, political party, or private business. A block-leader organization serving the whole community must be kept nonpolitical, nonsectarian, and nonpartisan.

If block leaders are to be general interpreters of the community organizations to the people, systematic orientation into the services, activities, programs, and personnel must be arranged. Leaders become effective screening and referral agents for social services as they develop firsthand acquaintance with the facilities of the community.

In-service training is required to keep leaders in close touch with the civic and organized life of the community and up to date on changes in services. In addition, every assignment requiring contact with block members must be thoroughly explained and understood. Before leaders spread information, survey their blocks, interpret a plan, discuss an issue, or pool opinions, they must have opportunity to discuss the matter thoroughly with competent authorities and examine closely any printed materials to be used or distributed. This preproject training is usually given in a community-wide or zone meeting held immediately before a campaign is launched.[31] Home visits for assignment may be used in some cases. With experienced and well-organized leaders, assignments can sometimes be given by mail or telephone.

Organization and Supervision of Block Leaders

A *block* sometimes refers to a city block, to two sides of a street between intersections, or to some geographic segment. More often it refers to a number of families with whom a leader maintains communication. A block of five to ten families, with one of their number as leader, seems to work best if associations are to be at all close. The typical block leader cannot maintain close and continuing contact with twenty or more families, although that many may be included in a single interview or solicitation. Incomplete coverage, high leader turnover, and general inefficiency usually accompany heavy loads. Where leaders are responsible for a small number of families, efficiency and morale are likely to be high.

From five to ten blocks constitute a sector. A similar number of sectors make up a zone. Districts and larger areas are built up when the size of the community makes this necessary. Units at each level in the hierarchy have leaders carrying line responsibility and titles arranged in rank—lieutenant, captain, and major, or block, sector, and zone leaders.

[31] For more detail, see Gladys Gallup, *Training Neighborhood Leaders*, U.S. Department of Agriculture Extension Service Circular 397, November, 1942.

An executive working under the direction of a committee usually tops the system. When democratically operated, a sector leader and his block leaders serve as a sector committee. This committee system can be repeated at each level of the hierarchy.

In comprehensive systems a professional staff and training service are desirable. Marginal-time, volunteer executives cannot hold the organization together when it grows beyond a moderate size. Because activities

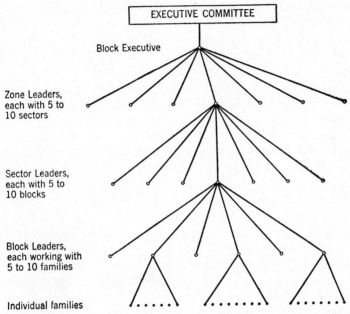

Fig. 9. Model block organization. (Source: Modified from *The Block Plan of Organization for Civilian War Services,* U.S. Office of Civilian Defense Publications, September, 1942, p. 8.)

vary so widely, no standards for volunteer-supervisor ratios have been set up. Some systems have one executive serving as many as 200 or more leaders.

The executive committee of a council of social agencies, a welfare council, a volunteer bureau, the PTA, a school board, or other parent body may direct the block-leader organization, provided that enough time can be given to it. In these cases an advisory committee which can pay close attention to block-leader activities may be of material assistance. In a few cases the block-leader system is essentially autonomous, with its own controlling committee consisting in part or wholly of its own members. Aside from their general responsibility for organization and public relations, the biggest task of executive committees is to examine, modify, and approve the projects and other matters with which leaders will be concerned. To do this wisely and democratically, to enlist broad community support, and to keep down charges of undue favoritism require board members of a high type approximating a true cross section of the community. Control and administrative relationships must be carefully worked out to prevent the system from reflecting the interests of too narrow a group.

Supervision, aside from that given the whole organization by the central staff, is a responsibility of the line officers. Assignments are made down the line, and reports of field activity are collected and consolidated by sector leaders before being passed on to zone leaders, who send them on through the proper channels. On certain projects one or more steps may be bypassed and information centralized directly in one spot. Block, sector, and zone leaders keep in touch with one another by face-to-face contact, by telephone, and by mail. Zone and sector leaders depend upon added experience and greater ability to be of service in helping block leaders with their problems of interviewing, gaining participation, organizing social activities, and interpreting information. Extra in-service training for the higher echelons and their participation in experiments and research can materially strengthen the competence of these line officials.

Organizational structure, of course, is useful only if it facilitates the flow of communication in the interests of all the people. The best education occurs only when the block system operates within the framework of democratic human relations, which permits neither open nor hidden manipulation of people. Likewise, effectiveness is usually lost when the system operates in a formal fashion.

Informal contacts between leaders and block members are the heart of the block-leader idea. They may be both planned and incidental. Usually, soon after a new campaign, survey, or other project gets under way, informal conversations are held with all members individually in their homes or during casual contacts around the neighborhood. These usually are face-to-face conversation, but at times, after rapport has been established, the telephone can be used for brief instructions.

Block parties and block discussions, either regularly or on call, help strengthen ties within the block and facilitate democratic processes.[32] Absent members can be followed up individually. Speed usually is not essential. On one occasion, however, one elementary-school block system contacted by telephone all available member households within an hour. In urban areas efficient organizations can contact a majority of homes within a few days.

Morale can be built and maintained at a high pitch as blocks strengthen personal ties and become natural groups. This was one of the significant

[32] See Ralph McAllister and R. A. Luke, "Chicago Block Discussion Program," *Adult Education Journal,* 2:170–172, October, 1943.

benefits of the intensive block activity of World War II, especially in England. Block plans which have survived during the postwar years usually have been those which developed the most social activity of a club nature.

Morale of leaders is high when they feel that their work is important and that it is appreciated both by the members served and those higher up. Clear purposes, explicit directions, and shared information on project results help keep morale high. Good block executives provide ample recognition of good work, giving earned credit and public praise freely. As with all volunteers, these are the coins of payment.[33]

Some Educational Tasks

A great many educational tasks can be carried out on an individual or small-group basis by neighborhood or block-leader systems. While work assignments must be specific, there seems to be no reason for not developing block systems for comprehensive educational service under the auspices of the public school or other public agency. The experience of the cooperative Extension Service indicates that such programs can be very successful. Examples of special educational tasks which might appropriately be undertaken by block systems sponsored by the public schools in conjunction with other community agencies are:

1. Dissemination of any information in the public interest, especially from government departments and community agencies

2. Revelation of educational and social services of the school and community agencies to the whole community through publicizing regular and special activities

3. Preliminary discussion of public policy, proposed legislation, tax issues, and other public affairs

4. Operation of small discussion groups centered around discussion guides on radio and TV programs

5. Interpretation of local campaigns such as bond issues, health drives, referenda issues, and other civic problems

6. Organization of new-voter preparation programs; stimulating young people to register and vote, provided that this activity is kept nonpartisan

7. Visiting newly arrived immigrants; orienting them into community life; inducting them into English and citizenship classes and other adult-education and social activities; tutoring of those who cannot attend classes

8. Welcome-wagon activities—visiting and orienting newcomers

[33] For further information, see *To Have and to Hold Volunteers in Community Services, Volunteers in Community Service: A Bibliography,* and *Volunteer Viewpoint,* an occasional newsletter, all issued by Community Chests and Councils, Inc., New York. See also L. Crile, *Suggestions for Building and Maintaining Interest and Enthusiasm of Neighborhood Leaders,* U.S. Department of Agriculture Extension Service Circular 400, 1943.

9. Community surveys of opinion and fact

10. Teaching of skills related to the home, farm, safety, health, neighborhood cleanliness, etc.

11. Maintenance of education activities and other social services among the aged and infirm

12. Operation of parent-education programs

While considerable experience has accumulated about neighborhood and block-leader systems, organizations developing them for the first time should realize certain dangers. First is the danger of being misunderstood. The democratic participation of all affected by the system in developing clear objectives and procedures is the best safeguard against this possibility. If powerful groups begin to think that the block organization is a clever way of putting something over on them or on the community, the system is unduly—perhaps fatally—handicapped.[34]

Block-leader systems structurally are similar to efficient political machines, although the motives and principles of operation differ in some respects. If the whole community is to be served, one needs to be sure that public block-leader organizations are not used for political, religious, sectarian, or commercial purposes.

Inept personal relations and an overaggressiveness in block leaders can lead to much ill will. Good pre-and in-service training is needed to build a clear concept of purposes and methods. Rapid growth is especially likely to result in bungled work, short-lived projects, and loss of confidence in the leadership. Slow growth, constant sensitivity to and evaluation of the human-relations side, and ready adaptation of strategy and tactics help ensure success.

No blueprint can be drawn in advance to outline the specifics of a block-leader system. The details have to be worked out in each situation anew—carefully, imaginatively, professionally, and yet practically. For maximum results the developmental engineer in this field should be well acquainted with the pertinent theory and findings in community organization, cultural anthropology, group work, human relations, social psychology, sociology, and sociometry. The block-leader approach offers both a promise and a challenge to the finest abilities of any director of adult education.

EVALUATION

The ease of assessing work with autonomous groups and neighborhood-leader systems depends upon the specificity of objectives. The organization of block leaders permits the systematic collection of many data as an integral part of the continuing activity. The block structure and number of contacts in relation to the total number of households show the

[34] See W. C. Phillips, *Adventuring for Democracy,* Social Unit Press, New York, 1940.

coverage. As assignments and campaigns have specific objectives, it is relatively easy for either the block leaders or outsiders to check later on changes in behavior made by people visited. The success of bond issues, registration and voter turnout, the number who try better practices, and the number of immigrants induced to enroll in more formal activities are types of indexes useful in assessing the effectiveness of neighborhood-leader programs.

Where work with autonomous groups is supplemented by mass media, experimental and control groups may have to be set up to determine differences in behavior change. In programs with multiple or comprehensive objectives, such as the Peckham experiment, the work of the Extension Service, or activity among the Harlem street gangs, part of the evaluation may be only a comparison of the sum of many specific indexes with similar data at a previous time. Any comprehensive evaluation should include assessment of the feelings and attitudes of the autonomous-group members, as well as the degree to which they increase their participation in larger groups—if that be an objective.

SELECTED REFERENCES

Coon, C. S.: "The Universality of Natural Groupings in Human Societies," *The Journal of Educational Sociology,* 20:163–168, November, 1946.

Doddy, Hurley H.: *Informal Groups and the Community,* Teachers College, Columbia University, New York, 1952.

Festinger, L., et al.: *Social Pressures in Informal Groups,* Harper & Brothers, New York, 1950.

Homans, G. C.: *The Human Group,* Harcourt, Brace and Company, Inc., New York, 1950.

Jennings, H. H.: *Leadership and Isolation,* Longmans, Green & Co., Inc., New York, 1950.

The Journal of Educational Sociology, May, 1946, and November, 1946. Both issues deal with autonomous groups.

Moreno, J. L.: "Organization of the Social Atom," *Sociometry,* 10:287–293, August, 1947.

———: *Sociometry and the Cultural Order,* Sociometry Monographs, no. 2, Sociometric Institute, New York, 1943.

Morgan, A. E.: *The Small Community,* Harper & Brothers, New York, 1943.

Whyte, W. A.: *Street Corner Society,* University of Chicago Press, Chicago, 1943.

See also General References: [35] Ely, pp. 143–158.

[35] The General References are listed in full at the end of this book.

CHAPTER 10 *Special Approaches*

Directors who use a variety of special approaches in the education of adults maintain the largest programs and provide learning opportunities for the maximum number of adults. Conventional classes typically attract only a minor portion of the total adult population. Program services to organized groups will stimulate many adults to learn throughout life. Educational services to informal groups can induce even more adults to participate in learning activities. Numerous special approaches, however, are necessary if the educational needs of other great segments of our population are to be served. Some of these by their nature must embrace the whole community and affect the whole population; others are useful with smaller groups. A few are individual.

INDIVIDUAL APPROACHES

"Feature writing! No, we don't offer that. We advertised short-story writing some time ago, but only three signed up. I'm sure there wouldn't be enough for a class in feature writing. However, we'll take your name and if enough request it, we'll try to find a teacher."

This is a typical registration-desk story. Every year unknown thousands of adults with specific learning desires are turned away because there are not enough for a class in that subject. Some find help in other agencies, but many never do. Turning away a prospective learner merely because too few others have requested the same course hurts the individual, the school, and adult education in general. Since there are many ways of serving individual interests, there is little need for this refusal. Most professions do not insist upon serving groups only. A doctor ministers to the individual patient; a lawyer will serve a single client; a judge hears a particular case. Can professional educators do less than assist all who desire to learn? This situation points up the need for special ways of educating adults for whom scheduled class study is neither attractive nor appropriate.

Tutorial Services

The great teachers have always relied heavily upon individual instruction, sometimes depending upon it almost solely. Through a sequence of penetrating questions Socrates led the individual to rational conclusions. Jesus often taught his disciples singly. Oxford and Cambridge gained their reputations largely through their tutorial systems. The story of Mark Hopkins sitting on a log meeting the mind of his student who sat beside him has become legend.

Personal tutoring is not only the oldest approach to education but in many respects the most efficient. In fact, some skills can be learned in almost no other way. Tutoring is especially effective in developing manual and mental skills, teaching foreign languages, and providing remedial instruction after specific weaknesses have been diagnosed. In a certain sense, of course, learning is always individual. Tutoring permits the closest interaction of minds and the most personal demonstration, offers the greatest opportunity to adapt the speed and level of instruction to the learner, and thus eliminates much waste of time. Many a modern Socrates, Mark Hopkins, or ordinary instructor can be at his exciting best in a one-to-one tutoring situation.

Tutoring is not used extensively in American schools. When the public demanded a system of education which would provide all the children of all the people with 8 to 12 years of schooling, economy and the shortage of trained teachers forced the adoption of group approaches. As a result, adult-education directors with public-school backgrounds are likely to overlook the importance of the individual approach. If tutoring is suggested, high cost will usually be given as the reason for not adopting it. True, costs may be high for completely individualized tutoring. When its greater efficiency over group methods is considered, however, the expense may not seem too far out of line. Where costs are prohibitive, variations can often be introduced to make this approach more economical. Wherever financially possible, tutoring is to be highly recommended.

In ordinary usage, the tutoring of small groups is an intermediate approach between teaching classes of normal size and individual coaching. Tutoring small groups cuts expense. When a few persons are under pressure to master a skill quickly or to prepare for an examination, they may have a need sufficiently crucial to warrant use of tutors. In skilled hands, such instruction may approach the coaching or cram sessions held before college examinations. For such purposes intensive tutoring may be useful, although if it is not preceded by adequate study, it is likely to result primarily in temporary learning. Also, small groups needing remedial instruction or review of fundamentals before starting an advanced course can often be brought up to par quickly by skilled tutors.

Tutoring may be combined with correspondence study or with the use of home-study materials. Individuals or small groups who cannot spend much time with an instructor may receive large blocks of work to do with clearly written materials and study guides. They may send lessons and examinations to the instructor and meet with him at infrequent intervals for checking progress, seeing films, discussing difficult concepts, and receiving further assignments.

Another advantage is that tutoring and home study can make effective use of volunteers. A paid professional teacher may assign self-teaching materials and instruct cadet teachers or other helpers in their work with students. Helpers may be relatives, friends, or neighbors. Lay helpers have been used successfully in tutoring near-illiterates and the foreign-born in home-study courses. Such arrangements may materially reduce the time normally required of the professional tutor.

The each-one-teach-one approach, popularized by Laubach in the literacy campaigns of the East Indies, has been used widely in Asia, Latin America, Africa, and other areas.[1] It makes use of volunteer leaders who have learned a specific lession which they teach to another person or to several others individually. These in turn teach one or more, and the program continues in chain-letter fashion. When this method is used in its simplest form, the teachers are only one lesson ahead of their pupils, and some loss in effectiveness undoubtedly occurs as each new link in the chain is reached. Theoretically, if no loss occurred, an educational campaign could sweep through a population. In practice its application is limited largely to simple skills, the teaching of which does not require much professional understanding or insight. Some of the work of the Extension Service of the U.S. Department of Agriculture is done through neighborhood leaders who at times use essentially the each-one-teach-one method. One major weakness stems from the fact that errors are cumulative. Constant and careful supervision is required to minimize this danger. Under stimulative supervision, considerable progress can be made with highly motivated leaders.

Guided reading is another variation of tutoring. A counselor, teacher, or readers' adviser may suggest a reading course, but the student progresses largely on his own. There is likely to be little discussion of its content with one who knows the field. The worth of this approach depends largely upon the care with which readings are selected to fit the interest and background of the reader. Courses suggesting sequences of titles in given fields are often available in libraries, and readers' advisers may suggest a list of books to fit individual interests. A few state libraries, such as those in Illinois and Oregon, set up noncredit reading courses, distribute the lists on request, and lend the books if they are not

[1] Frank C. Laubach, *The Silent Billion Speak*, Friendship Press, New York, 1943.

available locally. Several reading clubs, such as the Chautauqua Literary and Scientific Circle, systematize the reading and grant certificates for completion of a specified number of books. Among 2,684 school districts in the United States having adult-education programs, 118 reported provision of directed individual reading in 1947–1948.[2]

Correspondence Study

Toward the end of the last century President Harper of the University of Chicago and an editor of a mining journal in Pennsylvania encouraged the development of home-study courses. Both universities and private correspondence schools have offered home-study courses for over 60 years. *Accredited Higher Institutions*[3] lists 124 institutions which are reported to have a correspondence enrollment of 164,569.[4] Complete reports from resident institutions would probably show 150 of them having an enrollment of nearly 200,000. Thousands of high schools and dozens of junior colleges use correspondence courses to enrich their curricula. Private home-study schools have enrolled millions of adults and out-of-school youth. One such school alone has enrolled over 6 million.

For decades the Armed Services have used correspondence courses to teach enlisted men and officers in both regular and reserve status. During World War II more than 1,250,000 men and women enrolled in the U.S. Armed Forces Institute (USAFI) courses. An additional three-quarter million used USAFI study materials in locally organized groups.[5] During the 1952 calendar year USAFI processed 338,836 course enrollments; the Air Force, 57,044; U.S. Navy correspondence schools, 293,725; and the U.S. Marine Corps Institute, over 35,000. The Army and Coast Guard also have large programs.

Correspondence study is also used extensively at all educational levels in Australia, Canada, New Zealand, and in several other countries having sparsely settled areas. Even in thickly settled areas it can serve specialized needs. At peak enrollment in home-study citizenship courses, nearly 10,000 aliens were preparing for the naturalization examination by this method. Correspondence study with its variations and flexibility has proved itself worthy of a place in the repertory of any director of adult education.

Home study is the most practical and inexpensive way known to provide educational opportunities to a wide range of adults who find it in-

[2] Homer Kempfer, *Adult Education Activities of the Public School: Report of a Survey, 1947–48*, U.S. Office of Education Pamphlet 107, 1949, pp. 6–7.

[3] U.S. Office of Education Bulletin 1952, no. 3.

[4] *American Universities and Colleges,* American Council on Education, Washington, 1952.

[5] C. O. Houle et al., *The Armed Services and Adult Education,* American Council on Education, Washington, 1947, p. 96.

convenient or impossible to attend residence instruction. Prosser and Quigley [6] recognize it as a major educational approach in a democracy:

High on the list of institutions that are democratizing education stand the correspondence schools, most of which offer training both in general education and in vocational subjects for many different occupations. Their offerings cover a wider range of courses by mail than are available as residence courses in most any community, large or small. The repertoire of every correspondence school is available through the post office, to every student not only in the United States but in the world. The student does not travel to school. The school comes to him.

Only by means of the correspondence school will it ever be possible to give vocational education through schools to more than a comparatively small minority of the citizens of this or any other country. These schools though operated for profit, have become among the most effective democratizers of our educational institutions.

Home study can be thought of both as a supplement to other forms of education and as a major approach in its own right. Home study cannot do everything that personal tutoring or well-conducted classes and discussion groups of moderate size can do. In turn, they cannot do all that home study can do. The values of stimulation through face-to-face instruction or group discussion, of personal interaction with classmates, and of timely explanation are either absent or difficult to arrange in home study.

Correspondence study is essentially an adult way of learning. Public and private home-study schools offer every director of adult education the use of their extensive resources, which may well become an integral part of his regular educational program. Through home study, directors can offer educational opportunities which they cannot possibly provide in any other way.

Home study is for the isolated, the traveler, the man whose work conflicts with class schedules, the homebound, the person desiring a special course, the man who cannot leave his family or afford to quit his job for a year or two of special training, the man in mid-life who needs to prepare for another occupation, the working older person desiring to retire to a second career, and the middle-aged housewife needing to brush up her knowledge or to learn new, salable skills. Home study is for the would-be watch repairman located where there is no watch-repair school. It is for the industrial-accident victim gaining a second start through vocational rehabilitation. It is for a hundred other special cases which residence schools are not able to serve.

To the individual, home study offers these unique advantages:

1. It can be pursued at any time and place without regard to class

---

[6] C. A. Prosser and Thomas H. Quigley, *Vocational Education in a Democracy,* American Technical Society, Chicago, 1949, pp. 528–529.

schedules. Serious-minded adults with well-established study habits often find home study the most practical way of achieving an educational objective.

2. The student sets his own pace; he is not in lock step. A student can progress according to his own interest, work load, and ability.

3. To complete a home-study course, a person must master all parts of the course. Although certain weaknesses may sometimes be overlooked in group methods, there can be no sliding through a correspondence course. A person with a home-study diploma has demonstrated important character traits. By its very nature, home study has been a contributing factor to the lives of many well-known self-made men and to countless others.

4. Home-study students can learn while they earn and enjoy normal family and community life.

5. Instructional materials are usually self-teaching. Many private schools prepare their own texts, write them clearly, use illustrations profusely, and constantly improve their materials by revision.

6. Evaluation of a student's actual achievement is often more reliable and fairer than it is in a residence class.

7. Fees for home-study courses are usually lower than in residence schools. In addition, costs of travel and living away from home are eliminated.

Local directors of adult education and adult counselors are in key positions regarding the whole home-study field. If they have properly established themselves as educational advisers, their counsel will be sought by out-of-school youth and more mature adults who are thinking about signing up for a home-study course. Far more people register for correspondence courses each year than enter the freshman classes of all the colleges in the country. Guidance departments, therefore, certainly have a responsibility for offering advice in this field. Since most enrollments occur some time after people leave school, every school should assume the responsibility of informing its students before they leave of its home-study advisory services. Completion rates among those who receive sound advice from their counselors are higher than among those who enroll without such assistance.

In regard to home-study schools, directors of adult education, members of their registration and counseling staffs, and secondary-school guidance personnel should know that:

1. With few exceptions, private home-study schools, often concerned with adult trade and professional education, are accredited differently from the correspondence departments of higher educational institutions. Courses in the latter are usually expressed in semester or quarter hours or in high-school units. Most private schools gear their instruction primarily to the requirements of the trades and professions, although several

institutions offer standard secondary-school courses based upon widely adopted textbooks or specially written materials. Graduates of one large school have entered over 500 institutions of higher education.

2. Three agencies set standards for private home-study schools:

a. A number of states have laws and regulations governing home-study schools, although they vary widely in effectiveness. Some states inspect and supervise proprietary schools carefully, while others pay little attention to them. Regulations and laws of Illinois, New Jersey, New York, and Pennsylvania are among those providing the highest standards. Legal regulations at best can assure only minimum standards and cannot assure educational service of high quality or the wisest personal expenditure of time and money.

b. The Federal Trade Commission has established trade practice rules for private home-study schools in an attempt to foster and promote fair competitive conditions in the interest of the schools and the public. They apply to schools engaged in interstate commerce. Counselors should be suspicious of schools which violate these rules. Reputable schools, for instance, do not guarantee employment, promotion, or increases in pay.

c. The National Home Study Council in Washington is the only voluntary approval and accrediting agency serving the private correspondence schools. The council was established in 1926 to promote sound educational standards and ethical business practices within the home-study field. It has established standards of educational service, ethical operation, and financial responsibility, and its membership includes only institutions of the best repute.

Organization of the council was stimulated by a study financed by the Carnegie Corporation and made by Dr. J. S. Noffsinger, who served as executive director of the council for 26 years. The council works closely with the Federal Trade Commission, state education departments, and approval agencies to establish and maintain standards. The council exercises a healthy self-discipline among both its members and nonmembers in matters of promotion, enrollment, and services, although one of its chief contributions is in raising educational standards through research, experimentation, surveys, and evaluative procedures. The council cooperates with better business bureaus, chambers of commerce, the Post Office Department, and other official bodies in suppressing diploma mills, fly-by-night schools, and fraudulent and irresponsible schools. Its *Home Study Blue Book* is a ready reference for every director of adult education and student counselor.

3. A wide variety of credit and noncredit courses are available at high-school and college level from many colleges and universities.[7] A few schools provide courses of elementary level. At some private and public

---

[7] See Helen Duncan and W. S. Bittner, *Guide to Correspondence Study*, National University Extension Association, Bloomington, Ind.

schools home-study materials are available, under certain circumstances, for purchase without correspondence privileges.

4. There are often limits to the amount of home-study credit that high schools, colleges, professional schools, and licensing boards will accept. Counselors and students should find out in advance about the acceptability of any particular course.

5. *A Guide to the Evaluation of Military Experiences in the Armed Forces,* issued by the American Council on Education, provides credit recommendations for USAFI and other military courses accepted by civilian institutions.

6. An estimated 10,000 courses are available from home-study schools. They train for a high percentage of all recognized occupations. A sizable proportion of those who pass occupational licensing examinations prepare for them through home study.

7. Courses for the foreign-born studying citizenship and for near-illiterates are available from the U.S. Immigration and Naturalization Service and are particularly useful where helpers can be arranged.[8]

8. Rates of completion may be somewhat lower than in resident schools. About 10 per cent of those registered in USAFI courses during World War II completed them.[9] College home-study departments have a better record than USAFI, partly because they attract a more select group. Completion rates among private home-study schools vary widely according to the subject field and many other factors. While they are often less than 50 per cent, occasionally they are as high as 75 per cent.

9. There is fully as much variation among home-study schools as among resident schools, and perhaps more. While the best schools employ competent educators and utilize sound self-teaching instructional materials and study guides, other schools may not maintain a similar quality of service. Even where only schools of high quality are being considered, several basic questions should precede registration:

a. Does the prospective student have adequate educational background to profit from the instruction?

b. Does he have the necessary study skills to do the work and enough motivation to pursue it?

c. Does he have a sufficiently clear and compelling objective that may be satisfied by taking the home-study course?

d. Will he schedule sufficient time to work on the course?

10. Additional information can be obtained from state education departments, state university extension divisions, the Federal Office of Education, and the National Home Study Council.

Mortality rates among correspondence students can be materially re-

---

[8] N. C. Turpen, "Home Study for Foreign-born Applicants for Citizenship," *Higher Education,* 3:3–5, Jan. 15, 1947.

[9] Houle et al., *op, cit.,* p. 97.

duced if home study is brought under school supervision. This form of study was worked out a generation ago for broadening the curriculum of the high school.[10] It is particularly valuable in small communities, although it can be used profitably in programs of any size. Over 10 per cent of 2,684 adult programs claimed to use this approach in 1947–1948.[11] Its adoption by adult schools was stimulated considerably after World War II when the Veterans Administration approved correspondence courses for GI Benefits. While only a few adult programs reported offering such courses in a 1951 survey, those which did so rated home study among their more effective methods.[12]

Supervised correspondence study is a plan in which the school provides guidance, administrative, and certain educational services to the student without being directly responsible for his instruction. The school advises on courses and enrolls the student in the desired course from whichever correspondence school seems to offer the most suitable instruction. A regularly scheduled time and room are provided for study under the supervision of a teacher or supervisor of correspondence study, who acts as a liaison between the student and the correspondence school. The supervisor keeps track of progress, gives encouragement, arranges for necessary laboratory or shopwork, sometimes makes appointments with other teachers for assistance with problems, and otherwise helps maintain productive study conditions. Regularly scheduled meetings at which the student's attendance is expected help overcome the human tendency to procrastinate.

If only a few adults are enrolled, each possibly in a different course, they may all study at the same time in one room. If more than a roomful study at the same time, those in similar fields may be grouped together under a teacher qualified in one of them. In this case the teacher may take a more active part in instruction, moving from group to group as necessary. If home-study materials are purchased without instructional service, a teacher may use them as self-teaching texts, review the exercises worked out, carry on personal instruction or coaching where necessary, and let the students progress as rapidly as they individually are able. In this way one teacher can handle several related subjects or courses being studied by individuals or small groups.

Ordinarily, however, the supervisor does not attempt to teach, although he may occasionally help students over rough spots according to his ability. Students use the home-study instructional materials provided through

[10] S. C. Mitchell, *Supervised Correspondence Study for Individual Pupil Needs,* International Textbook Company, Scranton, Pa., 1939.

[11] Kempfer, *op. cit.,* pp. 6–7.

[12] Division of Adult Education Service of the NEA, *A Study of Urban Public School Adult Education Programs of the United States,* National Education Association, Washington, 1952, pp. 55–56.

their enrollment and maintain the usual relationship with their instructor by mail.

This plan makes the extensive resources of both private schools and correspondence departments of universities conveniently available to any person wanting to study. Even small communities can offer practically any course likely to be requested. Courses may range all the way from short units which can be finished in a few days to complete curricula demanding years of study. Courses can even be built up to meet individual needs. Accelerated academic training qualifying students for elementary- and high-school equivalency certificates can often be operated on a supervised home-study basis. The biggest advantage, however, is in opening up broad fields of study that could never be offered through any normal group approach.

While in a few cases correspondence instruction services are purchased by a school and provided free to adults, in most instances the cost of the course is borne by the registrant. A few private home-study schools have made instruction under local supervision available at monthly or per-lesson rates. Bills are submitted according to the number of students in active enrollment or the number of lessons submitted.

Occasionally, especially in the Armed Forces, groups use home-study materials for discussion purposes under local leadership or supervision. Open-book examinations are then completed individually. There may also be a tie-up with radio or TV broadcasts. In either case the regular feature stimulates a more rapid completion of courses.

Adults may study self-teaching materials for their own improvement or in preparation for examinations without partaking of correspondence privileges. An unknown number of regular home-study registrants follow this plan. After paying for the course and receiving all the materials, they may study as far as they need without sending in lessons. When an adult wants to study a subject without preparing the written assignments, the director may recommend correspondence instruction materials. A course from a reputable school is likely to consist of well-selected and understandable content with a minimum of irrelevant or out-of-date information. It is likely to be easier to learn than are materials prepared for resident use.

A few large city schools and state education departments offer home-study courses to those who, for satisfactory reasons, cannot attend classes. Scores of homebound aliens in New York City have prepared for their naturalization examinations in this way. On request the Board of Education sends out instructional material and study guides, reviews and returns lessons received, and arranges examinations.

Occasionally an adult school provides other home-study courses, such as program aids for club chairmen, literacy instruction, and elementary-

and high-school courses. It permits the local adult department to maintain a close service relationship with the student rather than to lose it to a more distant agency. Basic instructional materials are often purchased from some outside agency, although supplementary instructions are usually written locally. Ordinarily the handicaps inherent in small volume make local correspondence study less efficient and less satisfactory than the services offered by schools operating nationally.

GROUP APPROACHES

Most adult education in America is organized on a group basis. As most group approaches are discussed elsewhere, only two special types will be treated here.

Educational Trips

As a supplement to systematic instruction, the educational tour or field trip is widely used. Such trips, however, usually hold a minor place in the total repertory of methods. Classroom methods are often supplemented by a few excursions to add reality and interest to academic learning situations.

Until recently the planned group trip had little general use as a basic approach to education. True, a few selected classes in conservation, engineering, agriculture, geology, geography, and advanced social sciences for years have been conducted as field courses or "traveling classrooms." Likewise, a number of higher institutions have conducted summer terms of domestic or foreign travel, either with or without credit. A dramatic use of the excursion was the "flying classroom" originated at Michigan State College. In it groups of school administrators traveled from city to city by air for study of employment procedures, training methods in industry, human relations, public relations, occupational adjustment, and other educational aspects of business and industry. Similar values are gained on a local scale on BIE or BIEL (business, industry, education, and labor) days, during which teachers tour selected local businesses and industries in order to become better acquainted with problems and expectations of this phase of community life.[13] The process is profitably reversed by having business and industrial leaders learn about the schools by visiting them in operation.

The organized educational excursion now occupies a respected place in adult education, and it seems to be growing in favor. Among 2,684 districts recently reporting adult education, over 9 per cent claimed to sponsor conducted excursions.[14] Whenever practical to manage, such a trip is an interesting and usually an effective approach to learning.

[13] Further information can be obtained from The National Association of Manufacturers, New York.
[14] Kempfer, *op. cit.*, p. 8.

In groups or singly, adults can go on specific missions to interview people and to see industrial installations and processes. Most profit comes when the director knows the field intimately enough to make a wise selection of the places or persons to be visited and to direct the visitor to look for the most significant features. The next best arrangement is to refer the adults to experts in the field who can map itineraries and give advice. While this type of directed visiting without an accompanying guide may seem quite informal, actually it has often produced good results. Many foreign visitors learn a great deal by following itineraries built up by those who know a field. Through directed visiting, observation, interviews, and participation in conferences, they undoubtedly gain much more than they could through formal study. In many situations this approach is highly useful for adults who can explore learning opportunities within a community or region. The chief drawback is the time consumed in planning itineraries and the time demanded of busy authorities, especially when the visitors come individually or have individual interests. For this reason, whenever possible, directed visitation and observation should be planned as a group activity.

In a few places systematic courses have been built up using the directed visit, observation, and interview as the basic approach. Newcomers to a community may be escorted around town to the city hall, the health department, schools, historic points, and other places of interest where officials can orient them to the community. At least two Chicago YMCAs offer courses of the excursion type. One course, called Touring the Town, offers an opportunity for Chicagoans to see the marvels of science, industry, and arts and crafts—the cultural institutions and the medical centers—things which people come from all over the world to see. In another course, entitled Visits with Interesting People, the group members on successive weeks visit informally in the homes or offices of leaders of art, business, education, journalism, labor, politics, religion, and science and discuss their work with them.

Adult schools, community councils, advisory committees, study commissions, and similar groups may go on trips to gather information for special study-for-action projects. Members of a committee studying a problem are prepared to seek the specific information most pertinent to their concern. In one community, committee members filled two cars and visited several small libraries to pick up ideas on how to finance and improve their village library service. Visits to study recreation programs, housing developments, health programs, agricultural developments, or new adult schools can be aimed at finding out how others achieved good results. Such visits are usually made to pilot projects, experimental developments, and to outstanding programs. Visits often yield new insights for solving a problem or making a community improvement which cannot be obtained easily in any other way. Field visiting facilitates the gathering of pertinent data, the observation of actual conditions, and face-to-face discussion with local leaders.

Several adult schools provide extended educational tours of a day, a weekend, or a longer period. They often are planned to study history, geology, flora and fauna, or the social and economic life of a region. Extended tours are especially good ways of combining education and recreation during vacation periods. Such tours may be preceded by considerable preparatory reading and discussion. Transportation and other costs are usually financed by the members on a flat-fee basis.

The Adult School at San Jose, California, has sponsored educational tours for the past 15 years. They were started in the belief that true patriotism and love of country grow out of firsthand knowledge of it. A number of trips of 2 or more days have been made in the West. These are typical:

Tour	No. of days	Cost per person
Yosemite and wild flowers.....	2	$ 20.00
Coast and lakes..............	3	29.50
Oregon cascades and coast....	7	90.00
California deserts............	8	106.00

In 1951 three busloads of adults left San Jose and crossed the continent by a southern route. Stops were made at historic spots. The itinerants spent a full week in historic Virginia and returned by the northern route. This trip was scouted the preceding year by the leader, David L. Mackaye, director of adult education.

Applicants fill the places on the longer trips well in advance. The leader gives each registrant a detailed itinerary and a syllabus before the trip starts. On the trip the members take colored pictures to provide a permanent record for sharing with friends and potential members of future trips. Those who have taken such tours and those booked for future trips constitute "The Vagabonds," a club which meets monthly to enjoy the pictures, discuss past trips, and plan future ones. At least one trip resulted in the publication of an authentic guide to the flora of the region.

State education departments, state adult-education associations, and adult-education councils sometimes sponsor annual educational trips. Often teachers relate the trip to classwork in a broad field. Washington, D.C., and its environs are the objective of many of these trips, with the state capital a second favorite spot. Special excursion trains and all-expense trips are sometimes arranged.

For over 30 years, except in wartime, Connecticut evening-school students, teachers, and their friends have made an annual pilgrimage to Washington. From 300 to 1,000 usually go. Teachers of the foreign-born especially have the opportunity to focus their instruction during the year on the trip to the nation's capital.

Pilgrimages sponsored by the supervisor of adult civic education in Massachusetts include from 275 to 1,200 people. Classes all over the state prepare for the trip by looking at visual aids and discussing anticipated sights. Community libraries tie in by featuring a display of books on Washington during the weeks before the trip. In Delaware, civic groups often help finance trips to historical spots in the state. Rhode Island groups sometimes go to Boston for a weekend.

In South Carolina, as many as 3,000 to 4,000 adults, traveling by cars, busses, and trains, go on an annual Sunday trip which includes Charleston, Columbia, and other places in the state. Adult students in continuation schools and literacy classes are invited on a tour which studies the history, geography, natural resources, industries, and economic and social problems of the state. The itinerary and schedule are planned by the state supervisor of adult education. In preparation, adults save for the trip and discuss such topics as a suitable wardrobe, courtesy on the trip, balanced lunches, safety, and first aid. During the excursion each adult traces his route on a state map and writes in or marks towns through which he passes. Information gathered on the tour is used later in letter writing, conversations, discussion, and public programs.

Mass pilgrimages, like the crusades of medieval times, can take people out of their limited daily existence and broaden their horizons immeasurably. In spite of the high mobility of many people, a great many more, especially in the lower economic groups, seldom travel beyond their immediate neighborhoods and communities. To them a trip to a big city 100 miles away may be a special event. For many people a visit to Washington, New York, or another big city can be among the most stimulating experiences of a lifetime. Some adults will never be the same thereafter. Such a trip can be the focus of instruction for years in advance and the stimulator of learning for years afterward. With adequate preliminary planning and proper follow-up such pilgrimages can be an important educational approach.

For decades foreign educational tours have been sponsored by colleges and universities. In recent years such travel has become a valued part of certain adult-education programs and gives promise of further growth.

The community-ambassador program developed in New York State and in New England makes maximum use of foreign travel for developing international understanding.[15] Several communities send selected

---

[15] *The Community Project in International Understanding,* New York State Education Department, Albany, N.Y., 1948.

young people, each to live in a home abroad for a few summer weeks. Before going, the young people are thoroughly briefed on the history, organization, and nature of their community. They are prepared to explain the operation of American democracy at the community level. The young adult enters into the normal life of the foreign family and community as much as possible. He represents his community to the foreign village and may supplement discussion with home movies, and still pictures. Upon return, each tourist becomes a resource person for organization programs in the community. He is invited to appear before numerous groups to discuss his experiences and observations. While the individual may lack the authenticity of comprehensive surveys of economic and social conditions in the country, he certainly carries a down-to-earth, human interest which stirs the imagination of many more people back home in regard to peace and world understanding than do more academic approaches.

While the idea works especially well with young people, it can be used with older adults as well. Recently, a civic club in a Missouri town sent a popular postmaster to England and thereby facilitated a two-way flow of information. A common man reporting back home on his talks with common people abroad stimulates local interest that newspaper reporters and diplomats can seldom equal. Certain local and state UNESCO groups have carried on similar projects. This type of approach, multiplied many times over, offers much hope in building international understanding.

Financing such foreign tours usually becomes a cooperative venture. Older adults may supply a portion of the necessary funds, but community organizations often provide for all the expenses of young people. In Niagara Falls, 105 organizations including parent-education groups, mothers clubs, church societies, student groups, and general organizations joined in raising nearly $2,000 to send two young adults as community ambassadors to Europe in 1950. Such organizational tie-ins assure a wide degree of involvement with and interest in the visitor, both while he is abroad and on his return. Likewise, cooperative sponsorship by community organizations of such trips builds favorable attitudes within their own membership.

The Department of State, the Department of Commerce, the Office of Education, and other government agencies sponsor groups of adults from foreign countries who visit this country to study American agriculture, business, education, government, industry, and other aspects of our national life. Private organizations likewise bring over thousands of foreign visitors each year. Through planned itineraries of visits and conferences, the foreign guests learn under rather favorable conditions.

A golden opportunity for further education of our foreign visitors lies in direct contact with American home life. Firsthand understanding of our family and community life can best be gained through visiting, dining, and staying all night with typical American families. As the visitors associate with American families, living through their daily routines, they gain significant insights into what the non-Hollywood version of America is really like. They begin to understand something of what freedom and democracy in the family, the neighborhood, and the community mean to us. The stability they observe in American life may counterbalance the disturbing headlines of conflict among government leaders. Evaluative interviews with foreign visitors before departure reveal that visits in American homes are extremely significant.

Educational Camps

While educational camping began over 90 years ago, it has grown most during the past generation. By 1950, the departments of agriculture, biology, engineering, geology, geography, forestry, physical education, health, and science in fifty colleges and universities were conducting camps. Usually these provided field experience in certain courses or served as complete courses in themselves.

Organized camping is rapidly gaining recognition as an approach which provides participants with significant opportunities for education in an outdoor group setting. Among public schools, the Michigan State Department of Public Instruction, stimulated by the Kellogg Foundation, has demonstrated considerable leadership in this field; sixty schools in that state were providing camping experiences in 1950. California and New York both have legislation authorizing school-operated camps.

A great many private camps were established long before the schools evidenced much interest in such a venture. Even 20 years ago over 5,000 camps for boys and girls were in operation, and there are considerably more today. Camps of all kinds probably number 20,000. They are operated by churches, clubs, social agencies, police departments, the Ys, cities, 4-H clubs, and other character-building agencies, as well as by private individuals. While most camps serve youth of in-school age, educational camps for out-of-school youth and adults offer significant learning experience.

The Civilian Conservation Corps of the 1930s provided more experience in educational camping than any other venture except military camps. The Federal government established these camps during a period when millions of youth were unable to find work. In exchange for work on public projects, the CCC camps provided subsistence, a modest wage, experience in group living, certain health services, and a variety of opportunities for educational guidance and training. The camps were closed early in World War II, when the economy absorbed the young men.

Before the outbreak of the Korean War in 1950, unemployment among young adults again seemed in the offing. Bills were introduced in Congress to provide for the reestablishment of work camps for young adults.

This situation stimulated considerable thinking in Michigan and elsewhere among school people who disliked the idea of direct Federal operation of educational programs. They felt that if states and localities could gain experience in operating camps for out-of-school youth, decentralized governmental units could better insist on administering the camps if unemployment came.

Future Farmers, Future Homemakers, 4-H clubs, YMCAs, and religious fellowships frequently sponsor camps for out-of-school youth. Since they are often attended primarily by the local youth leaders, they offer programs of leadership training. Religious organizations and social agencies sometimes sponsor work camps, intercultural camps, and institutes. Fifteen to twenty thousand people, chiefly young adults, annually take hiking or bicycle trips sponsored by American Youth Hostels.

Many of the values claimed for in-school camping experience hold for young adults. Camping offers the benefits of social living in a group of peers, and this experience is profitable during the young-adult years, as well as at earlier ages. Camps provide a number of democratizing influences. Also, they can provide time and circumstance for health examinations and for instruction in hygiene and sanitation. If economic conditions do not offer a gradual transition from full-time schooling into full-time work, camping can provide a graduated work experience.

Direct educational values for young adults can run the gamut. Camps give the natural setting for study of conservation, weather, flora and fauna, geology and geography, and land use. Here young adults can study the reasons for shifting population, develop some of the skills of survival, and gain experience in planning and reporting, surveying and mapping, and using tools to build bridges and cabins. Camps offer more opportunity for concentrated attention to music, arts, and dramatics than do most other settings. This combination of education and recreation makes learning pleasant and interesting.

Educational camps for middle-aged and older adults have been sponsored on a limited scale by several agencies. In some states the cooperative Extension Service and the home and farm bureaus conduct summer camps for farm women. Labor unions, the Farmers Union, various colleges, and similar organizations conduct educational camps especially during the summer. Camp sessions, which are usually 1 or 2 weeks long, compete for the vacation time of participants. Longer sessions are held by groups interested in music, painting, writing, dramatics, and similar arts. A number of family camps are held under church leadership. The Salvation Army has long been a leader in family camps, and one of the most famous of all institutions of adult education—Chautauqua—grew out of a camp setting.

Camps for older adults provide a way of combining education with recreation. A fair percentage of adults can be encouraged to spend their regular vacations in camp settings having educational features. Adults can be especially attracted to weekend camps in the mountains, at the seashore, or other scenic spots. Educational activities in arts and crafts, music, dramatics, public affairs, family-life education, and a variety of similar fields can be arranged. The Chautauqua institution and dozens of other adult camps have demonstrated the necessary techniques for organizing and administering the educational program.[16] As these programs are largely self-sustaining financially, the techniques can be adapted and applied as a part of the public-school adult-education program.

MASS MEDIA

A part of education involves the exchange and dissemination of information. The media of mass communication—the press, radio, television, and cinema—provide the best means yet available for the spreading of information to large populations. The ease and economy of reaching large numbers through mass media, however, have led some educators to place too great a value upon them.

Powerful and important though they are, all mass media have one inherent weakness: they provide essentially a one-way flow of communication. Psychologically, learning is an activity which changes behavior. While members of an audience can respond to the stimulation of mass media, they have limited opportunity to interact either with one another or with the stimulator. Letters and telephone calls to newspapers, authors, and program directors at best lack the flexibility of face-to-face discussion. Despite this fundamental disadvantage, however, these means of mass communication are highly important approaches to the education of adults. Alert directors will use them whenever possible.

The Press

Local and metropolitan newspapers are widely used in promoting adult education, but few programs utilize the press in other educational ways. On 3,313 returned check lists in a 1948 nationwide survey, only 215 schools reported using newspaper columns or features for purposes other than public relations.[17] A subsequent inquiry, however, revealed that only a few of the 215 were systematically using newspapers to present content.

The educational opportunities offered by the press, however, are considerable. The population reached is often excelled only by the radio and television audience. Recently at Rochester, New York, for instance, the public and parochial schools jointly prepared attractive and clearly

[16] Margaret Willis and Mary J. Alton, *Adult Study Camps*, Franklin Press, Louisville, Kent., 1951.

[17] Kempfer, *op. cit.*, pp. 6–7.

written information on nominations, elections, and functional and structural aspects of government. This information appeared serially in the daily papers as a contribution to the civic education of the public. A few schools in other communities have presented materials on family life, parent education, recreation, health, safety, literature, and science as regular features, columns, or panel cartoons.

Adult schools which cannot assign staff to prepare material can sometimes encourage newspapers to carry syndicated features having educational content. As newspapers cannot afford to deviate very far from reports of readership surveys, encouragement to carry more educational features may have to be accompanied by promotional campaigns to enlarge readership of those features. Advisory committees, community councils, PTA councils, and other clusters of organizations sometimes are more successful in this encouragement than are individual directors. Newspaper reports on local public-opinion polls and community self-analyses often have high reader interest and contribute materially to public-affairs education.

In recent years the development of pocket books, pamphlets, and comic books has opened important adult-education possibilities. Tens of millions of Public Affairs Pamphlets have been sold. Pamphlets on child care and other subjects of popular interest are among the best sellers from the Government Printing Office. Farmers' Bulletins enjoy a wide distribution. Numerous national and state organizations are finding that inexpensive reproduction of their educational materials and extensive mass-distribution systems are effective means of reaching the public. Inasmuch as no material for national distribution can deal adequately with matters of purely local concern, there is always a need for clearly written information on state and local problems. In large cities and other places where volume can be sufficient, adult schools and other educational organizations could issue local informational materials for mass distribution.

Studies of readership show that comic books and strips reach a sizable portion of the adult population. While comics seem to make special appeal to men, young adults, and people in the lower educational levels who often avoid extensive use of other printed materials, people of all intelligence, educational, socioeconomic, and age levels find them interesting. They can be used to disseminate information widely and quickly. They have a more primitive and fundamental appeal than does unillustrated textual material. Before man was able to express himself in written words, he communicated through pictures. As clear line drawings with appropriate captions often teach more effectively than straight prose, the fundamental concepts and simpler elements of many subject fields can be advantageously presented in comic-magazine form. Thus far, labor unions, parent-education groups, churches, and organizations promoting intercultural and international understanding have been among the more extensive users of comics. They have potential value, however, in a great many other fields.

Academicians in schools and libraries may revolt at using a vehicle which became popular first as a commercial entertainment medium for children. As most people have only a few gross, generalized concepts in fields outside their occupations, any device which will help them gain broader understandings should not be ignored because of its origin. If line drawings and color can help adults conceptualize easily about many of the problems facing them in a complex world, the adult educator should not hesitate to use the comic-book approach wherever it can serve an educative purpose. Comics are among our best visual aids, and once they are in print, they require no mechanical equipment to be used effectively.

Motion Pictures

Experiments with films have shown that they increase the efficiency of learning. The extent of this increase, however, varies widely; films may offer only a slight advantage, or they may improve efficiency by 200 per cent or more. Through such devices as animation, time lapse, slow motion, miniature, and microphotography, skills sometimes can be taught two or three times as fast as they can by usual methods. In general, motion pictures can be counted on to:

1. Expedite acquisition of skills, facts, and understanding of principles
2. Provide an excellent medium for communication across language barriers
3. Stimulate interest and further participation
4. Affect materially the development of attitudes
5. Reach a broad audience
6. Offer a cultural force which can facilitate the change in habits of thinking and action from one generation to another

Valuable though films are, adult programs have not yet made full use of them. Adult educators seem to face special handicaps in the use of films. Even so, a persistent director is able to overcome most difficulties in connection with film showing.

The need for equipment presents a cluster of problems. Actually, projectors are available in nearly all school buildings used by adult educators; but if the adult program has no projector of its own, the problem may be one of arranging to use public property. Except in specially equipped rooms, the projector, screen, and speaker must be set up and tested in advance. The teacher must either learn how to operate the equipment or arrange for another person to do so. The elements of projector operation are so simple that even part-time teachers can be taught the use of the equipment.

Procuring films is often a more difficult problem, but systematic organization can solve it. Except in larger communities films may be too costly to buy. Extensive libraries including films for adult use can be built up where sufficient use warrants purchase of a sizable stock. When not locally available, the desired film may be obtained from one of the 2,660 film libraries which have been listed by the Federal Office of Education.[18] Whether films are obtained locally or from a distant library, whether rented or borrowed free, problems of obtaining the right titles at the right times and places are largely problems of anticipating need. Such needs can often be identified as soon as courses are scheduled and planned, long ahead of actual opening. When the film arrives, arrangement for a preview is necessary for planning its best use.

Films are useful in home study. As early as 1929 one private correspondence school was sending out projectors and animated films to teach the elements of electricity. A university has recently started using films as a supplement to correspondence instruction. Students in an area are invited to a center periodically to see related films and discuss high points of the course.

As most of the problems in using films exist regardless of the number of people attending, directors of adult education are inclined to show them to larger-than-classroom groups. Films are still sometimes used as bait to induce attendance at a lecture or other educational activity. They may convey information to large audiences, but unless accompanied by other educational procedures, they often represent a relatively low-grade educational activity. If explorers, travelers, or scientists accompany their silent films with a lecture or discussion, the values are enhanced. Travelogues alone may be little more than entertainment, or they may build significant insight into the problems of other peoples.

The advent of documentary films in the 1930s stimulated the film forum. In such a forum a film is used to present a problem or issue for discussion. Purely informational, instructional, or industrial films seldom provide adequate stimulation. For forum use the best choice is a short film of good technical quality that presents a human situation or point of view and arouses and sustains interest by its dramatic and artistic value. Broadly speaking, the human-relations field supplies most of the problems suitable for film-forum discussions. The most usable films are specially made for discussion purposes, although at times social-problem scenes in commercial entertainment films can be cut out and used in film forums.

The basic functions of the film are to portray a situation of interest to the audience and to raise questions and issues which will induce maximum discussion directed toward finding satisfactory answers. Film

[18] *A Directory of 2,660 16 mm Film Libraries,* U.S. Office of Education Bulletin 1953, no. 7.

forums can be used with large or small groups. After the initial showing, participation can be extended through normal forum and discussion techniques.

Films not designed to stimulate discussion can sometimes be adapted to forum use by affixing a trailer, either at the end or somewhat before, that incorporates a number of pertinent discussion questions. If this is impractical, a discussion guide based on adequate previewing can be used for the same purpose.

In recent years, especially through the stimulation of the Film Council of America, film users in many communities have organized themselves into film councils. A film council facilitates the pooling of resources. If a cooperative film library can be maintained at a museum, a library, or board of education office, only films of very frequent use need be owned by any one agency. A council, aware of the common resources and of the plans of member agencies, can promote the use of films throughout the community. Also, with the cooperation of member agencies, a council can train users of films, projector operators, and film-forum discussion leaders; arrange previews for potential users; evaluate films; prepare study guides; sponsor film festivals; plan and carry out research; and conduct education-by-film campaigns on specific problems in such areas as civil defense, health, safety, and government.

Radio and Television

Radio and television are the two most important developments in mass communication since the advent of the printing press. Neither has yet fully utilized its educational possibilities.

Educational broadcasting began early. Nearly a generation ago universities and land-grant colleges began to establish broadcasting stations. At one time approximately 175 educational radio stations were operating. Often they served primarily as training facilities for science and engineering departments. Radio instruction supplemented an occasional correspondence course in music or literature, but for the most part the stations gave little attention to providing educational programs for the adult public. A few programs thought to be of interest to school children were broadcast, but for the most part the requirements and possibilities of the new medium were not understood by educators. Insufficient funds usually hampered program development. By 1934 all but a handful of the educational stations had given up their licenses, usually to commercial stations. Only those stations survived which had learned through hard experience how to put on educational programs of wide appeal. This experience during the late 1920s and 1930s showed the necessity of good programming.

Awareness of the educational and cultural utility of educational broadcasting developed during this period. Several schools of the air were started, sometimes over educational stations but often over commercial stations. The principle of school participation in educational programming for educational stations is now widely accepted, but commercial broadcasters cannot afford to lose their listeners by conducting specific educational programs which appeal to a limited audience. Consequently, educational programs often find it impossible to gain favorable broadcasting time in the evenings, when adult programs would have most listeners.

These past experiences in program production, broadcasting, and utilization have convinced educational institutions that they must have their own stations if they are to be able to serve specific educational needs. The development of FM broadcasting offered educational institutions a whole new opportunity to reenter the radio field. When the educational FM band was allocated in 1945, many schools began to take advantage of their second chance. By 1952 approximately 130 AM and FM educational stations were in operation. One state has its own educational FM network. Most stations offer significant programs for the adult public and give the director of adult education an important outlet for good program features. The National Association of Educational Broadcasters operates a tape network which supplies several hours of educational, informational, and cultural programming per week to member stations desiring it. While there is little opportunity for educational institutions to get into AM, the FM field is still wide open. Any director of adult education not already using educational radio can do well to investigate the possibilities of FM and join with other appropriate educational agencies in using existing facilities or in establishing new ones.

Television is largely a postwar development. It grew so rapidly that the Federal Communications Commission in 1948 temporarily stopped granting licenses until it could have time to review its TV channel-allocation policies. At that time only one educational TV station was in operation—WOI-TV at Iowa State College. Under the leadership of the Office of Education, several national educational associations, fearful that all TV channels might be preempted for commercial use, formed the Joint Committee on Educational Television, which is affiliated with the American Council on Education. Largely through pleas of the JCET, the FCC in 1951 reserved a block of 242 TV channels for educational purposes. This is over 10 per cent of all channels now available for TV. Reservations were guaranteed for a year, ending June 2, 1952, with the challenge given educators to show definite progress toward plans for use of the channels. Two-thirds of the population of the country are within range of these allocations. A single institution can qualify as a licensee provided it agrees to make time available either free or on a cost-sharing basis to all other educational, cultural, and public-service agencies. This plan probably will be utilized primarily by universities and large school systems, especially if they have been operating regular radio broadcasting stations.

Progress is being made toward utilizing the allocated channels. In many localities, the cost of constructing and operating a TV station will probably be more than any single educational institution can afford. For example, the cost of building even a modest TV station will easily run to $200,000, while minimum annual operating, depreciation, and programming costs will run to $100,000 or more. Accordingly, in some communities, a number of educational and cultural organizations are forming nonprofit, cooperative associations to hold the licenses and operate the stations. While the latter arrangement takes more time to perfect, it has certain advantages in building an integrated community program of educational TV service. As one station can consume an enormous amount of program material, it is advantageous if a number of educational organizations are available to contribute to the programming.

Pooling of resources both within and outside the community offers considerable advantage in TV. Statewide networks are being planned in some states. A distinct setback came recently when a commission studying educational television in New York State turned down a proposal calling for public financial support of a network of stations which would practically blanket the state. The current reaction against high taxes, the financial needs of other segments of education, and the eagerness of commercial interests for certain of the educational channels are making the fight hard for educational TV. The creation of regional networks and possibly of a national network which could exchange or relay programs by microwave relay, coaxial cable, direct pickup, motion-picture films, or kinescope recordings might be advantageous.

A number of schools and institutions of higher education are producing programs over commercial TV stations. In the beginning these programs were often designed to serve public-relations purposes, although experimentation is going on in several content areas. As might be expected, there has been a certain amount of fumbling and inept programming, but educators, in general, are learning the limitations and requirements of the media.

Television combines most of the advantages of radio and motion pictures and possesses much greater flexibility than the latter. Television can show widely scattered concurrent scenes with a speed that transportation-bound spectators can never hope to equal. While the TV audience sees a live program, kinescopes can be made for showing at any future time, either on a screen or on TV.

Because of these characteristics, the educational possibilities of television are almost beyond comprehension. When fully developed with color, TV undoubtedly will be several times as effective as radio. Results so far have been dramatic, and no doubt the educational advantages discovered to date will be further multiplied as educators and technicians learn more about the medium.

The following assets of educational TV are shared only in part by radio:

1. A large audience can be reached. A very great percentage of all adults have access to radios, and a large majority listen at times of high drama. By 1960 an estimated 50 million TV sets will be in operation. A clear majority of our population can then see and hear history in the making. While few educational programs may win as large an audience as entertainment features, audiences for the former need not be small. Size of audience, however, should be only one consideration in educational broadcasting. Already certain educational network programs have over a half-million viewers.

2. TV can teach effectively. A number of experiments and studies present convincing evidence that under certain circumstances TV is as effective as classroom teaching. In fact, in some studies, the better preparation and the fascination of the medium were thought to be responsible for the superior results with TV. TV can present to a very large audience scientific demonstrations that otherwise could be seen only by a small group. Certain types of scientific and medical knowledge, for instance, can be spread more easily to large numbers.

3. TV can go to its audience. Adult educators have long recognized the desirability of conducting educational activities where people live. TV is the ultimate in intimacy and informality; it goes into the homes. All the personal fears of entering a new group, of facing strangers, and of being embarrassed are avoided. No time, money, or energy is spent in travel to a school. TV can be available at all times of the day or night, whenever housewives, working men and women, or shift workers and others have time for it.

4. Resources can be better utilized. The best teachers, performers, demonstrators, authorities, talent, instructional materials, and apparatus can be made available to many more people than could be reached through other means. In agricultural extension work, for instance, one county agent in a few minutes over TV can reach more farmers than he could in weeks of travel and demonstration in rural areas.

5. Current material carries more interest. The contents of today's newspaper are usually hours old when received. Films are always edited, fixed, controlled, and necessarily deal with the past. TV, even when rehearsed and planned, is alive. Current events can be seen as they actually happen; and history can be acted out with an authenticity and interest that can never be captured in words on a page.

An adult-education program has several major uses for radio and TV. Certain educational activities can be planned around available programs, which can either be brought into the classroom or seen or heard during out-of-class hours. Directed viewing is a distinct possibility, as is directed listening. Organization of informal radio-listening and TV-viewing groups, however, may be a better plan. In Cleveland, for instance, over 200 home groups of neighbors were known to listen to the educational broadcasts of Western Reserve University and to discuss them afterward. At times some of the national radio network programs on public affairs have had thousands of listening groups. In large cities and rural regions a director can plan a number of simultaneous groups and have a hand in shaping the program.

For formal study, radio and TV are easily combined with various forms of correspondence study. Radio is valuable chiefly in such courses as music appreciation and literature and in spot news reporting. TV can effectively serve a much wider range of courses, although both media probably should broadcast only material of relatively wide appeal unless a closed circuit is used. Western Reserve University charged regular fees for a TV course in literature, which included a syllabus, parallel reading materials, and an on-campus examination. Students sent in notes three times during the semester. Noncredit listeners could buy the syllabus for $5. In 1951 Brooklyn College started a combination TV and home-study course in human relations. In 1952 the Federal Office of Education found that eighty-six colleges and universities, thirty school systems, and five medical schools were producing TV programs.

Another important use of TV is in bringing educational and cultural experiences to adult members of the community who are unlikely to enroll in formal courses. The range of such programs is limitless. Programs showing the economic life of the community, historical background, contributions of ethnic groups, work of governmental departments, interests of professional and trade associations, new materials in museums, dramatic productions, civic orchestras, resources of libraries, scientific demonstrations, hobbies, and home arts are only a few of the possibilities. The relationship shown between the local, regional, national, and international aspects of the same field can build a sense of integration with the whole human race.

Television can serve practically all content fields, and it is often less expensive than motion pictures. TV is especially effective in such areas as art, current events, citizenship, dramatics, economics, health, history, languages, literature, occupational information and guidance, safety, science, and speech.

Closed circuits provide a way of limiting the audience to specified groups. This type of transmission is already being used for upgrading in the professions and for orientation and in-service training in large companies and in the Armed Forces.

Television can draw upon a wide range of resources for programming. Fully three-fourths of all educational films produced prior to the advent of TV have been released for use in television broadcasting. Nearly all currently made nontheatrical films are available for showing. Films can be obtained from governmental agencies at all levels, from nonprofit organizations, from industries and commercial firms, and from commercial sources of educational films. Over 1,000 educational films are made every year.

Films are especially useful to fill in program time during the early stages of station operation before sufficient live-program resources have been developed. Many films, of course, are inherently good and worthy of TV showing at any time. Telecasting feature films seems to reduce demand for rental, but showing educational films over TV seems to increase the demand.

Much of the normal activity around an adult school can, with a bit of staging, be televised directly for public-relations purposes. In the content areas an occasional activity can be telecast directly, although most programs require special preparation for the TV audience. A number of early programs consisted of awkward adaptations of classroom techniques. Gradually, however, educators and technicians collaboratively have improved presentations in a number of fields.

One of the greatest uses of both TV and radio is in bringing our education up to date—in helping us to learn what we need to learn when we need to learn it. This applies to all fields, but especially to public affairs, where the possibilities of this service stagger the imagination. Its potential contribution to democracy is tremendous. The "Town Hall of the Air," "Chicago Round Table," and a score of other popular radio forums can be made still more attractive and effective over TV. Telecasting of congressional investigations, the political conventions, and the inauguration of presidents have brought millions of additional people to the ringside to see politics and government in action. When a great issue arises, it can now be discussed both nationally and at the grass roots within a few hours.

Visualize this as a possibility: An emergency situation of Pearl-Harbor import arises. Within a few hours, highly placed leaders, in government and out, can be discussing it over TV. Immediately afterward groups all over the country can discuss it. Technically it is possible during the following hour for TV cameras to pick up for a nationwide audience a succession of shots of discussions going on in Austin, Bangor, Calumet, Yakima, Yonkers, Yuma, and a score of other places. After an hour or so, a poll of opinion in these groups could be taken, phoned to headquarters, and the results reported to the public. If the poll were based on pre-designed, representative, cross-sectional groups, in a representative cross section of American communities, the results would be a public-opinion poll as reliable as those normally reported in the press. Authorities could have the benefit of knowing how the public felt and could let this element enter into their further deliberations and decisions. The public would have participated in making the decision.

Most public problems can be seen arising months or years in advance. With more time, top authorities in the problem field and TV casting experts could combine to do an educational job as sound as could be done through any mass approach. Although the public may be largely unfamiliar with South Africa, Tunisia, or the social meaning of a new scientific development, competent authorities could provide ample information. The educational merit of programs could be greater than that provided by most commentators and news analysts. With such a tie-up between media and subject matter, we could acquire much of our public-affairs background for policy making as we go along—as need arises. We should no longer have to depend upon the reservoirs of knowledge presumably filled in our youth by an educational system designed for days now past.

At the other extreme is the use of radio and television in fundamental education. Television, especially, can disseminate information in such fields as agriculture, homemaking, small home industries, health, and child care among nonreaders in undeveloped countries. In a half-illiterate world this is significant. Literacy is not necessarily the first step in fundamental education. Much useful information can be taught before reading skills are acquired. The absence of telecasting and receiving sets in undeveloped areas is an economic problem which might well receive attention.

Even in this country we have a sizable literacy problem. We have three kinds of nonreading adults. Several million have never learned to read. Millions more can read but seldom do so. Other millions can and do read but seldom read anything of significance. As a large portion of all three groups follow routine occupations and never go to lectures or serious meetings, any medium which provides them with educational stimulation is important.

While we have a fundamental education problem in this country, a greater problem is that of general education for adults. It is the problem of helping the great majority of our adults come abreast and keep abreast of the general content areas that all should know. Science and technology change our world so fast that one cannot expect to keep up through the usual processes of searching out and reading pertinent literature on all matters about which he should be informed. Television with its pictorial presentation of concepts can hasten general education materially. With good selection and organization of program materials, the average man can do a much better job of keeping up with essential information than if he had to depend upon reading. In a world in which change piles up geometrically, we must utilize the most efficient methods we know for keeping abreast of the times. TV provides a quick way for bringing essential and timely information to millions.

Exhibits

Exhibits belong to the mass media. While many directors of adult education use them in promotion, few use them extensively to disseminate information in the content areas. County agents, industrial trainers, and librarians, however, use them a great deal. Exhibits have proved to be instrumental in inducing a significant number of changes in behavior.

Attractively prepared, advantageously located, and frequently changed exhibits can reach large numbers of people quickly, permitting them to control their own study time. As many people spend little time with exhibits, the pictorial, graphic, and verbal stimuli need to be simple enough to be comprehended at a glance. Exhibits are most effective when reinforced with some other medium, such as a loud-speaker, a demonstration, or an animated film.

EVALUATION

Individual approaches are evaluated largely by the progress that they occasion. Test results, examinations passed, licenses obtained, promotions gained, and new skills acquired are visible evidence of success. Program-wise, home study is often judged by the percentage of enrollees who graduate and the percentage finishing a significant part of the course.

The mass media are harder to evaluate. Such elementary yardsticks as readership, number of listeners and viewers, circulation, and attendance are widely used. Mass-media people with educational purposes are seeking better ways of testing results of their activity. Occasionally a dramatic result testifies to the effect of a single program or edition. More often results come from the cumulative effect of many programs and editions and often from a combination of many media. For example, the significant increase in percentage of voting in 1952 could not be claimed by any one medium, although most of them contributed materially.

Evaluation of mass media often requires experimentation. Sampling of behavior and attitude before and after an educational campaign may be productive if other significant elements are not influencing the expected changes in behavior. Matched groups are not easily arranged, for the audience of a mass medium is difficult to control unless the experiment involves moving pictures. The most desirable evaluation is that which appraises the kind and amount of behavior change resulting from the medium being evaluated.

SELECTED REFERENCES

Adam, T. R.: *Motion Pictures in Adult Education,* American Association for Adult Education, New York, 1940.

Allion, Helen, and Homer Kempfer: "New Developments in Correspondence Education," *Adult Education,* 4:76–80, January, 1954.

The Bulletin of the National Association of Secondary-school Principals, special issue on Supervised Correspondence Instruction in the Secondary School, 36:1–151, December, 1952.

Bryson, Lyman: *The Communication of Ideas,* Harper & Brothers, New York, 1948.

Clarke, J. M.: *Public School Camping,* Stanford University Press, Stanford, Calif., 1951.

Council of National Organizations of the AEA: *Television: A New Community Resource,* Wells Publishing Company, Leonia, N.J., 1953.

Dunham, F., and R. R. Lowdermilk: *Television in Our Schools,* U.S. Office of Education Bulletin 1952, no. 16.

"Educational Television: Special Number," *Higher Education,* 7:169–184, Apr. 1, 1951.

Gaumnitz, W. H.: *Suggestions Relating to Home and Correspondence Study,* U.S. Office of Education Circular 309, June, 1953.

Hudson, R. B.: "Adult Education and Mass Communications," *Adult Education,* 3:101–104, March, 1953.

Kempfer, Homer: "Easier Reading Materials Needed for 50,000,000 Adults," *School Life,* 32:115, May, 1950.

—— (ed.): *Home Study Blue Book,* National Home Study Council, Washington, 1953.

—— and Grace S. Wright: *Selected Approaches to Adult Education,* U.S. Office of Education Bulletin 1950, no. 16.

Klapper, J. T.: *The Effects of Mass Media,* Columbia University Press, New York, 1949.

Morton, John R.: *University Extension in the United States,* University of Alabama Press, University, Ala., 1953.

Olson, O. J. (ed.): *Education on the Air,* The Ohio State University Press, Columbus, Ohio, 1953.

Press, Radio, and Film, 1951–52, UNESCO, Columbia University Press, New York, 1952.

Schramm, Wilbur: *Communications in Modern Society,* University of Illinois Press, Urbana, Ill., 1948.

Seldes, Gilbert: *The Great Audience,* The Viking Press, Inc., New York, 1950.

Soop, E. J.: "The University of Michigan Television Hour," *Adult Education,* 2:113–116, February, 1952.

Stein, L. S.: "An Experiment in Correspondence Training of Trade Union Leaders," *Adult Education,* 1:176–183, June, 1951.

Waller, J. C.: *Radio: The Fifth Estate,* 2d ed., Houghton Mifflin Company, Boston, 1950.

Wierman, A. E.: *The Mechanics of Correspondence Instruction,* Prentice-Hall, Inc., New York, 1947.

Wittich, W. A., and C. F. Schuller: *Audio-visual Materials: Their Nature and Use*, Harper & Brothers, New York, 1953.
See also General References: [19] Beals and Brody, pp. 395–397; Ely, pp. 15–16, 222–224, 259–268; Essert, chap. 4; Kempfer; Sheats, Jayne, and Spence, chap. 9.

[19] The General References are listed in full at the end of this book.

PART THREE

*Problems of Organization
and Administration*

If a school system seriously accepts responsibility for adult education, it needs to provide for the definite organization and administration of the program. Staff members must be assigned responsibility for program planning, promotion, and operation. Leaders must be procured, oriented, and supervised. Activities must be financed and funds must be accounted for. The whole operation must take place within a framework of policy.

THE PLACE OF ADULT EDUCATION IN THE SCHOOL AND COMMUNITY

Responsibility of the Superintendent and Board of Education

Potentially, the most influential person in the development of local programs of adult education is the superintendent of education. If he believes deeply in lifelong learning and looks on the school as an institution serving community needs, an adult-education program can thrive. If he thinks of adult education as an appendage to the central work of the school, it is likely to remain only that. Superintendents vary widely in their leadership in this field.

Good public-school programs of adult education are found largely where superintendents are active in procuring adequate funds, outlining the organization, selecting the professional leadership, giving it a clear-cut assignment, supporting plans, and granting freedom to develop and carry out a program. The role that public schools will play in total community programs of adult education is directly related to the thinking of superintendents and boards of education. As the superintendent has certain responsibilities for the education of the board, his position is doubly important.

To a considerable degree, boards of education are likely to reflect the leadership of their superintendents and to accept the advice of representative advisory committees. Historically, boards of education have materially expanded the scope of their concern. After the establishment of the common school, they came to realize the need for universal secondary education. Many have since established junior and community colleges. In addition to lengthening the span of schooling, they have broadened their authority to include related social and educational services. If boards of education during the next generation tend to become public-education authorities, they will probably extend comprehensive opportunities for learning to all age groups. American education has grown strong through such civic leadership.

Few public-school adult-education programs start without prior approval of the board of education, and none should. Before the first group of adults is organized under school auspices, the superintendent needs to discuss the step with the board of education. Official consent should be obtained. In the early stages, as the program expands generally or in specific directions, the board should have opportunity to approve or disapprove the proposed expansion. Out of these early discussions and actions will emerge a set of policies setting the general guidelines of development. If both the superintendent and the board maintain a distinction between policy and administrative detail, only a fair share of board-meeting time need be concerned with adult education. In an established program the superintendent periodically makes progress reports and brings up new matters for policy decisions.

Policies ought to be kept general, simple, and flexible, especially during the early stages of a program. Flexibility is a primary characteristic of good adult education, and it should not be contravened by too many detailed and ironclad rules before experience proves them necessary. Only minimum essential policies should be formulated in the beginning. Others can develop as experience warrants. Eventually, in a comprehensive and expanding program, policies will have to be settled on matters such as these:

1. Scope of program—program areas
2. Kind of educational activities and approaches employed
3. Primary population segments for whom program is intended
4. Acceptable sources of leadership; qualifications and remuneration of leaders
5. Financial support—amount from taxes, fees, other sources
6. Places in which adult education may be held
7. Degree and kinds of cooperation with community organizations—leadership and services extended, cosponsorship, financial arrangements, and sharing of facilities
8. Treatment of controversial issues
9. Degree and kinds of promotion
10. Relationship of adult education to other parts of the educational program

The tone of the whole program is influenced greatly by the degree of support expressed in the policies of the board of education. The board of education can give a dignity and stability to adult education which can be achieved in no other way.

The Director of Adult Education

If adult education is to assume its proper importance, its direction must be in the hands of specialized personnel. A broad and varied adult program requires fully as much organization and leadership as are needed in the secondary and elementary schools. In the judgment of experienced state directors of adult education and other qualified observers, the position of director of adult education in the organizational structure should meet these criteria:

1. The position should have a status and pay equivalent to that of the top positions in elementary and secondary education.

2. The director of adult education should be responsible directly to the superintendent or, in large systems, to the top general administrative officer in charge of instruction. This permits maximum articulation and integration with the remainder of the educational program.

3. The director of adult education should be responsible for the administration and supervision of all adult-education activities of the school system.

The several commonly found organizational patterns meet the above criteria in varying degrees. Identified organizational arrangements include the following:

1. A district-wide director of adult education responsible to the superintendent. In large districts this director may be an assistant superintendent in charge of adult education. This is generally the most favored plan.

2. A director of adult education or an evening-school principal responsible to a building principal. In this system, the director is sometimes the vice-principal of the high school or junior college in charge of extension activities. Unless the institution serves the entire district, the position may carry no responsibility for other areas or may need to be coordinated with similar positions in other buildings. The greatest danger is that the adult program, and often the budget, tends to be dominated and restricted by the educational thinking of the administration and faculty of the institution to which it is attached. Some programs organized along these lines are excellent, however.

3. A double or multiple directorship. In the most common arrangement of this type, a director of vocational education and a director of adult education have coordinate roles, and both are responsible to a general administrator. A director of family-life education or of citizenship education may also be in the picture. Since much vocational education is adult education, this plan may result in partial duplication, neglect of certain areas, poor economy, uncoordinated programs, and other ills. Much of the weakness can be reduced, of course, if the directors work in harmony.

4. The superintendent serving as director of adult education. This is

very common in small districts. The breadth of responsibility carried by the superintendent prevents him from becoming the specialist in adult education that the field requires. A better solution can be worked out by larger, consolidated districts or through the patterns suggested below.

5. A shared director. Where the practice is legal, two or more small districts may engage a more competent director of adult education than either could alone. Sometimes several adjacent villages or consolidated districts share a director who spends an agreed-upon portion of his time in each. In every case, unless some other arrangement is established, he works under the local superintendent. The intermediate district and the boards of cooperative educational services, as developed in New York State, provide ways of obtaining a shared director.

6. A joint director. Two or more agencies jointly employ the same person as their local director of adult education. In certain California communities, for example, a college, the state university extension division, and the local school all pay a portion of one director's salary. He welds the resources of the different agencies into an integrated program to meet the needs of the community. Presumably, if a number of local agencies cooperated in supporting a director, he could truly become a director of community adult education.

7. A county director. Certain Southern states having schools organized on a county-unit basis employ a staff member to direct adult education. As he is responsible to the county superintendent, this system is similar to the first mentioned. In New York State several county boards of vocational and adult education employ a director of adult education responsible to the board instead of to county or district superintendents.

A number of variations of these patterns exist. In connection with the veterans' education program following World War II, certain Southern states used a system of district and area supervisors employed directly by the state education departments.

Evaluative studies almost invariably show programs having full-time directors to be superior in all significant respects to programs with part-time directors. One cannot expect to find well-developed programs run on the marginal energies of a day-school staff member who is interested primarily in some other assignment. Nevertheless, small communities and many larger ones can start an adult-education program even when only a part-time director is available. The least satisfactory arrangement is to load responsibility for adult education upon a staff member already carrying a full assignment. Under these circumstances, adult education is likely to be given only perfunctory attention. The extra remuneration usually is not enough to command a desirable share of the director's energy. A better plan is to lighten the regular load of a staff member appreciably and to pay him a regular salary with some supplement for the adult program. This plan is likely to work even better if someone is especially hired for this assignment, and his duties are agreed upon when he is engaged. This agreement helps the person with a divided field to develop more balanced loyalties. Part-time assignments are most successful if they are filled by people desirous of devoting full time to adult education and if the positions can be expected to grow into full-time jobs.

Integration and Articulation within the School System

While adult education ought to have status equivalent to other major levels of the school system, it should be closely articulated with them. On the one hand, it should be free to serve its own clientele, to develop its own approaches and methods, to break with tradition, and to pioneer new ideas. At the same time, many of its fundamental purposes are the same as those held by other levels of education. In so far as their purposes are similar, the different levels need to coordinate their work.

In relation to children, parents and schools have many objectives in common, although different methods are used to achieve them. Presumably both desire the maximum development of each individual along accepted lines. Parents should know what the school is trying to do, and the school in turn should know what parents desire. There should be full agreement on purpose. Ideally, the staff of elementary and secondary schools should also be adult educators. In addition to showing competence in the classroom, teachers and principals should be skilled at developing a two-way understanding of the purposes and methods used by both the school and the home. It is indeed a weakness in social policy to permit children to be educated toward certain ends in school that may be negated by the out-of-school environment. Since children are in school only a relatively short time, the effectiveness of the education they receive there depends in part upon the degree to which the greater community cooperates to achieve the same purposes.

Adult education has a responsibility for helping keep parents and the larger community abreast of the educational work done with children in schools. Adult educators often have approaches, methods, and techniques useful with parents and community groups which elementary and secondary teachers may not possess. Nursery-school and kindergarten teachers are usually trained for work with parents. If they cannot provide all, they can provide a part of the parent education necessary for those who have very young children. The adult program in family-life education has opportunity to work so closely with teachers of the lower grades that an outsider may be unable to detect which level is responsible.

Similar working arrangements should exist through all the years of full-time schooling. Paralleling the education of children and youth should be a program of adult education designed to keep parents abreast of the growth of their youth. Parents should become aware of the content and methods used in the education of their children. Likewise, they should acquire an understanding of the developmental stages through which their children grow. Their education, at times, can be a truly co-operative enterprise. Often children, youth, and parents can consider together the problems and issues of citizenship. They can work together on community problems of health, safety, economic development, and community improvement. Parents and children can learn together in many fields. In too many cases the adult-education program operates separately from elementary- and secondary-school programs. It is the responsibility of both these services to work together toward common ends. In so far as subject specialists in high school may be untrained in working with adults, adult educators may have to carry a greater part of the load for a time.

Another reason for close articulation is the need to build into youth the concept of lifelong learning. The atmosphere around most schools is still that education ends with high-school graduation except for the few who go on to college. High-school graduation is thought of as the sharp terminal point of systematic education for must youth. Inherent in adult education, however, is the concept of lifelong learning. Through close articulation of adult with elementary and secondary education a genera-tion of youth could be brought up fully aware of both the need and the opportunities for lifelong learning. Here are some things that the director of adult education and school principals could do jointly to facilitate the building of this concept into oncoming generations:

1. See that all teachers and other staff members are fully acquainted with the local adult-education opportunities both in the school and out-side of it. Within the school system this is partly a public-relations job, which may be approached by involving staff members as participants and teachers in the adult program so that they can experience and enjoy it.

2. Train teachers to develop in children and youth the concept of lifelong education—through precept, example, and an information pro-gram. Develop in every teacher the specific habit of referring school-leaving youth to adult-education activities.

3. Be especially sure that guidance counselors know about adult-education opportunities and that they habitually guide graduates and dropouts toward these activities.

4. Arrange for pertinent data on dropouts to flow from the guidance offices to the director of adult education. Follow up the dropouts in an effort to draw them into the adult program.

5. Encourage classroom teachers to use adaptations of adult methods whenever feasible—especially discussion group and forum procedures. Provide in-service training in these procedures.

6. Help high-school students to develop long-term educational plans which include adult-education activities, especially when all desired

courses of study cannot be crowded into the schedule before graduation.

7. Encourage seniors to get a taste of adult education before graduation by entering into selected adult activities, provided adults in these groups do not object to the presence of younger people.

8. Explain to high-school students, especially to seniors, the opportunities in the adult-education program—the richness, the flexibility, the fun. Do a selling job. In cooperation with the guidance department, make an annual spring survey of seniors to determine their interest in continued education and use this as a partial basis for program planning.

9. Plan to continue high-school interest groups with a minimum carryover of traditional secondary-school regulations. Develop young-adult bands, orchestras, choral groups, science clubs, athletic teams, and shopwork groups. Make a smooth transition by enabling the groups with the happiest associations to continue in the activities most enjoyed.

10. Design and develop activities to meet the needs and interests of out-of-school youth; provide programs for young adults. Such activities can be most easily developed in the vocational, civic, family-life and parent-education, recreation, and guidance fields.

11. Induce parents to participate in adult education early, so that they will come to regard lifelong learning as a regular adult responsibility.

Relationship with Junior Colleges

Where the junior college is a part of the public-school system and its head is responsible to the superintendent, logic suggests that there be one director of adult education for the entire system. His staff can develop adult activities in the junior college, in the high schools, and in the elementary schools. The junior college may be given the task of providing adult education for the whole system, in which case it may call itself a community college. It may draw resources from all parts of the system and beyond and serve most or all educational needs of adults, regardless of their previous schooling.[1]

Separate junior colleges and high-school districts can provide adult education in the same geographic area with least overlap and friction if they will agree to divide the fields served. This division may be by level of difficulty. That is, the junior college may restrict its program to classes and activities of junior-college level, either credit or noncredit, and the public school can agree to offer only courses below the college level. Sometimes they divide on the basis of the specialities and competence of their staff resources.

[1] See two articles by Homer Kempfer and William Wood, "The Community College: A Challenging Concept for You," *School Life*, 32:129–130, 140–141, June, 1950; and "Community College Education: A National Need," *School Life*, 33:29–32, November, 1950.

Relationships with Higher Education

State universities, land-grant colleges, and other state institutions usually have both the right and duty to provide adult education, through their extension divisions, anywhere they may be called upon within the state. Although legally they may usually operate in any community, good practice favors a close working relationship with the local educational authorities. The director of adult education who thinks of such outside resources can often identify a need for service which cannot be met locally. If he is alert in helping identify the need and in drawing on the higher educational institutions, he is on the road to developing good cooperative relationships. Staff members from colleges and universities in some cases can be engaged directly to provide tailor-made services to a community. Many institutions, however, prefer to have these arrangements made through their extension divisions. The smart local director finds out the terms and preferences, as well as the resources, of all institutions within whose service area his educational system functions.

Relationships with Supervisors

Two general plans of supervision are common:

1. Where day schools employ subject supervisors, such as for industrial arts, homemaking, and social studies, these supervisors may also be given responsibility for supervising their fields in the adult program. If initially they are too academic-minded and subject-centered, they may need to learn approaches useful with adults, or run the risk of restricting growth of their field. When supervising adult work, such staff members work closely with and under the direction of the director of adult education, much as they assist administrators of high- and elementary-schools and junior colleges. Vertical supervision facilitates close integration of adult education with other levels.

2. In some large districts, the director of adult education has one or more supervisors on his staff who work entirely with adult and out-of-school youth programs. They may work in such fields as family-life education, public-affairs education, Americanization, recreation, adult vocational education, and adult homemaking. In addition there may be program counselors, young-adult counselors, guidance specialists, and forum moderators. These often are in addition to adult-school principals. Such supervisors are in a good position to develop special competence with adult groups. Unless they work closely with other parts of the school system, they are likely to develop programs poorly related to the day schools.

The Comprehensive School-Community Program

Some schools provide good school programs of adult education largely unrelated to the rest of the community. Others not only do this but also furnish leadership for a community program of lifelong learning. Some of the country's larger programs are operated by schools having little connection or cooperation with the nonschool educational activities of their communities. Well-rounded programs, however, result when there are many coordinating, cooperative, and integrating relationships with other agencies.

Proper orientation for leadership in a community program of adult education begins with the realization that the whole community ultimately has responsibility for its own education and that, in most instances, many different organizations and agencies are providing adult education. Some agency programs have been created officially; others have seen a need and have started to meet it. Such insight should lead any director, superintendent, or board of education to accept the principle of cooperation and realize that most progress is made when all agencies are working together toward the same ends.

Building cooperative relationships between the school and other community agencies has been treated in other parts of this book (Chapter 4, in particular). The school's greatest contribution can be in providing sustained leadership without domination and in offering services unselfishly to other organizations. If the board of education can adopt liberal policies of cooperation along these lines—as liberal as state laws and regulations will allow—a director with vision can go far in helping the entire community engage in continuous learning activities.

ORGANIZATION AND ADMINISTRATION OF ADULT SCHOOLS

While directors of adult education are usually responsible for a variety of program activities, the adult or evening school is the most common institutionalized educational unit under their supervision. About half of all directors of adult education administer their schools personally; the remainder delegate the responsibility to a principal. While the trend is clearly toward the development of comprehensive community programs of adult education, adult schools in some form probably will continue to be the most important organized provision for adult education under public-school auspices. In addition, a number of YMCAs, YWCAs, local colleges, municipal universities, libraries, trade schools, business colleges, and other agencies, both public and private, have evening schools or divisions of adult education. In a 1948 survey, the public schools in approximately one-half of all communities above 2,500 in population reported having an adult school, evening school, Americanization school, opportunity school, evening elementary school, evening high school, or similar organized unit.[2] Large cities, of course, usually have more than one center.

The exact number of adult schools is unknown. Incomplete returns showed 1,601 districts with adult or evening schools. A projected total embracing communities of all sizes and all adult schools in larger districts would have given an estimate of close to 2,500. If districts with one, two, or three adult groups in a vocational, agricultural, homemaking, recreational, or similar activity are included, the number of schools becomes much larger.

Organization

A number of large cities employ full-time administrators for their adult schools. In Los Angeles, under general supervision from the central office, these administrators act much as large-neighborhood directors of adult education. A majority of adult schools enrolling 1,000 or more have full-time principals.[3]

Most adult-school principals, however, work only part time, even in districts having full-time directors of adult education. Often the position entails income in addition to a regular salary for a full daytime work load. One large city recently set up an evening-school principalship, the duties of which include a last-period class in high school, after-school activities, and supervision of the building—all for a unified salary. Where full-time principals are not warranted, half-time arrangements are next best, provided competent people can be induced to accept evening work in exchange for free mornings. Part-time principals come from the ranks of high-school teachers, assistant principals, and other staff positions.[4] Occasionally a substitute teacher or a person following an outside occupation is employed to head the adult school. In small schools and in annexes to larger schools "teachers in charge" and teacher-principals are common.

Half the principals have little or no responsibility for adult-education activities during daytime hours.[5] Sometimes morning or afternoon classes, club meetings, and other activities require the principal's presence. Such responsibilities can be included in the schedule of full-time principals, but they conflict with schedules of principals otherwise fully employed during the day. For part-time principals, nonscheduled activities—such as preparing the annual report, arranging exhibits, planning promotion, keeping records, and maintaining community contacts—must be taken care of during evening hours or squeezed in at other times.

[2] Homer Kempfer: *Adult Education Activities of the Public Schools: Report of a Survey, 1947–48*, U.S. Office of Education Pamphlet 107, 1949, p. 8.

[3] Homer Kempfer and Grace S. Wright, *100 Evening Schools*, U.S. Office of Education Bulletin 1949, no. 4, pp. 27–28.

[4] *Ibid.*, p. 28.

[5] *Ibid.*, p. 29.

Adult schools enrolling 1,000 or more usually are assisted by two or three nonteaching staff members. Their titles and assignments vary widely—assistant principal, coordinator, registrar, department head, supervisor, and counselor. Smaller schools typically have less administrative help. Adult schools usually have from 2 to 3 hours of clerical help per week per 100 adults enrolled. Large schools seem to have more clerical help per teacher than do the smaller ones. A shortage or even an absence of such help is common in small schools.

The proper ratio of full- to part-time adult-education workers is a question in the minds of most general administrators. Only a rule of thumb can be suggested in a field as unstandardized as adult education. For public-school programs Paul Essert recommends 1 full-time worker for every 100 hours per week of part-time professional service.[6] Professor Essert lists these functions for full-time workers, which part-time workers can perform only inefficiently, if at all:

1. Keep abreast of the best knowledge and practices in the field.
2. Extend public school services to other adult education agencies, clubs, and study groups, in materials, program planning, and educational consultations.
3. Identify voluntary group associations and implement their efforts to develop educational objectives.
4. Organize, evaluate, and reorganize the public school program in the light of changing needs.
5. Develop and service a community adult-counseling and group-life center in cooperation with other agencies.

These functions help build a strong case for having one full-time professional person instead of two or three part-time principals. In large districts, several full-time principals are likely to develop a better program than can be developed by many part-time principals. The recent NEA study clearly showed that programs with adequate administrative time are superior to those without it.[7]

Program Organization

Most educational activities of adult schools are set up as classes. Forums, concerts, lecture series, radio and TV programs, tutoring, supervised correspondence courses, and other activities are often organized as a part of the adult school, although they may be operated independently or affiliated with other phases of the adult program.

The following tabulation of 4,825 instructional groups in *100 Evening Schools* shows the relative popularity of subject fields.

[6] Paul Essert, *Creative Leadership of Adult Education*, Prentice-Hall, Inc., New York, 1951, pp. 183–184.
[7] Division of Adult Education Service of the NEA, *A Study of Urban Public School Adult Education Programs of the United States*, National Education Association, Washington, 1952.

Field	No. of sections operating
Business education.............................	948
Trade and industrial education..................	839
Arts and crafts................................	691
Homemaking....................................	590
English and speech.............................	322
Health, safety, physical education, and recreation...	226
Mathematics...................................	195
Foreign languages..............................	161
Immigrant education...........................	152
Music...	137
Social studies..................................	137
Science..	94
Miscellaneous..................................	92
Family-life education...........................	84
Psychology and personal development.............	70
Agriculture....................................	60
Elementary education..........................	27

SOURCE: Homer Kempfer and Grace S. Wright, *100 Evening Schools*, U.S. Office of Education Bulletin 1949, no. 4, pp. 27–28.

The median school in this study had nearly fifty operating groups. The 100 schools, however, were not strictly representative of the evening schools of the country.

In the NEA study, curriculum areas were classified differently, with the results shown in Table 10.

The majority of evening schools in the U.S. Office of Education study provide for earning high-school credit, although relatively few offer elementary education or an eighth-grade diploma. Often credit can be obtained in only certain subjects, and it is usually transferred to a day high school where it can count toward fulfilling graduation requirements. About a fourth of the evening schools, however, offer a full high-school curriculum and grant a diploma upon successful completion of the required work.

Both evening and day junior colleges offer classes for adults. Almost invariably they include credit courses which are transferable to day institutions. A few institutions grant junior-college diplomas on the basis of work completed entirely in evening classes. Whether credit courses are conducted on an accelerated or regular basis depends upon the regulations of the appropriate state education department or accrediting association. A few schools offer only credit courses and curricula.

All except a few adult schools offer noncredit courses. These afford a major field for expansion, whereas credit courses leading to degrees and diplomas will be a part of adult education only as long as the general public places a premium upon such evidence of education. There is

Table 10. Percentage Distribution of Adult-education Classes and Groups According to Content or Curriculum Area, by Size of City, 1950–1951

Curriculum area	School systems in cities of—			Total
	Over 100,000	30,000– 100,000	2,500– 30,000	
General academic education..............	16.0	9.7	7.8	13.7
Americanization and elementary education.	10.6	5.2	3.9	8.6
Fine arts..............................	3.2	4.8	7.0	4.0
Practical arts and crafts................	3.3	10.4	12.6	6.0
Commercial and distributive education.....	19.4	11.9	14.6	17.0
Agriculture...........................	0.3	1.1	3.8	0.8
Vocational and technical education other.. than agriculture......................	16.7	18.5	13.8	16.9
Homemaking education..................	12.0	17.8	13.7	13.7
Parent and family-life education..........	5.3	3.7	2.4	4.6
Health and physical education............	6.5	5.3	4.7	6.0
Personal improvement..................	0.5	1.0	0.6	0.6
Recreational skills......................	2.6	3.2	3.3	2.8
Safety and driver education..............	1.9	4.5	9.0	3.2
Remedial, special education..............	0.2	0.5	0.4	0.3
Miscellaneous classes or groups...........	1.5	2.4	2.4	1.8
Total.............................	100.0	100.0	100.0	100.0

SOURCE: Division of Adult Education Service of the NEA, *A Study of Urban Public School Adult Education Programs of the United States*, National Education Association, Washington, 1952, p. 12.

nothing inherently good in a credit course that cannot be included in a noncredit activity. As adult education, to be successful on a voluntary attendance basis, must first serve real educational needs, activities often start and flourish without regard to standards of accrediting agencies. In many cases a satisfied clientele is the criterion of merit. In recent years the greatest growth in adult education has occurred in the noncredit field. As adults come to value the inherent merit of courses tailored to serve their specific needs, the trend toward noncredit courses will no doubt continue.

In spite of sporadic promotional efforts, student activities are not nearly as well developed in adult schools as in secondary and higher institutions. Probably not over a third of the adult schools have any student-conducted activities. Even fewer have student councils, newspapers, field trips, athletic events, dances and social activities, fashion shows, and art and music festivals.

Several reasons account for the lack of special activities. Part-time administration and the feeling that adult schools are in borrowed quarters handicap their development. Short sessions, short terms, irregular schedules, and part-time activities result in a student body with little of the cohesion that develops among people who spend many hours a week together.

Attitudes of participants, however, are the greatest handicap to the initiation of student activities. Being adults, they have serious responsibilities at work and at home. Many who come to school with specific purposes are likely to resent any deviations from these aims. Their interest in learning is often high, but they must see the connection between any activity and their desired objective. Therefore, they are not easily induced to lose time in reaching their own goal in order to engage in something that seems extraneous.

However, even if students have this natural reluctance to deviate from their chosen course, the adult school has a responsibility for broadening their vision. It should not only provide the kind of education they want but expose them to other fields in the hope that they may cultivate new tastes. Specifically, the school should help all who enroll to develop broader civic and cultural interests and sympathies. It can provide many significant social experiences for such a development. Many men and women attend partly, or largely, out of a need for human association, companionship, and the stimulus given by the interaction of different minds and personalities. This human need provides a basis for leading them beyond their initial specific interests into broader cultural activities.

A few schools do this systematically. Each teacher is trained in specific ways of inducing adults into other phases of a field and into new fields. Every person who continues to enroll in a succession of different areas of knowledge year after year is accepted as evidence of success in providing an enriched program. Administrators of these schools point with pride to records showing that some students have enrolled without a break for 10, 15, and 20 years and that a growing number have registered for 5 or more years. While continuous enrollment is not the only evidence, certainly it is incontrovertible proof that the concept of lifelong learning is being realized.

Organization of Classes

The programs of adult schools are usually built upon educational needs determined by some combination of the methods discussed in Chapter 4. At times, proposed courses represent only armchair judgment, but registration and continuance in courses test the methods used.

Determination of content within a course follows no fixed pattern. In most cases the teacher knows reasonably well what he plans to teach. He may modify the course somewhat in terms of the interests and needs of those enrolled. However, in the more conventional activities, especially in credit courses, the prescribed content may often have priority both for instructor and students. Where state aid is given, state education departments often require that a syllabus be filed in the principal's office or, at times, in the state education department.

Classroom procedures are likely to be more informal with adult groups than with high-school students. Methods of instruction vary widely according to the course and the objective of the students. Credit courses and other formal offerings are often taught by conventional methods, which include lectures, demonstrations, questions and recitation, supervised practice, and laboratory work. In noncredit activities, the various techniques of discussion are more often brought into play.

In any case, the methods used often have a positive and definite effect on the popularity of schools. Those run by conventional methods and staffed largely by day-school teachers ordinarily enroll only a tiny percentage of the adult population. However, those that utilize a variety of approaches, have leaders acceptable to adults, provide desirable courses, and give adequate publicity, are likely to attract a far greater number.

Policies on class size vary widely. Some cities attempting to serve many people on limited budgets may require enrollments as high as forty or fifty for each class in the hope that an attendance of thirty or more will be maintained. The minimum size is usually much smaller—occasionally twenty, more often fifteen or twelve, and sometimes as low as eight. New York State requires an average attendance of eight if a class is to qualify for state aid. Maximum size is occasionally specified.

Practice in the assignment of homework varies considerably. Except in credit courses and supervised correspondence study, much less homework is usually asked of adults than of high-school or college students. Experience has shown that, when it is assigned, often it is not done because of distractions and interferences of home and job. On the other hand, motivation, maturity, and accumulated life experience enable the adult to get more out of class activities than do school-age people. Instead of daily assignments to be worked out, homework is likely to consist of recommended reading, studying pamphlets, and trying out new things learned. In some courses, such as Great Books Discussions, assigned reading is a requisite to intelligent participation.

Library service is often an underdeveloped part of the adult school, possibly because of the practice of assigning little homework. In the study mentioned previously, only one-half of those offering high-school diplomas kept their libraries open at night.[8] Slightly more than one-fourth of all adult schools kept their libraries open during the evening. As may be expected, large schools are more likely to offer library service

[8] Kempfer and Wright, *op. cit.*, p. 21.

than are small ones. In many places the public library is probably used much more by adult-school students than is the school library.

Schedules

As emphasized earlier, flexibility of schedule is a characteristic of good adult schools. Rigidity of schedule typifies the weak school and the limited program.

Frequency of class sessions is determined largely by willingness of adults to meet, although optimum learning conditions remain a factor. Academic, vocational, and English and citizenship classes for the foreign-born are likely to meet most frequently—often twice a week, and sometimes three times. In recent years, as participation has increased and the scope of activities has broadened, there has been a marked trend toward fewer sessions per week. Experienced adult-school principals know that many adults would rather devote one evening of 2, 3, or even 4 hours to an activity than attend two or three shorter sessions. In the 100 evening schools studied, fewer than 20 per cent of the classes met more than twice weekly. Informal groups and discussion groups seldom meet more than once a week. Most Great Books Discussion groups meet every 2 weeks.

Two-hour sessions are by far the most popular; 1- and 3-hour periods are next most frequent; and 4-hour sessions are found occasionally. While state regulations may make other lengths awkward, actually there is no reason why 90-minute and 150-minute periods should not be common. Most classes of 2 hours or more have a mid-point intermission of 5 or 10 minutes, whereas a 90-minute session would not require one.

A typical adult school uses more than one length of period. Typewriting, shorthand, lecture classes, and academic subjects are more often given in short periods. Shop courses, arts and crafts, and sewing usually require longer ones.

Terms have been growing shorter in recent years. Full semesters are seldom observed, except with academic subjects—and not always with them. Twelve-week, ten-week, and eight-week terms are popular. A fall term usually starts sometime in September or early October and ends before Thanksgiving or Christmas. A winter term may end before Easter, and an increasing number of schools then offer a spring term of 6 or 8 weeks. Fewer than a fifth of the adult schools have a summer term, but the number seems to be growing. Occasionally a school will schedule certain classes for one long term right through the winter or through the entire calendar year, making allowances only for holiday seasons. The evening elementary schools of New York City, for example, operate 3 nights per week for 100 nights.

Most schools organize their terms according to the habits of the people of their communities. As organizational activity declines in most com-

munities during the summer, terms are usually planned to stop before
attendance slumps too greatly. However, certain classes with high interest may continue beyond the regular closing date.

While terms with definite starting and stopping dates simplify administrative problems, increasingly principals are learning that many activities should not be fitted into a rigid term pattern. Some activities should
run a shorter or a longer time. Likewise, others should start when the
group is ready and meet on schedules that are convenient to most of
the participants. The practice of starting courses before and after the
regular term-opening dates increases the total administrative load in
some respects but also spreads it more evenly. Whereas regular schedules permit routinizing much of the work, irregular schedules give more
opportunity for professional supervision, teacher orientation, and tailor-
ing the activity to the needs of the group. A compromise is to operate
terms of two or three lengths concurrently. For example, in the fall one
set of courses might run for a semester, another set for 11 weeks, and
another for 6 weeks.

Division between terms is not always sharp. Many courses continue
through the second or third term. Usually some end, and a number of
new ones are started. Whether or not new registrants are accepted in
continuing courses for the second term depends largely upon the nature
of the subject.

Large schools usually are open four or five nights each week. In
small communities, evening schools are likely to be open less often,
although with expanding programs the week is lengthening. Few adult
schools hold classes on Saturday night or on Sunday. A long week permits service to a larger enrollment, permits certain teachers to teach
two or more groups, and gives the public greater opportunity to participate in some activity. Because certain adults find evening attendance
difficult, a number of schools offer part-time morning and afternoon
courses.

Housing

Most adult schools are housed in buildings occupied by day schools.
A few large ones, like the Emily Griffith Opportunity School at Denver,
have buildings of their own in which they operate more or less the year
around, with either full- or part-time activities filling morning, afternoon,
dinner, and evening hours. This makes maximum use of the school plant.
Where a day school has first priority on the building, the adult school
can, at most, schedule only a few morning and afternoon classes, although
more space becomes available in the late afternoon. It may schedule day
annex classes in other places in the neighborhood, however.

High-school buildings are favorite locations for adult schools, partly
because they serve larger areas but chiefly because they are more likely

to have shops, typewriters, sewing machines, gymnasiums, laboratories, rooms with movable adult-size furniture, and other facilities. Junior-high and elementary schools rank next in order.

There is a growing tendency for certain adult-school activities to be scheduled away from the main building. Hoover Evening High School in San Diego, for instance, in 1952 was offering adult courses in ten school buildings in the area, two churches, a settlement house, a community building, a YMCA, and a playground. The Berkeley Evening School utilizes nine school buildings. Nearly half the activities at Greenwich, Connecticut, are scattered in ten locations away from the main building. Other facilities may be more usable, and decentralized locations enable the school to reach more people. Other places used are airports, cafés, churches, clubrooms, hospitals, housing projects, homes, libraries, parks, recreation halls, shops, stores, swimming pools, and industrial and business locations.

School programs operating on nonschool property need a set of clear policies and administrative procedures. Understanding needs to be reached on questions of rent, responsibility for injury, availability to the general public, control of the space, custodial care, hours of use, type of activities permitted, and related problems. The board of education should formulate flexible policies on these matters. Some boards limit activities to other public buildings and do not authorize holding sponsored activities in homes or on private property. Such a policy, however, may unnecessarily limit program expansion.

Routines

There are three general plans for registration.

1. Many adult schools, especially the smaller ones, register on the night that classes begin. Teachers may sit behind tables under big signs around a gymnasium wall to counsel adults and take registrations. If the procedure is simple, teachers can be in their rooms to receive adults, counsel with and register them, become acquainted with their interests and needs, outline the courses, assign materials, and otherwise get started. If publicity encourages everyone to come at a stated time, a maximum number of enrollees will be in attendance during the full session. This plan is especially workable where no registration fees are collected.

2. Some schools do not hold classes on registration night. The regular office and counseling staff may be supplemented by department heads and teachers who assist with advice and registration. This permits spreading the work of registration and gives more time for balancing classes, finding teachers for additional sections, changing schedules, and ironing out other wrinkles. Some schools using this plan provide an opportunity to register by mail, although this system is likely to result in more drop-

outs and more dissatisfied students. A long registration period permits more thorough counseling.

3. Adult schools often permit students to register for and enter non-credit courses at any time.

Registration forms should be as simple as possible. Since many adults hesitate to give much personal data, many directors ask only for the information required in state reports. Some schools never ask adults to state their age; others ask them to indicate only their general age group. Principals who desire to make an occasional detailed analysis of their registrants can obtain the necessary data by questionnaires distributed to all students or to a representative sample during the term or at registration.

Practically all adult schools keep attendance records in some form. Keeping classbooks and submitting daily or weekly reports to the office are common practices. Some schools have worked out a standard 8½-by-11-inch card providing space for attendance and performance data for a whole class. These are more convenient to file permanently than are classbooks.

Rules for dropping registrants vary widely as do methods for determining the average attendance and the percentage of attendance. These details usually follow state practice. Few attendance regulations exist for adults except in credit courses, where an attendance of 75 or 80 per cent may be required. A recent study in 331 public-school adult-education programs reported a median percentage of attendance as follows:

Course	Per cent attending
Academic high-school subjects....	64.5
Arts and crafts.................	68
Business education.............	67
Homemaking...................	68
Trade and industry.............	68.5
Human relations...............	70
Americanization...............	58
Vocal music...................	70

SOURCE: Grace S. Wright, *Persistence of Attendance in Adult Education Classes*, U.S. Office of Education Circular 353, October, 1952.

Attendance rates in specific subjects half the time fell between 48 and 82 per cent. In noncredit courses average attendance often ran between 50 and 80 per cent of the active enrollment. Artificial penalties were usually not attached to irregular attendance, except for credit courses and related apprentice training.

Permanent records are usually kept of the credit work completed; those for noncredit work are often maintained only as registration or class reports. Sometimes permanent records are only the accumulation of registration cards with attendance and marks entered upon them. The use of large permanent cards carrying cumulative data is fairly common. Only an occasional school maintains a folder system of permanent cumulative records.

Where day-school buildings are used, the adult-school principal is often assigned a separate room or suite with its own outside telephone. In programs of any size, minimum facilities should include a private office, an inquiry counter, storage and file space, and work areas for the necessary clerical help. Counselors also need separate rooms. A pigeonhole mailbox for teachers is almost a necessity.

When only evening classes are scheduled, offices are usually opened 15 to 30 minutes before the first class starts and stay open a few minutes after the last class closes. For the protection of the custodial staff and the budget, rules must usually be made regarding the time of departure from the building—unless a night custodian stays on.

ORGANIZATION IN SMALL COMMUNITIES

The community-school concept offers small communities an unusual opportunity to provide a program of lifelong learning. Given adequate leadership, nearly any village—even a rural high school—can have, as a minimum, several classes, study groups, and a few other activities each year in its adult school. Imaginative leadership can add to this by welding a corps of teachers into a leadership team which can literally revitalize the whole community. The broadest concept of the community school is that it shall provide opportunity for children and adults to learn how to solve their individual and group problems together.

Illustrative of adult education in the community school is the story of Ascension Parish, Louisiana. Although little or no formal adult education has existed there during the past quarter century, the school staff, led by a wise superintendent with vision, has materially lifted the level of life of the whole area. Children in school and parents on committees, in workshops and institutes, and in community gatherings have studied problems of health, diet, agriculture, water supply, sanitation, and homemaking. Together they have learned better ways of doing things and mapped out campaigns for improving specific phases of life. Evaluations have shown significant improvement in such areas as dietary habits, sanitation facilities, health, and farm practices. Academic subject matter has taken second place, has become a resource to be drawn upon as needed. Immediate problems have set the tone of the curriculum for both children and adults. Solution of them has resulted in satisfactions which have led to further and continuous learning.

SELECTED REFERENCES

Administrators Adult Education Handbook, Superintendent of Public Instruction Bulletin 334, Lansing, Mich., 1945.

Adult Education Handbook for Administrators, New York State Education Department, Albany, N.Y., 1953.

Crawford, Will C.: *Survey of Purposes and Personnel Administration of Adult Education in California,* California State Department of Education Bulletin 11, July, 1942.

Engelhardt, N. L.: *Planning the Community School,* American Book Company, New York, 1940.

Houle, C. O., et al.: *Universities in Adult Education,* Columbia University Press, New York, 1952.

Hunter, Guy: *Residential Colleges: Some New Developments in British Adult Education,* Occasional Papers, no. 1, Fund for Adult Education, New York, 1953.

Jones, Leo: *Handbook on Continuation Education in California,* California State Department of Education Bulletin 19, March, 1950.

Mann, Arthur F.: *Bridging the Gap: A Handbook for Adult Educators,* Department of Public Instruction, Adult Education Division, Honolulu, Hawaii, n.d.

Mann, G. C.: *Handbook on Adult Education in California,* California State Department of Education, Sacramento, Calif., May, 1949.

—— and J. W. Getsinger: *Development of Adult Education in California,* California State Department of Education Bulletin 22, Sacramento, Calif., 1953.

Mumma, R. A.: "Public School Administrators and Adult Education," *Adult Education,* 1:12–18, October, 1950.

Nolte, J. M.: "Role of State Universities in Adult Education," *National Association of State Universities Transactions and Proceedings,* 1952, pp. 57–70.

Regional Committee on Adult Education: *Now . . . In Our Town: Emerging Administrative Practices in Adult Education in Public Schools and Colleges,* American Association of School Administrators, National Education Association, Washington, 1945.

Sharer, R. E.: "Community's Program of Continuing Education," *Adult Education,* 3:59–62, January, 1953.

Smith, R. G.: *The People's Colleges,* Cornell University Press, Ithaca, N.Y., 1949.

Spence, R. B., and B. Shangold: *Public School Adult Education in New York State, 1944–47,* New York State Education Department, Albany, N.Y., 1950.

See also General References: [9] Division of Adult Education Services, chaps. 5, 11, 17, 22; Ely, pp. 196–213; Essert, chap. 10; Kempfer; Kempfer and Wright; Knowles, chaps. 5, 8; Sheats, Jayne, and Spence, chap. 7.

[9] The General References are listed in full at the end of this book.

CHAPTER 12 *Selection and Development of Leaders*

"There are no poor teachers of adults . . . not for long." This statement, though perhaps a slight exaggeration, is largely true. Adult education is the free enterprise of the educational world, and its leaders must meet their competition—fatigue, family and occupational responsibilities, the world of entertainment, and the thousand and one other interesting things that appeal for the time of adults. Possibly adult education, more than any other level, depends upon competent leadership—the ability, not only of principals and program directors, but of every leader in every group. Adults simply will not waste time with leaders who fail to give them what they desire—something worthwhile in palatable form. Under our compulsory system, elementary and secondary schools can operate with mediocre teachers and principals if none better are available. Pedantic and uninspiring college and university professors can still have classes to teach, particularly in required courses. Adult education, undertaken voluntarily, will not thrive under such conditions.

DEVELOPMENT OF DIRECTORS

The director is the key leader in any adult-education program. If given adequate administrative backing, he—more than any other person—determines whether a program thrives or withers. Like the superintendent of schools, the director of adult education should have a broad background, vision, the potential for creative leadership, and the technical ability to organize and supervise. In addition, he should have extensive experience in educational administration and in community organization and a driving passion for continuous self-development.

Educational Background

In a rapidly growing field many newly appointed leaders are inevitably limited in preparation. This is particularly true where the directorship of adult education is a part-time assignment.

A decade ago, for example, the full-time directors of general adult education in New York State could be counted on the fingers of one hand. Today several hundred communities have adult programs, several dozen

314

of which are headed by full-time directors. With (1) almost no full-time directorships available a decade ago, (2) only a few university curricula offered as preparation for such positions, and (3) a rapid postwar growth in adult education, new directors with adequate preparation are hard to find. Even today key state education department and university adult-education positions are sometimes filled with promising candidates who, however, have little background in the adult field.

As might be expected, this lack of broad background is most evident in newly appointed directors. Many of them—in some states most—come from the ranks of directors of vocational education. A common practice is to give responsibility for general adult education to the vocational director or to the supervisor of distributive education, trade and industrial subjects, or agriculture. In the beginning such men are often handicapped in the general field, although adult work in the vocational fields is likely to thrive. With their specialized training and their habit of thinking in vocational terms, these men often go about developing other areas in conformity with the vocational pattern. Regions and states where this practice is common often find it difficult to develop a broad, liberal adult-education program.

Similar difficulties show up when a new director has nearly any other special background, whether education for the foreign-born, work with young adults, the homemaking field, or a high-school academic area. Possibly a broad-gauge guidance person has less trouble than most others, provided he is not tied to the approaches of particular subject areas.

The required educational background is, of course, broader than one can acquire in 4 or 5 years of college. Even so, a diversified curriculum is preferable to specialized training. The social sciences and sciences of human development are recommended fields of study. Some acquaintance with the vocational fields, shop subjects, the arts and crafts, and science, as well as a good background in professional education, is desirable. After the director has acquired a broad grounding in these fields, advanced study in psychology, sociology, and education, especially as they relate to adult education, should add to his competence. While not referring specifically to public-school directors of adult education, Professor W. C. Hallenbeck suggests that the content of training for adult educators include the following: [1]

History of adult education, not as such, but rather to discover the place it has held in various times and in various cultures, the objectives and purposes under which it has operated, the forms it has taken, and its accomplishments; the precipitate of history in the adult education of the present day; the factors which have made adult education effective in the past and their relevance today.

[1] W. C. Hallenbeck, "Training Adult Educators," *Adult Educational Journal,* 7:4–10, January, 1948.

Philosophy of adult education: the character of purposes and objectives and how they are determined, both ultimate and immediate; the ideas with which to work; principles derived from experience; the necessity for and the purposes of developing a "working philosophy."

Functions of adult education deduced from an analysis of the social scene, involving a knowledge of the chief characteristics of American culture and an understanding of the place of adult education in that culture, the conditions imposed on adult education by democracy, the relation of the cultural function to community functions.

Administration of adult education including the organizational structure of American adult education, the roles of various institutions, practical problems of organizing and operating a program, the community approach, problem of integration.

Emotional requisites for adult educators: belief in people and a better world, sense of mission, genuine interest in adults, broad interests, and experience in rich living.

Community and community organization. This area of study would include a basic knowledge of sociology and the techniques of community study; an acquaintance with sources of data about communities; the theory and facts about community organization and community planning; a practical understanding of the relation of adult education to community organization and community planning and of group life and cooperative activity.

Psychology of adults. Factual data about adult learning; deductions regarding the peculiarities of education of adults; implications for methods in adult education.

Methods and materials. How to meet the conditions of adult learning: individual attention and group experience, informality; attitude toward and character of methods. Methods found useful by experience: cooperative participation; discussion of various types; workshops; psychodrama, etc. Problems of materials: readability; printed matter; uses of mimeograph, radio, films, discussion outlines, etc.

Experience

A broad educational background can provide only a base for the development of a director of adult education. Higher competence comes from diversified and rich experience. The following kinds of experience are recommended:

1. Adult-group leadership in a variety of areas using discussion methods

2. Teaching adult groups in laboratory, shop, and academic areas

3. Participation, as a member and leader, in the program and educational committees of community organizations

4. Close association with a variety of experimental, research, and trial adult-education projects

5. Diversified occupational experience and a variety of interests outside the field of education

6. Reasonably extensive travel

This experience can be acquired in two general ways:

1. For capable but inexperienced persons, internship can follow training. Even though the internship pattern is not yet widespread in adult education, it offers several advantages. Starting with undergraduate supervised teaching and group leadership, internship could be a significant part of a fifth-year training program. A 2-year program of full-time internship, combined with study, could lead to a master's degree. Internship offers an opportunity to develop under supervision. Interns can gain an especially rich experience if they are apprenticed to outstanding practitioners or placed in well-selected agencies. Apprenticeship gives maximum assurance that the insights and practices of creative leaders will not be lost. Internship facilitates continuity of leadership provided the intern stays on as a staff member. Finally, this method stimulates the continued growth of both the leader and the neophyte.

2. Potential directors can acquire experience by performing a succession of paid teaching, group-leadership, supervisory, and administrative services as they move up the occupational ladder. Ambitious individuals usually combine these duties with additional part-time training or alternate periods of work and schooling. Some who are employed during the academic year may study during the summer. On the other hand, summers between academic years of study can be used to gain varied occupational experience, although there is little opportunity for experience in adult education during the summer months. Alternating a semester or year of work with a like period of study may be more practical for those who are forced by economic circumstances to combine the two. The interweaving of theory and fully responsible work has much to commend it, even though the individual, left without supervision, must make his own integration of theory and practice. A director of adult education is foolish if he ever thinks he has completed his preparation. Such an attitude is inconsistent with the philosophy of lifelong learning.

If a new director coming from any specialized field seriously intends to serve the whole scope of adult education, he faces the problem of gaining familiarity with all its other aspects. A man trained in vocational education, for instance, needs to learn his way around in family-life and parent education, intercultural education, forums and public-affairs education, the foundation and academic fields, the liberal arts, arts and crafts, consumer education, education of the foreign-born, and adult guidance. Possibly, he must also become familiar with the recreation field, community councils, programs for the aging and for young adults, and several other phases of adult education. Summer sessions, specialized institutes, state and national conferences, advisory committees, home-study courses, magazines in special fields, self-directed reading, and a plan of extending personal contacts give the new director an opportunity to become acquainted with the other parts of his responsibility. An administration sympathetic to his need for professional growth will try to provide time, incentive, and travel expenses so that he can take advantage of available resources.

To help ensure continued development, the Fund for Adult Education has embarked upon a program of fellowships which enable experienced adult educators to take leave from their positions for a few months of travel and observation of outstanding programs. This tends to break down provincialism, spreads good practice, and helps build unity in a movement.

Extending acquaintance in the wide range of adult-education fields is enough to absorb one's professional energies throughout life. In addition to this requirement, however, is the need to keep up with new developments. In a flexible and growing field new developments come in rapid succession. Not only are educational needs of adults constantly changing, but the philosophy of adult education is emerging anew. This calls for new approaches, new methods, use of new media, and the constant retraining of leadership. Most of all, it requires continuous development of the directors and supervisors. The top leader who does not keep growing can become the Rip Van Winkle of his profession in less than 20 years. Such training oportunities as are offered by the summer sessions of the National Training Laboratory at Bethel, Maine; several labor-management institutes; intercultural education workshops; the Survey Research Center at the University of Michigan; study and research projects of the Institute of Adult Education at Teachers College, Columbia University; The Human Dynamics Laboratory at the University of Chicago; the Materials Research Center of the Fund for Adult Education; and other research and training centers can help the director keep up with the new developments.

State Responsibility

State education departments have a responsibility for training local directors of adult education along the lines discussed earlier. One example of leadership training for local directors is that of New York State.

In 1951, a new training qualification for directors of adult education went into affect in New York. During the preceding academic year, in order to ensure at least a minimum of training, the State Bureau of Adult Education had provided 10 hours of workshop experience, spread over 2 consecutive days, in each of fourteen locations. More than 90 per cent of all local directors attended. In addition, a sizable portion of the annual State Conference on Adult Education is given over to in-service training. It is hoped that eventually schools of education will take over most of the training functions. The state has laid down certain course requirements that must be met within a specified time if a local program desires state approval. A number of summer sessions now offer the appropriate training.

In addition to providing formal training, a state education department can stimulate or conduct regional institutes in a number of special fields, with emphasis on problems of local directors. The state department can likewise identify a variety of special training opportunities, help shape them so that they can be of maximum service to local directors, and encourage directors to attend.

Another major service of value to local directors is state leadership in developing cooperative planning among state agencies concerned with adult education. State libraries, universities, museums, and departments concerned with health, agriculture, conservation, recreation, industry and business, and labor often have little incentive for working together toward common ends. Each is likely to feel responsible to the state legislature for carrying out its own assignment with little regard for other agencies.

In a few cases the state education department has been able to bring representatives of the several vested interests together to discuss their problems, to exchange information, to set common goals, and to plan cooperatively a united program of action. The problem is a difficult one, hedged about with all sorts of legal rigidities, jealousies, and complacency. However, if anything like a state council on adult education or community development can be established and certain forms of cooperation can become apparent at the state level, the director will find the development of cooperative relations easier at the local level. Where the state administration is dominantly of one party, good strategy suggests that the governor should assume the leadership or give his blessing. In some cases, however, the state superintendent of public instruction is the logical person to take over this responsibility.

Similar moves have been tried, with moderate success, with state offices of nongovernmental voluntary agencies. While such attempts may not be greatly handicapped by legal restrictions, they lack the advantage of political unity.

GROUP LEADERS

As most adult education takes place in groups of varying sizes, leaders of these groups form the chief cadre in most adult-education programs. What are the characteristics desired in an educational leader of adults? He need not be a superman, but he must possess certain definite qualities:

1. He must have the ability to participate actively and cooperatively in the challenging adventure of learning. This holds true even when he is teaching routine skills—devising the most effective ways of helping each individual adult gain adequate facility. He is not merely teaching a skill

or subject; he is engaged in reaching individual men and women who may differ widely in background, ability, and motivation.

The need for a joint adventure in learning is even more necessary in the nonskill fields. Dispensing information, although often necessary, is not enough. It is only one part of one step in the educational process. The leader must understand what education really is: a process by which people find better solutions to their problems of living. When education is considered in this light, no leader in a democracy can do other than acknowledge that he does not have the answers, that there are no pat answers. All he has to offer is a process by which answers may be found, together with some knowledge of resources and some skill in organizing and leading. The leader, too, must wonder what the answer may be, where the evidence may lead. He must be less one who knows the answers than one who is constantly seeking them. He leads best who goes through the process with his fellows.

2. The successful leader of adults must be able to establish an informal and friendly atmosphere in the group. To do this, he looks for the good, the pleasant, the successful, and organizes the learning experiences in such a way that the participants feel achievement. This is the principle of reinforcing learning through reward. He respects the attitudes, feelings, and backgrounds of his students as he would those of his closest friends. He shows no air of superiority. He knows that knowledge and schooling are relative, and he realizes that every adult present is in some respects superior to him. He is fully aware, too, that the members of the group function as responsible adults at home, at work, in the community, and in their social and political associations.

3. The good educator of adults is a specialist—an expert along some line. He must know something well or perform something well—something that other adults want to know or do. When adults are invited to list the characteristics most liked or desired in a teacher, knowledge of subject usually ranks first.[2] The method of leadership is important, but there is no substitute for specific and accurate knowledge of the subject or skill which he is teaching.

4. A good leader must know how to relate his specialty to the whole of life. Almost by definition the advance toward maturity is a struggle to integrate specific, usually incomplete experience into consistent wholes. From where we stand, all of us tend to see life in pieces. A leader who is only a specialist can merely reveal other pieces. Adults desire a leader

---

[2] Administrators of adult education in twenty-one cities reported that the following personal qualities ranked highest, in the order named, as attributes of the successful teacher: (1) thorough knowledge of subject, (2) attractive personality, (3) adaptability, (4) thorough teaching preparation, (5) sympathy with adult students, (6) practical experience, and (7) cooperativeness. W. C. Crawford, *Survey of Purposes and Personnel Administration of Adult Education in California*, California State Department of Education Bulletin 11, July, 1942, p. 13.

who can help them relate the fragments of their lives to a larger setting. He must help adults see relationships—among individuals, among groups, between an act and a whole social movement, between the past and the present, between the present and the future, among institutions, between geographic locations, among people everywhere. The ability to see these relationships is a distinguishing characteristic of an educated and mature person.

5. A leader of adults must be able to see the community as a whole, not only its special aspects. Politicians see a community in terms of its voters. Social workers see the underprivileged and maladjusted. Ministers, merchants, and mayors see the community from their special vantage points. The adult-education leader must see the community in all these perspectives and more. He must see the duplication, the competition, and the gaps in community organization; recognize the needs of all socioeconomic levels; and think about how to meet them.

In addition to these general characteristics, the leaders should have ingenuity in planning learning activities, in using a diversity of methods, in engendering enthusiasm, and in maintaining a high level of interest in the group. He should also possess ability to work cooperatively with his fellows, familiarity with the total adult-education program, and competence in handling reports and housekeeping routines promptly.

The requirements of lay and professional leaders are not essentially different. If lay leaders do not already possess special ability, they will need to acquire it. As they are usually not paid for their part-time work, their *esprit de corps* depends largely on how clearly they see its importance in the whole picture.

Recruitment

"I could start 100 more classes tomorrow if I could find the right kind of teachers." So reported a city director recently. A good majority of his counterparts and many evening-school principals consider that finding and holding well-qualified teachers are major and constant problems.

Day-school teachers constitute the most convenient pool of certified and experienced leadership for a director to draw upon. Their experience in dealing with children and youth, however, cannot be automatically counted as an asset. Day-school teachers may or may not be successful with adults. Nonetheless, the regular faculty lists often provide a reservoir of teachers for activities similar to their day assignment. In addition, a survey of other professional qualifications of teachers, as well as their experience, hobbies, and interests, is likely to unearth potential leaders for a number of other activities. After survey results are catalogued, the director has a list which can be drawn upon as need arises. Such surveys need not be limited to the home district. Staffs of surrounding districts may have equally rich leadership resources.

Former teachers can often be induced to take part-time work as leaders of adult groups. Teachers who have married and left the profession, retired teachers, and those working in another occupation may have time to help out. Staff members from nearby colleges and universities can often be approached. Graduate students often welcome part-time teaching both for the experience and for the income.

About one-half of the staffs of public adult schools are made up of day-school teachers.[3] Large schools seem to draw more from outside the regular teacher group than do the smaller ones. In part, the reason may be that urban centers have a greater variety of personnel resources. Also, large schools are more likely to employ full-time principals, who have time to search afield for teachers and to become acquainted with certification procedures and regulations. Part-time principals usually take those most readily available.

An NEA study shows that three-quarters of the teachers of adults have had training as teachers.[4] Not even one out of every eight, however, has had special training as a teacher of adults. Professions other than teaching can also supply faculty members. Much that adults want to know can be taught by doctors, lawyers, certified public accountants, nurses, social workers, librarians, and others. The skilled trades and management occupations are another source of potential adult-school teachers.

The problem, often a difficult one, of locating a specialized leader not on the school staff can be attacked in several ways. Day teachers frequently know the community leaders in their field. General community leaders of long residence can often make suggestions. Local trade-union officials can identify top craftsmen with leadership ability. Trade and professional association secretaries can name leaders in their fields. Hobby groups have among their members or acquaintances the local authorities in their areas of interest. Operators of specialty stores are likely to know who is who in their fields. Even a director new to a community can begin to trace down potential teachers by prudent inquiry of sources listed in the classified section of telephone directories.

Some directors maintain constant watch for leaders at every luncheon, group meeting, school function, or social gathering. They note articles about local people with special talent and save clippings. They maintain lists of leads for further inquiry. They have all teachers who inquire about possible positions file an application, giving fields of competence and background. Occasionally, if no other way seems to reveal the desired specialist, they may run an advertisement in the local paper. Leads

[3] Homer Kempfer and Grace S. Wright, *100 Evening Schools,* U.S. Office of Education Bulletin 1949, no. 4, pp. 32–37.

[4] Division of Adult Education Service of the NEA, *A Study of Urban Public School Adult Education Programs of the United States,* National Education Association, Washington, 1952, p. 66.

on people to fill part-time positions are only occasionally obtained from teachers' agencies or institutional placement offices.

In time of teacher shortage and general high employment, an adult school may not have many applicants. Then, as at other times, the director may find it rewarding to use aggressive methods for finding the best possible teachers wherever they may be. After locating them, he may need to persuade them to join his staff. Added income is sufficient attraction to some people but by no means to all. Appeals may have to be based on the rewards of social service, on the prestige inherent in teaching, on occupational benefits, on the basic satisfactions derived from teaching, and on the fact that other key people have recommended them.

Selection and Appointment

The procedures for selecting teachers of adults are neither as uniform nor as standardized as they are for selecting regular day-school teachers. Most candidates have not come through a well-defined and systematic course of preparation similar to that for elementary and secondary teachers. After a potential teacher is identified, the director must ascertain whether or not the person can lead or teach adults. This is not always easy, but several practices are helpful in evaluating candidates.

Examination of the application form should reveal whether or not the candidate has had any extensive experience in leading adult groups. A careful check of references may indicate strengths and weaknesses. In a personal interview, the director can determine the applicant's general thinking in regard to adult education by asking for his views on how to handle adult groups and what to include in the course. Paul Durrie, formerly director at Des Moines, used this method especially with those not trained as teachers. If personal characteristics seem favorable, the interchange between the director and the candidate can stimulate enthusiasm and produce ideas for a successful course.

If there is any doubt, other administrators and department heads may be asked to interview the applicant. A few directors ask the candidate to outline tentatively the content of the proposed course or to write a publicity item for it. This helps reveal imagination, organizing ability, and cooperation. If the candidate is a teacher, the director or a supervisor should observe him on his regular assignment.

Teachers cannot usually be put on the payroll until they have been approved by the board of education. While the board may take an active part in teacher selection in small communities, in the larger ones the appointments are usually made from the list of candidates selected and submitted by the superintendent. This list is often approved without extended discussion provided it has been prepared and the teachers have been chosen in conformity with the regulations of the board. Formal competitive examinations are sometimes set up for specific types of positions. In addition to written tests, the examination may include voice and personality ratings, evaluation of academic preparation and experience, an interview by a panel, and submission of special studies. Large cities often have detailed rules and regulations governing the selection and appointment of teachers. In New York City, for instance, when a list of adult-teaching positions is to be filled, the Board of Examiners sets up qualifications, publicizes the vacancies, holds examinations roughly similar to civil-service tests, and prepares lists ranking the candidates in order of merit. The Board of Education makes appointments from the list on recommendation of the superintendent.

In some states the law demands a formal contract. Otherwise, letters of appointment specifying the term, rate of pay, and the assignment are usually used, especially in medium-size and small communities. Other documents, such as a copy of the board regulations, a teachers manual, an oath of allegiance, and a withholding tax slip, usually accompany the letter if they have not been distributed earlier.

While volunteers are not ordinarily asked to sign contracts, volunteer bureaus and other supervisory agencies have found virtue in specific letters of agreement. Such letters setting forth duties, limits of authority, expected standards of work, hours, supervisory relationships, and resources for technical assistance are often issued as letters of assignment at the end of initial training.

Almost without exception, state laws and regulations require that public-school teachers shall hold valid credentials. This rule is usually applied to teachers of adults, although occasionally exceptions are made for part-time teachers. The following data show the types of certificates required by adult-education teachers in 375 cities as reported by an NEA study:

Type	Per cent
Day-school *or* adult-education certificate	25.9
Day-school certificate	20.8
Adult-education certificate	13.9
Day-school or special vocational certificate	6.9
Day-school or special Americanization certificate	1.6
Certificate for certain courses only	14.1
Different types of certificates required for different subjects	1.1
No certificate required	15.7
Total	100.0

SOURCE: Division of Adult Education Service of the NEA, *A Study of Urban Public School Adult Education Programs of the United States*, National Education Association, Washington, 1952, p. 66.

Certification is a two-edged sword, which may both facilitate and handicap the proper development of an adult program. Certification requirements may protect the director from having to add to his staff un-desired and unqualified persons promoted by politicians, friends, and enthusiastic cosponsors, but requirements are a handicap wherever nar-row regulations or rigid interpretations prevent the employment of com-petent leaders. While certification helps ensure the quality of elemen-tary- and secondary-school teachers, formal state regulations usually re-quire a specific minimum number of semester or term hours in subject matter and professional education courses which may have little meaning for adult education. Many competent leaders of adult groups have not been trained as teachers and do not qualify for a regular teaching certifi-cate. Inasmuch as they are mature adults following other occupations, they are not likely to enroll in a college teacher-training curriculum to qualify for a part-time assignment teaching adults. Their services will be lost unless some arrangement can be made to put them on the pay-roll. Fortunately, experienced directors are aware of several ways of using such nonprofessional leadership.

1. As most states do not require special certificates for teaching adults, often any valid certificate will suffice. A special regulation, or the absence of a rule, may permit regular teachers to teach on a part-time basis in other than their day assignments.

2. States often certify temporary, part-time, or substitute teachers with qualifications lower than those of regular teachers. Many potential lead-ers of adult groups can qualify for part-time work under regulations which would prohibit their working full-time with youth. Concurrent enrollment in professional courses in education may or may not be re-quired.

3. Special regulations may be set up for teachers of adults whereby persons of a specified general education and with the required years of experience can be certified. This pattern comes from the vocational field, but it is applicable to others. In one state, for example, a ninth-grade edu-cation, with 9 years of journeyman experience in a trade, and enrollment in certain professional courses qualify an individual for certification. A sliding scale permits certification on less experience, but with more gen-eral education.

4. Occasionally a certificate can be issued to a person with sufficient years of schooling if he completes one or two specified professional courses in education. These are usually courses in methods or in prin-ciples and practices in adult education.

5. If a desired leader cannot be certified, there are still several ways of utilizing his services:

a. He may "assist" a certified teacher. The trained teacher may advise on methods and techniques while the assistant handles the subject matter.

b. He may carry the instructional load while a certified supervisor is nominally in charge of the group.

c. He may be engaged for part or all of the course as a noncertified consultant and be paid on much the same basis as an assembly speaker is paid.

d. He may volunteer his services or be paid from funds not under the control of the board of education.

Whatever way is used should conform to the possibilities in a given state and locality. The ultimate answer, of course, is to develop state regulations which adequately recognize the variety of leadership backgrounds needed in adult-education programs. This calls for flexible regulations, which permit procurement of competent adult leaders from any source. At the same time, they should give adequate assurance of competence. Any kind of closed-shop regulations which tend to limit leadership to professional educators will unduly restrict the proper development of the adult field.

Retention

The employment status of teachers of adults varies widely over the country. A great many are appointed on a term or an annual basis and reappointed only as long as their services are needed. The lack of stability of offerings in some areas often makes it administratively unwise to encourage too many part-time workers to expect permanent status. Day teachers on tenure retain it, of course, when they take additional part-time adult work. When the laws provide for tenure, part-time workers with adults are sometimes prevented from acquiring permanent status by the board's expedient of dropping them before the end of the probationary period. In some cases permanent status is allowed for part-time teachers. Those on a full-time basis in regular academic and vocational fields, often with combined day and evening schedules, are likely to be on tenure. Directors, supervisors, evening-school principals, and similar personnel usually occupy the same status as do other full-time employees of the district; that is, they have tenure in their adult position or in another position if they devote only part-time to adult education.

Full-time employees in adult programs usually enjoy the same retirement system as do other staff members engaged by the school district. Those on part time are seldom included in the retirement system, although they are usually covered by Social Security.

Often there is considerable turnover in adult staffs—far more than course changes alone would suggest. Many directors have found that it pays to work at keeping good teachers. Among the means used to retain the best instructors are:

1. Commending them on their successes and minimizing their failures
2. Letting them share in policy making, guidance, and placement activities, in so far as possible

3. Encouraging them to try their own techniques, approaches, theories, and methods

4. Raising their salaries after each year of work and otherwise rewarding outstanding service

5. Answering promptly their requests for equipment, supplies, and visual aids

6. Keeping rules and regulations to a minimum

7. Arranging for adequate substitutes, for sick leave, and for retirement benefits

8. Cutting down paper work, red tape, and other impediments

9. Assigning a reasonable work load

10. Promoting from within the system

These add up to a reduction of anxiety, an increase in self-confidence and creativity, and a feeling of responsibility on the part of all leaders for the advancement of the program.

DEVELOPMENT OF LEADERSHIP

The adult educator cannot be simply a person of good will and generous impulses—and large ignorance. He must know something well. Neither can he be simply a person who knows something well but who is profoundly ignorant about the mental and emotional make-up of the adult human being and of the society in which he resides. Nor can he be simply a schoolman in the traditional sense of that word, a person trained in pedagogy and in not much else. To train anyone, including oneself, to become a genuine adult educator is a large order. For the adult education expert must be in a sense two or three experts rolled into one. He must have specific and accurate knowledge about something. He must know people and human society. And he must know the special hopes and problems of his educative profession.[5]

Preservice Training

The Federal Smith-Hughes and Smith-Lever Acts a generation ago provided for the preservice training of county agents, teachers, and supervisors of vocational education. No comparable development has stimulated educational opportunities for leaders in the general adult field. Until recently, only a few public-school adult educators obtained any specific training for their work before being assigned to it. A common excuse given by schools of education for not developing training programs in adult education has been the lack of specific job opportunities. With the rapid growth of adult education, the situation is gradually improving, although even today many of the leading adult educators in the country and an even greater percentage of teachers have had little

---

[5] Harry A. Overstreet and Bonaro W. Overstreet, *Leaders for Adult Education,* American Association for Adult Education, New York, 1941, p. 38.

or no undergraduate or graduate education directly focused on the education of adults.

At present, several dozen colleges and universities offer professional courses in adult education. Nearly one-half of them are parts of the vocational-education programs of land-grant colleges; most of the remainder are single courses offered as electives in curricula for librarians, public-health workers, social workers, and teachers. In 1953, John A. Spence, a graduate student at Ohio State University, found fourteen universities with well-organized professional curricula supported by sufficient related work to warrant their giving a graduate degree in adult education. As paid positions become more plentiful, the number of such curricula undoubtedly will grow, but a great many adult-education workers will still have to learn on the job. Volunteers usually obtain their preservice training in workshops, institutes, or short courses.

In the land-grant colleges most vocational teachers-in-training receive instruction in adult education either as an integral part of methods courses in the subject-matter field or in special adult-education courses. In addition, graduate courses in adult education may be available. Such courses nearly always deal with adult education within the vocational-education framework. Students preparing for high-school teaching in the social studies, English, science, mathematics, or other academic fields seldom find anything in their methods courses on instructing adults. Very few undergraduate teachers-in-training elect courses in adult education. In large cities, preservice courses are sometimes given by universities prior to a specific examination for prospective adult-school principals, evening elementary teachers, and teachers of the foreign-born.

The professional courses most commonly available to undergraduates and graduates are concerned either with a general introduction to the field or with organization and administration, principles and philosophy of the movement, psychology of adult learning, or methods and materials. Occasionally, more specialized courses in community organization, intergroup relations, human relations, family-life and parent education, public affairs, education for the aging, or use of mass media are available. Beyond these specific courses the potential teachers of adults in the typical institution may round out their preparation by taking and adapting related courses in such fields as anthropology, sociology, social work, secondary or higher education, psychology, and the content fields. As professors in most of these fields are oriented to secondary or higher education or to research, they can usually give only limited help to students interested in work with adults.

Except in the vocational fields, few teachers have any preservice opportunity to teach adults under supervision. Instead, practice teaching during the college years is nearly always with children and youth. In contrast, The People's College of the University of Stockholm offers hundreds of university students the opportunity first to apprentice themselves to the leaders of adult groups and later to take over their leadership directly. A great many of the graduates moving into secondary-school positions are thereby qualified by extensive, supervised experience and training to assume concurrent leadership in adult education.

As adult education grows, no doubt more colleges of education will include curricula combining formal instruction, field observation, and internship designed to develop these competencies:

1. Ability to identify and define the learning needs, interests, and capacities of adults

2. Ability to organize suitable learning activities to serve these needs

3. Familiarity with a wide range of educational approaches, and ability to select and use appropriate ones with the necessary instructional techniques

4. Ability to develop appropriate instructional materials

5. Methods of helping a wide range of community groups to develop better educational activities

6. A practical knowledge of the psychology of adult learning

7. Knowledge of current literature bearing on the special adult fields

8. Ability to locate and use appropriate resource personnel

9. Competence in dealing with controversial issues

As adult education develops into the fourth great segment of education, with its own characteristics and clientele, training programs for educators will need reorientation. The entire profession will need a general acquaintance with adult education, just as educators now, no matter what their work, need to be familiar with the general outline of elementary, secondary, and higher education. In addition, a worker in any subject area can expect to spend an increased portion of his time in adult education. A good third of the work of nursery-school staffs has become parent education. Elementary and secondary teachers all have the responsibility of working both with parents and with other adults.

Even now, the development of adult education in public schools is held back by the lack of awareness among educators of its social significance. G. W. Garrard, late principal, Evening High School, Bakersfield, California, gathered evidence (unpublished) showing that the attitudes of teachers toward adult education are distinctly less liberal than those of certain lay groups. He obtained ratings on four statements of proposed principles favorable to adult education from 123 elementary, 269 high-school, and 66 junior-college teachers in 18 communities in 10 states, and from 140 members of Bakersfield business and professional groups.[6]

---

[6] The four principles were: (1) "Adult education should be an integral part of the total educational responsibility of the state"; (2) "equalization of educational opportunities for all should be insured"; (3) "financial stabilization of the program should be guaranteed through continuous, adequate support from combined state

Fewer than one-half of the 458 teachers agreed wholeheartedly with the principles while over two-thirds of the business and professional people expressed complete agreement. A majority of the teachers accepted the theory of equal educational opportunity for all ages but hesitated to accept the claim of adult education for tax funds. Elementary teachers expressed least approval of adult education.

In light of this widespread feeling within the educational profession, adult educators often feel that they are crying in the wilderness. They are discouraged by the lack of understanding among superintendents, principals, and teachers of the actual and potential importance of the adult field. In some respects, superintendents are more aware of the significance of adult education than are others in the profession, but most of them lack both experience with and training for work in the adult field.

While general courses in the organization and administration of elementary and secondary education have long been required of school administrators, only occasionally does a curriculum in school administration require a course in adult education. When professional preservice curricula have produced a generation of teachers who are sufficiently aware of the philosophy, principles, approaches, and methods of adult education and of its position as an integral part of all education, then a generation of people can best be made aware of the necessity of lifelong learning.

In-service Training

As few professional adult educators prepare directly for their work before entering upon it, in-service training is ordinarily far more important than preservice preparation. Even so, one glaring shortcoming of a great number of adult-education programs has been the absence of any effective in-service training. Directors too long have depended upon finding reasonably well-qualified leaders and having them learn largely unaided on the job.

In-service training starts when a director interviews an acceptable candidate. Most directors hold one or more individual conferences with each new teacher, some time after he has been engaged but before work has begun, to go over plans, develop ideas, clarify assigned responsibilities, and answer questions. While this is time-consuming, it is one of the most effective ways of helping a new teacher get off to a secure start. It gives an early opportunity to establish a favorable relationship and mutual understanding between the director and the new staff member. In large schools much of this orientation can be delegated to supervisors and department heads.

and local sources"; and (4) "adequate administration of adult education should be provided at the state and local levels."

A few directors and department heads assign inexperienced teachers as observers of the best teachers in their departments. Later the new teachers may serve as assistants to carry certain parts of the instructional load or to work with certain subgroups. Such apprenticeship provides excellent orientation under public-school conditions, but it can seldom be arranged for long periods.

All-school or all-department staff conferences are sometimes held prior to the opening of a term, although occasionally such conferences are confined to new teachers. A committee is useful in informally orienting the newcomers by arranging a social period, making introductions, showing them the building, and assisting them with social and community contacts. A danger in preterm conferences lies in wasting the psychological moment for inspiration by droning through administrative matters.

A growing number of directors are finding that special bulletins and teachers handbooks are useful ways of systematically orienting new teachers concerning relationships, requirements, rights, privileges, schedules, textbooks, and other organizational and administrative matters. A staff manual, which is useful for older teachers as well, provides a ready reference throughout the year.

The ideal orientation cannot confine itself to a single conference and rely on written communications thereafter. The initial orientation should set the stage for regular staff meetings at which teachers can discuss problems and work out solutions. Written manuals, while useful for administrative purposes, can never disperse information or solve the immediate problems of staff personnel as effectively as can live discussion and genuinely friendly personal relationships.

Volunteer leaders are usually oriented in instructional groups, workshops, discussion groups, or a series of informational meetings. Individual conferences with supervisors at time of selection or later are also common. Written instructions are prepared in most volunteer programs of any size.

Department heads, adult-school principals, directors of adult education, and, in small communities, general administrators have responsibility for the supervision and in-service training of leaders and teachers of adults. On occasion, staff members from the state education department have supervised local leaders directly or have given special help to the local supervisor. Direct supervision from the state department seems to be less frequent than it was formerly, when area supervisors, or organizers, were fairly common in adult education.

Supervisors need to pay close attention to inexperienced teachers during their first few sessions in order to diagnose any apparent weakness and, if necessary, to offer practical remedial help at once. A supervisor who overlooks this responsibility early in the term runs the risk of soon finding teachers without classes. In spite of all selective procedures, a director who takes a chance on an inexperienced leader in order to get an activity going is bound to make an occasional error. Sometimes elements of weakness in leadership, if identified early, can be corrected, and the major portion of the group can be saved. If they cannot be corrected, the director may either see the group dissolve, admit his mistake and try to substitute another teacher, or transfer the students to another group.

Some principals follow the practice of making the rounds every night to see how things are going. They try to spend a few minutes discussing problems with a succession of teachers before class, at intermissions, and after hours. A few evening principals and directors of adult education make systematic period-long observations of classroom activities and follow them with teacher conferences focused on improvement of instruction. Such supervision is more likely to be a function of a department head, however, who spends his time primarily with new teachers serving on a coleadership or apprenticeship basis. New teachers are likely to be especially receptive to help in teaching techniques, in selecting and using instructional material, in handling individual differences, and in keeping records.

Prevention through careful selection and adequate orientation is, of course, preferable to remedial work after difficulties have appeared. The director must consider the effects not only on the group, but on the leader or teacher himself and on the rest of the teaching staff. Resort to corrective measures during the term cannot be considered a substitute for foresight and prevention.

Corrective supervision, while rather widespread in adult education, is generally less profitable than is a more positive approach. At its best, supervision becomes creative in-service training in which the participants work together with specialists on their common problems.

Adequate supervision is essential in programs carried on by volunteers. Supervision itself may be volunteer, if the director is sufficiently interested and devotes enough time to the task. Most voluntary organizations have found limits beyond which they cannot operate successful programs without paid professional supervisors or consultants who assume supervisory responsibility. The ratios of paid staff to volunteers vary widely according to the nature of work, the inherent interest of the volunteers, the time they give, the traveling distances involved, and numerous other variables.

Professionals who work with volunteer workers say that lack of control makes their supervision difficult. However, this viewpoint may express an undemocratic perception of the respective roles. Volunteers often have a vague sense of responsibility and little training. Allegiance must be built up inherently; it cannot be commanded. Initial enthusiasm leading to the volunteer's offer of service often wanes under the rigors of the assignment. Short-lived interest induces heavy turnover, with its accompanying load of recruitment, training, and administrative headaches. On the other hand, the selfless devotion and the enthusiasm of many volunteers and the values of widespread participation and interpretation are rewards beyond those often obtainable from paid workers.

Until recently, only a few in-service training programs for teachers of adults have existed outside heavily populated areas. Such programs as were developed often were designed for special groups, such as forum moderators, discussion leaders, teachers of the foreign-born, vocational instructors, and parent-education leaders. Since World War II, however, a growing number of localities have initiated orientation and training programs for adult-education leaders. In New York State, local districts must provide a specified minimum amount of in-service training as a condition for receiving state aid.

Until recently, local programs have consisted chiefly of a few late afternoon and evening sessions of general orientation in the philosophy, principles, and modern role of adult education; in the psychology of adult learning; and in general methods. At times they have been largely inspirational. Sometimes the content has been concentrated into three or four all-day sessions spaced a month or so apart. At other times an intensified 1- or 2-day workshop or teacher institute has been organized.

Only a few adult-education administrators hold regular meetings for the total staff, although the number could well increase. Admittedly an adult staff often presents difficulties that do not exist with a day-school faculty. Programs with a high percentage of part-time leaders on staggered schedules commonly have a minority of the total staff available at any given hour. Staff meetings calling for special trips, extra evenings, and irregular schedules raise the question of extra compensation for workers paid by the hour. A few schools pay for one or two extra meetings per semester.

If a staff is to become a team working toward broad, integrated objectives, staff meetings would seem necessary.

Without such a chance, each worker remains a psychological atom who happens, for a certain clock-measured period each week, to occupy a certain room in a certain building, where he instructs a certain group of men and women in a certain subject that may or may not have any relationship to anything else going on in the building at the same time.[7]

In their efforts to solve the problem, administrators have tried occasional socials, all-school assemblies, monthly meetings, beginning- and end-of-term meetings, and even repeat meetings for those present on given evenings. The problem is admittedly difficult. Possibly meetings

[7] Overstreet and Overstreet, *op. cit.*, p. 176.

focused on the objectives of the entire program and the problems of staff members could include sufficiently worthwhile content to attract most teachers a few times per year. If extra pay is not given, perhaps a clear understanding at appointment time and a favorable over-all pay rate would encourage the attendance of most teachers.

Training for specialized workers has been organized in communities of moderate size, in counties, and occasionally in intermediate districts, or by two or more school districts jointly. A specialist in language teaching may be brought in for instruction in a system of language study. A family-life expert may train mothers for volunteer leadership of parent-education discussion groups. A specialist in community organization may lead a self-study group of community leaders through experience in surveys, community analysis, and action research. In the late 1940s six city discussion-leader training projects of the National Institute of Social Relations demonstrated the values of such training for a wide range of community leaders. This demonstration and other projects stimulated a number of communities to set up discussion-leadership training programs.

In rural and village areas the small number of workers often make in-service training in specific subject or service areas impractical, except on a county or regional basis. Teacher-training institutions and state education departments at times arrange in-service training for special groups on an area basis.

Community organizations and private agencies may provide their own in-service training, either alone or through their councils. Public agencies often serve specific common training needs of other groups. A great many voluntary agencies take advantage of the training services of the extension divisions of universities and land-grant colleges.

While most training programs depend upon group approaches, training can also be provided through individualized approaches. If time can be found to locate, procure, and organize materials for a professional library, a directed reading program can be beneficial. Teacher-training institutions provide home-study courses, with or without credit, in a number of specialized fields. Courses likely to draw too few enrollments within a state can be publicized and made available throughout the country. Individuals or teams can be sent to summer sessions and workshops to work out specific problems or to plan educational activities in a given field. Leaders can be sent on visits to neighboring communities to see outstanding programs, experiments, or demonstrations. Attendance at professional meetings, encouraged by giving time off and contributing toward expenses, can stimulate professional growth.

The whole question of the kind of training needed warrants a more definitive investigation. The directors and superintendents covered in the NEA study reported these needs:

| | Per cent |
Training needed	mentioning
In use of methods and aids............	65.9
In understanding needs of students.....	59.7
In understanding needs of community..	37.6
In subject matter....................	6.7

SOURCE: Division of Adult Education Service of the NEA, *A Study of Urban Public School Adult Education Programs of the United States*, National Education Association, Washington, 1952, pp. 66–67.

Training in understanding the needs of students and in methods and aids was especially needed in large cities. The need for reorientation in method is emphasized in the following data, compiled from the same study (pp. 54–56):

Method or procedure	Rank in effectiveness	Rank in frequency of use
Workshops.................	1	5
Demonstration laboratory.....	2	1
Forums....................	3	7
Correspondence courses *......	4	10
Informal group discussion.....	5	3
Panel discussions............	6	6
Teacher-pupil recitation.......	7	2
Formal lectures..............	8	4
Home study (individual)......	9	8
Debates....................	10	9

* Defined as "Direct contact between learner and the school by mail, or [it] may involve supervision by adult-education teachers even to the extent of administering tests."

With so little relation between effectiveness of method and frequency of use, one is tempted to guess that teachers of adults use procedures learned in nonadult contexts. Surely teacher-pupil recitations and formal lectures would not be so common if teachers were sensitive to their relative ineffectiveness. A more detailed study is needed to delineate the training needs more clearly.

The problem of providing certain types of intensive in-service training in rural and village communities is best solved by organizing larger geographical units. General orientation and specialized training are sometimes provided on a county basis, especially where the county is the unit of school organization. A few states—such as New York, with its County Boards of Vocational and Extension Education—occasionally provide county supervisors of adult education who are responsible for leader training.

During the early developmental stages state education departments have frequently assumed responsibilities for initiating and conducting in-service training programs for group leaders. Inasmuch as state laws and regulations provide the general framework within which public education develops, state education departments have a direct responsibility to develop such programs. Several of the more professional state departments also have enough staff to provide considerable leadership and promotion. Among them have been those of California, Florida, New Jersey, New York, Rhode Island, Wisconsin, and a half-dozen other states. California in particular has demonstrated an integrated approach.[8]

In 1947, under the leadership of the state department of education, the University of California Extension Division, in cooperation with the university schools of education and the two professional organizations of public-school adult educators, started conducting classes at a number of centers throughout the state. The state department's announcement of new credential requirements to replace emergency credentials stimulated many teachers to enroll. As part-time teachers are reluctant to attend weekly sessions, intensified schedules were worked out. One training period opened with a 3-hour session on Friday night, followed by 6 hours on Saturday. Four such concentrated programs were scheduled about 2 months apart. Another plan utilized six scattered Friday nights for classes, each followed by a 4-hour session on Saturday morning. As other public agencies contributed services and resource personnel, the university was justified in reducing its tuition fees. A series of several courses to be given in rotation was projected. A methods course and a course in the psychology of adult learning were developed and tried out first. While the content was designed to benefit all teachers of adults, the organizational pattern is adaptable to any specialized training which may be needed.

While preservice training is primarily a function of teacher-training institutions, state education departments have an important complementary role to play in assisting such institutions to develop a training program in harmony with the objectives of the state program. As a statewide program of adult education develops, it is not unusual to find state departments and college teacher-training staffs holding somewhat different concepts. Indeed a college faculty set up to train elementary and

---

[8] A few state education departments, adult evening colleges, and state adult-education associations issue handbooks, circular letters, or other materials for aiding teachers of adults and directors. In addition to those listed at the end of chaps. 11 and 12, see also *Handbook in Adult Education: A Guide for Personnel and Course Goals,* New Jersey Association for Adult Education Bulletin 1, September, 1950; and *Better Teaching: Our Common Goal,* Washington University, University College, St. Louis.

secondary teachers may include no one competent in the adult field. The faculty, oriented toward a different kind of education, may have limited initial usefulness in training teachers for adult education.

Under these circumstances, the state education department staff can well afford to work closely with the most appropriate people on the college faculty in developing a suitable curriculum. Instead of theoretical discussion and preparation of courses, better mutual understanding can be developed through coleadership of classes, directed observation and field work, joint research projects and studies, and joint supervision of interns. Outstanding local directors serving as resource people in workshops can also help develop a clear understanding of adult education as conceived by the schools. Otherwise, a university or college type of adult education may develop with too little practical emphasis on the community approach.

EVALUATION

Evaluation of leaders and of programs for their development can best be a joint responsibility of the director and the entire leadership staff. One means of self-evaluation is through check lists or self-rating scales which can be developed by staff committees. If developed in a way that does not threaten staff members, such instruments and evaluative processes can lead to further growth and improvement. A staff, sometimes in cooperation with a committee of the adult student body, has occasionally developed a rating scale whereby the students can rate their instructors anonymously. While this may have limited merit, it can be useful in a larger pattern of evaluation.

Low staff turnover and high morale, the satisfaction of students, and persistent attendance are indexes of good leadership development. In fact, steady growth of the entire adult program is one of the best indications of a good staff. The readiness of teachers to participate in cooperative research projects, training programs, and all-school activities is another index of success of previous training.

SELECTED REFERENCES

Anderson, Presco: "In-service Training for Directors of Adult Education," *Adult Education,* 1:223–228, August, 1951.

Cologne, Rose: "Training Workers for Community Service," *Adult Education Bulletin,* 9:141–145, June, 1945.

Deming, R.: "Method in Adult Teaching," *Adult Education Bulletin,* 13:186–188, August, 1949.

Dickerman, W., et al.: "A Methods Course for Teachers of Adults," *Adult Education Bulletin,* 13:164–172, August, 1949.

――――: "Inservice Training for California Teachers of Adults," *Adult Education Bulletin,* 13:99–103, April, 1949.

Eckert, R.: "The Psychology of Adult Learning: An Inservice Course for Adult Teachers," *Adult Education Bulletin,* 14:55–59, December, 1949.

Hallenbeck, W. C.: "Training Adult Educators," *Adult Education Journal,* 7:4–10, January, 1948.

Kieffer, J. C.: "A Leadership Education Project," *Adult Education Bulletin,* 11:41–55, December, 1946.

Lippitt, R.: *Training in Community Relations,* Harper & Brothers, New York, 1949.

Mumma, R. A.: "Effective Instruction in an Evening Program for Adults," *Adult Education,* 1:183–189, June, 1951.

Overstreet, Harry A., and Bonaro W. Overstreet: *Leaders for Adult Education,* American Association for Adult Education, New York, 1941.

Ponitz, H.: "Competencies Required of Adult Education Teachers and Group Leaders," *Adult Education Bulletin,* 14:124–125, April, 1950.

Spence, John A.: *Opportunities for Professional Training in Adult Education,* Ohio State University, Bureau of Special and Adult Education, Columbus, Ohio, 1953.

"Spotlight on Leadership," *Adult Leadership,* 1:1–32, June, 1952.

Sworder, Stanley E.: *Handbook for Teachers of Adults,* California State Department of Education Bulletin 20, May, 1951.

Van Sant, T. A. (ed.): "In-service Training for Adult Education," *Adult Education,* 2:153–184, June, 1952.

Zander, Alvin: "Student Motives and Teaching Methods in Four Informal Adult Classes," *Adult Education,* 2:27–31, October, 1951.

See also General References: [9] Beals and Brody, chap. 3; Division of Adult Education Service, chap. 11; Ely, pp. 243–252; Knowles, chaps. 3, 4; Sheats, Jayne, and Spence, chap. 12.

[9] The General References are listed in full at the end of this book.

Adequate publicity and promotion are vitally important in building a successful program of adult education. Most influences which ensure participation of children and youth in educational activities do not operate with adults. Compulsory attendance laws, attendance officers, and custom ensure the enrollment of practically all children of school age. Requirements for entrance to specific types of work and other socio-economic pressures carry most youth through high school and a smaller number through college.

In contrast to the widespread belief in free education for children and youth, there is no general sentiment in favor of adult education. A negative feeling is more likely to be found, particularly among the educationally underprivileged and among those who live in isolated regions. In some communities a majority of adults of low educational background may be timid and hesitant about enrolling in educational activities because they are ashamed to admit their deficiencies. These circumstances call for a particularly sensitive and skillful kind of promotion.

At any given time only a minority of adults feel a strong need for education, and even fewer feel the need keenly enough to spend any considerable amount of energy hunting for it. Others who want education fail to find the kind they want, either because they are inept at looking for it or because it is unavailable. Inevitably, too, vocational and family responsibilities and many other interests are competing for attention. If an adult program is to thrive in competition with these interests, it must be promoted. New programs with good leadership may fail to materialize or may struggle along weakly because of ineffective and insufficient promotion. Established programs may coast along on previous reputations for a while with minimum publicity, but if new programs or expanded features of old programs are to succeed, the public must be made aware of them.

Promotion Policies

Two extremes of thought, stemming from prevailing educational philosophy, are evident in current promotion policies. Under one policy little effort is made to publicize educational activities for adults, on the theory that adults with felt educational needs will respond without having to be urged. Promotion may consist of bare announcements in a newspaper or on indiscriminately placed placards. The resulting lack of enthusiasm is often interpreted as proof that adults do not want to be educated. In extreme form, of course, only those activities are provided which are requested by a sufficient number, through petition or otherwise. Under this policy those enrolling are likely to have a pressing serious academic or vocational purpose.

The other policy assumes that all adults have educational needs and that everyone should be informed about available learning opportunities. All media and methods helpful for this purpose are likely to be used in an effort to enlist the participation of everyone who has a trace of interest. Underlying this activity, of course, is an attempt to identify the educational needs and interests of as many adults as possible and to design appropriate activities. In any normal community, only the latter promotion policy is likely to yield a flourishing program.

Selling versus Involving

Many directors of adult education think of promotion as selling. Courses, lectures, and other activities are their merchandise. In many respects promotion is to adult education what advertising is to business. Certainly the public must be informed, convinced, and persuaded to participate. Many methods and media widely used today are those of the advertiser, the salesman, and the publicist. This chapter will be concerned largely with the distribution of information about programs and with the promotion-as-selling concept, for these ideas are most widely understood. Likewise, they often provide easier, although usually more artificial, ways of promoting a program, at least in its earlier and more elementary stages.

Astute educators of adults, other able educational leaders, people of deep insight in human relations, and, of late, businessmen are beginning to recognize that conventional publicity and advertising, no matter how aggressively carried on, have their limitations.[1] Their one-way flow of ideas is based on assumptions which are becoming less and less valid as our culture and the relationships between people become more democratic. In the long run, directors who depend upon old-line publicity are likely to find it becoming relatively less effective. Many agencies and most community leaders of adult education will no doubt continue to use several of the media and many of the devices of advertising and public relations. Nonetheless, a growing number of directors are promoting their programs by involving adults in all stages of these programs, from the preliminary research to the final appraisal. Adults are involved in identifying and defining their own educational needs, in planning the

[1] Holly Whyte, "Is Anybody Listening?" *Fortune*, September, 1950.

desired educational activities and experiences, in developing them, and in evaluating them. By such processes, they integrate learning with living and abandon the dualism of the seller and the buyer, the teacher and the student. Important learnings accompanying this basic democratic process include human-relations skills and an increased sense of self-reliance and community responsibility. Involvement is a much more fundamental concept, in that the participants develop an emotional commitment often lacking among those who are merely sold a program. Earlier parts of this book deal with various ways of involving adults which go far beyond ordinary promotion techniques.

Strategic Timing

Promotion, like all other phases of a director's work, is most fruitful when systematically planned and scheduled. Experience has taught business and industrial groups, community-organization officials, politicians, and successful directors of adult education that a combination of year-round promotion and special campaigns is best.

A constant promotional effort has several advantages. By making friends throughout the year, it is not as likely to provoke criticism as is a new campaign. It permits the steady building up of public confidence in adult education as a permanent part of community life. It encourages maximum capitalization on such effective general program themes as "Learn While You Earn," "Learning for Living," and "Lifelong Learning." It produces a dignified picture of adult education as a whole much more successfully than does an emotional selling campaign. It permits the use of a wider range of media and publicity approaches. Direct announcement of activities can be supplemented with news of personnel and activities, special features, human-interest stories, pictures, radio and television broadcasts, and other types of publicity. Continuous promotion spreads the work load. It is usually less expensive in the long run because much year-round promotion is free, whereas special advertising campaigns cost money.

Special campaigns, however, are necessary. Usually they are used (1) to call special attention to the opening of a new term, or (2) to prepare the public for a new type of activity. Special publicity is usually most effective if it is started some weeks before a term opens. An occasional announcement or story during the preceding months can build a general expectancy in the public mind. Successful directors often time their campaigns to begin at least 2 or 3 weeks in advance of the registration date and to continue until late registration is no longer encouraged or until the membership of classes and groups stabilizes. A late start usually prolongs the settling down period and may cut enrollment. The amount of news and advertising space, radio time, and other publicity usually increases until the campaign reaches a peak during the week preceding registration. If local policies permit late registration, publicity for a few days after the registration period should stress this fact.

Campaigns to prepare the public for a new type of activity are usually longer and less intensive—except during the last 2 or 3 weeks—than those before registration. Campaigns to sell tickets for a lecture or concert series and other money-raising campaigns may have to be timed months in advance—in the spring for fall opening—if a favorable booking contract can be obtained only by a cash guarantee. Such special promotion should continue well into the first season to help establish the activity firmly in the public mind.

As promotion is only one of many responsibilities of most adult-education administrators, they often plan to provide the public with a steady flow of information that requires minimum energy but produces maximum effects. Better plans can usually be made if a promotion or publicity calendar is used, especially if its major features are filled in 6 months to 1 year in advance, subject to changes as new stories come up. Special campaigns can be spotted and various types of stories, pictures, and other activities planned for the intervening months. Radio time, deadlines for preparing and distributing materials, and dates with community organizations can be scheduled in time to give best results. Details may change as time moves on, but a promotion calendar helps greatly to avoid the hand-to-mouth type of publicity that so often plagues a young program.

UTILIZING MASS MEDIA

Newspapers

In many quarters the newspaper is the favorite, occasionally the only, and usually a relatively easy publicity medium to use. Fully four-fifths of all school and college programs and nearly all private-agency adult-education programs are publicized through newspapers.

Most adult-education publicity appears as news. Stories range from bold-headlined front-page spreads to small items among the advertisements on the back pages. Since newspapers are an important medium, program directors can well afford to spend a few hours studying the arts of the journalist and publicist. Several references listed at the end of this chapter are concerned with news and feature writing, technical preparation of copy, relations with the press, and similar points. The following suggestions, however, should help program directors make the best use of news columns:

1. Develop all possible publicity outlets. General daily and weekly newspapers reach most people, but the alert director does not overlook the neighborhood weeklies, shopping guides, trade journals, labor papers, house organs, club and church bulletins, civic organization circulars,

and the newsletters of professional societies. Where feasible, items should also be placed in foreign-language papers, since they often influence an audience otherwise difficult to reach. A list of locally published periodicals can usually be found in city directories and the yellow pages of telephone books. Ayer's *Directory of Newspapers and Periodicals*, available in many libraries, reports circulation and other data.

2. Become personally acquainted with newspaper reporters and editors. Through such acquaintance, directors can discover local preferences in news and its preparation—whether a paper wants fact sheets, prepared releases, or opportunities for reporters to prepare their own stories. Editors and reporters appreciate sincere thanks for favorable editorials or especially good treatment of stories.

3. Give morning and afternoon papers and other competing papers an even break on news. Become acquainted with deadlines and alternate the breaking time of important stories. Separate releases should be written for each paper, but if only one version is prepared and mimeographed for distribution to all papers, it must be assumed that each paper will cut and rewrite the story as it sees fit. Schedule some stories for days of light news, such as Monday.

4. Develop a nose for news. In addition to announcements of opening dates, places, and course titles, timely stories on budgets, staff appointments, policy changes, anticipated program developments, enrollment data, and much other information are newsworthy. Inspection of adult-education news reveals too many meek and barren course lists on back pages and too little variety.

5. Watch for human-interest stories and opportunities for pictures. Enrollment of new immigrants, activities of the oldest registrant, grandmother-mother-daughter enrollments, whole-family participation, a 20-year consecutive enrollment, a lifetime educational ambition realized, a safety award to a recent driving-class member, departure of community ambassadors, and many similar opportunities provide material. Invite a paper to send a feature writer and photographer to cover such events, or develop writing skill and submit a story with photos.

6. Cultivate the acquaintance of local columnists and feed them material. As they are usually widely read, space in their columns is often better than straight news.

7. Arrange for a "box" or a calendar on the front page or elsewhere in weekly or Sunday papers and keep it filled with announcements of special events of the week and new activities. The public will develop the habit of looking for it.

8. Provide newspapers with prepared stories of general interest, as well as items especially slanted for the woman's page, financial page, sports section, travel page, church sections, and other departments. Furnish a dozen or more one- or two-sentence fillers for use at any time.

Example: "Over 2,800 adults are attending day and evening classes in the Mills Adult School each week."

9. Slant news to the audience of each paper. Mastheads sometimes mean little. Acquaintance with a staff member gives opportunity to learn the general interests and characteristics of the paper's readers.

10. Write concise, accurate, vigorous stories. Short, fact-packed items are preferred. Write in the style desired by the paper. Remember that names make news, especially in small communities.

11. Encourage adult-school classes in journalism, feature writing, and public relations to assist with promotion.

12. Try to include a newspaper man on an advisory committee. He may volunteer valuable advice and material help.

The use of paid advertising varies widely with the type of adult-education agency. No doubt advertising will be used increasingly as adult education becomes established as an accepted function of the public schools. Nearly all private programs use newspaper and magazine advertising. These suggestions, used with discretion and adapted to the local situation, will help the adult school get the most out of its advertising dollar:

1. Schedule advertising on the promotion calender and spread it widely among the news outlets, without regard to the news and editorial treatment that the school has received from each paper.

2. Use advertising primarily as part of the promotion campaign leading up to the opening of a term or the starting of a new service.

3. Help a paper to issue an annual school or adult-education edition carrying numerous news stories, features, and advertisements relating to adult education. The layout for display ads can sometimes be reprinted in fliers, folders, or schedules prepared for supplemental distribution.

4. In small communities having one widely read weekly paper, almost complete coverage can be gained with a full- or half-page display ad a few days before registration. This is especially advantageous to comprehensive programs. Smaller ads may have much less effect. Good news write-ups and an editorial on adult education can often be carried in the same issue.

5. In most communities small, frequently run display ads give better dollar returns than occasional large ads. General ads can be placed on the educational page or anywhere, but ads aimed at a specific group should be located in the appropriate section, such as the page devoted to world news, real estate, finance, or women's interests.

6. Ads placed in Sunday city editions may be especially useful, as people have more leisure to read them.

7. Display ads should list and briefly describe activities in an attractive

and easy-to-read type and layout. Advice on this can be obtained from the newspaper or from specialists in public relations.

8. Ads in specialized journals and other publications with selected audiences are more effective if written to appeal to the particular interests of readers.

9. Use classified ads written to cover specific courses, curricula, or areas of vocational training. Classify them under "instruction," "educational opportunities," or other appropriate heading so that they will appear where they are most likely to be seen by special groups of readers.

Catalogues, Bulletins, and Pamphlets

The adult-education programs of practically all colleges and private agencies and of most public schools are publicized by printed or processed materials prepared for mail or personal distribution. Besides listing and describing activities, these materials usually carry descriptions of activities and information on location, registration, schedules, general regulations and procedures, and fees charged, if any. In a few cases such materials also carry commercial advertising which may pay part or all of the printing and distribution costs.

Large adult-school programs in some cities issue a general catalogue listing all activities by name and location. In addition, each local center has its own supplemental publicity material. Likewise, large programs often issue a separate piece of publicity material for each curriculum, each field, or each type of activity. For example, the Cass Technical Evening High School in Detroit recently issued two general announcements and nine other pamphlets, each covering a department. Separate announcements are often available for forums, lectures, and concert series; for recreational activities; for vocational departments; and for guidance and other special services. Publicity matter is sometimes written in a modified newspaper style and issued on newsprint in a miniature or regular-size newspaper format. The Shorewood, Wisconsin, Opportunity School and a few others use slick paper.

Agencies with comprehensive programs sometimes use periodic newsletters to keep their registrants abreast of current developments. If they are intended primarily for circulation within the agency, they may take the form of a house organ or a student-faculty newspaper. *Modern Knight*, a monthly at Central Night High School in Atlanta, provides an outlet for writing talent, gives some journalistic experience, and carries news and promotional material. A weekly mimeographed bulletin supplements the monthly with current information on the curricular and extracurricular life of the school. The *News*, published by the American School of Chicago, carries student news and inspirational material. The four-page weekly *Night Letter* of the San Jose, California, adult program is full of information about current and coming activities. Some newsletters have widespread circulation outside the student body and help maintain contact with former registrants.

Newsletters can be sent to leaders of community organizations and to personnel directors of industrial concerns. They provide a way of keeping community leaders continuously aware of what is going on in the adult-education field. The Adult Education Council of Denver each week circulates *Educational Opportunities,* a calendar of adult-education events reprinted from the *Monitor,* to a selected mailing list. Councils in New York; Cincinnati; Hamilton, Ohio; and other places prepare monthly calendars of adult-education events and circulate them to strategic persons for reference and for posting on bulletin boards.

Primarily for reasons of economy much promotional material is reproduced by offset, multilith, mimeograph, hectograph, and similar processes. Care on the part of the local director can do much to ensure more effective publicity materials. Well-prepared and skillfully arranged copy may take more time, but not more money. Likewise, when printed materials are used, time in planning stock and layout and in examining proof is usually well spent. Illustrations can be planned and photos assembled in advance of need. (Early preparation is one advantage of using a publicity calendar.) Snappy line drawings, stick figures, and plenty of white space brighten print. Two-color effects can be obtained by use of colored ink on tinted stock.[2]

Captions and descriptions are extremely important, whether courses are listed together or in single announcements. When skillfully written, they can help attract potential enrollees and lighten the counseling load at registration time. The total publicity piece makes the first impression, but the course caption is next to catch the eye. The ideal caption combines brevity, uniqueness, and interest. If possible, it should indicate the focus of the course. Law for the Layman, Behind the Headlines, Cooking for Two, and Personal Typing are examples which fill most of these criteria. Such captions as Arithmetic, Consumer Education, English, Homemaking, and Dramatics are almost meaningless in their generality. When A Pre-high-school Program was used as the caption for a course of study at Parker Vocational School, Dayton, Ohio, a sizable number enrolled, but only a few had been attracted to the same course when it was labeled Elementary Education. Only a handful of veterans enrolled in Psychology when it was offered after the War at Florence, Italy, but 1,100 enrolled when the title was streamlined. An examination of current publicity materials will give other practical ideas.

Brief course descriptions following the title should indicate content and further slanting. They should help the reader answer such questions

[2] For other effective uses of color, see L. Cheskin, *Colors: What They Can Do for You,* Liveright Publishing Corporation, New York, 1947.

as these: At what level is the course pitched? Is it too elementary or too technical for me? Will it begin where I am and help me progress? In addition, the description should arouse the reader's interest and induce him to take the course. The paragraph should be effective sales copy. Here are two samples that do all these things:

Stenography Refresher

This course, popular with ambitious career girls, will concentrate on review and building up more accuracy and speed in Gregg shorthand. Dictation will be given at varying speeds, from 60 to 120 words per minute. Try out the old saying: "Time spent in whetting your axe is never lost."

Your Income Tax

Here's a practical course timed to answer your questions and help you prepare your own income tax form for 1954. You'll review the latest regulations as they affect several types of citizens: the unmarried person, the married person with one or more dependents; persons with a business; persons with income from estates and other sources. Exclusions, exemptions, deductions, and capital gains and losses will be analyzed and applied to your particular tax problems. Limited to 25.

A few directors ask instructors and group leaders to write the first draft of course descriptions indicating the material covered, the group for whom it is planned, and similar information. These may be rewritten to give desirable uniformity in style and length. Cleverness in writing captions and descriptions, if not overdone, pays dividends.

Inexpensive fliers, leaflets, and simple folders promoting a single activity are popular in large programs as supplements to comprehensive lists. They are especially useful for activities organized after comprehensive lists have been issued. They are good, too, for publicizing co-sponsored projects; the names of two or more cooperating agencies included in these promotional pieces do not imply sponsorship of other activities, as they might if they were given in a more comprehensive list. People are more likely to read fliers than to read catalogue descriptions, even when the content is the same. Public-school programs are making increasing use of fliers.

Printed leaflets are preferred, although multilithed and mimeographed announcements are most common. Attractive color and layout, an appropriate descriptive line drawing, and a brief facts-of-life description are required ingredients. A size convenient for mailing, for leaving on counters and desks, for placing in books, leaving on reading tables, and for hand distribution is best. When printed on cardboard of proper size and sufficient weight, some materials can be mailed without envelopes. A few programs use mimeographed or printed postal cards for this purpose. In addition to use with special mailing lists, these cards are an inexpensive means of answering inquiries about specific courses.

As adult-education agencies have come to recognize that they are serving a common cause, more of them have learned to promote that cause cooperatively. Occasionally they jointly produce a comprehensive directory of activities for extensive distribution. Usually this is done through an adult-education council. The Council at Cincinnati, for example, in 1949–1950 issued a *Directory of Program Resources,* which listed 142 local sources of program aid, and a *Directory of Vocational Classes.* It also issued a *Directory of 16 mm Films* available in the community. The Film Council at Des Moines and similar councils in scores of other cities and counties list films available locally and promote their use among community organizations. All activities of both public and private programs listed in the directory issued by the Adult Education and Training Council of Hamilton, Ohio, are indexed for ready reference.

Condensed annual reports can be widely distributed. Constituencies like to know what has taken place and what is being planned. If the whole scope of past and planned operations can be condensed annually into a readable folder in which various points are illustrated with pictures, line drawings, and graphs, this thumbnail sketch can be given the widest distribution. One annual report, undoubtedly read by nearly all who received it, came in the mail to the author as a printed postal card; 10,000 were sent to ensure complete family coverage.

If the layout is attractive enough to encourage reading, more extensive reports may be designed for a list of community leaders, staff members, and business offices. The board of control and advisory-committee members, of course, should have still more complete reports.

The Radio and Television

Radio and television offer important opportunities for promoting adult education. The public-service responsibilities of commercial stations make them receptive to cooperation with public adult-education agencies. Much good practice in newspaper publicity applies, with adaptation, to the air. However, special skills in script writing, program planning, dramatization, and production are required for extensive work with these media. Local stations can frequently help with these processes. The usefulness of the following suggestions depends largely upon the broadcasting facilities available.

1. Use spot announcements to open promotion campaigns. Aim them at obtaining mail or telephone inquiries or attendance at specific meetings.

2. Seek plugs by special commentators; use the "Woman's Page of the Air," and similar programs to supplement news and advertising.

3. Advertise adult-department activities through daily or weekly public-school broadcasts.

4. Promote adult-education services related to educational programs

by tying in publicity with these programs. A local radio or television forum permits reference to courses, discussion groups, further reading opportunities, and other activities in public-affairs education. Radio and TV broadcasts on family problems, child development, consumer problems, and similar fields often can refer to other adult-education activities.

5. Experiment with tape recordings of discussion-group and classroom activities. Use these recordings as parts of spot announcements or prepare them for longer periods of air time. Run some of these during morning and afternoon hours for the housewife audience.

6. Set up a series of short broadcasts of "inside scenes" or "on-the-scene pickups" of interesting program features—an Americanization class, a woodshop, a cooking class, a nursery-school observation group, a lively round table, a choral-reading class, a dramatic group, a camera club, or an educational tour.

7. Arrange interviews with staff members, participants, guest speakers, advisory-committee members, and important out-of-town guests visiting the program. Play up human-interest angles.

8. Remember that effective radio and TV educational programs in themselves reflect favorably on the sponsor. Multiply them, run them through all seasons, and capitalize on the opportunities they provide to publicize other phases of the total program.

Motion Pictures

Because preparation of a reel of professional-quality film is expensive in skill, time, and money, not many programs in small communities have used locally developed motion pictures in promotion. The Los Angeles Adult Education Administrators Association has prepared "Self-realization," a 20-minute 16-millimeter sound film of high quality showing scenes in their 24 adult centers. Akron, Ohio; Highland Park, Michigan; and a few other cities have done likewise. Films of top quality can be very effective when shown widely to community organizations. The inspiration they furnish and the possibilities they suggest to those who have antiquated ideas of education undoubtedly are a powerful influence both in increasing participation and in building public support.

Amateur productions of acceptable quality sometimes can be made at reasonable cost. They make good projects for advanced motion-picture photography classes. If they fall too far below acceptable standards, however, their value before community groups is severely limited.

Motion pictures prepared in other communities offer rich opportunities for initiating or expanding adult-education and community-development programs. Advisory committees, boards of education, town councils, community organizations, and the general public are more likely to catch a vision of the possibilities of adult education after seeing activities in other communities not too dissimilar from their own. In small communities, short programs with oral presentation of filmstrips, slides, opaque-projector materials, and similar visual aids can be worked up without too much expense for publicizing local programs to community groups.

Exhibits

Exhibits usually show what has been made by participants in adult-education courses. Arts and crafts, homemaking, trade and industrial, business, and science classes offer the most visible products, but enlarged pictures can portray certain other activities. If permanent display space can be arranged in museums, libraries, and similar places, exhibits should be changed frequently.

Individual courses and lecture series can be promoted through exhibits. Window dioramas, table models, and other three-dimensional displays in miniature, supplemented by brief printed information, can promote such courses as How to Plan a House, Interior Decoration, Dressmaking, Gardening, and Flower Arrangement. Exhibit users have made these additional suggestions:

1. Exhibits, especially if they utilize light, color, motion, or sound, interest some adults who do not respond to printed or broadcast appeals.

2. Downtown bank and department-store windows, lobbies, corridors, and other places the crowds pass are favorite locations.

3. Because window space for a week represents a considerable expense, it is well to publicize by radio or newspaper the location of such exhibits.

4. In downtown exhibits big pictures of the institution and, in metropolitan areas, a map showing bus routes to the school help identify and locate it.

5. Portable exhibits for display at fairs, conventions, and large meetings can help keep the public informed.

6. Outdoor billboards have been used to advertise large city and state-wide programs.

7. Lighted schoolhouses themselves have promotional values. More than one director schedules classes first in rooms facing the streets and turns on the lights of all other such rooms during the first week, whether used or not, to give the impression of activity.

8. An educational building usually has enough passersby to warrant the location of a glassed-in bulletin board, neon sign, or exhibit on its own premises. This has the advantage of associating the location with the activity.

9. Exhibits and displays inside the entrance of large schools help inform participants and visitors about activities of which they may be unaware.

If used wisely, posters and placards can stimulate inquiries and registrations. These suggestions will improve results:

1. Use posters where costs prohibit extensive use of other mass media or where complete coverage of the population by direct mail is not practical. They may also be effective where the program offered is of little interest to the total public, provided they can be selectively placed. For instance, a course in television repair in a large city might well be advertised through posters located where many young men will see them.

2. Cards in streetcars and buses serve essentially the same purpose as posters. The size of the public reached varies widely from city to city.

3. Because some of the posters will be seen at considerable distances, they should display less print than an advertisement of the same size. Course descriptions usually must be short or omitted altogether.

4. Reply cards in pockets or perforated and stapled at the bottom of the placard often bring many requests for catalogues from sincerely interested people, as well as some from the mildly curious.

5. Distribution to bulletin boards, selected plant and store personnel departments, offices, libraries, public buildings, social agencies, churches, and organization secretaries is most effective if handled personally. Interviews with a list of key people can open the way for mailing posters to them later. If these key people are provided with catalogues and their names are individually imprinted on the posters, they can serve as initial information and contact points for prospective registrants. School officials should keep in touch with these people personally, whenever possible, or by telephone.

6. An integrated series of three or four posters, changed weekly, improves results.

7. Use colored ink and tinted stock if it will attract without loss of dignity. Print on two stocks—light weight for posting on bulletin boards and heavier for standing alone.

8. Posters made in an art department can be used locally for building interest in and informing present clientele of new activities.

Festivals and Open House

A display of activities, together with an exhibit of products, can be planned for an annual all-school affair. If such affairs are planned to bring in large numbers of outsiders, they can provide quite effective promotion, especially in small communities. Practically all aspects of a program can be displayed. These suggestions can be adapted to local situations:

1. Hold an open house or visiting night after the middle of the term with products on display in the workrooms, where instructors and participants are busy with materials and equipment. Encourage outsiders to visit widely.

2. Display and demonstrate products in a gymnasium and use the auditorium for music, dramatics, public speaking, and similar activities.

3. Hold an agricultural, homemaking, athletic, musical, or dramatic festival that sponsors competition within the school and with outsiders. Plan a nationality festival to show the many contributions made by immigrants in music, foods, language, traditions, and the other cultural elements.

4. Hold style shows to display products of dressmaking classes.

5. Build a complete evening program. Make it a community affair. Exhibits can be open from before dinner until late evening. Dinner can be planned, prepared, and served by meal-planning, foods, and cooking classes. Americanization classes and intercultural groups can prepare and serve dishes of other lands. After-dinner entertainment can be furnished by music, dancing, dramatics, and public-speaking classes. Science and vocational classes can put on demonstrations to large groups or small. Continuous demonstrations of processes in arts and crafts, business, trade and industry, homemaking, and similar fields can fill the free hours. Instructors and students of academic subjects can demonstrate how their activities bear on contemporary life. A small adult school in New York State, on its closing evening, holds a banquet, gives time for visiting shops and classrooms, and provides an hour of magic, music, and variety acts, all put on by the students currently enrolled. The evening is closed with social dancing for those who care to remain. Many variations of this program are possible.

6. Induce visitors to participate in activities wherever possible—in folk dancing, singing, lathe operation, weaving, typing—nearly anything. Give elementary instruction that leads to visible progress. Learning is fun, and participation makes it infectious.

SYSTEMATIC COVERAGE

Widespread distribution is necessary to make well-prepared publicity materials maximally effective. Inexperienced directors often overlook this point, and their efforts, consequently, have a poor response. Usually the desired audience is the total adult public, although special activities may appeal to selected groups. In the latter case the aim is total coverage within the group.

The audiences of newspapers, TV, and radio are relatively fixed and beyond the control of the local director. Time on the air and sometimes the newspaper edition can be selected. Otherwise, control is limited by choice of medium. The audience of exhibits is determined largely by location. Control of other media and methods, however, can often be maintained to ensure desired coverage.

Direct Mail

Direct mail, although costly in time, money, and energy, is a favorite way of publicizing adult education. The mass media are often used to build general receptivity, which is capitalized on by pinpointed direct mail. Mass-media promotion need not be as heavy when direct mail is extensively used.

Mimeographed, multilithed, or multigraphed form letters written especially for certain groups are often effective. Form letters, if accompanied by descriptive folders, should be concise and focus on the enclosure. If used alone, they must necessarily be long enough to include all the essential information. In either case they should be slanted to the interests of a particular group.

Because of the cost, individually typed letters are seldom used except to key leaders. Personally typed letters as a follow-up to mimeographed form letters sent, during World War II, to aliens of long residence in New York State brought only a few more to Americanization classes. Such letters may be feasible for selected groups, however, if automatic typewriters are available.

Common mailing lists available for occasional use are:

1. Newly arrived immigrants—for invitation to orientation activities and English and citizenship classes (see chap. 6).

2. High-school graduates and dropouts—for acquainting them with general or specific opportunities available.

3. Parents of kindergartners or first graders—for invitation to activities in family-life education related to their child's development.

4. New residents and parents of new registrants in any grade—for invitation to participate in any phase of the adult program. (Names may be obtained from moving companies, public-utility lists, and bureaus issuing building permits.)

5. Those who have completed a specific course—for special invitation to join an advanced course, a club, or an association with educational purposes.

6. Newlyweds and new parents—for invitation to family-life education or other special activities. (Names are available from bureaus of vital statistics, marriage-license bureaus, or newspapers.)

7. Any occupational or other group for whom certain activities may have special appeal.

A growing number of directors with community-wide programs attempt to circularize their communities completely, at least annually, by mailing announcements to every household. Materials addressed to the "Occupant" of each street address or to all boxholders may give the most complete coverage but may not receive the attention of mail that bears the occupant's name. City directories, although they may be 90 to 95 per cent accurate within a year or two after publication, will eventually deteriorate, with addresses of homeowners and other long-time residents remaining most stable. Lists of registered voters and taxpayers sometimes represent only a minor fraction of the adult population. Telephone directories and other public-utility lists are likewise less complete than is often assumed. The availability of public and private lists varies widely among localities. Directors of public programs sometimes have wide access to public lists. At times arrangements can be made to use addressograph plates free or at cost. Small announcements, leaflets, or reply cards requesting catalogues can sometimes be enclosed with gas, electric, telephone, or water bills.

While complete coverage is often desirable, selected mailing lists usually bring greater returns per dollar spent. General announcements are most often sent to former registrants and the accumulated list of inquirers. A number of experienced directors send announcements of an individual activity or of activities in a particular field to specialized occupational groups. Mailing lists for announcements of brush-up and other timely courses of interest to building superintendents, service-station operators, florists, realtors, or members of professional and trade groups can be obtained from classified sections of telephone directories and secretaries of organizations. Many useful lists, classified by income, home ownership, occupation, or other characteristics, are available commercially.

An example of excellent use of special mailing lists recently occurred in connection with a forum series on international affairs. Although publicized by mass media, the first meeting of the series drew a very low attendance. The punched cards used for circulation analysis in the library supplied the names of people who had drawn books on international relations. By mailing an individualized form letter to this list, the forum director was able to build his second session into a sizable audience.

If enough clerical help is available, a program can build and maintain its own lists. Lists used for publicizing program services are often valuable for other types of promotion. Chambers of commerce, telephone directories, city directories, councils of social agencies, and public libraries are common sources for lists of major organizations, although usually a great many smaller groups can be added by conscientiously checking the newspapers for notices of organization activities. Opinion is divided on the value of the secondary publicity which may result from using such lists—that is, on the value of promoting programs among leaders who—by making an announcement, giving personal advice, or posting information—may induce others to enroll. No doubt many blindly mailed matter hits the wastebasket. Selective mailing, however, can be built into an effective system if the director extends his personal acquaintance among the recipients of his promotion material. For example, one director annually sends announcements and posters to several hundred key organization leaders of whom he personally knows about 200. Individually typed letters, handwritten notes, and phone calls accompanying mailed publicity material add the personal touch which stimulates cooperation.

Mailing lists need to be kept up to date. A reply card sent to organization secretaries annually in late spring or early fall, or better still immediately after the organization's annual election, can bring desired minimum data: the names, addresses, and telephone numbers of new officers. Special lists of all inquiries should be accumulated as a nucleus for starting new activities or publicizing the old. Members of current adult groups can be encouraged to add names of potentially interested persons to this list.

To be most useful, lists must be classified to permit selective mailing. Schools, libraries, social agencies, newspapers, radio stations, business and industrial house organs, clergy, PTAs, personnel managers, unions, and community organizations of all sorts are common categories. In small communities most names are kept in typed lists, on 3- by 5-inch cards, or on perforated carbon copies of gummed labels. In larger communities, it may be more frequently used lists on addressograph plates. Names kept on Keysort cards can be alphabetized and yet divided easily with a hand tool into numerous previously coded categories.

Users of direct mail can often save money by familiarizing themselves with current postal regulations and possibilities before designing publicity materials. First-class mail, of course, receives most attention by both the postal service and the recipient. It is also the only class that will be forwarded or, if no forwarding address is available, returned. Certain lower rates require special permits, quantity mailing, and special bundling, and delivery of material sent at lower rates may be delayed.

Hand Distribution

Many public-school directors send publicity materials home by school children. This practice often works best with elementary-school pupils, especially in the lower grades. In some communities, little cooperation is obtained from youth in the upper grades and in high school.

The effectiveness of this system depends upon the traditional home-school relationships and the care with which the distribution is organized. Usually fewer than one-half of all households have children in grades 1 to 12. Even if cooperation were perfect, no more than one-half of the homes would be reached. The coverage can be extended by having children take the materials to nearby neighbors who have no children in school, if doing so does not result in exploitation. This practice should be organized on some systematic or block-leader basis which prevents duplication. Efficiency depends in part upon the relationships built up with day-school teachers. Notices placed in teachers' mailboxes without instructions may be distributed routinely and enlist little enthusiasm among the children. If the director or local principal builds understanding and strong cooperation on such matters, teachers may help ensure almost complete community coverage.

Where homes are compactly located, publicity materials may be distributed house to house either by volunteer or paid workers. Boy Scouts, Girl Scouts, and other volunteers are sometimes willing to give this type of service, especially if special recognition can be given the group. Occasionally such distribution may be tied in with cookie or doughnut sales. Both paid workers and volunteers need to be instructed carefully, and the reliability of the former may need checking if they are paid by the job. Careful distribution may give coverage almost as complete as the best mailing lists. In this case, the decision to use one or the other method will be based primarily on the question of cost.

Lack of help or funds may prohibit complete personal or mail distribution. Under such circumstances, distribution of quantities of material to strategic spots may be a partial answer. Banks, city offices, doctors' offices, lunchrooms, social agencies, welfare offices, and church exits are favorite places to leave stacks of attractive folders. Library clerks and grocery checkers can sometimes be induced to pass out leaflets or catalogues. Distribution at plant exits may be useful, although promiscuous handing of fliers on the street may detract from the dignity of the program. Distribution with home deliveries of milk is likely to be spotty, but it is often better than nothing.

PERSONAL APPROACHES

Promotion through mass media, direct mail, and hand distribution can never be as effective as personal approaches. In fact, it is probable that many adults will never become personally involved in significant learning activities until they are induced to do so in a face-to-face relationship. There is no substitute for word-of-mouth promotion.

Group Contacts

Short informative talks before all community groups with whom arrangements can be made go far in spreading the gospel of adult education and in outlining the specifics of the local program. Some successful directors and their chief assistants do this very systematically and find that it pays ample dividends. An offer to show a film or filmstrip may help the director gain a speaking engagement. Such program appearances can be strengthened materially if publicity material supplements the talk.

The minimum results desired are threefold: (1) acquaintance of the group with the adult-education program so that members can speak intelligently about it as occasion affords; (2) the establishment of a friendly relationship between group members and the individual representing the institution or program—the reduction of the psychological barrier that exists in regard to a strange program; and (3) eventually, the registration of group members in specific adult-education activities.

If advance arrangements can be made, these appearances permit the speaker to involve his audience in the initial stages of the educational process, as discussed in Chapter 4. Interests and needs of the group as a whole or of its individual members can be discussed. After seeing some of the possibilities of an adult-education program, a group may start thinking about an educational activity of its own, possibly on a co-sponsorship basis. It may ask for consultation help, direct leadership, or some other form of educational service. If such ideas do not develop, the advice of the group can be sought on types of educational activities which should be provided. For a short period, small groups can act as advisory committees for program planning. Even if their ideas are not all usable, the experience helps sensitize them to adult education in the community and may give them a mind-set favorable and responsive to future developments. Extensive use of involvement techniques can result in a sounder program and can build substantial public sentiment for it.

Successful directors of adult education cannot live in isolation. Membership in community organizations is important, even though the director should conserve his energy by not accepting time-consuming leadership responsibility in most groups unless it is related to education. Membership in several key community organizations gives opportunity for (1) keeping the adult program before the community, and (2) injecting the educational process into the activities of the organizations. The adult administrator having the widest personal acquaintance and membership in community groups is likely to have the most serviceable program.

For these reasons, directors often encourage members of their administrative and instructional staffs to join community organizations, both those of a general nature and those relating to their special interest. These group contacts often exist anyway, but with cooperative planning they can be made to yield important dividends in program promotion.

In some communities, it is customary for school staffs to visit representative business firms and industrial plants to become better acquainted with the economic life of the community. The practice is applicable to adult programs, too, and it should include visits by businessmen and industrialists to school shops, studios, and other educational facilities. The Technical School at Phoenix, Arizona, in cooperation with the Personnel Club, holds an annual forum in which discussion of major personnel problems provides an opportunity to show the resources of the school. One year the school invited, in turn, each of nine service clubs to a noonday inspection tour of the school plant, which includes an extensive outlay of equipment. After a short luncheon, small groups were led through the various departments by staff members. In this way some of the possibilities of adult education were revealed to 800 leading men of the community. The state legislators were also invited to inspect the school.

Adult-school directors and department heads find that personal contacts with businessmen, members of the chamber of commerce, foremen's groups, labor leaders, and plant managers are among their most valuable associations. In addition to providing for integration of education and community life, such contacts help keep leaders in the economic community aware of the varied services of adult education. Chapter 4 discusses in more detail the uses which can be made of field people in this regard.

Person-to-person Methods

Several directors of public-school programs have organized telephone campaigns. For example, twenty-five women at Hamilton, Ohio, telephoned 308 persons listed on assigned pages in the local directory and asked whether or not they had recently attended classes. Activities were briefly and informally explained to them, and an inquiry was made concerning their interest in further education. Nearly one-half of those approached in this way were sent further information at their request. This sample represented one of every fourteen adults in the city. Suggestions received led to the offering of six new courses, five of which materialized.

In communities without a daily paper or a radio station, telephone calls may occasionally be used to announce hurriedly developed events or opportunities of outstanding quality, such as the unexpected opportunity of hearing a famous speaker. Telephone campaigns are best adapted to small communities where personal acquaintance runs high.

Personal home visits by staff members are seldom used for promotion except by private or proprietary institutions. In a few communities a worker is assigned part- or full-time responsibility for becoming acquainted with all war brides, DPs, and other newly arrived foreign-born in an effort to induce them to participate in immigrant-education activities. Volunteers are sometimes used to do this interesting work.

Sufficient staff time is seldom available in public agencies to permit extensive visiting, although volunteer visits have been used occasionally. In a few communities modifications of the wartime block-leader system (see chap. 9), operating under the auspices of the PTA, the council of social agencies, some other agency, or independently, are available for distributing printed and oral information in regard to selected tasks. In one community the block-leader organization had good results from publicizing a family-life institute by personal contact. Organized volunteers are potentially of great value, and their use in adult education should be broadened.

In the final analysis the best promotion is based on a good program. The best possible publicity for an adult school is a high percentage of satisfied customers. Once a person has joined an adult-education activity and is pleased with the result, he will tell others. When enough participants become enthusiastic about what they are getting, word-of-mouth publicity becomes effective. Some principals of extensive programs claim that it is responsible for over half their enrollment.

This type of publicity is not subject to much organization or control, although there are a few ways of encouraging it. This slogan is still good: "If you like what you are getting here, tell others; if not, tell us." The foreign-born in immigrant-education classes can be urged to bring others who, although wanting to learn English or to prepare for naturalization, may be too timid to come alone. Similar encouragement should be given in literacy classes, elementary-education groups, and certain others. Married people can be invited to bring their spouses or whole families for either a variety of classes or family-night activities. Some principals challenge those requesting certain courses to find and bring in enough others to warrant a class. Occasionally this method brings results.

When adults become alert to educational activities, they provide much of their own promotion. The ideal in promotion is reached when the program is so good that the world beats a path to participate in it.

PROMOTION WITHIN THE SCHOOL SYSTEM

Although many educators have talked about lifelong learning, neither the public nor professional educators are yet thoroughly imbued with the spirit of lifelong learning. The attitude around most schools is that education has stopping points—that it ends with graduation from high school except for the few who go on to college. In the thinking and behavior of students, faculty, and community alike, commencement is the sharp terminal point of systematic education for most young people. If principles of growth were followed, youth would move gradually from full-time schooling to full-time remunerative work or homemaking, but they would continue to maintain a part-time connection with education.

Close articulation between elementary and secondary schools is the accepted practice. Records are forwarded, visiting days are arranged to help orient pupils to the next higher institution, principals visit lower schools, and a general liaison is effected in numerous other ways. Likewise, articulation is relatively close between high school and college. Only adult education seems to live apart. Too many adult programs are built and publicized without the benefit of close cooperation with the day schools.

Directors of adult education and elementary- and secondary-school principals have a joint responsibility to remedy the situation. From their first days in school, children should live in an atmosphere which expects that systematic education will be available throughout life and that they personally will continue their learning as long as they live. Chapter 11 lists a number of specific things that directors of adult education and day-school principals can do to instill the concept of lifelong learning in the thinking of both staff and youth.

EVALUATION OF PROMOTIONAL ACTIVITIES

Unless publicity and promotional activities are evaluated repeatedly, time, energy, and money are likely to be wasted. Evaluation can be from two vantage points: (1) an inventory of what is done, and (2) an appraisal of the effect it has. Both approaches can lead to improvement.

What Is Done?

By keeping a promotion calendar, a clipping file, or a scrapbook, in addition to other simple records, a director can systematically accumulate the data basic to appraisal of his promotional activities. Thoughtful answers to such questions as these will begin to indicate wherein promotion may be improved:

1. Are promotional activities an integral part of a larger program designed to involve people in lifelong learning?
2. To what extent are promotional activities well planned?
    a. Is promotion continuous and systematic?
    b. Is a promotion calendar used to ensure proper sequence and timing?
3. Is promotion sufficiently intensive?
    a. Are enough well-chosen modern media of communication used?
    b. Is coverage of the desired population adequate?
    c. Are sufficient personal and group contacts maintained?
    d. Is the school staff thoroughly acquainted with available adult-education activities?

Answers to questions of this type, though helpful, may lead to armchair conclusions. Promotion activity in itself is not enough. Expenditure of energy is not the best criterion. The effect on the program is what counts.

What Are the Results?

1. *Is the community aware of opportunities for adult learning?* A representative sampling interview study can find out. Spot checking by asking a specific question of a dozen or score of adults, selected at random downtown, will begin to reveal the answer. In one community, after a campaign of radio and newspaper publicity on immigrant education, only one of the first dozen adults who were asked about opportunities to prepare for the naturalization examination referred the inquirer to the evening school. Questions asked of a representative sample of 100 or 200 adults in residential interviewing can show some of the gross aspects of this ignorance and indicate the outlines of the promotion job to be done.

2. *Is the public convinced of the merit of the program?* Sampling studies similar to the above can help answer this question. Other clues are available. If a high percentage of the adult population is enrolled, if participation steadily increases, or if a growing number of adults return year after year, possibly the program has been well promoted. Desirable results, however, may stem largely from the quality and scope of the program, economic conditions, or other causes and may not clearly indicate merits of the promotional activities. Continued willingness to pay taxes or to increase them for the support of an adult program may be evidence of good promotion.

3. *Is the promotion economical?* Is too much or not enough money spent on promotion? Few usable standards are available to help answer this question, although observation of public-school programs indicates that much less money is spent on their promotion than is spent by private educational agencies. The maximum result at minimum cost of time and money is the goal. Directors want to know which media and promotional activities bring people to the registration desk. A simple way, but sometimes deceiving, to find out where people first learned about a program is to inquire at registration time. Inquiry later is not as valuable. Although questions requiring recall are likely to yield more reliable data than are check lists, the desire to give an answer may interfere with accurate recall.

Simple experiments can be set up to test the effectiveness of media. For instance, assuming that mass media reach all alike, announcements can be mailed to odd-numbered houses only. If no other activities complicate the picture, any increase in enrollment from houses having odd numbers may be attributed to direct mail. Testing direct mail by geographic sections of the community does not take socioeconomic differences into account.

If registrants are encouraged to bring in advertisements or to register by mail on forms clipped from newspapers, keyed symbols on each can facilitate comparisons of the pulling power of each paper. Tests of the effects of different colors, layouts, styles of presentation, and distribution schedules are feasible if materials are randomly distributed. Many other checks of specific features and media can be devised. Advertisers are constantly measuring the results of their efforts. Directors of adult programs need to do likewise.

Directors with comprehensive promotion programs should change them only when pilot-project data show that some methods are better than others. Most methods reinforce one another in ways not revealed by simple tests. Complete abandonment of mass media, for example, in favor of complete coverage by direct mail may be unwise, although a reduction in mass advertising intensity, and cost, may be warranted. While constant evaluation of promotional activities should be made as a basis for developing the best possible program in a given community, no director can afford the luxury of feeling that he has discovered the ultimate answers. The motives of adults and the nature of adult education are too dynamic to permit continued success with standardized publicity.

SELECTED REFERENCES

Becker, R.: "Promotion through Service," *Adult Education,* 1:190–194, June, 1951.

Cheskin, L.: *Colors: What They Can Do for You,* Liveright Publishing Corporation, New York, 1947.

Durrie, P.: "An Adult Education Pantomime," *Adult Education Bulletin,* 11:83–84, February, 1947.

Fine, B.: *Educational Publicity,* Harper & Brothers, New York, 1943.

"Getting and Keeping Members," *Adult Leadership,* special issue, 1:1–32, November, 1952.

Gilbertson, H. W.: *Educational Exhibits: How to Prepare and Use Them,* U.S. Department of Agriculture, Miscellaneous Publications, no. 634, 1948.

Hand, H. C.: *What People Think about Their Schools,* World Book Company, Yonkers, N.Y., 1948.

Horn, G.: *Public-school Publicity,* Inor Publishing Company, Inc., New York, 1948.

Kempfer, Homer: "Let Your Caption Sell Your Course," *Adult Education Bulletin,* 11:20–22, October, 1946.

Modley, R.: *How to Use Pictorial Statistics,* Harper & Brothers, New York, 1937.

National Publicity Council for Health and Welfare Services, Inc., New York. A series of how-to-do-it pamphlets on publicity and public-relations techniques: *Annual Reports: How to Plan and Write Them* (1946), *How to Make a Speech and Enjoy It* (1944), *How to Turn Ideas into Pictures* (1950), *Pamphlets That Pull* (1948), *Planning Your Exhibit* (1948), *The Public Relations Committee: What and How It Works* (1949), *Public Relations Programs: How to Plan Them* (1950), *Radio: How, When and Why to Use It* (1946), and *Working with Newspapers* (1943).

Pedersen, C. E.: "Adult School Publicity," *Adult Education Bulletin,* 11:19–20, October, 1946.

The "PR" Guide, Division of Press and Radio Relations, National Education Association, Washington, 1950.

Public Relations for America's Schools, Twenty-eighth Yearbook of the American Association of School Administrators, Washington, 1950.

Reck, W. E.: *College Publicity Manual,* Harper & Brothers, New York, 1948.

Rowden, D.: "Before Going to Press," *Adult Education Journal,* 5:123–126, July, 1946.

Widutis, Florence B.: *Here's How It's Done: A Popular Education Guide,* The Postwar Information Exchange, Inc., New York, 1945.

See also General References: [3] Kempfer; Knowles, chaps. 9, 10; Sheats, Jayne, and Spence, chap. 16.

[3] The General References are listed in full at the end of this book.

CHAPTER 14 *Finance*

Few issues in adult education are discussed perennially with more vigor than are its sources of support. Social policy with regard to sources of funds is important because the sources and the conditions attached, more than any other factor except leadership, determine the size of the program, the population segments involved, the nature of activities conducted, and the purposes which the program serves.

THE MAJOR ISSUE

The major sources of money available for public-school adult education are local, state, and Federal taxes, and fees paid directly by adults. Contributions from foundations, business firms, and other agencies, and fees paid by organizations for services rendered are important in a few communities. Only occasionally does money come from any other source. Whether it is better for adult education to be supported from public taxes or from fees paid directly by participants is the primary issue which must be resolved at both state and local levels. Ultimately the answer lies with the public and with those to whom they have delegated policy-making responsibilities.

Opinion Studies

Among professional personnel, the opinion of the superintendent regarding the methods of financing adult education is most important, for in guiding educational policy, he is the key leader in the community, in the board of education, and in the school staff. In connection with a nationwide survey of public-school activities in adult education, the U.S. Office of Education asked local superintendents in all states except California and New York this question: "In general, how far do you think the public school should go in providing education for adults and out-of-school youth?" [1] Provisions were made for objective responses to questions covering twelve subject fields or types of activity. The answers of 2,479 superintendents, including 468 from schools not then providing programs of adult education, were distributed as follows:

[1] *Financing Education for Adults and Out-of-school Youth: Views of Superintendents,* U.S. Office of Education Circular 319, October, 1949.

	Per cent
Response	
The school should use tax money to pay:	
All costs. Activities should be entirely free to adults and out-of-school youth..	28.5
All costs except nominal registration fee......................................	19.7
Half the costs. Students should pay half.....................................	5.0
Some of the costs. Students should pay the major portion.................	8.7
Only for heat, light, and custodial services. Students should pay the remainder..	19.1
Adult education should not be a responsibility of the public school...........	10.8
Expressed no opinion..	8.2
Total..	100.0

While approximately half of the superintendents who expressed opinions (48 per cent of the total group) believed that public-school adult education should be completely, or almost completely, free to participants, it was apparent that, in 1948, a significant number of educational administrators (30 per cent of those included in the study) opposed free education for adults and out-of-school youth. The extent to which this opposition reflected the attitudes of the boards of education in their home communities, the shortage of funds for elementary and secondary schools, or the basic beliefs of the educators themselves was not revealed by the study.

Interestingly enough, the presence or absence of adult-education programs in their community seemed to make little difference in the attitude of superintendents. Within the total group of 2,011 superintendents from districts offering adult education, 49 per cent felt that tax money should be used to pay all, or nearly all, the costs, and 11 per cent felt that such programs should not be the responsibility of the public schools. Among the 468 superintendents from districts not offering adult education, 45 per cent believed that tax money should be used for all or nearly all of the costs, while 16 per cent opposed adult education as a public-school responsibility.

This survey did show, however, that the attitude toward free adult education is related to the availability of state aid. In fourteen of the nineteen states which provided aid during the year studied, the superintendents were more favorable toward free education for adults than were those throughout the nation as a whole. Superintendents in only eight of the twenty-seven states providing no aid were more favorable toward free adult education than was the group as a whole. The opinions of the superintendents within each state seemed to have no relationship to the per capita income or the educational level of the population. While opinions did not differ widely in relation to the size of the community, the proportion of superintendents favoring free public education for adults was higher in large communities than in villages and rural areas.

The fact that these administrators' opinions did differ considerably regarding the financing of specific types of adult education can be seen from the following data compiled during the same study:

Subject or type of activity	Per cent responding	
	Use tax money for all or nearly all costs	Not a responsibility of the public school
Literacy instruction..........................	70.9	6.3
Americanization...............................	69.3	7.0
Vocational- and educational-guidance services.......	55.9	6.2
New-voter preparation programs..................	55.8	12.7
High-school subjects...........................	53.1	5.1
Weekly child-study groups......................	48.4	8.4
Education-for-marriage groups...................	46.1	12.2
Open forums on civic affairs....................	45.4	12.1
Educational consultation services to club leaders.....	40.3	15.2
Public-affairs radio-listening discussion groups.......	34.7	17.8
Community-band instruction.....................	33.8	16.6
Arts and crafts groups..........................	29.6	9.6

No similar analysis of the opinions of directors of adult education or of members of boards of education has been made. However, in 1951 Guy Garrard, principal of the Bakersfield, California, Evening High School, found that among 122 members of the California Association of Adult Education Administrators 93 per cent agreed completely with the statement: "Financial stabilization of the program [adult education] should be guaranteed through continuous, adequate support from combined state and local sources."

Public sentiment regarding the use of tax money for adult education has not generally been clearly identified. Indeed, the question has never been raised in many communities. However, as opportunities for adult education become more widespread and as participation in lifelong learning becomes more common, it will be possible to identify the general attitude of the public toward this important question with greater clarity. One of the most definite indications of public opinion concerning the provision of adult education on a state-wide, tax-supported basis came in 1953, when the Senate Interim Committee on Adult Education of the California Legislature held public hearings on the question. Such interest was aroused among various groups of citizens that those desiring to reduce the adult-education program of the public schools were soundly defeated.[2] Apparently a great many Californians had either benefited personally from the policies of public support and liberal state aid or had otherwise come to believe in the principle.

Opinion Surveys as a Basis for Policy

Until adult education becomes an accepted part of the American culture, states and communities will probably differ widely in their attitudes toward its support. The existing differences are quite likely the result of interaction among the usual factors which operate in the formulation of public policy—a trend toward liberality or conservatism, the tax structure and load, economic conditions, educational level, past and present leadership, religious outlook, age distribution of the population, and many more. The influence of each factor on attitude toward support and the interrelationships of the various factors are, however, still matters for research.

In view of this wide divergence of opinion, local superintendents, directors of adult education, school boards, and other officials might well take pains to keep themselves informed of the current thinking of their fellow citizens concerning financial policy. Situations similar to that which arose in California can be avoided or more easily handled if policy makers have adequate knowledge of the public will. Such time-worn methods of ascertaining public sentiment as letters to local officials or to newspapers, resolutions passed by organizations, visits from representatives of various groups, or expressions of opinion at public hearings are still useful, but they have their limitations. Because of the bias often represented by articulate, organized minorities, improved methods of taking the public pulse have come into increased use in recent years. Systematic opinion surveys are among the newer methods. While they are subject to misuse and misinterpretation, in the hands of trained and ethical people they undoubtedly represent an important extension of democracy. Further, they offer a systematic means by which administrators can discover public attitudes toward financing adult education and toward other important aspects of the program.

Unless a thorough exploration of sentiment is to be attempted, it is not usually necessary to set up a special survey, since a few questions on the support of adult education may be included as part of a more comprehensive study. If the city council or budget office makes an occasional or an annual opinion survey on the spending of tax money, questions on adult education may often be included. Surveys of need, as discussed in Chapter 4, also offer an excellent opportunity to check opinion on finance. Sometimes a local newspaper operates a local opinion poll based on a representative sample of the population. Surveys by or for the com-

2 *Partial Report of the Senate Interim Committee on Adult Education,* California State Senate, S. Res. 185 (1951), 1953.

munity chest, a council of social agencies, the board of health, a community council, or some other public or private agency may include questions on financing adult education. A primary precaution is to see that the population sample is soundly designed. If the base population is the list of property owners, of telephone subscribers, or of some other fraction of the total population, the survey may still be made, but results should be interpreted with a full awareness of their limitations. In such cases usually the amount and sometimes even the direction of bias are unknown.

Some questions on adult education were included in a 1947 public-opinion poll directed by the author in Erie County, New York (where the city of Buffalo is located). A representative sample of 600 residents aged twenty-one and older were asked: "Do you think the public schools should use tax money to provide education for all adults who want to learn, or should every adult have to pay directly for his own education?" Substantial backing for public support was evident in that 57 per cent of the respondents said tax money should be used, but 38 per cent thought that adults should pay directly for their own education, while 5 per cent offered no opinion. Among those expressing opinions, 60 per cent favored the use of tax money.

The same question was asked of another representative sample of adults in Montgomery County, Maryland, in the spring of 1949. The county was faced with a heavy influx of postwar children and with mounting taxes to pay for buildings and to employ teachers. In this instance only 26 per cent of the sample wanted to pay for adult education with tax money, while 54 per cent thought that adults should pay directly for their own education, and 20 per cent expressed no opinion. Thus, only one-third of those in Montgomery County who expressed opinions favored complete public support.

These widely divergent results emphasize the need for knowing the temper of local opinion. The National Commission on Adult Education Finance, which was set up by the Adult Education Association in 1953, recognized this need and began developing procedures whereby communities could better face the financial issues and arrive at a decision democratically.

SOURCES OF SUPPORT

Local Taxes

Boards of education in every state use local tax money, either directly or indirectly, for the support of adult education, although statutory authorization to allocate funds for this purpose in some cases does not exist. Table 11 shows the states in which local boards of education had authority, in 1949, to spend local school funds for eight specific areas of

Table 11. Areas of General Adult Education for which Local School Funds May Be Expended by States

State	Foundation areas				Nonacademic general adult education			
	Non-citizens	Literacy	Elementary subjects	Secondary subjects	General cultural education	General civic education	Personal and family living	Recreation and avocational education
Alabama		x	x	x	x	x		x
Arizona	x		x					
Arkansas		x						
California	x	x	x	x	x	x	x	x
Colorado	x	x	x	x	x	x	x	x
Connecticut	x	x	x	x	x	x	x	x
Delaware								
Florida	x	x	x	x	x	x	x	x
Georgia		x		x				
Idaho	x	x						
Illinois	x		x	x				
Indiana			x	x				
Iowa	x	x	x	x	x	x	x	x
Kansas	x		x	x				
Kentucky			x	x				
Louisiana			x	x				
Maine	x		x	x	x	x	x	x
Maryland	x		x	x	x	x	x	x
Massachusetts	x	x	x	x	x	x	x	x
Michigan	x	x	x	x	x	x	x	x
Minnesota	x		x	x				
Mississippi		x	x	x				
Missouri								
Montana	x		x	x	x	x	x	
Nebraska	x	x	x	x				
Nevada	x		x	x				
New Hampshire	x	x	x	x	x	x	x	x
New Jersey	x	x	x	x	x	x	x	x
New Mexico		x						
New York	x	x	x	x	x	x	x	x
North Carolina	x	x	x	x	x	x	x	x
North Dakota	x		x	x				
Ohio	x		x	x				
Oklahoma	x		x	x	x	x	x	x
Oregon	x		x	x	x	x	x	x
Pennsylvania	x	x	x	x	x	x	x	x
Rhode Island	x	x	x	x	x	x	x	x
South Carolina	x	x	x	x	x	x	x	x
South Dakota	x	x	x					
Tennessee	x		x	x				
Texas								
Utah	x	x	x	x	x	x	x	x
Vermont	x	x	x	x				
Virginia	x	x	x	x	x	x	x	x
Washington	x	x	x	x	x	x	x	x
West Virginia	x	x	x		x	x	x	x
Wisconsin								
Vocational and adult schools	x	x	x	x	x	x	x	x
Public schools *	x	x	x	x	x	x	x	x
Wyoming	x	x	x	x				
Total	37	28	41	40	25	25	24	25

* Not counted in totals.

SOURCE: Leon F. Miller, *Statutory Provisions for Public School Adult Education and Their Implementation*, doctoral dissertation, University of Chicago, Chicago, 1950, pp. 45–46.

adult education.[3] Laws in three states apparently provide no authority whatever for local taxes to be used for the support of general adult education.

The proportion of support for adult education derived from local taxes varies fully as much as it does for elementary and secondary education—from 0 to 100 per cent, with only a few cases at either extreme. Except for limited programs, such as literacy education and classes for immigrants, boards of education seldom support adult education entirely from local taxes. If other public aid is not available, at least partial support is usually obtained from student fees. The fraction of cost borne by local taxes depends, of course, upon the amount of money available from other sources. In a study of 100 representative evening schools, those receiving a significant amount of state aid derived 23 per cent of their support from local taxes, while those receiving little or no state aid derived 42 per cent of their income from local taxes.[4] In a later nonrepresentative study, about one-third of the support of adult education in twenty-eight public schools and community colleges came from local taxes.[5] Local taxes supplied 10 to 50 per cent of the income in half of the schools, but never accounted for more than 80 per cent of a school's financial support.

The amount of support received from local funds is often deceivingly low because it seldom reflects local contributions for building operation and maintenance, fixed costs, capital outlay or proportionate rent, general administrative overhead, and similar expenses. Integrated operating budgets make it difficult to segregate the income received by the school and public expenditures for adult education.

Next to professional leadership in the state education department, provisions for state financial aid have the greatest influence on the development of adult education in public schools. Experience and observation bear this out. Of the twenty-four states involving relatively large percentages of adults in educational activities, fifteen provide state aid. Among the remaining twenty-four, those serving a smaller percentage of adults, only six provide state aid.[6] States with the highest enrollments—California, Wisconsin, and New York—all provide financial aid for adult education in local districts. The Wisconsin State Board of Vocational and Adult Education was set up in 1911, and local boards under its supervision received funds from the start. State aid for adult education in

---

[3] Leon F. Miller, *Statutory Provisions for Public School Adult Education and Their Implementation,* doctoral dissertation, University of Chicago, Chicago, 1950, pp. 45–46.

[4] Homer Kempfer and Grace S. Wright, *100 Evening Schools,* U.S. Office of Education Bulletin 1949, no. 4.

[5] Homer Kempfer and William R. Wood, *Financing Adult Education in Selected Schools and Community Colleges,* U.S. Office of Education Bulletin 1952, no. 8.

[6] Homer Kempfer, *Adult Education Activities of the Public Schools,* U.S. Office of Education Pamphlet 107, 1949, back cover.

California dates back a generation. After New York started aiding local districts in 1945, its adult enrollment in public-school programs multiplied fivefold in the first 4 years.[7]

The influence of state aid is clearly shown by studies of the types of adult education provided locally. Massachusetts, for example, provides aid to local districts primarily for adult civic education, which is interpreted as immigrant education. Only a few communities, such as Springfield, have comprehensive adult programs. In Pennsylvania, where the law provides that money shall be available to the schools for recreational activities and social services, many schools offer such activities. Aid is available in South Carolina for adult literacy education, and few county school systems in that state have any other organized adult programs.

All states, of course, match Federal funds granted for vocational education. Consequently, aside from recreational programs, more schools have programs of vocational education for adults than any other kind. With only two or three exceptions, aid-granting states have the most highly developed programs and define adult education most liberally.

Apparently only twenty-three states currently allocate funds to local districts for one or more areas of general adult education. Several other states have legislative authority to grant such aid and have provided funds in certain past years but not in 1953, the latest year for which statistics were available at the time of writing. Table 12 shows the areas in which state aid was made available in the twenty-four states that granted aid in 1949. Two state education departments retain the funds to operate their own programs and do not allocate money directly to local districts.

In addition to supporting vocational education and the areas of general adult education listed in the table, individual states often authorize financial assistance for various other fields and for special types of activities. All states provide for the education of World War II veterans, either independently or in connection with Federal laws pertaining to the education of veterans. In twenty states, there is at least one full-time member of the state education department to supervise veterans' education.[8] In some states this is largely a state program having little connection with local schools. In Mississippi, for example, the state is administratively responsible for the program. The state provides district and area supervisors, who work closely with the local superintendents. In Florida, county veteran institutes were set up under county boards of education soon after the war. For the most part these arrangements provide opportunity for veterans to complete their elementary and high-school educa-

[7] *Preliminary Annual Report of the Education Department for the School Year Ending June 30, 1949*, New York State Education Department, Albany, N.Y.
[8] Miller, *op. cit.*, pp. 50–52.

Table 12. Areas of General Adult Education Provided with State Aid

State	Foundation areas					Nonacademic general adult education		
	Non-citizens	Literacy	Elementary subjects	Secondary subjects	General cultural education	General civic education	Personal and family living	Recreation and avocational education
Alabama..........................		x	x		x	x		x
California.......................	x	x	x	x	x	x	x	x
Connecticut.....................	x	x	x	x	x	x	x	x
Delaware........................	x	x				x		
Florida..........................	x	x	x	x				
Maine...........................	x		x	x	x	x	x	x
Maryland........................	x		x	x	x	x	x	x
Massachusetts...................	x	x	x			x		
Michigan........................	x	x	x	x	x	x	x	x
Nebraska........................	x							
Nevada..........................	x		x	x				
New Hampshire..................	x	x						
New Jersey......................	x		x	x				
New York.......................	x	x	x	x	x	x	x	x
Oregon..........................	x		x	x	x	x	x	x
Pennsylvania....................	x	x	x	x	x	x	x	x
Rhode Island....................	x	x	x	x	x	x	x	x
South Carolina..................		x	x	x	x	x	x	x
Tennessee.......................			x	x				
Utah............................	x	x	x	x	x	x	x	x
Vermont.........................								x
Virginia.........................	x	x	x	x	x	x	x	x
Washington......................	x	x	x	x	x	x	x	x
Wisconsin Vocational and adult schools...	x	x	x	x	x	x	x	x
Total.........................	20	16	20	18	15	17	14	16

SOURCE: Leon F. Miller, *Statutory Provisions for Public School Adult Education and Their Implementation*, doctoral dissertation, University of Chicago, Chicago, 1950, pp. 48–49.

tion and to acquire vocational competence. In most cases nonveteran adults are permitted to enter the program upon payment of fees. In many instances, as the veteran enrollment declined, these programs have evolved into general adult-education programs.

A number of states provide education for adults in certain state-operated schools or through programs designed for specific population groups. Thus, twenty-seven states provide educational services for blind adults through institutions or through traveling libraries of Braille books, records, and other materials. In about half of these states, responsibility for the program is assigned to the state education department, and in the remainder, to some other state agency. Eleven state education departments have responsibility for the education of deaf adults, and in nine additional states some other agency is responsible.[9] Public schools in most states have not been tied in closely with this work. A few states have schools of noncollege grade open to adults in specialized fields. New York, for instance, has five agricultural and technical institutes and five state-operated institutes of applied arts and sciences, with educational programs for both older youth and adults.

Nearly all states encourage adult education by authorizing local boards of education to open buildings for public use. Purposes for which school facilities are made available vary widely, but they usually include public discussions, political meetings, recreational activities, entertainments, meetings of classes, and meetings of civic and community groups. Activities for which admission is charged and meetings otherwise limited in attendance are often under slightly greater legal restrictions. For the most part, however, the unlighted schoolhouse is more the result of limited local leadership and vision than of state disapproval.

Local boards differ greatly on policies regarding expenses. Most boards absorb the extra costs of operating and maintaining school-connected activities, including adult education. Often they extend the same privileges to community organizations with educational programs open to the public. Rental fees become more common as the purpose of the activity becomes less educational. Occasionally a board of education feels it must charge a rental fee for an adult-education program operated by a PTA or some other local community group. Many factors, no doubt, enter into local policy, but it would seem in harmony with the ideals of free public education for a board to extend the use of public equipment and facilities as widely as possible.

Schools in a majority of states have authority, either independently or in connection with other local agencies, to establish recreational programs for adults and out-of-school youth.

In sixteen states school libraries may be used by adults under varying restrictions. In ten states certain schools are authorized to establish public libraries, either independently or in cooperation with other municipal bodies.[10] In fewer states, boards of education accept responsibility for operating public libraries.

Public schools in 9 states have been authorized to conduct workers' education. Eight states authorize local boards to provide free lectures, either in connection with regular adult-education programs or independently. Correspondence instruction is provided in four states, either by state education departments directly or by certain local districts. Three states authorize local districts to provide home instruction for adults on an individual basis.[11]

9 *Ibid.*, pp. 21–22.
10 *Ibid.*, pp. 58–59.
11 *Ibid.*, pp. 54–55.

Patterns of State Aid

The amounts of state aid, the purposes for which it is granted, and the methods and conditions of its distribution vary widely among the twenty-four states which assist local districts. In only sixteen states does this aid amount to as much as one-quarter of the local expenditure. A synopsis of practice in the twenty-four states reveals the variety. Unless otherwise noted, the following discussion applies to general adult education and omits adult vocational education, vocational rehabilitation, separate veterans' education, and other special types. Certain data given below, being of more recent origin, differ slightly from those reported in Table 12.

Alabama. State aid, amounting to $12,500, is distributed to certain counties primarily for literacy classes as agreed upon with local superintendents.

California. A minimum reimbursement of $120 is guaranteed for each unit of average daily attendance. The actual amount of aid received depends upon an equalization formula based upon local support and assessed valuation. The average daily attendance is computed by dividing the total days of attendance (180 minutes) by 175. No more than 15 clock-hours of attendance per week per adult can be counted, except in trade and industrial courses. A full-time administrator is required for 200 units of ADA, and half-time nonteaching service is required for each additional 200 units. In 1953–1954 the state appropriated $8,864,548.86 to local districts.[12]

Connecticut. The state reimburses one-half of the salaries of local supervisors up to a limit of $1,500. Attendance is reimbursed at the rate of 2⅔ cents per pupil clock-hour. Aid amounted to $51,801.38 in 1951–1952.

Delaware. A director is provided and aid is given for foundation education (education for the foreign-born and illiterates) outside of Wilmington. The adult-education allocation for 1953–1954 was $8,250.00.

Florida. Reimbursement, based on instructional units, is allowed for each qualified teacher employed for a full load of 900 class-hours. Fractional parts of units are allowed. The average instructional unit draws $2,900 for salary, $400 for capital outlay, and $300 for current expenses. A minimum average attendance of twenty is required, except in isolated areas, where the minimum is fifteen. Aid in 1952–1953 amounted to $1,332,000.

Louisiana. Legislature appropriated $100,000 in 1952 for aid to parish programs of adult education.

Maine. Fifty per cent of local instructional costs are reimbursed. Aid in 1951–1952 amounted to $21,952.51.

[12] Includes aid for vocational adult education.

Maryland. The General Assembly appropriated $75,000 in 1952–1953 to reimburse county boards of education for instructional costs up to a limit of 100 per cent of the minimum salary level.

Massachusetts. One-half of the local supervisory and instructional costs of adult civic education were reimbursed in 1952–1953. The amount was approximately $90,000. State-operated university extension classes, correspondence instruction, and audio-visual services required a subsidy of $134,116.19, in addition to the $155,485.17 collected in fees. An appropriation of $18,000 covered the high-school equivalency certificate program.

Michigan. State appropriated $300,000 in 1952–1953. Reimbursement is based on a membership year of 720 clock-hours of attendance in noncredit courses by those under twenty-one years of age; half reimbursement is provided for those over twenty-one. Reimbursement covers about 35 per cent of the total cost.

Nebraska. In 1952–1953, state aid of $3 per hour of instruction was granted to 112 immigrant-education classes. Aid covered about 80 per cent of the cost.

New Hampshire. No special grants were made, although general school aid is available for literacy and Americanization instruction.

New Jersey. No special appropriations were made in 1952–1953, but instruction of adults in evening academic high schools is eligible for general state aid.

New York. Each 40-minute period of approved instruction draws $2.50 state aid. An average daily attendance of eight per class is required, with exceptions. Aid in 1951–1952 amounted to $3,298,690, including funds for vocational education outside of New York City.

Oregon. No special grants were made, but adult classes may be counted in general state reimbursement. The basic provision of 20 cents per 6-hour day applies pro rata to adult classes below college grade.

Pennsylvania. Aid for educational, social, and recreational services for out-of-school youth and adults is based upon a required minimum salary of $2.50 per hour multiplied by the equalization fraction of the district concerned. Aid ranges from about 30 per cent to 100 per cent, averaging about 83 per cent.

Rhode Island. Teachers may be paid full salary from state funds, one-half salary from state funds, or entirely from local funds. Aid in 1953–1954 amounted to $53,610.

South Carolina. The annual appropriation for general adult education is $59,720. Aid is apportioned flexibly to counties on the basis of interest and need, number of illiterates, previous support, and local contribution. ADA of nine per class and an enrollment of twelve are required to qualify a course for full reimbursement. The State Opportunity School was supported separately by an appropriation of $139,500.

Tennessee. There were no special grants. Approved night schools, however, are eligible for general state aid.

Vermont. A limited program of arts and crafts is supervised and supported by the state education department. Adults can attend.

Virginia. In 1952–1953, state aid of $32,190.10 covered one-half of instructional costs.

Washington. No special grants were made. Adult education draws 7 cents per clock-hour of attendance, plus additional equalization needed to guarantee a minimum of 20 cents for each day's attendance. Six hours of attendance equals one day. An additional minimum of $700 is appor-

Table 13. Methods of Apportionment of State Aid for General Adult Education by States

State	Ex-penses	Flat grants	Attend-ance	Match-ing	Ses-sions	Equal-ization	Other
Alabama							x
California		x	x			x	
Connecticut	x		x				
Delaware					x		
Florida			x		x		
Maine	x						
Maryland	x						
Massachusetts				x	x		
Michigan			x				
Nebraska	x						
Nevada					x		
New Hampshire						x	
New Jersey						x	
New York					x		
Oregon			x			x	
Pennsylvania					x	x	
Rhode Island	x			x	x		
South Carolina	x						
Tennessee			x			x	
Utah							x
Vermont	x						
Virginia	x						x
Washington		x	x			x	
Wisconsin Vocational and adult schools	x			x			
Total	9	2	7	3	7	7	4

SOURCE: Leon F. Miller, *Statutory Provisions for Public School Adult Education and Their Implementation*, doctoral dissertation, University of Chicago, Chicago, 1950, pp. 86–87.

tioned for each full-time certificated employee, based on the number of educational units.

Wisconsin. No aid for adult education is available to public schools. Within limits of appropriation, the state pays up to one-half of the costs of instruction and supervision in schools of vocational and adult education, with limitations granted by size of city. In 1952–1953, aid was $420,000, including vocational-education funds for persons aged fourteen and above.

Federal Aid

Under the Smith-Hughes and George-Barden Acts, every state and certain major possessions receive Federal funds for vocational education. These funds are available in five areas for the education of those aged fourteen and above who meet certain broad qualifications. While both Acts require that the Federal appropriation be matched by state funds, the amounts contributed by states and localities in recent years have usually been much greater than the Federal expenditure. In 1952, every dollar of Federal money was counterbalanced by $4.66 from other sources. Comparative expenditures for that year were as follows:

Source	Amount *	Per cent *
Federal.......	$ 25,862,968.21	17.7
State.........	47,818,415.61	32.6
Local.........	72,784,298.75	49.7
Total.......	$146,465,682.57	100.0

* Provisional figures subject to final audit of state reports.

SOURCE: *Digest of Annual Reports of State Boards for Vocational Education to the Office of Education*, U.S. Department of Health, Education, and Welfare, 1952, p. 9.

No separate accounting is made of Federal vocational funds spent on the education of adults and out-of-school youth. Although these students constitute 56 per cent of the total vocational enrollment, programs for these groups cost far less because they are operated almost entirely on a part-time basis. The enrollment and Federal funds (provisional figures) spent in each of four fields of vocational education during the fiscal year 1952 are given in Table 14.

Federal funds are available to local districts in accordance with plans drawn up by state boards of vocational education and approved by the Federal Office of Education. Such plans usually specify qualifications for instructional and supervisory personnel, approved activities, and other regulations. These state boards have general supervisory responsibility

Table 14. Enrollment and Distribution of Federal Funds in Four Areas
of Vocational Education

Area	Federal funds distributed to states	No. of adults and out-of-school youth enrolled *	No. enrolled in school full time
Agricultural education..........	$10,148,313.86	319,620	426,782
Home economics education.....	6,256,588.18	659,576	731,813
Trade and industrial education..	8,637,339.92	586,456	206,757
Distributive occupations........	820,726.25	207,575	27,409
Total......................	$25,862,968.21	1,773,227	1,392,761

* Includes evening and part-time enrollment in agriculture; evening and part-time enrollment in home economics; evening and part-time trade-extension, part-time trade-preparatory, and part-time general-continuation enrollment in trade and industrial education; and evening and part-time extension enrollment in distributive occupations. All other types of classes were classified as in-school enrollment.

SOURCE: *Digest of Annual Reports of State Boards for Vocational Education to the Office of Education,* U.S. Department of Health, Education, and Welfare, 1952, p. 10.

for the federally aided vocational programs. As the state plans differ considerably, detailed information on them can best be obtained directly from the state boards.

Individual Fees

About one-tenth of the income of public-school programs of adult education comes from student fees. A great majority of formal and some informal adult-education programs are supported in part or entirely in this way. Programs operated by private agencies, such as YMCA, YWCA, clubs, settlement houses, correspondence schools, private schools, and private colleges, are usually supported entirely by fees. Extension divisions and evening colleges in publicly supported institutions of higher education usually charge fees for much, if not all, of their credit and noncredit work, although a number of junior and community colleges receiving liberal state aid charge relatively little. Public libraries usually make no charge for their services except, occasionally, for film or projector rental, rental of popular books, and an initial fee or deposit for a library card. The cooperative Extension Service of the Department of Agriculture requires no fee for the services of county agents or for educational materials.

Practice with regard to fees in public schools is closely related to the amount of state and local aid available. Most public schools charge fees, although in many cases they are small and do not bear any major portion of the instructional costs. In a 1949 study of 100 representative evening schools, one-fourth charged no fee for attendance, and another fourth charged a registration fee of only $1 or $2.[13] In a study of forty-five schools and community colleges "fees paid by enrollees furnished significant support (20 per cent or more) in about one-third of the cases. In seven of thirty-nine communities student fees supported half or more of the total costs." [14]

Within limits the size of fees depends upon their purpose. In a program supported entirely in this way, fees may be based on the total budget. One means for determining the size of the fee is to divide the total anticipated expenditure by the expected enrollment and make adjustments for exceptional activities. Often this is reduced to a class, semester, or clock-hour basis and may become standardized for the whole program. Proprietary institutions usually add enough to this amount to yield a reasonable profit. University extension divisions and evening colleges have been known to turn over to their parent institutions sums from fees collected far in excess of divisional operating costs. The reverse may also occur.

In some programs surplus income from large classes may help support the costs of small classes. In other programs, however, every activity must enroll enough adults to pay all the costs incurred. This practice is especially prevalent where rates of pay for leadership differ widely. The former policy, of course, gives greater flexibility and usually results in a larger, more comprehensive program.

Private agencies which depend heavily upon fees may find a maximum fee rate beyond which they cannot go without severely reducing enrollment. For nonvocational classes even maximum fees can often defray only 50 to 75 per cent of the total operating cost. The remainder must be made up in some other way.

Where the board of education or parent institution absorbs the costs of building operation and maintenance, the salaries of administrators and office help, and other overhead costs, fees may be necessary to cover only instructional costs. In this situation, administrators, knowing the rate of pay of instructors, are likely to work out the prorata costs per clock-hour and set fees according to the length of each course. Some directors depart from the standard in certain activities, raising or lowering the rate according to what the traffic will bear, the importance of the activity, or some other criterion.

In practice, fees often vary considerably within the same program. Immigrant-education courses and often literacy classes are free. Federally aided vocational courses often require a low fee or none at all. Fees for credit courses are often higher than for noncredit activities, and occa-

[13] Kempfer and Wright, *op. cit.*, p. 49.
[14] Kempfer and Wood, *op. cit.*, p. 23.

sionally the same course taken for credit will carry a higher fee than if audited or not taken for credit. When students have registered for one course, a few schools offer them the privilege of taking additional courses at reduced rates. Sometimes a single fee permits the registrant to participate in as many activities as the schedule permits.

Aside from these variations, graded scales are not common. If fees are based on the nature of the activity, the following three classifications are probably the most desirable from the point of view of sound social policy. They may also bring least public criticism.

1. Tuition-free group. Activities which are fundamental to the maintenance of our democracy; activities which are included in the birthright of every American child: literacy education, elementary and high-school instruction, citizenship education, and immigrant education.

2. Moderate-fee group. Activities concerned with vocational competence, health, homemaking, family-life and parent education, psychology, and personal development.

3. Full-fee group. Activities which seem relatively less essential; education for recreation and social activities: arts and crafts, ballroom dancing, card playing, dramatics, music; activities which are commercially available.

One can easily imagine the perpetual arguments arising from such a classification. Since a sound case can be made for putting all activities on the same cost basis, the above is recommended for consideration only where local sentiment strongly favors a graded-fee system.

In practice there may be little distinction between tuition fees and registration fees. They are often lumped together under the same name. In theory, however, tuition fees help defray the cost of instruction, and registration fees carry certain overhead costs. Some principals defend charging at least a small registration fee on the grounds that it pays for the cost of processing an enrollment regardless of future attendance. They feel that insincere registrants who drop out almost immediately add unnecessarily to the cost without receiving any educational return.

In the NEA study 59 per cent of the schools reported charging registration fees; 12 per cent, tuition on an hourly basis; and 29 per cent, tuition on a course basis. The median hourly tuition rate was 52 cents, and the median course tuition rate was $4.45.

The cost of consumable materials is commonly, but by no means universally, charged to the enrollees. For the sake of simplicity, it is sometimes standardized and paid as a flat fee; at other times the cost is individually determined by the instructor responsible for money collection and record keeping. Texts are sometimes provided free and sometimes for a fee, but most often they must be purchased by the student. Special fees for lockers, laboratory privileges, use of equipment, and similar costs are occasionally charged, but they are usually combined into one over-all sum. Public adult schools seldom charge an activity fee; in fact, they are unlikely to have extraclassroom activities.

Practices in privately supported evening colleges, however, are somewhat different. Among sixty members of the Association of University Evening Colleges, Neuffer [15] found that seventeen charged registration fees; fourteen charged activity fees; six, library fees; twenty, matriculation fees; forty-two, late registration fees; twenty-five, fees for deferred payment; and nineteen, fees for program changes. In addition, nine had a special fee for auditors.

Practice varies widely on returning fees to those who withdraw after starting a course. Policies are often flexible and sometimes are related to the reasons given for withdrawal. Evening colleges charging sizable fees often refund them. Of the sixty university evening colleges surveyed, 97 per cent refunded fees in whole or in part if the student withdrew because of illness or employment. Over half of these institutions refunded fees as late as 8 weeks after the term started; nineteen had a refund period of 5 weeks or shorter.[16] Most public schools charging fees make no return unless the original fee was large. Small registration fees are almost universally retained or are not returnable after a specified time. A few administrators return fees on demand. With larger fees a rapidly reducing scale of return is occasionally used, so that withdrawal at midterm or later often yields no refund. Fees should invariably be returned to all who enroll in courses that are canceled by the school. Many directors encourage enrollment in another course at this point, however.

Schools drawing local tax funds sometimes charge a higher fee to nonresidents and are justified in doing so. Nonresident fees are usually based on the prorata total costs of the activity, whereas resident fees are usually designed to pay only the difference between the total cost and that covered by local appropriations. State aid provides no justifiable basis for a fee differential if nonresidents can be counted in claiming state aid. Sometimes local enrollment alone is not great enough to warrant maintaining an activity, but nonresidents usually represent fewer than 10 per cent of the total enrollment.

Returnable fees and deposits seem to be on the wane. In 1933, a nationwide study [17] covering 124 cities of all sizes found 23 per cent requiring returnable deposits. Sixteen years later, only 10 of 100 evening schools required deposits. A Pennsylvania regulation permits the collection of a $5 fee but requires its return on 75 per cent attendance.

Opinions of administrators differ on the influence of deposits in main-

---

[15] Frank R. Neuffer, *Survey of Administrative Problems and Policies: 1947–48*, Association of University Evening Colleges, p. 13. (Multilithed.)

[16] *Ibid.*, p. 14.

[17] E. E. Clark, *A Study of Fees and Deposits in Adult Education*, National Commission on the Enrichment of Adult Life of the NEA, Washington, 1933.

taining regular attendance, although valid evidence seems lacking. In the 1933 study 35 per cent favored deposits. Lack of clear evidence leads one to think that returnable deposits may have less effect on attendance than administrators sometimes claim. No doubt, a deposit encourages attendance in some individual cases. Unless the amount is sizable, however, certain ordinary causes of irregular attendance are not likely to be affected. Since deposits penalize even those unable to anticipate unavoidable absence, sizable amounts may keep out, not only triflers, but others as well. The practice in one city of requiring a $1 deposit in each course with 50 cents returnable upon 80 per cent attendance is said by evening-school principals to be more of a nuisance than an aid to regular attendance. Added record keeping is the big argument against the practice. The finding of the 1933 study that deposit-charging schools enrolled a slightly higher proportion of the population than did other schools is probably not statistically significant.

Effect of Fees

Until tax support of adult education becomes much more widespread and liberal, fees will continue to bear a sizable fraction of the cost. Private agencies, of course, probably will continue to be supported largely on a fee basis indefinitely, although they may benefit from foundation funds, gifts, and similar sources.

Despite the fact that public opinion, antiquated tax systems, and similar realities make fees a necessity, the arguments against fees and for free public adult education seem overwhelming. The major points can be summarized briefly as follows:

1. Free public education has long been an American ideal. Historically, the concept of free education, at first restricted to the elementary grades has been extended upward until a high-school diploma is now within the reach of all youth. The extension of this concept to the total adult population through the community-college and adult-education programs is only a logical conclusion. Free public adult education extends the ideal of equal opportunity to all throughout life without setting age deadlines.

2. A democratic state in a world of rapid change must assure its perpetuation by providing opportunities for lifelong learning to all its citizens. The challenge of competing ideologies, coupled with the fact that technological developments have far outstripped social controls, makes lifelong learning for all doubly imperative.

3. The merchandise theory, which holds that education should be paid for directly, was abandoned long ago in elementary and secondary education and in many other social services. The fact that adults are of income-earning age is not a valid reason for requiring direct payment for educational services. Adult citizens have the American right of purchasing

educational services for themselves cooperatively through taxes whenever they put this social policy into law.

4. Fees reduce the numbers enrolled. Although this is less true in times of high employment than in economic depressions, it operates at all times.

The effect of fees on enrollment and attendance needs examination in light of the philosophy of lifelong learning for all. In the previously cited study conducted by Clark in 1933, data from 95 cities showed little difference in the proportion of adults respectively attending free and fee programs. Free cities maintained an average attendance of 48 per cent of those enrolled, and fee cities maintained an attendance of 61 per cent. Opinions of the respondents were equally divided in regard to the desirability of charging fees and returning deposits.

Wright [18] found that states providing no financial aid enrolled only one-third as many adults as did states providing considerable state aid. The median persistence of attendance, however, was 82 per cent in the former and only 61 per cent in the latter.

No doubt the availability of liberal state aid encourages the development of extensive local programs. Even so, the presence or absence of fees does make a difference in the number attending. Within the limits of financial necessity, policy makers can decide whether it is better to encourage large numbers of adults to participate in adult education at the cost of less regular attendance or to obtain more regular attendance in small programs by charging fees.

5. Fees limit the content of programs. Programs supported by fees tend to be deficient in the foundation and elementary fields, even though the communities have many adults who need that level of education. People of little education usually do not appreciate its value and, often being in the lower economic levels, are neither eager nor able to pay for instruction in reading and writing, better homemaking practices, consumer buying, child care, occupational skills, and similar basic training. If there is a choice between paying for baby's shoes and a term of evening school, the shoes win. Ignorance breeds ignorance, and when fees are charged, this cycle is hard to break. Under the fee system those able to pay buy the kind of education they want, while the poor cannot purchase even the fundamental tools of learning. Fees, therefore, run counter to our democratic ideals.

6. Fees limit the type of activities provided. People with money will pay for activities which make a strong personal appeal, but they often resent paying for activities which they seemingly can have without charge. Thus, adults will pay fees for authoritative lectures, whereas few are willing to pay for the privilege of discussing problems in a group,

[18] Grace S. Wright, *Persistence of Attendance in Adult Education Classes,* U.S. Office of Education Circular 353, October, 1952, p. 5.

even though the learning values of the latter may be considerably higher. They feel that they can discuss their problems anywhere without paying. Many adults will not engage in certain effective types of learning activities in parent education, citizenship, consumer education, safety, and health if they must pay fees.

Fees are impractical in many instances. They work best with activities requiring classroom attendance. Educational programs using radio, television, and certain other mass media cannot be easily supported by fees. Community-wide and informal programs in safety, health, citizenship, intercultural education, thrift, consumer education, or any other field requiring a mass approach cannot depend upon fees. If a program must rely solely upon fees, it must either make sufficient profit on classroom activities to pay for other types or, as it true of most fee programs, restrict itself to traditional methods and avoid modern, broader approaches.

If the local philosophy is to limit educational activities, fees help. Certainly private programs may purposely work with a selected group, but a democratically oriented adult educator interested in lifelong learning for all cannot afford to confine his efforts only to persons having a well-defined purpose. He should welcome all comers, regardless of their level of motivation and interest. Returnable deposits may have some slight value in stimulating attendance, for they offer, in effect, a monetary reward for continued participation. Fees and deposits provide a screen which lets in only those who have considerable motivation and enough cash.

Many administrators feel that fees encourage attendance and are therefore warranted for their psychological value, even if adequate public funds are available. Nonreturnable fees, in themselves, probably do nothing to increase interest or attendance; they merely keep out adults with low motivation. Individuals enrolling under fee systems usually have a stronger motivation, feel more intensely about specific educational needs, and consequently maintain a higher average attendance than those enrolling in free courses. It undoubtedly is easier and more satisfying to serve the former group. However, persons of less sharply defined purposes may have equal educational needs and probably a greater need for counseling and other assistance in self-development. The policy adopted in regard to fees will depend in part upon the nature of the responsibility accepted by the adult school. It would seem that if the right kind of education is good for all people in a democracy, then everyone ought to be encouraged in every way possible to enter into educational activities.

Other Sources

Foundation funds partly or completely support adult-education and community-development programs in a few communities. These are usually administered by public schools, public libraries, or private agencies, which use the grants according to the conditions laid down in the agreement. The Test City Program of the Fund for Adult Education is the most extensive current project of this nature. Occasionally a local, state, or national foundation operates the adult-education program directly, although more often money is given for special research, a demonstration, or a leadership-training project. A few agencies, including an occasional school or library, are endowed with permanent funds which may be used for adult education. The alert director of adult education will not overlook the possibility of securing foundation assistance, especially for imaginative projects which may bring advances in approaches, methods, or techniques.

Business and industrial firms are frequently willing to pay lump sums for classes, testing and counseling, training, and other educational services for their employees. Sometimes these services are desired specifically for their workers, although lately companies have become more liberal in paying the costs for families of their employees, their friends, and even the whole community. The narrow view of supporting strictly work-related education is broadening to include general and cultural fields.

Public agencies need to establish policy on the extent to which they will provide services at the request of a company which pays either a lump sum or the individual fees of its employees. Occasionally a firm wants the instruction to be given on its property for the exclusive benefit of its employees. As a matter of principle, the public school cannot exclude people from classes on the grounds that they are not employed by a given company. Willingness to provide similar educational opportunities at the school and to make them available to all firms desiring them may result in an uneconomical program. Modern equipment in business and industrial plants often provides an aid to learning that cannot be furnished by schools. Although payment of the cost of instruction carries with it considerable implication of control, public schools should permit adults not on a specified payroll to receive the instruction given company employees, especially if the company does not supply enough registrants to close registration on that account. Sound policy based on experience holds that it is best for the school to accept the use of outside educational facilities only when it can retain control of both the enrollment and the program.

Adult-education programs which lack adequate state and local aid from taxes could well exploit cooperative financial support more widely. A cosponsoring relationship often draws funds and thereby has a richer opportunity to involve members of contributing groups. Service clubs and other community organizations sometimes are sufficiently interested to contribute funds to support an educational program for adults. Especially in small and middle-size communities several organizations may be induced to throw in sums to help get a program started or to initiate some special project. One or more organizations interested in international affairs or civic education may underwrite or contribute funds to a lecture or forum series under school management. Members of these groups may sell season tickets and promote the activity in other ways. Cultural societies may assume financial responsibility for an artists' series, a little theater, or a community dramatics or music program. Sometimes a PTA will contribute money to sustain a parent-education program. Some superintendents and directors induce dozens of community organizations to give financial backing to specific projects within their fields of interest and in doing so build a truly community program—a program not only for the community but by the community.

Miscellaneous sources of income, such as the above, are reported by only a few schools, usually in negligible amounts. However, in some cases sizable sums are obtained from such sources. The fact that a few thriving programs depend substantially upon miscellaneous sources should be a challenge, especially to program directors unable to tap the more usual sources in sufficient amount.

EXPENDITURES

Comparatively few accurate data are available on expenditures for adult education, although the studies of the National Commission on Adult Education Finance of the Adult Education Association should soon provide more. Certainly few studies of expenditures, unit costs, and budgetary practice have been made of public-school adult programs. The great variation in state programs and in school programs within a state makes comparative data for adult schools much less meaningful than for grade schools, high schools, and colleges.

Debatin [19] attempted, with disappointing results, to gather data on budgetary procedures from 206 institutions. His survey included city schools, state education departments, colleges and universities, WPA adult-education projects, trade associations, adult-education councils, libraries, and several other types of organizations. Only eighty-one usable replies were received. Analysis of the data showed that systematic information on the financing of adult education is almost unobtainable. Because of the difficulties involved, few workers have been inspired to try analytical studies. The recent NEA study [20] found that "no uniform basis of reporting adult education expenditures was discernible in the reports submitted."

A major reason for the lack of systematic information is that data

[19] Frank M. Debatin, *Administration of Adult Education,* American Book Company, New York, 1938, chaps. XV, XVI.

[20] Division of Adult Education Service of the NEA, *A Study of Urban Public School Adult Education Programs of the United States,* National Education Association, Washington, 1952, p. 37.

relative to adult education are embedded in other budgets. Accounting systems often do not segregate income or expenditures for adult education. Federally reimbursed vocational education is an example. While statistics in vocational education are relatively detailed and subject to analysis, often only gross data on expenditures for adults can be obtained. Enrollment data can be broken down for in-school youth and adults. Expenditures, however, are reported only by fields, and any proportional division of expenditures according to enrollment gives misleading results,[21] since the expenditures for one part-time adult and one full-time youth are not comparable.

Amounts spent on adult education cannot be identified in school accounting systems in which the salaries of adult teachers, along with the salaries of elementary- and high-school teachers, are coded merely as instructional service. When a principal supervises adult education as a part of his regular assignment and receives no extra pay for this service, what should the records show for adult education? They usually show nothing. In one state with an extensive adult-education program including liberal state aid, the accounting system purposely does not segregate expenditures for adult activities. This practice is defended on the grounds that education is one, that the education of adults is as important as the education of youth, and that both are entitled to equal financial benefits.

A large library with an adult-education department may know the salaries and other expenditures of that department, but it is doubtful that this reveals the true cost of its services to adults. A settlement house which works with both youth and adults may record expenditures in one unified budget. While in many instances a detailed on-the-grounds study could segregate, with some accuracy, the costs of adult education, a questionnaire is not likely to bring complete or reliable data.

Another difficulty is the failure to segregate costs of plant operation and maintenance. Most adult-education programs utilize space, equipment, and custodial services which are provided primarily for other uses. Only occasionally is any attempt made to assign prorata costs to the adult budget. Likewise, capital outlay is seldom charged to adult education. In Wisconsin, where some communities have separate schools of vocational and adult education, these costs can be identified relatively easily and accurately. Even here, however, the researcher in finance would be plagued with the problem of assigning costs either to the full-time program for youth or to the part-time program for adults.

Another difficulty is the lack of standard definitions and forms. Every state and every agency, indeed every community, has its own definition of adult education. Activities which may be included or excluded vary

---

[21] See latest *Digest of Annual Reports of State Boards for Vocational Education to the Office of Education,* U.S. Department of Health, Education, and Welfare.

more widely than in any other branch of education. A number of state education departments collect no enrollment data, and even fewer collect financial data on adult education, except in those vocational fields where it is required by the Federal Office of Education. Financial and attendance data collected by the remaining states are comparable in detail only by coincidence. A step toward more uniformity in adult-education statistics, however, has been made by the Office of Education,[22] and it is hoped that the National Commission on Adult Education Finance will stimulate local schools and state education departments to keep more systematic and uniform records.

Additional difficulties include the hesitancy of some private agencies and colleges to reveal data which are considered confidential. The valued flexibility and fluctuating nature of adult-education programs also make data collection difficult. Certainly the desires of the statistician and the accountant for detailed information should not control the nature of adult education. However, more order must be obtained in this chaotic field, or many important questions will remain unanswered.

A few state directors of adult education have developed formulas, or rules of thumb, for estimating the true costs of adult education. Such formulas usually allocate to the adult program a justifiable portion of the costs of plant operation and maintenance and of general administration and supervision. They seldom include fixed charges, capital outlay, or debt service. When these formulas are used, from 1 to 3 per cent of the total school budget is usually found to be devoted to adult education, although individual programs may run higher or lower. Kempfer and Wood found that twenty-one school systems were spending slightly over 2 per cent of their total operating budget for adult education.[23] The figure for eight colleges was nearly 7 per cent. An NEA study [24] of public-school programs reported that adult-education expenditures equalled 1.8 per cent of the day-school costs.

Per Capita Expenditures

As might be expected, expenditures per participant vary widely among agencies according to the type of programs they offer. Comparisons of expenditures for adult programs in libraries, schools, evening colleges, private agencies, and community organizations are of little value unless the types of activity sponsored are similar.

The recent NEA study, covering the year 1950–1951, estimated the average expenditure per capita per year to be $24.03, with no consistent

---

[22] Paul L. Reason, et al., *The Common Core of State Educational Information,* U.S. Office of Education Bulletin 1953, no. 8.

[23] Kempfer and Wood, *op. cit.,* p. 25.

[24] Division of Adult Education Service of the NEA, *op. cit.,* p. 37.

difference among cities of different sizes. Cities having directors of adult education spent significantly more for adult education than did cities without directors, but the former, by virtue of large enrollments, generally had lower per capita costs. This was true in all but the very largest cities.

Total expenditures for public-school adult education rose rapidly after World War II. In the 4 years prior to 1950–1951 the 302 cities reporting in the NEA study increased their expenditures nearly 70 per cent. Seven in ten cities spent more in 1950–1951, while only 8 per cent spent less.[25]

Elements of Cost

It is generally thought that the administrative and supervisory costs in adult education are higher than in elementary, secondary, and college programs. This probably is true when the clock-hour of instruction is the base. However, some administrative processes in adult education, such as procurement and orientation of part-time teachers, require approximately the same energy as do the corresponding tasks in full-time schools. Certification, record keeping, payroll procedures, and similar office routines are equally time-consuming, per teacher, in both types of institution. Measured in amount of educational service rendered, however, three or more part-time teachers are required to equal a full-time staff member.[26] Publicity costs are usually greater in adult programs. Supervisory time may be on a prorata basis, although often the scattered locations of adult classes run the supervisory costs higher. Likewise, administrative energy spent in organizing short courses, forums, and other special activities is usually greater than in organizing courses of standard semester length. The common shortage of student-personnel services in adult programs may help counterbalance administrative costs. Usually, however, it can be shown that administrative costs of adult education are higher than those of programs serving or employing people on a full-time basis.

Variation in cost of professional and clerical service is considerable even in schools of comparable size. In one study among thirty-eight public evening schools enrolling between 1,000 and 6,000 persons, the administrative staff ranged from one part-time principal with 6 hours of clerical help to a full-time principal with two professional assistants, five registrars, one adviser, one guidance specialist, and two librarians.[27] Clerical assistance in these schools ranged as high as 156 hours per week, with a median of 40 hours. In the same study, reports from ninety-three schools showed that the amount of clerical help varied as follows:

[25] *Ibid.*, pp. 37–44.
[26] Calculated from data listed in the "Junior College Directory, 1951," *Junior College Journal*, 21:169–197, November, 1950.
[27] Kempfer and Wright, *op. cit.*, pp. 30–32.

No. of students	Hours of clerical help per 100 students	Hours of clerical help per teacher
1,000 or more.....	2.3	.86
400–999..........	2.8	.58
Fewer than 400....	2.0	.32

From such data one can understand the wide variations observed by Debatin. He reported that the proportion of the total budget spent for administrative costs in fourteen randomly selected institutions ranged from 9 to 45 per cent, with a median of 16 per cent.[28]

The proportion of budget going for teachers' salaries likewise varies widely. Whereas instructional services in a high proportion of public schools consume between 65 and 75 per cent of the total budget, instruction in some adult programs utilizes less than 50 per cent and in others more than 90 per cent of the budget. In a majority of adult schools instructional salaries account for over 60 per cent of the expenditures.

Most part-time instructional service under public-school auspices is paid for at hourly or session rates. The majority of large city school systems pay a flat rate, and this practice is even more common in smaller places. A substantial minority of large cities pay according to a sliding scale, with better rates going to teachers with superior qualifications or experience. Usually a teacher can reach the maximum rate appropriate to his training in 3 to 5 years. In recent years Thomas A. Van Sant of the Baltimore public schools, in cooperation with the Division of Adult Education Service of the NEA, has made an annual study of the salary rates for part-time teachers in public-school adult-education programs in cities of over 100,000 population. The data in Table 15 are taken from his findings.

Pay rates in public evening schools in 76 communities of smaller size are reported in Table 16. These rates are based on only the first 2 hours of instruction. Six of the schools reported a reduced rate of pay for instructional service beyond 2 hours of teaching in any one evening or in addition to 10 hours in any one week.[29]

A few other bases of pay have been worked out. One of the more interesting plans is used at Stockton, California, where part-time teachers are located on the regular salary scale according to training and experience. The annual salary for which they would qualify as full-time teachers divided by 1,400 (175 teaching days times 8 hours per day) gives the rate per working hour. Teachers are paid for both class and preparation

[28] Debatin, *op. cit.*, p. 352.
[29] Kempfer and Wright, *op. cit.*, p. 35.

Table 15. Hourly Rates of Pay for Part-time Public-school Adult-education Teachers below Junior-college Level, 1945–1950, in Cities above 100,000 Population

| Year | Flat rate | | Sliding scale | | |
	Median	Range	Median bottom	Median top	Range
1945	$2.03	$1.65–$3.00	$1.73	$2.54	$1.00–$5.00
1946	2.03	1.65– 3.00	1.73	2.54	1.00– 5.00
1947	2.50	1.50– 4.00	2.00	2.87	1.00– 5.00
1948	2.75	2.00– 4.25	2.25	2.87	1.20– 5.00
1949	3.00	2.12– 5.00	2.50	3.00	1.50– 6.00
1950	3.00	2.50– 4.25	2.50	3.20	1.50– 7.50
1951	3.00	2.25– 4.25	2.50	3.32	1.50– 7.50
1952	3.00	2.50– 5.00	2.50	3.25	1.50– 7.50
1953	3.00	1.50– 5.00	3.00	3.60	2.00–12.50

Table 16. Hourly Rates of Pay (Flat Rate) for Teachers as Represented by Seventy-six Schools Classified by Size of City

| Rate | Schools in cities of population of— | | | |
	100,000 or more	30,000– 99,999	10,000– 29,999	2,500– 9,999
High.......	$5.00	$4.00	$4.16	$5.00
Median....	3.30	2.65	3.00	3.00
Low.......	1.93	2.25	2.00	2.00

time. Assignments requiring heavy preparation draw 1½ hours of preparation pay in addition to each hour of class time. Assignments requiring less preparation, such as shop and laboratory courses, draw less preparation pay, with the minimum set at half an hour for each hour of class time. Under this plan a teacher at the maximum level who has a doctor's degree and who is assigned to a class requiring heavy preparation could earn as much as $17.50 for a 2-hour period. The minimum rate is $6.30 per session, and the average is about $7.50.

Occasionally, in both evening colleges and public-school programs, the rate is reduced for service after the first 2 hours, for the second class, or for large weekly loads. Sometimes afternoon rates are slightly lower than evening rates.

The use of volunteer instructors for formally organized courses under public-school auspices is relatively rare. However, an inquiry among thirty Iowa public-school, nonvocational programs enrolling 15,000 adults in 1948–1949 showed that only 63 per cent paid their teachers. This is an unusually low proportion. In the nationwide sample of 100 evening schools only three were found to pay nothing, and in a fourth case an honorarium was given at the end of the year.[30] The practice of not paying teachers of adult groups may gain impetus from the widespread practice of vocational homemaking and agriculture teachers who work with housewives and farmers as a part of their regular assignment without extra compensation. Usually their loads and schedules permit such work. Occasionally, in small schools with only a few adult activities, day-school teachers are assigned responsibility for adult groups on one or two nights a week without extra pay. This may be accepted as a responsibility for extraclassroom activities and may be in lieu of such day-school assignments. If compensating adjustments in the teachers' schedule are made, his work with adult groups can be remunerated by his regular salary. A normal load of work, whatever the ratio of adults to youth among the teacher's students, need not draw extra pay. Since compensation for part-time work is often looked upon as extra, the practice of incorporating part-time work with adults into regular assignments without extra pay helps give adult education a more desirable status. The latter practice is apparently a growing trend.

Pay rates in evening colleges usually run considerably higher than do those in public-school programs. In fact, where adult activities are sponsored by both a public school and a college, the public-school director often feels unable to compete in employing part-time teachers for similar work because of the rate differential. This becomes apparent when the school rates listed in Table 15 are compared with evening-college rates. In Neuffer's study [31] among AUEC members, professors were paid from $4.00 to $15.00 per class-hour, with a median rate of $7.50. The median rate for associate professors was $6.25; for assistant professors, $6.00; for instructors, $5.50; and for lecturers, $6.00. The range in ranks below the professorial level was from $3.00 to $13.00. For laboratory assignments the range was from $2.00 to $13.00, with a median of $4.00—except for professors, whose median was $5.00.

Allowances are sometimes given for extra travel or other unusual expenses. Thirty per cent of the evening colleges grant extra pay for

[30] Kempfer and Wright, *op. cit.*, p. 36.
[31] Neuffer, *op. cit.*, p. 18.

instructors of greater experience. Directors of both college and public-school adult programs occasionally engage outstanding lecturers and leaders at rates above the salary schedule. One has to be careful in doing this, however, as too much deviation from the regular salary scale without ample justification may undermine staff morale.

Variation of pay with size of class is not common in public schools, and in general it is to be condemned, for it tends to make each instructor his own recruiting agent with all the attendant dangers. If too few enroll, the class is usually dropped; or—if important to the participants—it is maintained, and the instructor is paid the usual rate. In a few cases, however, the instructor is given the option of dropping the course or of continuing with a small enrollment at a fraction of the remuneration he would receive for a class of normal size. This practice is more common in evening colleges. In Neuffer's study, 25 per cent paid the instructor less when class size was below the minimum, while only 14 per cent paid more when enrollment ran above normal.[32]

The following tabulation, compiled from data supplied by T. A. Van Sant and F. R. Neuffer, shows when public schools and evening colleges raised their pay rates during the postwar period:

Year	No. of public schools	No. of evening colleges
1945–1946		37
1946–1947		63
1947–1948	69	65
1948–1949	22	35

The materials required for instruction are another cost item. Textbooks are usually purchased by the adult student, although a few schools have established a rental system enabling a student to borrow all texts in a course for a small fee. Only an occasional school provides free textbooks to adults. Library materials, where they are available, can generally be used without charge. Most schools require participants to provide their own consumable materials, such as paper, arts and crafts materials, lumber, paint, textiles, and foods, which may be purchased privately or bought at the school. When such materials are used more or less uniformly, however, as in foods courses, a materials fee is frequently charged. Items of personal equipment, such as drafting instruments, are almost universally provided by the student, but materials consumed in teacher demonstrations must be provided for in the budget.

[32] *Ibid.*, p. 17.

In general, instructional materials constitute a relatively small budgetary item.

Many adult-education courses are conducted with equipment originally provided for day-school use. In fact, some programs, limited by such equipment, find it hard to push beyond the equipment boundaries set by the parent institutions. Although borrowing equipment helps keep the budget small, especially if no charge is attached, the practice increases dependency. As adult programs grow, they will certainly need equipment at times when it is in use elsewhere, and they will need more equipment or equipment in new fields. Eventually, therefore, the budget must begin to reflect expenditures of this type. Boards of education should supply equipment for adult use as well as for the use of children and youth and should spend as freely in one case as in the other, but sometimes special fees are levied for a darkroom, a kiln, a radio transmitter, or other equipment. In buying equipment, the director of adult education who takes the long view and spreads his purchases over several years keeps the budget load in better balance.

Operation and maintenance costs are also usually a minor item in the budget. The mutual benefits which a day school and an adult program share in using the same building, however, are seldom reflected in the budget. Often the parent organization maintains and operates the facilities and absorbs the costs. This is one of the simplest moves a board of education or other parent authority can make to promote adult education. Custodial service, heat, light, telephone service, and extra maintenance costs would change the budgetary picture considerably if special allowance had to be made for them. Debatin found that forty of eighty-one institutions did not charge the adult program for operation and maintenance. In some cases, however, the host institutions absorbed surplus income to help defray these costs.[33]

A few public schools insist that the adult-education division pay rent. In a community without state aid, this usually puts the entire burden of support on student fees. While one must favor clarity in budgeting and proper allocation of costs, a board that requires an adult-education program to pay the same rent it would ask of a private community organization tends to discourage broad programs of adult education.

As public-school and evening-college programs spread their activities beyond institutional walls, the problem of paying rent will arise more frequently. Satisfactory rent-free facilities cannot always be found, so that budgetary provision will have to be made for off-campus janitorial service and other operating costs.

[33] Debatin, *op. cit.*, p. 355.

Budgetary Practices

The budget is the financial plan which should reflect the over-all educational plan. Those who prepare the budget begin by mapping out tentatively how much each part of the educational plan will cost and where the money will come from. In general, detailed budgets are preferable to general ones, provided that the various items remain sufficiently flexible. After the budget is prepared, presented for discussion, and approved, it becomes the financial guide for the year's operations.

Inasmuch as most adult programs are sponsored by agencies which have other educational obligations, the director of adult education can expect to fit his budgetary procedures into the framework set up by the general administration and the board of control of the parent agency. In public programs the state law very often provides the general calendar within which budgeting takes place. State education departments and state university systems often outline the major details and procedures of accounting systems and sometimes provide the forms. Although the director will need at least general acquaintance with these features, he will be more particularly concerned with how budgeting is done in his institution, agency, or community.

While there are specific deadlines, good budgeting is essentially a year-round activity. That is, as the director and his staff continually plan the educational program, they should simultaneously convert its various features into a dollars-and-cents estimate, taking into consideration both costs and income. Budgeting usually operates on an annual cycle, but it also has its long-term aspects—salary increases, new equipment, new enterprises, and general expansion of the program.

The competent director realizes that the best budgeting is a democratic process in which staff members suggest their needs, plan new developments, and decide upon what will be proposed to higher authority. This helps make them budget-conscious. In their attempt to involve teachers intelligently in the budget-making process, as well as in its administration, some directors prepare a handbook on budget making, if one is not available for the system as a whole. Public hearings on the budget are welcomed as an opportunity for effective adult civic education.

The following budget of the Modesto, California, Evening Junior College illustrates the size of the task and indicates some of the mechanics of budgeting. The director of adult education can find further sources of information on budgeting procedures in the Selected References at the end of this chapter.

Modesto Evening Junior College
1953–1954 Income

Source of income	1952–1953	1953–1954
Beginning net balance.........................	$ 29,000.00	$ 39,000.00
From state apportionments....................	96,303.90	120,936.00
From government............................	2,000.00	1,600.00
From Veterans Administration.................	25,110.00	10,810.00
Tuition from other districts...................	8,000.00	8,000.00
Registration fees............................	2,900.00	3,000.00
Kiln-firing deposits..........................	500.00	400.00
Resale deposits..............................	5,000.00	3,000.00
Total......................................	$168,813.90	$186,746.00

1953–1954 Expenses

Account no.	Account name	1952–1953	1953–1954
100	Administration		
112A1	Superintendent's salary	$2,161.00	$2,295.00
123B532	Barnett's repair	5.00	5.00
Total—100...................................		$2,166.00	$2,300.00
211	Supervisors' salaries	$ 8,000.00	$ 8,050.00
212	Administrators' salaries	10,500.00	11,000.00
213.1	Teachers' salaries	97,518.00	88,683.00
213.3	Substitutes' salaries	350.00	350.00
221A11	T-and-I supervisor's secretary	1,100.00	1,048.00
222A01	Laboratory assistants	2,500.00	2,000.00
222A02	Music assistants	100.00	0
222A03	Swimming assistants	150.00	200.00
222A04	Driver-training assistant	500.00	650.00
222A06	Regular clerks	8,664.00	8,400.00
222A07	Special clerks	100.00	100.00
222A08	Tool clerks	3,000.00	3,300.00
231D-	Instructional supplies, broken down into 17 subject fields	4,722.00	7,200.00
231D39	Secretarial office supplies	2,500.00	1,500.00
231D51	Visual education	150.00	400.00
231D53	Radio and phonograph	0	50.00
231D59	Veterans' resale (books)	1,200.00	500.00
231D60	Resale	5,000.00	3,000.00
231D99	General	500.00	500.00

1953–1954 Expenses (*Continued*)

Account no.	Account name	1952–1953	1953–1954
233-	Library expenses, broken down into 13 subject fields	450.00	715.00
234.1B1	T-and-I supervisor's office supplies	150.00	125.00
234.1B5	Supervisor's outside travel	200.00	200.00
234.1B6	Supervisor's local travel	1,950.00	1,350.00
234.1B15	T-and-I supervisor's library	15.00	10.00
234.2B1	Principal's office supplies	600.00	1,000.000
234.2B4	Principal's conventions	350.00	500.00
234.2B5	Principal's outside travel	600.00	400.00
234.2B7	Principal's car upkeep	400.00	450.00
234.4	Citizenship graduation	150.00	100.00
234.5B1	Office	250.00	0
234.6-1D	Film rental—14 subject fields	0	425.00
Total—200		$151,669.00	$142,206.00
410	Custodians' salaries	$ 400.00	$ 350.00
432	Gas	150.00	150.00
433	Lights and electricity for welding	100.00	1,000.00
435	Water	100.00	100.00
436	Phone	450.00	550.00
440.4D01	Garbage—home economics	0	25.00
440.4D14	Garbage—homemaking	25.00	25.00
Total—400		$1,225.00	$2,200.00
505.1A		$1,227.00	$ 0
505.1B		364.00	0
505.2A		334.00	0
505.2B		316.00	0
513	Gardener	300.00	300.00
521	Maintenance painting	0	550.00
525	Repair of buildings	747.90	500.00
531	Repair of furniture	150.00	150.00
532D	Repair—11 subject fields	928.00	1,300.00
542	Replacements—8 subject fields	0	1,675.00
542D99	Replacement, general	0	100.00
543E07	Replacement of station wagon	0	1,600.00
Total—500		$4,366.90	$6,175.00

1953–1954 Expenses (*Continued*)

Account no.	Account name	1952–1953	1953–1954
612	Certified retirement	$ 300.00	$ 180.00
613	Noncertificated retirement	400.00	$ 500.00
624	Comprehensive insurance	217.00	385.00
641	Rents	5,000.00	5,000.00
Total—600...............................		$5,917.00	$6,065.00
1030.4	New construction	$ 0	$4,500.00
1041.2E02	New furniture	400.00	200.00
1042D	Capital outlay—10 subject fields	2,420.00	2,600.00
1042D99	Capital outlay—general	650.00	500.00
Total—1000...............................		$3,470.00	$7,800.00

	1952–1953	1953–1954
Undistributed reserve for possible refund to Veterans Administration................................	0	$ 20,000.00
Total...	0	$ 20,000.00
Total budget...................................	$168,813.90	$186,746.00

SELECTED REFERENCES

Burke, Arvid J.: *Financing Public Schools in the United States,* Harper & Brothers, New York, 1951.

Hendrickson, Andrew: "Planned Adult Education Programs Wait upon State Aid," *Ohio Schools,* 26:308–309, October, 1948.

Johns, R. L., and E. L. Morphets (eds.): *Problems and Issues in Public School Finance,* Bureau of Publications, Teachers College, Columbia University, New York, 1952.

Kempfer, Homer: "Sound State Policy in Public School Adult Education," *Adult Education Bulletin,* 14:12–15, October, 1949.

—— and William R. Wood: *Financing Adult Education in Selected Schools and Community Colleges,* U.S. Office of Education Bulletin 1952, no. 8.

Morphet, E. L., and E. L. Lindman: *Public School Finance Programs of the Forty-eight States,* U.S. Office of Education Circular 274, 1950.

Mort, Paul R., and Walter C. Reusser: *Public School Finance,* McGraw-Hill Book Company, Inc., New York, 1951.

Olds, Edward B.: *Financing Adult Education in America's Public Schools and*

Community Councils, Adult Education Association, National Commission on Adult Education Finance, Washington, 1954.

Partial Report of the Senate Interim Committee on Adult Education, California State Senate, S. Res. 185 (1951), 1953.

Pittenger, B. F.: *Local Public School Administration,* McGraw-Hill Book Company, Inc., New York, 1951.

Spence, Ralph B., and Benjamin Shangold: *Public School Adult Education in New York State, 1944–47,* New York State Education Department, Albany, N.Y., 1950.

Sworder, S.: "Financing Adult Education in California," *California Journal of Secondary Education,* 28:450–453, December, 1953.

See also General References: [34] Division of Adult Education Service, chap. 8; Kempfer; Sheats, Jayne, and Spence, chap. 18.

[34] The General References are listed in full at the end of this book.

CHAPTER 15 *Over-all Program Evaluation*

Evaluation is one of the most difficult and one of the most important tasks facing the director of an adult-education program. Any attempt to assess the results of a specific activity is difficult enough, but evaluation of a complex program of lifelong learning is several times more difficult and, therefore, frequently neglected. Yet, constant evaluation of the total program is necessary if it is to experience continuous and secure growth.

Although evaluation comes last in the sequence of steps that constitute the thinking and educative process—definition of the problem, data gathering, analysis, decision, action, and evaluation—it should not be looked upon as a final event. Instead, evaluation should permeate the entire program of adult education and function as an integral part of the total educative process. It should never be omitted. Ideally, evaluation is a continuous process, but specific data-collecting and appraisal points occur. Results at every stage, from changes in an individual to the progress of the entire program, should be evaluated. The plan for evaluation should provide for appraisal of the total program and of each important element in it. Since evaluation of specific phases of adult programs has been treated earlier, evaluation of the total program will be considered here.

PURPOSES OF EVALUATION

The basic purpose of evaluation is to stimulate growth and improvement. Whatever other worthy purposes exist are only facets of the all-inclusive effort to assess present conditions as a basis for achieving better ones. Evaluation that does not lead to improved practice is sterile.

An attempt to appraise a program by comparing it with another, or with several others, perverts the basic purpose of evaluation and usually leads to unsound conclusions. Programs differ in definitions, objectives, conditions accepted as desirable, data-gathering instruments used, and other variable and incomparable features, but comparisons between them tend to impose the objectives of one program upon another. Evaluation intended to show the effectiveness of an operation in order to win budget support, to justify program expansion, or to defend the current program can easily fall into the traps of program comparison.

Evaluation by direct comparison is also psychologically unsound. It accepts the average, or some other norm, as the desirable goal. If one adjudges his program better than the norm, he may gain satisfaction, but little stimulus to improve. Assessment of conditions in evaluation can best be made against a previous bench mark in the same situation or against an ideal—always in the light of accepted objectives.

THE EVALUATIVE PROCESS

In theory, the structure of the evaluative process is simple. Evaluation is the comparison of actual conditions or characteristics with the ideal. The specific steps in this process are as follows:

1. Agreement is reached on objectives—the desirable state of affairs—goals.

2. An assessment is made of the present state of affairs.

3. Something is done which presumably moves the situation toward the desirable state.

4. Another assessment is made to see how far the situation has progressed toward the ideal.

If a motorist decides to be in Denver tomorrow night and now finds himself in St. Louis, he may pursue any road which presumably leads toward his destination and check at a later time to see how far he has progressed toward his goal. He has evaluated. If he is satisfied with the road he has taken, he may continue on it; otherwise he may select anew.

The adult educator, like the motorist, spends most of his time driving —moving toward the goal. If repeated or constant evaluation is omitted, however, he may waste time or go off the road. The difficulties in evaluating adult education, as well as most other fields of applied social science, exist because the various steps lack specificity. Often no accurate and complete assessment has been made of conditions at the start. The motorist can get his bearings in a minute; the adult educator requires more time. The motorist can quickly decide upon, accept, or define an objective. Decision on goals in adult education often involves large numbers of people and develops slowly. The motorist has a road map showing how to get from here to there. Many maps in adult education are less specific. Much terrain—largely unexplored—has never been mapped. When the motorist stops along the way, he needs but a moment to discover how far he has traveled, whether he is on the right road, and what more he has to do. The adult educator must spend much more time in finding out where he is; even then, he may not know too clearly what progress has been made or whether any achievement is due to his efforts or to a dozen other cultural influences.

The Goals—Evaluative Criteria

Evaluation must always be in terms of objectives or goals. Goals serve best if they are ideal—as ideal as can be conceived at a given time. Educators of adults often err at this point by desiring to compare their programs with those of their neighbors or the average of the state or nation. Comparison with the average is dangerous because it sets up mediocrity as the goal.

Objectives may be immediate, intermediate, or long-term. Long-term goals are value judgments which arise out of social philosophy—out of the system of thought developed by a culture. They are what people think are important—maximum development of the individual, increased freedom, happiness, a high level of material living, good health, improved human relationships, happier homes, increased participation in deciding the conditions by which we live—in short, the good life.

Goals may be arranged in a hierarchy, with long-term objectives at the top. In a well-integrated value system short-term goals contribute to intermediate goals, which in turn help accomplish long-term goals. Lesser goals may contribute to more than one greater goal. Short-term objectives may, in themselves, be thought of as a sequence. In fact, a very great deal of learning is arranged in a sequence which contributes to intermediate or longer-range goals. The system of goals stretched through the adult years duplicates in most respects the developmental tasks discussed in Chapter 3.

Short-term goals may be accomplished in a few minutes, a day, a week, or longer. Teaching a group of women how to make buttonholes, teaching illiterates how to write their names, and preparing candidates for the naturalization examination are examples of such objectives in an adult-education program. Aside from contributing to larger goals, the achievement of short-term goals is necessary to give the required sense of accomplishment. The danger of thinking chiefly of immediate objectives, however, is that once they are reached, complacency may set in; one may be satisfied with a low level of achievement.

Intermediate goals sometimes require years for their accomplishment. Teaching apprentices an occupation or training a group in democratic discussion leadership are examples of intermediate goals. In working to achieve these lesser goals, long-range goals must be kept in mind. If long-range goals are overemphasized, however, energy may be wasted in wishing for the ideal without taking all the practical and possible immediate steps. A balance is required—one must keep his eye on long-range goals as he continuously works to accomplish immediate and intermediate objectives. As immediate objectives come within grasp, directors of adult education who have vision readjust their sights in line with longer-term goals.

The primary function of a goal is to give direction. In a very real sense, the best long-range goals recede. The director of adult education is never fully satisfied by achieving goals. Satisfaction comes primarily from the learning process, not from possession of an achieved goal. Goals give focus to the educative process.

There are both individual and group goals. The former arise from the biological and cultural motivations of men. The goals of a public-school or a community program of adult education or a community-development program should be determined through democratic group processes.

Evaluative criteria are standards for judging—tests, measures of a good program. Often they are specific indications that a goal is being reached. Thus, for young adults a low divorce rate, a low juvenile-delinquency rate, and extensive family-unit activity in community life may be accepted as measures of good family-life education. Exactly what constitutes *low* and *extensive* is a matter of judgment, and data on actual conditions would need to be compared with the ideal situation to determine the degree to which it has been realized.

In a democracy, goals—like policies—should, in theory, be determined by all affected by them. In fact, through policy-making processes a democracy is constantly making up its mind on its goals—always clarifying them, always maintaining a varying balance between decided goals and goals in the process of being decided. The onflow of new generations and the dynamic nature of our world require this.

The imposition of goals is authoritarian. Capricious desires of administrators, vested interests of specialists, or prejudices should not control the development of goals or the evaluative criteria used. On the other hand, if the formulation of objectives is left to individuals without control or agreement, on the principle of *laissez faire,* anarchy is the ultimate result. Such dangers emphasize the wisdom of involving as many people as possible in the evaluative process. In any comprehensive evaluation of a community program, the adult-school staff, members of advisory groups, the leaders, and the whole community should be included, both in setting the goals and in making the assessments. Through this type of involvement, the groundwork for maximum improvement is laid, and the emotional commitment to achieve it is developed.

Goals should be comprehensive enough to cover all aspects of individual and group growth and development. Criteria should not depend upon the availability of adequate measuring instruments. They should satisfy program-wide or community-wide purposes. General or long-term goals take on meaning only as they are spelled out in specific, realistic, and attainable behavior patterns. They should indicate specific growth which can be sought through learning processes.

For example, good citizenship may be all right as a general goal, but it has very little meaning until its component parts become specific. Specifics may include such items as these:

1. A high proportion of young adults, or all of them, register and vote as soon as legally possible.

2. A high proportion of adults participate in community and neighborhood groups concerned with civic improvement.

3. All newly arrived immigrants planning permanent residence receive instruction in citizenship.

4. Open sessions of policy-making bodies are attended by representatives of many citizens groups.

Practically, goals may be set by the local agency director, group leaders and teachers, the board of control, an advisory committee, the student body, the general public, or by others. Under the democratic philosophy, it is both unfair and impossible for any evaluation, either self-made or made by outsiders, to be conducted in terms of objectives not accepted by those in charge of and participating in the activity. While the objectives of a program can be criticized and judged, once agreement on them is reached, they provide the evaluator with ideals. Criteria can then be developed for assessing the effectiveness of the program. The goals, however determined, must be acceptable to both the program administrator and the evaluator, assuming that they are different people.

Methods of Gathering Data

After the goals or the objectives have been spelled out into evaluative criteria, the evaluative process requires the gathering of data which show the extent to which the objectives have been realized. The degree of success must be measured.

Data are useful in so far as they reveal actual conditions. Data may include such widely varying information as the following:

Press reports and editorials
Membership in community organizations
Numbers participating in adult-education activities
Votes at elections
Persistence of attendance in adult-education groups
Trends in vital statistics
Employment rates
Delinquency rates
Health indexes
Percentage of adults participating in adult-education activities year after year
Quantity of adult education provided
Types of adult education provided

Wherever possible, descriptions of actual behavior and conditions should be reduced to quantitative terms. Subjectivity can be reduced through use of analytical studies and surveys, anecdotal records, case studies, logs and diaries, check lists, rating scales, opinion polls, profile charts, inventories, sociograms, standardized and homemade scales, recordings and stenographic reports, and similar instruments. If desired information is not available, other data can sometimes be used, but their propriety should be well understood.

Quantitative data may be arranged in a simple table for comparative purposes. For example, in evaluating immigrant education in a community, these data might be included:

Desirable Conditions	*Actual Local Conditions*
All newly arrived immigrants should receive systematic orientation in American culture.	Twenty of fifty immigrants arriving in 1951 were involved in an orientation program.
A high proportion of all foreign-born adults should make educational preparation for naturalization within a reasonable time after arrival.	Sixty of two hundred immigrants settling in community X within the last 5 years have been enrolled in classes preparing for naturalization.
A high proportion of candidates for naturalization have had citizenship instruction.	Sixty-six of ninety-five candidates for naturalization in the past 5 years have been enrolled in citizenship classes.
Most newly naturalized citizens continue systematic study of citizenship.	Seven of ninety naturalized in the past 5 years have enrolled in citizenship classes after naturalization.
All non-English-speaking adults engage in systematic study of English.	Thirty-five of forty non-English-speaking immigrants who arrived in 1951 are systemmatically studying English. Twenty of two hundred who arrived before 1930 are in English classes.

This systematization of data makes it easy to see how well objectives of a given type are being reached. Weak and strong features stand out, but judgment is still necessary to determine where to put greater emphasis. After data are in, a change of objective may seem wise. The sights should not be lowered, however, merely to agree more closely with actual conditions. Usually more energy needs to be spent, or better ways designed, to accomplish the desired results. Such comparative data can be used effectively in public relations and promotion and can be presented to superintendents and school boards.

Cooperative Surveys—the Baltimore Experience

Over a period of years the Cooperative Study of Secondary School Standards has developed evaluative procedures which combine the benefits of self-evaluation with study by a committee of outside consultants.[1] Certain of these procedures were adapted by the Baltimore Cooperative

[1] See *Evaluative Criteria*, Cooperative Study of Secondary School Standards, Washington, 1950. Other materials developed by this study also merit examination by evaluators of adult-education programs.

Survey of Adult Education, which began in 1947.[2] This was probably the most ambitious attempt in recent years to evaluate the total adult-education program of a large metropolitan city. While in this instance the public school assumed the initiative, the entire project was a joint enterprise of the adult-education agencies of Baltimore and Region II of the Department of Adult Education of the National Education Association. The total survey consisted of three main parts—the preliminary data-gathering by local committees, a 3-day work-survey conference, and follow-up activities.

Early in 1947 all groups and agencies in Baltimore concerned with adult education were invited to work together in developing a general basic philosophy of adult education, a set of guiding principles, and a list of survey limitations. A local planning committee set up a committee on coordination and evaluation and convened eighteen local area committees representative of all organizations and agencies within their particular area. These areas were generally functionally determined, although in a few cases they were centered around organizations. Their areas of concern were:

Library services
Recreational programs
College and university extension
Public evening schools
Veterans education
Museum educational services, including scientific associations
Mass media of communication: press, radio, movies, and theater
Public and private trade and vocational schools
Men's and women's civic and social clubs
Parent-teacher associations
Music groups
Materials and instructional technics
Workers education
Industrial arts and crafts
Testing and guidance
Intercultural education
Parent education
Religious education

The eighteen committees worked several months gathering data about the local program facilities and the needs for adult education in their areas. They reflected need against facilities and reviewed plans for expansion or curtailment of services. In most instances a preconference report of findings was prepared.

[2] For a complete account, see the *Baltimore Bulletin of Education*, 25:153–248, January–March, 1948.

The coordination and evaluation committee gathered certain general data about the city as a whole, assisted area committees with their planning, reviewed their work, received the preconference reports for abstracting, and kept in touch with the chairmen and members of regional committees.

Paralleling local activity, nineteen regional teams—counterparts of each of the local committees, including the coordinating group—were set up from among the adult-education leaders planning to participate in the evaluation. Well over 100 regional specialists from seven states were enlisted. Chairmen of several regional committees met with chairmen of local committees late in the spring, corresponded with them during the summer, and met with them again in September for preconference evaluation of progress and adjustment of further plans.

In late October, the chairmen and members of regional committees met in Baltimore for 3 days with the chairmen and members of local committees. Group leaders and recorders met in briefing sessions during the afternoon and evening preceding the conference. The first day was devoted to general orientation, final organization of joint regional-local committees, and reports of local committees to their regional counterparts. The second day was spent in discussion, visiting facilities and programs in operation, and in action research. Regional-local committees worked out revised reports and fed them back in a summary session on the third day.

The entire project was conceived as a continuing attempt to improve the Baltimore program of adult education. Consequently, during the greater part of 2 years, the committee on coordination and evaluation—expanded by the addition of local-committee chairmen and interested lay leaders—held monthly meetings at each of which representatives of specific area committees appeared. The reports of the work-survey conference submitted by each area committee were considered in detail, and plans were discussed for further activity and improvement in program. Several committees gathered additional data, studied them, and made further plans. The participating agencies and organizations, stimulated to self-study by outside specialists, started a number of positive new activities.

Evaluation of this project resulted in several observations of value for similar undertakings in the future:

1. A high degree of cooperation can be attained if the initiating leadership begins and continues in a democratic fashion. All agencies and organizations interested in adult education must have opportunity to participate in the evaluation.

2. The time schedule should be longer and better arranged. Activities of local committees might better begin in September and work through a full year, with the work-survey conference coming during the fall of

the second year. This would permit more thorough data gathering, more detailed analysis, and better organization of preconference reports. Considerable time would remain for follow-up during the second year.

3. Machinery should be set up so that follow-up activities can be continued for some time after the conference. The conference will otherwise appear as a culminating activity instead of as a special focal point in a continuing plan of improvement.

4. Clear lines of communication should be established and maintained among local committees and between them and their regional counterparts. Abstracts of reports and an understanding of processes should be shared in advance of the conference.

5. Full advantage should be taken of the opportunity to involve scores and hundreds of lay leaders in consideration of the problems of adult education.

6. Local committees should be given full orientation in planning and developing criteria.

7. Ample work space and secretarial help should be provided, both to local committees during their months of work and to the combined committees at conference time.

8. The conference must be very carefully organized, with time-place-purpose charts kept up to the hour.

9. When committee and conference procedures are applied to smaller study groups, fewer committees may be necessary. If local committees do their work well, one well-selected general outside committee could conceivably hear and discuss local reports, visit activities, and help in cooperative direction finding. One general visiting committee may be more useful than several when the program of only one agency is being evaluated.

WHAT TO ASSESS

Comprehensive evaluation of a program requires that it be examined, both quantitatively and qualitatively, from at least two major points of view: (1) the amount and kind of activity and (2) the results.

Scope

The scope of a program refers to its quantitative aspects. In evaluating scope, such questions as these, and many more, are pertinent:

1. How comprehensive is the program? How broad is the range of educational services? How much activity goes on?

2. To what extent are all interests and educational needs of the community served?

3. What facilities are used? How much are they used?

4. What fraction of the adult population is involved? How much time are adults spending in learning activities?

5. What media, approaches, procedures, and methods are used?

6. What age groups are served? Educational levels? Socioeconomic groups? Ethnic groups? Occupational groups?

Sizing up the scope is sometimes not difficult. The range of fields served can be easily determined. The facilities, media, approaches, procedures, and methods used are usually common knowledge among agency heads and staff members. Generally the number of organized groups and the extent of their membership can be ascertained, although those not connected with the major agencies may present a problem. If the number of adults having defined educational needs and interests has been determined, the size of the program can be compared with the total task.

The Clock-hour Formula

The size of adult-education programs is commonly measured by the number enrolled and less often by the average daily attendance. Variations in length of term, length of sessions per week, average daily attendance, size of community, and other factors make such indexes of limited value, whether for comparisons within programs or between programs. The quantity of adult education provided in a community or by an agency can be determined, however, by the clock-hour index, in which one clock-hour of individual participation is the basic unit.[3] If it is assumed that all hours spent by participants in educational activities are of equal worth, the aggregate of participant hours becomes a basic quantitative measure. To make the aggregate most meaningful, it should be related to the size of the adult population of the community. The relationship may be stated as a fraction:

$$\frac{\text{Total clock-hours of attendance per year}}{\text{Adults in the community}} = \text{clock-hour index}$$

The numerator is the sum of all the time spent by adults in educational activities. It may be the sum of attendance hours in the activities of one agency or of all agencies and programs within a community. It may include all types of activities except those so informal in schedule that it is impossible to gather data on participation. Sessions and periods of varying length should be converted into standards of 60 minutes. For within-program evaluation, the total number of clock-hours of attendance per year can be worked out for each major area, such as citizenship or family-life education, and the areas compared with one another. Year-by-year comparisons can also be made of the whole program, or of parts.

The denominator of the fraction usually represents about seven-tenths of the total population of the geographic area served. In 1950, 69.4 per

[3] Homer Kempfer, "A Formula for Measuring Adult-education Programs," *Adult Education Bulletin,* 12:195–198, October, 1948.

cent of the people in the United States were aged eighteen and over. The percentage of adults in the various states diverged several points from the national ratio, and in communities variations were even greater. The director of adult education should determine the local figure, if possible, and use the same denominator from year to year until a significant change in the population occurs.

The index itself represents the time in hours which every adult in the community would have devoted to educational activities of the types included had all participated equally. It ignores the differences in educational quality of various kinds of activities and does nothing to show the diversity of fields, the intensity of activities, the number of adults involved in each, and similar important factors. All are melted down into one basic unit. The formula can include anything which the evaluator wants to classify as adult education. It works with any definition of adult education; consequently, comparisons based on different definitions lose their worth. Because of this, local directors who have had experience with the formula agree that it can be most advantageously used in year-by-year evaluations of their own programs.

The formula has been applied to several hundred public-school programs. If group leaders and teachers record and add up the total clock-hours of attendance or participation in each activity, application of the formula at the end of the year takes only a few minutes. During 1948–1949, fewer than 10 per cent of nearly 400 public-school and community-college programs were providing 5 clock-hours or more of educational service for the typical adult in their communities. Adult education is admittedly a party-time activity, but it is given only a very tiny fraction of the individual's time as compared with a standard of 900 clock-hours in a 9-month term for children and youth.

The distribution of service to the different educational levels, ages, socioeconomic groups, ethnic groups, and occupations requires more study. For larger communities and counties, census data are available showing the distribution of the adult population in these respects. Analysis of registration forms or questionnaires to the participants can furnish other data. Occasionally, items included on representative sampling surveys of the community can provide the desired cross-sectional data. For example, such a survey, though taken primarily for other purposes, can yield the distribution of religious faiths, the number of commuters, or the number belonging to organized groups of specified types—data which may otherwise be unobtainable. One can then compare the adult-education clientele with the normal adult population. Unserved or little-served groups may come to light.

The form for comparison of the major characteristics of the population served with those of the total adult population in a community may look like this:

Characteristics	Percentage distribution	
	Persons in the community (from census data on local survey) *	Adults Participating in educational activities of agency X
Age:		
18–19	3.1	
20–24	7.6	—
25–29	8.1	—
30–39	15.1	—
40–49	12.7	—
50–59	10.2	—
60–69	7.3	—
70 and above	4.8	—
Educational level (age 14 and above):		
Elementary school		
Fewer than 5 years	10.8	—
5 to 6 years	9.1	—
7 or 8 years	27.0	—
High school		
1 to 3 years	16.9	—
4 years	20.2	—
College		
1 to 3 years	6.2	—
4 years or more	6.0	—
Not reported	2.8	—
Median years completed	9.3	—
Sex:		
Men	49.4	—
Women	50.6	—
Nativity and race (age 15 and above—1940):		
Native (white)	82.8	—
Foreign-born (white)	6.7	—
Nonwhite	10.5	—
Employment status (age 14 and above—Nov. 5–11, 1950):		
In labor force	58.1	—
Employed	96.2	—
Unemployed	3.8	—
Not in labor force	41.9	—
Occupational classification (employed workers age 14 and above):		
Professional, technical, and kindred workers	8.7	—
Farmers and farm managers	7.7	—
Proprietors, managers, and officials, except farm	8.9	—

Characteristics	Percentage distribution	
	Persons in the community (from census data on local survey) *	Adults Participating in educational activities of agency X
Clerical and kindred workers.....................	12.3	—
Sales workers.................................	7.0	—
Craftsmen, foremen, and kindred workers.........	13.8	—
Operatives and kindred workers.................	19.8	—
Private household workers.....................	2.5	—
Service workers, except household...............	7.6	—
Farm laborers and foremen.....................	4.3	—
Laborers, except farm and mine.................	6.1	—
Occupation not reported.......................	1.3	—

* Percentages in this column show the national distribution based on 1950 Census data. They should be replaced by local data for each community in which an adult-education program is being evaluated.

An adult-education program can be large and can draw many types of people and still be narrow in scope. Large programs of adult vocational education, recreation, or film forums, for instance, may serve only a limited part of the total educational need. The comprehensiveness of a program may be examined from these points of view:

1. What fields are included? Are there activities to assist with all the developmental tasks of adults? Does the program include educational activities in the following areas? (Each of these areas can be detailed further, and others can be added.)

    a. Family-life education
        (1) Preparation for marriage
        (2) Prenatal care
        (3) Infant care and child development
        (4) Relationships with adolescents
        (5) Marriage adjustment
        (6) Adjustment to middle age and maturity
    b. Education for production and consumption
        (1) Vocational guidance—testing, counseling, and follow-up
        (2) Training opportunities in a broad range of occupations
        (3) Retraining and refresher opportunities available throughout life
        (4) Management of a home and income
        (5) Consumer education

    c. Public-affairs or citizenship education
       (1) Immigrant education
       (2) New-voter preparation for twenty-one-year-olds
       (3) Intercultural education
       (4) Continuous education for all, dealing with problems and issues at the local, state, national, and international levels
    d. Leisure-time education
       (1) Athletic recreation of many types for all ages
       (2) Nonathletic leisure-time activities: music, graphic and plastic arts, crafts, literature, dramatics, hobbies, etc.
    e. Foundation education
       (1) Literacy education
       (2) Elementary education for adults
       (3) High-school education for adults
       (4) Health and safety education

  2. Are educational experiences organized in enough ways to serve the needs of all? What approaches are used?
    a. Credit courses and curricula for those who need or desire them
    b. Noncredit courses
    c. Forums and similar large group meetings
    d. Lecture series
    e. Concert and artist series
    f. Film forums and film showings
    g. Conducted educational tours
    h. Radio broadcasts for adults in content fields
    i. Organized radio-listening groups
    j. Workshops, short institutes, or conferences
    k. Courses or educational activities cosponsored with industrial, business, or community organizations
    l. Clubs for adults or out-of-school youth sponsored by the school or other educational agency
    m. Supervised correspondence study
    n. Programs related to apprentice training
    o. Guidance services for adults
    p. Directed visiting, observation, and/or participation in activities
    q. Exhibits to the public—in content fields
    r. Organized participation in civic-improvement programs
    s. Consultant services to program leaders of community organizations
    t. Cooperative services with the community council
    u. Other organized approaches, such as special activities for the aging, use of newspaper columns for content material, training for community leadership, educational camps, block-leader organizations, little theaters,

community-center activities, directed individual reading, tutoring services, social activities, etc.

3. Are activities available at convenient times and locations?

a. Are activities offered during a variety of hours throughout the day? Morning hours? Afternoon hours? Evening hours? Other special times convenient to certain groups?

b. Are activities held on enough days of the week (including week ends) to involve most people?

c. Do activities start when participants are ready and run for as long as may be necessary without regard to standardized term or semester lengths?

d. Do learning periods vary according to the psychological characteristics of adults, their desires, the demands of the content, and other pertinent factors, or are sessions limited to the traditional length?

e. Are a maximum number of activities geographically and psychologically near the participants or potential participants? Are activities held in many geographical areas? On both public and private property that is open to the public?

Results

The truest test of the merit of an adult-education program lies in the results produced. Quantitative criteria—the amount of activity and the numbers of people involved—have already been discussed. Qualitative measures are concerned with the changes in behavior that are induced by the program. Essentially, what difference does the program make in the behavior of the participants?

From the community viewpoint, such questions as these are pertinent:

1. What difference does the program make in the life of the community?

2. To what extent is the community made a better place in which to live and make a living?

3. Is the community moving faster toward the democratic ideal as a result of the adult-education program?

4. Are the values of adults becoming more mature?

5. Are there fewer broken homes? Less delinquency? Stronger families?

6. Is there less discrimination based on age, color, sex, racial or national origin, and more discrimination based on merit, ability, and competence?

7. Is health improving? Is infant mortality going down? Is the incidence of disease declining? Is life expectancy lengthening? Is less time lost by illness?

8. Is employment high? Is poverty decreasing? Are living standards rising?

9. Is there a higher degree of cooperation among groups in community activities?

10. Are the recreational interests and activities of adults becoming more satisfying?

11. Are adults becoming more competent in solving both their individual and their group problems?

In regard to individuals, questions with more specific and often ascertainable answers are asked:

1. What growth is occurring in people? What desirable changes are people making?

2. Do adult-education experiences lead more people to participate in civic life? Do more vote? Do more participate in governmental and non-governmental policy making?

3. Are adults better able to select their leaders?

4. Are people more aware of the nature of their world? Of the impact of science on their daily living? Of the conflicting ideologies competing for the minds of men?

5. Are adults acquiring the knowledge, habits, and skills they want?

6. Are time, energy, money, and other resources, both natural and human, being used more wisely?

7. Are adults developing new and desirable interests?

8. Are adults gaining ability to take responsible leadership roles in a democracy?

General questions, like general objectives, must be broken down into specific ones before meaningful data can be assembled. Present conditions should be compared with both past conditions and the ideal, and data for this purpose are often readily available or easily obtained. Proving that any improvement is caused by adult education is sometimes a difficult task, however. Adult educators occasionally claim credit where the evidence is not clear, and they may as often contribute to changes without realizing the full impact of their efforts. The influence of such factors as economic trends, the general progressiveness of a community, the general educational level, educational influences outside the program being evaluated, and similar elements are often never known. While it may be that a reduction in the deaths caused by tuberculosis, desirable changes in dietary habits, and a reduction of traffic accidents are largely the result of extensive educational campaigns participated in by several agencies using many media over a long period of time, other factors undoubtedly contribute both positively and negatively. A great many educational programs and campaigns, especially those of a community-wide nature, are still carried out with no serious attempt at evaluating their results.

The clearest and soundest evidence of the effect of a program can often be obtained by setting up controlled conditions. Occasionally, before a community-wide educational program is started, a detailed representative sampling is taken of local knowledge and opinions. After the educational program has been carried out, a comparable survey is made.[4] The comparison of results can often be accepted as a relatively valid indication of change due to the educational program. However, the effects of day-to-day history must be considered, for events shape opinion. If there had been a nationwide campaign in late November, 1941, to induce an attitude favoring American participation in World War II, it might have claimed great results by mid-December. The American Institute of Public Opinion announced on October 4, 1941, that 21 per cent of the adult population thought that the United States should immediately enter the war, whereas ample evidence after December 7 showed strong approval for our entrance. The attack on Pearl Harbor, rather than any verbal barrage, caused this very material change in public attitude.

Experimental conditions using matched control and experimental groups are often desirable. In broad community-development programs and in educational campaigns dealing with current affairs, or other matters likely to be influenced considerably by events, carefully designed pre- and post-surveys may be necessary to assess the effect of the passage of time. If two communities are similar in the factors to be studied and in important related characteristics, and an educational campaign is conducted in only one of them, significant differences in the two that are revealed by post-campaign surveys can often be attributed to the experimental program—provided that national, regional, and other influences were the same on both communities.[5] Because of the costs involved in such an undertaking, its size, and often the long time required, few scientific evaluations of this scope, character, and refinement have been made. Experimental studies are highly important, however, if weaknesses

---

[4] After a 6-month campaign in Cincinnati to increase information about the United Nations, a comparison of pre- and postsurveys of local opinion and attitudes showed disappointingly little improvement in the level of information. Despite an intensive program that employed several mass media, approximately the same percentage as before (28 per cent in March, 1948; 30 per cent in September, 1947) seemed to be totally unacquainted with the main purpose of the United Nations. See S. A. Star and H. M. Hughes, "Report on an Educational Campaign: The Cincinnati Plan for the United Nations," *The American Journal of Sociology*, 55:1–12, January, 1950. In contrast, however, a 1-month educational campaign on foreign trade in New Brunswick, N.J., showed a considerable extension of knowledge and awareness among the citizenry.

[5] The Eight-year Study, involving thirty schools, represents an evaluation of this type. (See William Aikin, *The Story of the Eight-year Study*, Harper & Brothers, New York, 1942.) *Middletown* by R. S. Lynd and *Middletown in Transition* by R. S. and H. M. Lynd (Harcourt, Brace and Company, Inc., New York, 1929 and 1937) represent an assessment of conditions at two different times, but no unusual influences were injected. If an adult-education program with specific, yet comprehensive, purposes had operated in a parallel community, a comparison of the before-and-after assessment with the Middletown studies might have revealed the effects of the program.

in old procedures and methods are to be identified and more effective ones developed.

While it is often difficult to measure complex behavior changes, ways can more easily be devised to test the effects of specific educational approaches. Illustrative of this is the experimental comparison that was made of the two educational methods used in World War II to change meat-buying habits.

Six groups of women, two each from the high, middle, and low economic levels, were paired in an experiment designed to induce them to consume more kidneys, brains, and hearts—meats against which rather deep resistance is commonly found. The number who had served these foods in the past was determined by questionnaire.

Three groups were given lectures on the problem of nutrition in the war effort, the vitamin and mineral values of the three meats, and methods of preparing them to avoid their objectionable characteristics. Charts of food values were shown, and recipes were distributed. Both the economic and the health aspects were stressed.

A group-decision method was tried with three similar groups. In this method, the leader introduced the problem of nutrition in relation to the war effort and general health. He stressed the difficulties the government had in trying to change food habits and asked women how successful a direct appeal to housewives like themselves might be. Discussion from here on led the group to see the problem more concretely and to take responsibility for helping to do something about it. As the common reasons for rejecting the meats were discovered, an expert was introduced who discussed ways of avoiding the difficulties. The expert provided essentially the same information, though in condensed form, that was given in the lecture. After full discussion, the housewives voted on the question of trying one of the meats during the following week.

An interview follow-up a week later revealed that 10 per cent of the lecture group and 52 per cent of those in the discussion group had served one or more of the specified meats. Among women who had never served any of the meats before, 29 per cent from the discussion group and no one from the lecture group had served them during the first week.[6]

Such evaluations as these have far-reaching significance in regard to methods and approaches in adult education. One valid measurement yielding dramatic results is worth more than a dozen guesses. How else can one prove that new ways are better?

In a democracy the participants are often the final judges of the worth of an adult-education program. While few programs should ever be

[6] For a more complete description, see Kurt Lewin, "Forces behind Food Habits and Methods of Change," *The Problems of Changing Food Habits,* Report of the Committee on Food Habits, 1941–43, National Research Council Bulletin 108, October, 1943, pp. 35–65.

judged solely on consumer satisfaction, assessing student opinion is an important approach to evaluation.

Participants may indicate their estimate of a program in several ways.

1. Size of enrollment is itself an index of the degree to which a program seems worth the time of adults. Size, however, varies with economic conditions and with a dozen other factors not inherently connected with quality of program. Nonetheless, directors can use enrollment figures as a rough index of merit.

2. If lifelong learning is an accepted objective, the number returning year after year is an index of merit. A few directors, even of informal programs, keep permanent record cards, on which dates of courses taken are entered. A study of these will give data on the degree to which people are building habits of lifelong learning.

3. Interest in pursuing advanced courses, however demonstrated, is an index of good teaching and leadership.

4. Direct appraisal of the program by questionnaires to the participants is rather common.[7] They may be administered either to the entire group or to a representative sample, but distributing questionnaires to the total membership of selected groups, with other groups omitted, is likely to give a biased sample. Such questionnaires are usually developed locally and often seek information on such items as:

a. Purposes for which the adult is attending the activity

b. How closely the activity meets his needs

c. The adult's opinion of the quality of instruction or leadership

d. The adult's opinion on the favorable and unfavorable features of the program

e. Courses taken

f. Age, sex, occupation, educational level, and other characteristics of participants

The questionnaire may be set up as a rating scale, a list to be ranked, a check list, a series of multiple-choice items, a series of open-end questions, or in some other form. End-of-term questionnaires to be returned anonymously are sometimes used, either by the administrator for gathering opinions about the whole program or by instructors in evaluating their own work. Getting the true opinion rather than superficialities takes some skill in questionnaire design or in interviewing. Occasionally a group can be induced to evaluate an activity with the teacher absent and with the composite opinion channeled through a designated spokesman.

Participation appraisals are incomplete unless they include a study of nonparticipants and dropouts. A survey based on interviews gives the

---

[7] See *The Educational Consumer Appraises the Evening Schools,* Connecticut State Department of Education Bulletin 8, January, 1941, for methods, the questionnaire, and results in a study of five communities.

most useful and reliable results in studying these groups. To save expense and energy, however, first-class mail, providing for an anonymous reply, is a common approach to determining the attitudes of dropouts. It is less useful with those who have never been connected with a program. Signatures or other means of identification will be necessary if a follow-up is desired. Mimeographed or typed reply cards containing three to five questions are likely to prove reasonably effective. The data called for in connection with dropouts usually include their reasons for leaving and for failing to accomplish their purpose. The evaluator must be aware of people's tendency to give expected rather than honest answers, especially when the latter may be more complex or embarrassing. He must be able to convey his sincerity in wanting to know the real reasons so that the program may be improved.

Analysis of results often reveals places for improvement in preregistration counseling, in teacher selection, in the quality of instruction, in identification of need, in adapting instruction to needs, in administrative practices, and in as many other features as may be included in the questionnaire. Some dropouts are caused entirely by employment, family responsibilities, or personal situations beyond the control of the school or agency, but other reasons for leaving may point out appropriate points for improvement.

Good directors seek constantly to involve their clientele in programs of evaluation through systematic studies, advisory committees, and other ways. Participants can suggest significant means of improvement through paper-and-pencil methods; through personal interviews, formal or informal; or occasionally through a group interview. The dropout point is an excellent time to interview, but with adults this is often hard to arrange. The open-office-door atmosphere and extensive informal mixing among the participants may facilitate the collection of important data. Such data, however, may be hard to classify and weigh.

Directors of adult education need to know what the public thinks of their programs. Tax-supported programs, especially, often depend directly upon the local attitudes. Few directors, either of public or private-agency programs, will want to go far beyond the bounds of local approval. They will want to know whether a scathing letter to the editor denouncing instruction in social dancing, fly tying, or bridge represents crackpot opinion or a substantial portion of local thinking. This should be determined in advance through systematic exploration of community feeling. The competent director knows how his community feels on major matters of policy.

The degree of intensity or firmness of feeling about the program should be tested occasionally, since tacit approval in fair weather may not hold up in storms. The director will do well to know the strength of local support, as well as its numerical size. Directors of public programs need to know how support for adult education compares with support for the education of children and youth, for old age pensions, recreation, and other claims on the public purse.

Community attitudes can be determined in a number of ways:

1. The amount of community backing, especially financial support, gives clues to the public attitude toward adult education. While support for an adult program seldom comes to a separate vote, a generous school tax rate willingly voted is indirect evidence of a good program.

2. Follow-up studies of participants may give important evaluative data. Employers' opinions, obtained systematically or by accumulation of unsolicited letters, are worthwhile data. Percentage of placements, promotion records, discharge records, and similar data are evidence especially useful in the vocational field, provided that other factors can be properly weighed.

3. Members of boards of control are usually sensitive to public opinion, although they normally reflect the views expected of their background— business, the professions, politics, organized labor, or farming, as the case may be. Representative advisory committees may reflect community opinion more accurately.

4. Frank discussion with members of organized groups can sometimes yield valid judgments of an adult program. Few groups, however, will express unfavorable views directly to a director or his known lieutenants. Group opinion relative to special phases of a program can sometimes be channeled through an officer of the organization. Thus PTA members may express themselves on the parent-education or family-life program; unions may speak regarding the education provided workers.

5. Agencies may be induced to pass judgment on general areas or certain activities.

6. Opinion and attitude polls based on representative sampling procedures can give detailed information on public sentiment. One should be aware, however, that behavior is not always consistent with answers in an interview. Likewise, one must remember the probability of bias and the other dangers in voluntarily returned questionnaires. Many adults will have too little information to make valid judgments. This, in itself, constitutes an evaluation of the public-relations program. Through the use of screening questions, the opinions of those who have any given degree of acquaintance with the program can be segregated for study.

RESEARCH IN EVALUATION

Much research is needed in establishing criteria, in developing better instruments for gathering data, and in devising evaluative procedures which involve the maximum number of adults in growth processes. If surveys of the Baltimore type were made in a succession of communities of varying sizes and their procedures and results were carefully examined, better evaluative criteria and techniques could be developed. Many more communities ought to be involved in developing objectives, criteria, procedures, and measuring instruments in various fields. The results would be useful for evaluating both agency and comprehensive community programs.

Measurement of changes in individuals in many academic and vocational fields has been worked out in considerable detail. Educators know how to measure knowledge and skills, but appraisal of social attitudes, emotional maturity, competence in human relations, and ability to operate in a democratic group is less often attempted. Evaluation of broad, community-wide programs lags behind. Progress needs to be measured in the cultural development of a community, in consumer buying habits, in social-civic work, in intercultural understanding, and in various other fields. Schools and community organizations continue to spend much educational energy in these areas, but only rarely do they try to find out how much or how little their activities actually contribute to their stated objectives.

Evaluation of the methods used to change human behavior promises rich rewards. The effect of several methods has long been questioned. Methods and approaches need to be tested to determine the conditions under which they are most useful. New methods showing promise in one situation need thorough testing under varied circumstances. Evaluation of methods under both experimental and field conditions could help identify and define the approaches that are of most value with adults. Probably in no other aspect of adult education would careful research yield more productive results.

If we could agree upon and determine the characteristics of good community and school programs of adult education and find practical means and methods of evaluating such programs, we would gain deeper insight into the processes by which good programs develop into better ones.

SELECTED REFERENCES

An Evaluation of Local Programs of Vocational Education in Agriculture, U.S. Office of Education, Division of Vocational Educational Bulletin 240, 1949.

Benne, K. D.: "The Future of Work-survey Conferences," *Adult Education Bulletin,* 12:93–96, February, 1948.

Burch, G.: "Evaluating Adult Education," *Adult Education Journal,* 6:70–75, April, 1947.

Connecticut State Department of Education: *The Educational Consumer Appraises the Evening Schools,* Bulletin 8, Hartford, Conn., January, 1941.

Deming, R. C.: "Characteristics of an Adequate Adult Education Program," *Adult Education,* 1:25–26, October, 1950.

Dressel, P. L.: "Evaluation Procedures for General Education Objectives," *The Educational Record,* 31:97–122, April, 1950.

"Evaluating Program and Performance," *Adult Leadership,* special issue, 1:32, April, 1953.

"Evaluation of Adult Education," *Baltimore Bulletin of Education,* 25:153–248, January–March, 1948.

Finlay, G. C.: "How Do You Know You Have a Good School?" *Illinois Education,* 37:39, 60, October, 1948.

Hedlund, P. A.: "Measuring Public Opinion on School Issues," *American School Board Journal,* 116:29–31, April, 1948.

Kaplan, A. A.: *Socio-Economic Circumstances and Adult Participation in Certain Cultural and Educational Activities,* Contributions to Education, no. 889, Teachers College, Columbia University, New York, 1943.

Program Evaluation in Adult Education, Adult Education Association, Committee on Evaluation, Washington, 1952.

Stensland, Per G.: "Criteria of Adult Education," *Adult Education Bulletin,* 8:174–178, August, 1944.

Stratton, B. E., and L. Lipsett: "An Extension Division Evaluates Its Program," *Adult Education Bulletin,* 13:240–244, December, 1948.

Thorndike, E. L.: *Your City,* Harcourt, Brace and Company, Inc., New York, 1939.

Van Sant, T.: "The Baltimore Cooperative Survey and Work-survey Conference," *Adult Education Bulletin,* 12:87–93, February, 1948.

See also General References: [8] Division of Adult Education Service, chaps. 10, 19; Essert, chap. 15; Knowles, chap. 11; Sheats, Jayne, and Spence, chap. 19.

[8] The General References are listed in full at the end of this book.

General References

Beals, Ralph A., and Leon Brody: *The Literature of Adult Education*, American Association for Adult Education, New York, 1941.

Division of Adult Education Service of the NEA: *A Study of Urban Public School Adult Education Programs of the United States*, National Education Association, Washington, 1952.

Ely, Mary L. (ed.): *Handbook of Adult Education in the United States*, Teachers College, Columbia University, New York, 1948.

Essert, Paul L.: *Creative Leadership of Adult Education*, Prentice-Hall, Inc., New York, 1951.

Kempfer, Homer: *Adult Education Activities of the Public School: Report of a Survey, 1947–48*, U.S. Office of Education Pamphlet 107, 1949.

——— and Grace S. Wright: *100 Evening Schools*, U.S. Office of Education Bulletin 1949, no. 4.

Knowles, Malcolm S.: *Informal Adult Education*, Association Press, New York, 1950.

Sheats, Paul H., Clarence D. Jayne, and Ralph B. Spence: *Adult Education: The Community Approach*, The Dryden Press, Inc., New York, 1953.

Index

DATE D